INSTRUCTIONAL MEDIA
AND THE NEW TECHNOLOGIES OF INSTRUCTION

INSTRUCTIONAL

JOHN WILEY & SONS

New York
Chichester
Brisbane
Toronto
Singapore

MEDIA AND THE NEW TECHNOLOGIES OF INSTRUCTION

ROBERT HEINICH
Indiana University

MICHAEL MOLENDA
Indiana University

JAMES D. RUSSELL
Purdue University

Photo Research by Sibyl Weil and Teri Leigh Stratford
Photo Editor, Stella Kupferberg
Cover Photo by Geoffrey Gove
Cover and Text Design by Laura C. Ierardi
Production supervised by Elizabeth Doble
Copyediting supervised by Deborah Herbert

Library of Congress Cataloging in Publication Data:

Heinich, Robert.
Instructional media, and the new technologies of
instruction

Includes index.
1. Educational technology.   I. Molenda, Michael.
II. Russell, James D.   III. Title.

LB1028.3.H45   371.3'07'8   81-14630
ISBN 0-471-36893-8   AACR2

Printed in the United States of America

10 9 8 7 6 5 4

PREFACE

This book is intended for teachers at all levels, who place a high value on successful learning. The examples used emphasize elementary and secondary school applications because the majority of readers are most concerned with these levels. However, examples from college and adult out-of-school settings are also included, since there is a growing interest in applying media and technologies of instruction to these areas. We believe that the principles discussed are applicable to the whole range of school, college, business/industry, organizational, and institutional learning settings. Readers will have no difficulty in translating examples into their own particular situations.

We began writing this book with several convictions in mind. First, we believed that a rapprochement could be reached between the so-called "humanist" and "technological" traditions of the field. Second, our experiences indicated that students need a comprehensive treatment of instructional media and technology—one that covers both basic audiovisual skills and the pedagogical underpinnings of those skills. Furthermore, we thought that a treatment of this kind could serve both teachers-in-training and teachers who are beginning graduate study in the instructional media/technology profession.

Too frequently, lines are drawn between "humanism" and "technology," and they cause a choice of one or the other. Advocates of humanism reject technology as being "mechanistic," inordinately obsessed with the trivial. Advocates of technology dismiss humanists as being "soft-headed," hopelessly mired in amorphous language and ill-defined goals. We do not believe that these two approaches are inherently opposed; properly understood and used, each one can support the other. Technology can give rigor and reliability to the instructional process; the humanistic approach can help us not only to understand the individuals in the instructional process but also to ensure that technology serves them—not the other way around.

Coverage

One characteristic of our field is that the media of instruction frequently are also the mass media—films, radio, and television, for instance. Therefore, we consider, in Chapter 1, the role of the mass media in contemporary culture. We then discuss key psychological and theoretical foundations underlying the field. The relatively new concept of "technologies of instruction" is introduced. The broad instructional contexts for using media and the technologies of instruction are examined. The "humanism versus technology" issue is reconciled as well as the subsidiary issue of "flexibility versus structure."

Chapter 2 introduces the ASSURE model of instructional planning. This model is our own creation, and we think that it is most appropriate because it can easily be used to design a lesson as well as a complete instructional program. Readers who already are familiar with a "lesson planning" procedure will find the ASSURE model more familiar and congenial than the more technical models associated with instructional development. Chapter 2 explains the ASSURE model in reference to the domains of educational objectives. Finally, this chapter discusses general procedures for appraising, selecting, and using audiovisual materials.

Chapter 3 examines visual literacy from the viewpoints of interpreting and producing visual media. This chapter provides a theoretical context for Chapters 4, 5, 8, and 9.

Chapters 4 (graphic materials), 5 (projected visuals), 6 (audio materials), 7 (multimedia systems), 8 (film), and 9 (television) discuss the most commonly recognized audiovisual formats.

They are the "bread and butter" of the field. We treat these media and combinations of them in the context of the theory and research that substantiate their use. We call attention to the attributes of each media format—its strengths and limitations.

Chapter 10 deals with "media-ware"—the tools of the media trade. Teachers in both formal and nonformal education must have a basic knowledge of the equipment and techniques necessary for effective media presentations, as described in this chapter.

Chapter 11 defines "technologies of instruction" not as machines but as particular patterns of teaching-learning activities that put scientific principles of human learning into action. Programmed instruction, the Personalized System of Instruction, simulation/gaming, and other examples of this concept are examined in detail.

Two of these technologies of instruction—simulation/gaming and computer-assisted instruction—occupy our attention in Chapters 12 and 13. We have discussed them in depth because we believe that they will play more prominent roles in education and training in the 1980s. The age of the microcomputer is now upon us, and all instructional planners must consider the possibilities for computer assistance in their field.

We conclude (Chapter 14) with a look at certain trends in society and education and their likely impacts on the use of media and technology. New technological developments that may be important in the future, or that are useful to special populations such as the handicapped, are described. This chapter gives us a chance to reflect on what has been studied in the context of the future, and it ends with an overview of professional opportunities in the field, professional associations, and journals.

We reflect, in words and pictures, our own awareness of the diverse audiences that our readers deal with. Having worked as teachers and consultants ourselves, in many cultures outside of North America, we avoid the unconscious chauvinism of country or culture; we also avoid stereotyping based on gender. We are sensitive to the needs of teachers who deal with handicapped learners, and we make specific references to the roles of media in regard to various handicapping conditions.

Special Features

Many features are used to make the book more readable and practical:

- **Outlines.** Each chapter begins with an outline of the contents, thus providing a quick advance organizer.
- **Objectives.** A detailed list of performance objectives precedes the text of each chapter. These objectives have been popular with our own students as study guides and have alerted them to important points ahead.
- **Concrete examples.** "Close-Ups" show miniature case studies of media applications. "Media Files" show and describe actual AV materials in each media format. The materials shown in the Media Files were chosen because they are *typical* of a given class, not because they are necessarily *exemplary*. No endorsement of any kind is implied—nor even commercial availability.

- **How To...** Various media production and operation procedures are spelled out with clear, illustrated, step-by-step instructions. Each is boxed for easy reference.
- **Appraisal Checklists.** Separate checklists have been developed for appraising each media format. Users have permission to photocopy these lists for personal use. This makes it easy to preview materials systematically and to preserve the previews for later reference.
- **AV Showmanship.** This feature gives specific tips on delivering media presentations with flair and dramatic effect.
- **Flashbacks.** These are brief vignettes that lend a sense of perspective and often provide fascinating behind-the-scenes glimpses of historic developments.

Appendixes are at the back of the book, and they can be referred to frequently, even after the formal study of the text has been completed. Appendix A describes indexes and catalogs that identify purchase and rental sources for the media described in the text. Appendix B lists sources of free and inexpensive materials—an important consideration in these cost-conscious days. Appendix C deals with the Copyright Law of 1976. Although we point out the important restrictions of the law, we suggest that an intelligent approach to the spirit as well as the letter of the law can result in giving the instructor more "elbow room" than generally has been considered possible.

Instructors who adopt this book for a course or a workshop can obtain an *Instructor's Guide*, published separately. It contains suggested course syllabi, detailed outlines of chapters, transparency masters, and suggested sample test items.

Input from the Field

We benefited greatly by advice and feedback from professionals in the field and from our own students. The need for a book of this kind emerged serendipitously from a survey conducted in the mid-1970s by Indiana University for the purpose of determining what supplementary AV materials might be used in teaching AV utilization courses. The survey pointed out gaps that motivated us to write this book. After working out a rough draft, we went back to the field early in 1980 with a questionnaire for a nationwide sample of AV-course instructors. Their answers gave us a much clearer picture of users' interests and priorities. We are grateful to all of those who responded to this survey.

Class Tested

The real test of a book is how well it meets the needs of its users. As chapters were developed, we experimented with them in our own classes at Purdue University and Indiana University. Feedback helped us to improve the subsequent versions. When the first draft of the entire book was completed, we taught it and revised it again. We went through three major revisions based on tryouts in seven separate classes. We are grateful to the hundreds of students whose candid criticisms and suggestions helped us to do a better job.

During the tryout period we also sent draft versions to people who are experienced in the field. Their comments were invaluable, especially those of Merlyn McClure, University of Cincinnati; Donna McGrady, Purdue University; and Barbara Martin, Kent State University.

We are confident that all our formative evaluation efforts have resulted in a text that is well suited to your needs. We will appreciate *your* formative evaluation. Please send your comments to us so that we can shape a future edition that will be responsive to the demands of the times.*

Robert Heinich
Michael Molenda
James D. Russell

---

*Send the comments to Dr. Robert Heinich, Department of Instructional Systems Technology, School of Education, Indiana University, Bloomington, IN 47405.

ACKNOWL-EDGMENTS

Early drafts of the manuscript were reviewed by Ted Cobun, East Tennessee State University; Arni Dunathan, University of Missouri; Terry Holcomb, North Texas State University; Robert Hunyard, Northern Illinois University; Bruce Petty, Oklahoma State University; William Winn, University of Calgary. We also appreciate the help of some of these reviewers who reacted to final drafts.

The collaboration of many people is required for any publication, but one as complex as this one demands an even higher order of talent and teamwork. Some key contributors already have been acknowledged. In addition, the editorial, design, graphic, photographic, and production staffs of Wiley deserve special thanks. The editing of Jim Roers helped immeasurably in blending our three styles. We thank the media publishers and manufacturers who supplied photographs and gave us permission to use them.

Kristine Rinella, Michael Neff, Deane Dayton, Danny Callison, Jim Owens, and William Orisich of Indiana University and Doris Brodeur of Ohio University gave invaluable assistance, often under pressing circumstances.

For our treatment of computer-based learning, we are grateful to John Childs and Al Stahl of Wayne State University and to school people in the Detroit area, who were kind enough to help us learn from their experience. We thank Calvin Mether of the University of Iowa, head of the AECT archives, for the photos he supplied for Chapter 14. Our colleagues at Indiana University and Purdue University graciously provided feedback and moral support.

Finally, we thank our families for putting up with us during the years of effort that this book represents.

R. H.
M. M.
J. D. R.

CONTENTS

SPECIAL FEATURES

INSTRUCTIONAL MEDIA
AND THE NEW TECHNOLOGIES OF INSTRUCTION

CHAPTER 1

MEDIA AND INSTRUCTION

OUTLINE

OBJECTIVES

After studying this chapter, you should
be able to:

1. Identify the range of information
vehicles available for both education
and mass communication.

2. Distinguish between "differentiation"
and "integration."

3. Explain the "concrete-to-abstract
continuum" as presented in the text,
indicating how it can be used to aid in
the selection of media.

4. Relate differentiation and integration to the concrete-to-abstract
continuum.

5. Diagram and explain a communication model (Shannon, Shannon–
Schramm, or one of your own design).

6. Analyze a given instructional situation in terms of one of the communication models.

7. Describe the transactional nature of
communication.

8. Define or describe "technologies of
instruction" and cite an example.

9. Describe and distinguish between
CMI and CAI.

10. Discuss five roles or purposes of
media in the instructional process.
Your discussion should include an
example of media in each of these
roles.

11. Indicate the relationship between
"structure" and "flexibility" in instructional situations.

12. Demonstrate by examples the
relationship between instructional
media and flexibility in instructional
design.

13. Describe the role of instructional
media in the "out-of-school" setting,
indicating their function and types of
uses.

14. Discuss the relationship between
humanism and instructional technology
in the classroom.

THE PERVASIVENESS OF MASS MEDIA

Living as we do in a society in which instantaneous, worldwide communication of information is commonplace, we can easily forget that several decades ago such a phenomenon would have seemed preposterous, at best the stuff of dreams and poetry. Philosopher Ralph Waldo Emerson, for example, *could* stir the imagination toward poetic contemplation of such a notion as he memorialized the battle of Concord Bridge which signaled the start of the American Revolution: "Here once the embattled farmers stood, and fired the shot heard round the world." But never could our poet have imagined that a day would actually come when momentous gunfire could literally be "heard round the world."

In truth, of course, it took many months for this opening volley of war to be "heard" throughout the American colonies, and years for it to be "heard" around the world. Imagine, if you will, what would probably have happened if modern communications technology and mass media had been available in 1775. The whole world would have heard the shots and witnessed the scene at Concord Bridge via communications satellite. A few hours later, newspapers would have reported the incident in greater detail. Almost simultaneously, television and radio would have begun to present in-depth coverage of the event, complete with background information about relations between Britain and its American colonies, interviews with eyewitnesses to the battle, and statements by politicians and pundits concerned with its national and international implications. Newspapers and periodicals would continue to present the public with even more information

and details. Within a few weeks, speculative and informative paperback books about the battle would be ready for mass consumption, and a few months later more scholarly works exploring the deeper political, social, and military implications of the affair would be in print.

The notion of television cameras mounted on Concord Bridge in 1775, of Barbara Walters securing an exclusive interview with Sam Adams, of Mike Wallace interrogating that "rabble-rousing dirty little atheist Tom Paine" (as his Tory enemies called him) on *60 Minutes,* or of Dan Rather interviewing the patrician George Washington and the possibly mad King George III on worldwide tele-

Figure 1.1a Current satellite earth stations, such as those used for the Canadian Technology Satellite, are one-tenth the size of earlier receiving dishes yet they bring high-quality color television signals directly to viewers virtually anywhere in the world.

vision may make us smile, as may the notion of mass-market paperback accounts of the battle of Concord Bridge appearing on the shelves of colonial village stores and apothecaries. But the smile should be a thoughtful one, especially for those of us concerned with education. There can be no doubt that modern communications technology has vastly increased our ability to witness events as they happen and thereby has vastly increased our exposure to information and experience. The very pervasiveness of this technology in our everyday lives, however, tends to obscure the fact that this is a relatively new phenomenon, with implications for education that are only now beginning to be fully understood and appreciated.

Just as they do for adults, mass media today provide more and more varied sources of information for children than ever before. There are more magazines, newspapers, and books, not to mention textbooks and other printed instructional materials, designed specifically for children than ever before. Children today are rarely out of earshot of radio (witness, for example, the phenomenon of young ears seemingly glued to hand-carried transistor radios); and, of course, there is television.

There are children's television programs specifically designed to instruct as well as entertain— *Sesame Street, Mister Rogers' Neighborhood,* and *Captain Kangaroo,* for example. There are numerous programs primarily designed to attract young viewers for commercial reasons, but which nevertheless do provide information and experiences to which previous generations of children are unlikely to have been exposed. And there are the programs intended primarily for adults but watched by countless children.

Figure 1.1b *Sesame Street* is viewed by millions of children at home, in schools, and in day care centers in North America and abroad.

Figure 1.1c Microcomputers were designed to suit the needs of small businesses but also have become increasingly popular for home use.

With all these communications sources, learners today have absorbed more information and vicariously experienced many more phenomena than people of previous generations. They have witnessed the undersea world of Jacques Cousteau and have followed the adventures of man into space. The hidden world of our natural environment has been revealed to them through modern photographic techniques and devices such as strobe-light photography that stops action at a thousandth of a second, and microscopic and time-lapse photography that can reveal the wondrous formation of crystals as well as the equally wondrous blossoming and decay of a flower.

All of which is to say that learners of all ages are to some extent "different" today from learners of previous generations simply by virtue of their exposure to mass

Figure 1.1d The original mass medium, the newspaper delves into the events of the day more deeply than radio or television.

Figure 1.1e The clarity and simplicity of language in most news magazines makes them accessible to young and old alike.

Figure 1.1f Radio has evolved from a mass medium to a very individual, personal one.

media. There is no question of whether or not modern communications technology should be brought into the learning situation. It is already there, as it is in other aspects of society, in the experiential and environmental background of teacher and student alike. The real question is, How can we best use this pervasive technology for effective education? This book will help you answer that question.

In the remainder of this first chapter, we will present an introduction to and overview of the major premises and themes of this book. We begin with a brief review of certain key learning concepts, particularly as they relate to effective use of media for instructional purposes. From there we move on to a discussion of communication, for without appropriate communication there cannot be effective teaching. We then discuss the general concept of technology of instruction, with some emphasis on the germinal instructional technology that has emerged from applications of reinforcement theory. We then present a preview of some general educational strategies to which instructional media are particularly applicable, followed by a discussion of growing use of instructional media outside the formal educational setting. We close with an affirmation of the theme that pervades this entire book: properly and creatively used instructional technology and instructional media can provide us with hitherto unattainable opportunities to individualize and humanize the teaching/learning environment.

EPIGRAMS

It was the funeral of President Kennedy that most strongly proved the power of television to invest an occasion with the character of corporate participation. It involves an entire population in a ritual process.

Marshall McLuhan

In an electric information environment, minority groups can no longer be contained—ignored. Too many people know too much about each other. Our new environment compels commitment and participation. We have become irrevocably involved with, and responsible for, each other.

Marshall McLuhan

Today the world has shrunk in the wash with speeded-up information movement from all directions. We have come, as it were, to live in a global village.

Marshall McLuhan

Television is the first mass-produced, organically composed symbolic environment into which our children are born and in which they will live from cradle to grave...Television is a total cultural system (as was tribal religion) with its own art, science, statecraft, legendry, geography, demography, character types, and action structure.

George Gerbner

All man-made material things can be treated as extensions of what man once did with his body or some specialized part of his body. TV, telephones, and books which carry the voice across both time and space are examples of material extensions.

Edward Hall

It turns out that TV is a powerful educational medium even when it isn't trying to be, even when it's only trying to entertain. There must be millions of people who have learned, simply by watching crime dramas in the past few years, that they have the right to remain silent when arrested.

Herb Schlosser

The book is one of the first, and very possibly the most important, mass-produced product, and its impact demonstrates the falsity of the common notion that mass production per se brings about the massification of men.

David Riesman

Just as the printing press democratized learning, so the television set has democratized experience.

Daniel J. Boorstin

EPIGRAMS

Print created the drive for self-expression, self-portraiture (Montaigne, Rembrandt), but in time it rendered illegible the faces of men...Photography, film, TV, aided us in the recovery of gesture and facial awareness—a language of moods and emotions never adequately expressed in words and totally lost in print.

Edmund Carpenter

A child who gets his environmental training on television—and very few nowadays do not—learns the same way any member of a pre-literate society learns: from the direct experience of his eyes and ears, without Gutenberg for a middle man. Of course, they do learn how to read too, but it is a secondary discipline not primary as it is with their elders.

Howard Gossage

Today we immerse ourselves in sound. We've all become acoustic skindivers. Music is no longer for listening to, but for merging with.

Edmund Carpenter

Do you in fact think that television stops anybody from reading? Yes, I believe that middle-class children are less well-read than they were, although probably far better informed about public affairs.

Kenneth Clark

When we listen to speech, we need to wait until the end of each sentence to understand what is meant; while the act of looking at a landscape provides immediate and simultaneous information from an infinite number of sources.

Caleb Gattegno

Electronic media have made all the arts environmental. Everyone can avail himself of cultural riches beyond what any millionaire has ever known.

Edmund Carpenter

Some Basic Definitions

Medium; media (plural): In this book used in the general sense of a means of communication. Derived from the Latin *medium*, "between," the term refers to anything that carries information *between* a source and a receiver.

Film, television, radio, audio recordings, photographs, projected visuals, printed materials, and the like are media of communication. They are considered *instructional media* when they are used to carry messages with an instructional intent. The middle chapters of this text are concerned with instructional applications of media such as these.

Format: The physical form in which a medium is incorporated and displayed. For example, motion pictures are available in 35-mm, 16-mm, and 8-mm formats. Cassette tape is an audio format. Print is a verbal format.

Material: An item of a medium format; in the plural, a collection of items of a medium format or of several media formats, often used in a general sense. For example, *Instructional materials are available from many sources.*

Technology: This term has three meanings in this book; the meaning in each instance can be identified by the context of use.

1. Technology as a process—"the systematic application of scientific or other organized knowledge to practical tasks;"* the process of devising reliable and repeatable solutions to tasks.
2. Technology as product—the hardware and software that result from the application of technological processes. We must remember that a film is as much a product of technology as the projector that displays it. The book is as much a product of technology as the press that prints it.
3. Technology as a mix of process and product—used in instances where: (a) the context refers to the combination of technological processes and resultant products, for example, *Technology is constantly expanding our information delivery systems* implies both the process of invention and the devices that result; (b) process is inseparable from product, for example, the technology of computers is inherently an interaction between hardware and software (the program).

---

*John Kenneth Galbraith. *The New Industrial State*. Boston: Houghton Mifflin, 1967, p. 12.

Learning: A general term for a relatively lasting change in performance caused directly by experience; also the process or processes whereby such change is brought about. Learning is *inferred* from performance.

Instruction: Deliberate arrangement of experience(s) to help a learner achieve a desirable change in performance; the management of learning, which in education and training is primarily the function of the instructor.

THE "WHY" OF USING INSTRUCTIONAL MEDIA

Too frequently instructors use media without any reference to guiding principles of how the experiences contained in those media will be used by learners. *Without a good theoretical rationale, use of specific materials may become simply mechanical, with the fond hope that what is presented to learners will eventually become meaningful to them.* We will help you develop conceptual and theoretical bases on which to choose specific materials and methods by discussing the relationships between media, learning, and instruction in the following three contexts:

1. The developmental learning process of differentiation and integration.
2. The attributes of media in reference to developmental learning.
3. Communication models that can help you analyze and deal with human communication problems.

Differentiation and Integration in Learning

Very young children tend to react to situations as a whole. For exam-

Figure 1.2 Babies respond to sensory stimuli with their whole bodies.

ple, when a baby tastes something objectionable, the whole body tends to respond, not just the taste organs (Figure 1.2). Through experience children start differentiating their responses to the environment. They start distinguishing between mother and father and the other people they come in contact with, including siblings. They soon separate dogs from cats and then are aware of varieties of dogs and varieties of cats. These differentiations based on experience lead to the development of concepts, that is, the development of the ability to classify objects by characteristics they have learned to identify. At this point, verbal labels have some meaning. Prior to the acquisition of experience, verbal labels may lead to a diffuse and confused response.

The children's next step in the process of mental growth is to integrate those differentiations into generalizations and abstractions. Once again responding to the total environment but from an entirely different point of view, they now start organizing their differentiations into series of constructs that enable them to deal more effectively with their environment. One of the aims of education is to help students achieve working generalizations. The children who were going through the process of differentiating first dogs from cats and then certain dogs from other dogs are now in a position to deal with the class, dog, in a much more meaningful and useful way.

Thus far we have talked primarily about the development of a child's ability to differentiate. However, the same principles apply to *any* learner of *any* age who happens to be naïve in a particular subject area. For many years, the theme of a visitor from another planet having to make new differentiations and integrating them into appropriate constructs has provided playwrights *(Visit to a Small Planet)*, novelists *(Stranger in a Strange Land)*, and TV writers *(My Favorite Martian* and *Mork and Mindy)* opportunities to make humorous and perceptive comments on our own culture (Figure 1.3). Adult learners can usually make new differentiations more quickly than children but instructors need to remember that adults still have to make them.

People handicapped by sensory impairment have a particularly hard time with making accurate and consistent differentiations. The hearing impaired, for exam-

Figure 1.3 Stories involving visitors from other planets, such as the *Mork and Mindy* television series, remind us of the many and complex differentiations that must be learned to cope with modern life.

ple, have difficulty in mastering the spatial meanings of prepositions such as above, below, by, behind, at. Instructors need to be prepared for learning problems of handicapped students whose experiences have been distorted by inadequate sensory abilities.

The Concrete—Abstract Relationship

Thus far we have discussed differentiation—integration in reference to learning. But learning is guided by instruction, and instruction is the job of the teacher. Hoban once pointed out that the business of education is not learning, but the management of learning, that is, instruction. The teacher organizes the experiences of learners in a way that helps them change their performance in a meaningful way.

The psychologist Jerome Bruner, in developing a "theory of instruction," proposes that the instruction provided to a learner should proceed from direct experience, through representations of experience (as in pictures, films, etc.), through symbolic representation (as in words).* He further states that "the sequence in which a learner encounters materials" has a direct effect on achievement of mastery of the task.† The development of instruction should parallel the differentiation—integration learning process. Bruner carefully points out that this applies to all learners, not just children. When a learning task is presented to adults who have no relevant experiences on which to draw, learning is facilitated for them when instruction follows a sequence from actual experience through symbolic representations.‡ As we

will discuss later, an important first step in instruction is to determine the nature of any learner's current level of experience. The principles that Fleming and Levie derive from research underscore Bruner's position.* Concrete experiences facilitate learning and the acquisition, retention, and usability of abstract symbols.

Instructional media not only provide the necessary concrete experiences, but also help students integrate prior experiences. Many students have watched various aspects of the construction of a highway or a street. They have seen the machine that lays the asphalt down; they have seen graders at work; and they have seen a number of other aspects of road building. However, they need to have all these experiences integrated into a generalized notion of what it means to build a highway. A film that can show all of these processes in relation to each other is an ideal way to integrate their various experiences into a meaningful abstraction.

In the beginning of this chapter, we mentioned that children today, because of television and movies, have acquired many mediated experiences at a much earlier age than children of previous generations. These experiences are extremely helpful to them in making the kinds of differentiations referred to above. However, we cannot assume that those differentiations have been achieved, or that they are accurate. The teacher should check to make sure those differentiations have been made on a sound basis, and should help students integrate the experiences that they have acquired into meaningful constructs.

Historically, improving the relationship between concrete and abstract learning experiences was a key reason for using instructional media. However, current research questions the nature of the distinctions between media made by earlier authors. The relative concreteness and abstractness of various media and methods and their comparative effectiveness in learning is not as clear-cut as we once believed. Most instructional materials use a combination of presentation forms that vary in their degree of realism; for example, films (motion pictures) or filmstrips (still pictures) may be captioned or narrated (verbal symbols). In certain circumstances, line drawings (visual symbols) have been shown to be more effective than realistic photographs (still pictures). It now seems clear that a second key to effectiveness is learner response—what mental processing or overt practice is conducted in response to the audiovisual stimuli. Regardless of the appeal of a mode of presentation, the ultimate test is learner response and performance.

Decisions regarding trade-offs between concreteness of a learning experience and time constraints have to be continually made by the instructor. In general, as you move up Dale's Cone toward the more abstract media, more information can be compressed into a shorter period of time than at the lower end of the cone. It takes more time for students to engage in a direct purposeful experience, a contrived experience, or a dramatized experience than it does to present the same information in a motion picture, a recording, a series of visual symbols, or a series of verbal symbols. For example, a field trip

*Jerome S. Bruner. *Toward a Theory of Instruction.* Cambridge: Harvard University Press, 1966, p. 49.
†Ibid.

‡See Flashback, page 12.

*Malcolm Fleming and W. Howard Levie. *Instructional Message Design.* Englewood Cliffs, N. J.: Educational Technology Publications, 1978, pp. 107-111.

Flashback: Dale's Cone of Experience

In one of the first textbooks written about the use of audiovisual materials in schools, Hoban, Hoban, and Zissman stated that the value of audiovisual materials is a function of their degree of realism. In developing this concept, the authors arranged various teaching methods in a hierarchy of greater and greater abstraction, beginning with what they referred to as "the total situation" and culminating with "word" at the top of the hierarchy.[a]

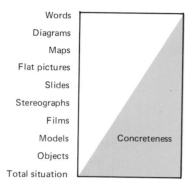

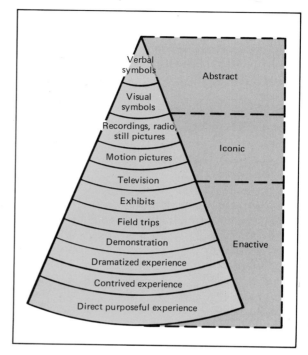

DALE'S CONE OF EXPERIENCE. From *Audio-Visual Methods in Teaching*, Third Edition, by Edgar Dale. Copyright 1946, 1954, © 1969 by Holt, Rinehart and Winston. Reprinted by permission of Holt, Rinehart and Winston. p. 108.

In 1946, Edgar Dale took the same construct and developed what he referred to as the "Cone of Experience."[b]

In the Cone of Experience, we start with the learner as participant in the actual experience, then move to the learner as observer of the actual event, to the learner as observer of a mediated event (an event presented through some medium), and finally to the learner observing symbols that represent an event. Dale contended that learners could make profitable use of more abstract instructional activities to the extent that they had built up a stock of more concrete experiences to give meaning to the more abstract representations of reality.

It is interesting that psychologist Jerome Bruner, working from a different direction, devised a descriptive scheme for labelling instructional activities that is quite parallel to Dale's. As shown here, Bruner's concepts of enactive,

iconic, and abstract learning may be superimposed on Dale's Cone. Bruner, though, intended to emphasize the nature of the mental operations of the learner rather than the nature of the stimuli presented to the learner.[c]

[a]Charles F. Hoban, Sr., Charles F. Hoban, Jr., and Samuel B. Zissman. *Visualizing the Curriculum.* New York: Dryden, 1937, p. 39.
[b]Edgar Dale. *Audio-Visual Methods in Teaching.* New York: Holt, Rinehart and Winston, 1969, p. 108. From *Audio-Visual Methods in Teaching*, Third Edition, by Edgar Dale. Copyright 1946, 1954, © 1969 by Holt, Rinehart and Winston. Reprinted by permission of Holt, Rinehart and Winston.
[c]Jerome S. Bruner, op. cit., p. 49.

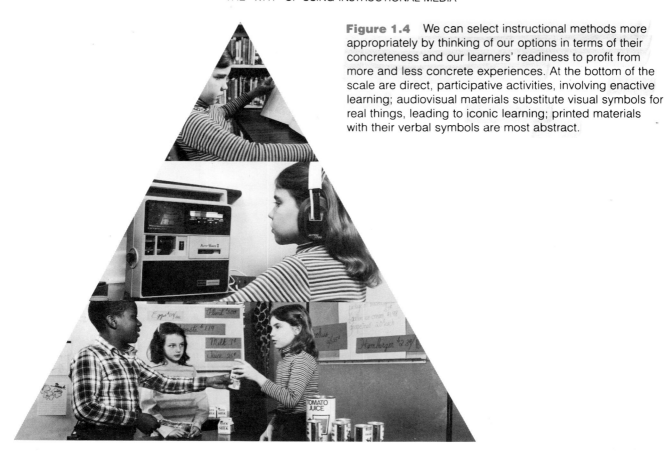

Figure 1.4 We can select instructional methods more appropriately by thinking of our options in terms of their concreteness and our learners' readiness to profit from more and less concrete experiences. At the bottom of the scale are direct, participative activities, involving enactive learning; audiovisual materials substitute visual symbols for real things, leading to iconic learning; printed materials with their verbal symbols are most abstract.

Figure 1.5 Learning effectiveness depends not only on the media selected for presentation but also on how the learner *uses* the information presented.

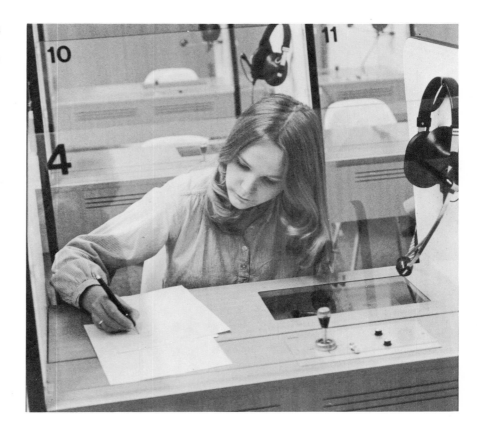

can provide a learning experience relatively high in concreteness, but it also takes up a good deal of instructional time. A motion picture depicting the same experiences as the field trip could be presented to the students in a much shorter period of time and with much less effort. Similarly, a simulation (a contrived experience) such as the game "Ghetto" can help students relate to new situations and solve new problems, but such a simulation game does take more time than a more abstract learning experience such as watching a brief television documentary about ghetto life. In such cases, the instructor must decide whether the particular nature of the experience is worth the extra time it may take.

The instructor must also decide whether or not the learning experience is appropriate to the experiential background of the student. The greatest amount of information can be presented in the least amount of time through printed or spoken words (the top of the concrete-to-abstract continuum and cone). But if the student does not have the requisite experiential background and knowledge to handle these verbal symbols, time saved in presentation will be time lost in learning. As mentioned before, the instructor finds out if the right match has been made by relying on what is perhaps *the* basic principle of instruction: learning means appropriate change in response, or performance. Because of this, emphasis in contemporary instructional research is placed on analysis of learner response as the key to choosing appropriate instructional experiences.

As Dale has pointed out, a model such as his Cone of Experience, while not an accurate representation of complex relationships, is, nonetheless, a practical guide to analyzing the characteristics of instructional media and methods and how these media may be useful.

This book will not cover all of the media and/or methods shown in the concrete-to-abstract continuum. We will be concentrating primarily on those methods that incorporate instruction into some media format. You should remember that the media discussed in the following chapters are not the answers to all instructional problems.

Figure 1.6 Are high school students likely to develop greater interest in and appreciation for social problems by participating in a simulation than by watching a television documentary? What other differences might there be in learning outcomes? Are these differences sufficient to justify the greater time expenditure of the simulation game?

Communication Models

Instruction is the arrangement of information to produce learning. The *transfer* of information from a source to a receiver is called communication. Because new learning usually depends on taking in new information, effective instruction cannot take place unless commu-

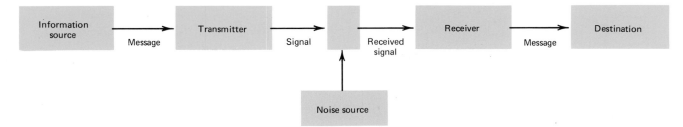

Figure 1.7 A message is selected by an *Information Source*; for example, a recording of a top 40 tune by a radio station. That message is then incorporated by the *Transmitter* into a carrier wave. The signal is then received by an individual's radio set (*Receiver*) and transformed into the message reaching your ear (the *Destination*). Acting on the signal as it is being transmitted are various distorting factors that Shannon called "*Noise Source.*" In the case of AM radio transmission, for example, the signal is subject to distortion caused by electronic disturbance in the atmosphere. To use another example, if you were showing a film in your class, the reception of both image and sound by your students would be affected by a number of external "noise sources," such as excessive light in the room interfering with the image on the screen, noisy heating units, loud conversation in the hallway, and the trumpet lesson in the room next door. Noise is any distortion of the signal *after* it has been transmitted and *before* it is received.

nication takes place. It is, therefore, helpful to know something about the communication process if we are to use instructional media effectively.

How do we communicate with one another? More importantly, how do we communicate so that the message we wish to communicate is correctly received by the person for whom it is intended? A number of attempts have been made to analyze communications by use of mathematical or verbal models as means of representing key elements in the communication process.* We will use one of the most seminal of these, the Shannon model, to help you analyze and solve instructional problems.

The model was developed by Claude E. Shannon of the Bell Telephone Laboratories. Warren Weaver, as coauthor of a book with Shannon, is the popularizer of the model.* When Shannon developed his communication model, he was interested solely in the technical aspects of communication and this is very clear from his definitions (Figure 1.7). He was interested in what happens to messages when they go through mechanical or electronic information transmission systems and not in the *meaning* of the message. Whether the radio station in our example in Figure 1.7 selected Beethoven's Fifth Symphony or one of the Top 40 pop tunes makes no difference.

For instructional purposes, however, the meaning of the message and how the message is interpreted are of paramount importance. The Schramm† adaptation of the Shannon model incorporates Shannon's concern with the technical aspects of communica-tion, but its central concern is with communication, reception, and interpretation of meaningful symbols. This is at the heart of instruction (Figure 1.8).

Let us examine the Shannon–Schramm model, first as it applies to communication per se in a television newscast, and then as it applies to communication in the instructional situation.

Newscast Communication.
Television stations receive much of their newscast content from wire services via teletype machines. The stories that will be broadcast are selected and edited by station personnel, transmitted by the television station, received by television sets, and emitted as image and sound to the receiver.

On the technical level, the Federal Communications Commission with its technical regulations and standards, the individual television stations, and the manufacturers of television sets and equipment do their utmost to make sure that the signal is transmitted and received accurately.

---

*For a discussion of communication models, see John Ball and Francis C. Byrnes (eds.). *Research, Principles, and Practices in Visual Communication.* Washington, D.C.: Association for Educational Communications and Technology, 1960.

---

*Claude E. Shannon and Warren Weaver. *The Mathematical Theory of Communication.* Champaign, Il.: The University of Illinois Press, 1949, p. 7.
†Wilbur Schramm. "Procedures and Effects of Mass Communication," in Nelson B. Henry (ed.), *Mass Media and Education.* The Fifty-Third Yearbook of the National Society for the Study of Education, Part II. Chicago, University of Chicago Press, 1954, p. 116.

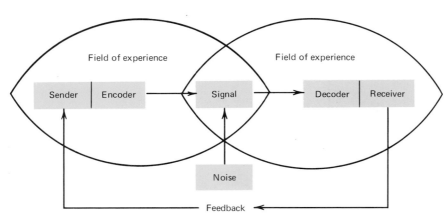

Figure 1.8 Schramm's adaptation of the Shannon model emphasizes that only where the sender's and the receiver's fields of experience overlap is there communication; for example, a spoken word—the signal—may be understood by both but will communicate only part of the richness of meaning that both people have for that word.

We must remember, however, that technical limitations can affect the visual and audio quality of transmitted and received signal and hence the quality of its interpretation. For example, antenna requirements for good reception vary considerably, depending on distance from source, land contour, and other interference factors. We should keep in mind that Shannon's "noise" factors affect "technical" quality; for example, an ambient light level suitable for the average viewer might prevent a vision-impaired viewer from seeing a screen image clearly. Or, a low sound level suitable for most listeners might cause message deterioration for a listener with hearing problems.

On the meaning level, the communication process starts with the station news staff's selection of stories they think will be important and interesting to the viewers. Now the decision has to be made as to the form the newscast will take. Should a particular story be delivered exactly as received from the wire service or should it be rewritten with a local flavor? Should film clips or graphics be used to help give the story more meaning? These are decisions of the *sender*, who then *encodes* the message according to those decisions. How members of the news staff perform this function depends on their knowledge and skill—that is, their *field of experience*. The transmitted signal is then decoded by those viewers

(receivers) tuned to the station. How the receiver interprets the message depends upon his or her knowledge—that is, *field of experience.*

Encoding and decoding can function effectively only in reference to the nature of the accumulated experiences of sender and receiver. Obviously, a receiver who has a poor grasp of standard English or a very low level vocabulary will have difficulty in correctly interpreting (decoding) the newscast message. Or let us say the signal (the encoded message) is about politics in Great Britain. To correctly interpret the message, the receiver must have some knowledge (experience) of international politics and of Great Britain itself—that is, the signal must be within the receiver's field of experience.

It is important to keep in mind that "meaning" per se cannot be transmitted. What are actually transmitted are *symbols* of meaning, such as words and pictures.

Figure 1.9 Like the journalist selecting from among various stories, the film editor selects from among various shots to construct a movie sequence, *encoding* the message to communicate most effectively to the viewer.

As authors of this book, for example, we cannot directly transfer to you the personal "meanings" we have built up in our own minds about instructional media. (We even have trouble doing so among ourselves!) The most we can do is to transmit verbal and graphic symbols from which you can evoke your own "meanings." The most we can hope for is that our skills and knowledge will enable us to encode our messages in such a manner that your skills and knowledge can be used to decode and interpret them correctly.

Instructional Communication. The principles of communication which help us analyze a television newscast can also be applied to the instructional situation. If you are using television for instructional purposes, either as an individual or as a member of an instructional television team, you will likely be called upon to help select and encode curricular content into meaningful symbols to achieve learning objectives. How successful the instruction will be depends upon the same factors that influence the "success" of a television newscast. For example, success will depend on your skill in encoding symbols that are meaningful to the students (the receivers) and on their skill in decoding them. Obviously, if the signal (the message) is within the field of experience of both you and your students, the opportunity for successful communication is at its optimum.

Unlike the newscast, however, instructional television is intended to *instruct* and not merely to communicate information. *Instruction is communication specifically designed to broaden and extend the field of experience of a learner.*

As a classroom teacher, for example, you would prepare your students for the instructional telecast (with a preliminary discussion of the topic, an overview of content, etc.), and you would design follow-up activities to reinforce and extend the range of what has been learned through the telecast.

Ideally, material presented to a student should be sufficiently within his or her field of experience to learn what is needed to be learned but enough outside the field of experience to challenge and extend that field. How far the instruction can extend beyond the student's field of experience before confusion sets in depends on many factors. Perhaps the most important of these is the ability of the student. Able students can assume more of the responsibility for extending their own fields of experience than less able students. Slower students will need instructional content more within their field of experience in order to be successful. Most retarded learners will require instruction that is almost entirely within their relatively limited field of experience. In Chapter 2, we will discuss the determination of "specific entry characteristics" of a student. This is a technical concept. The term specifies that part of a student's field of experience be pertinent to the learning task at hand.

There will be times when the learning task (message) may not be within the field of experience of the *instructor*. When this occurs, both instructor and student seek to extend their respective fields of experience, and the instructor should not feel peculiar about being in this position. Some of the most effective learning takes place when instructor and student must seek the answers together.

Another very important distinction between television (or any other medium) as a communication medium and television as an instructional medium is feedback from the receiver (see Figure 1.8). We usually think of feedback as some form of test, but many other techniques are available to indicate to the teacher how students are receiving instruction. Classroom discussion, conferences with individual students, homework, responses on short daily quizzes, body language, etc., are all forms of feedback. Not only does feedback help us to ascertain whether instruction has been successful or unsuccessful, but it also tends to take the burden off the student and place it where it more appropriately belongs—on the sender of the message (the instructor). Instructors are frequently tempted to blame the student when instruction is not successful. The real problem may be that the instruction has not been designed or delivered appropriately.

If feedback (evaluation) indicates that instruction has been less than fully successful, the Shannon–Schramm model and Dale's Cone of Experience (concrete-to-abstract continuum) can help us identify the source or sources of the problem and can suggest remedies. If "noise" unduly interfered with your signal, instruction can be repeated under more favorable conditions. If you made an error in appraising your students' field of experience, the concrete-to-abstract continuum may suggest a more appropriate entry level for your particular group. If the message was not

Figure 1.10 After viewing the prototype of a telelesson, the students provide feedback to the producers by telling their reactions during an "instant replay."

sage encodes it according to his or her skill and knowledge (field of experience) and the receiver decodes it according to his or her field of experience. In the feedback process, however, the receiver (student) does more than decode the message. He or she must also encode his or her interpretation of the signal for relay back to the sender (teacher), who, in turn, must decode it. In effect, receiver becomes sender and sender becomes receiver. And both interpret the message according to their fields of experience (Figure 1.12).*

This is an extremely important point for teachers to keep in mind. You must decode your students' feedback signals according to *their* interpretation of instructional content, which may or may not be the same as yours, and which will very likely differ, at least in detail, from student to student. For example, instructional information about

encoded properly, the continuum can help you identify more suitable materials, or you can adjust your utilization of the materials to produce more effective instruction.

Transactional Nature of Communication

We emphasize that communication is an interpretive transaction between or among individuals. As noted above, the sender of a mes-

*Wilbur Schramm, op. cit., p. 119.

Figure 1.11 The picture on the left shows one of the classic demonstrations of the transactional nature of visual perception. The right-hand head appears to be larger than the left-hand one. However, the second picture shows that the heads are actually the same size but that the shape of the room and size of the windows have been manipulated. Our past experiences with right-angle walls and equal sized windows leads us to interpret the image incorrectly.

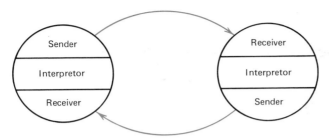

Figure 1.12 A transactional model of the communication process shows that during human communication when the receiver responds to the message he or she becomes the sender and vice versa. And both sender and receiver *interpret* the other's signals based on their past experience.

the labor movement in the United States may be interpreted one way by the child of a business executive and another way by the child of a union member. Black students and white students may interpret a film on slavery quite differently. The limited sensory abilities of some handicapped students may lead them to interpret instructional content differently from those of nonhandicapped children. Students raised in other countries will bring their cultural assumptions with them. For example, in the United States, the owl is often used as a symbol of wisdom, but in one region of Nigeria, the owl is an omen of evil. As an instructor, you must always be sensitive to the fact that student response to a communication signal is a product of student experience.

TECHNOLOGIES OF INSTRUCTION

Up to this point we have been discussing ways in which audiovisual media and materials can help improve communication and thereby improve instruction. The emphasis has been on the "things" of instruction—the *products* of technology. But instruction is more than communication alone, and technology *as a process* is a powerful tool for analyzing and solving instructional problems.

The principal definition of *technology* used in this book refers to "the systematic application of scientific or other organized knowledge to practical tasks."* Adapting this definition to the instructional situation, we may define *technology of instruction* as the application of our scientific knowledge about human learning to the practical tasks of teaching and learning. A technology of instruction, thus, is a particular, systematic arrangement of teaching/learning events designed to put our knowledge of learning into practice in a predictable, effective manner to attain specific learning objectives.

Over the years, many such arrangements have been devised, including programmed instruction, computer-based instruction, audio-tutorial systems, modular instruction, and simulation/gaming. Some technologies of instruction incorporate audiovisual media, others do not. Some employ electronic or mechanical devices, but others, such as programmed books and simulation games, may involve no such devices. (Specific technologies of instruction are discussed in detail in Chapter 11.) However, they all have one thing in common: they focus on the learner and on scientific principles of human learning.

Figure 1.13 Listeners with different cultural backgrounds may derive different meanings from the same message.

*John Kenneth Galbraith, op. cit., p. 12.

Figure 1.14 The "teaching machine" was one of the first outgrowths of the programmed instruction movement. The learner makes an overt response and checks the correctness of that response before proceeding to the next item.

immediate feedback to the student as to the correctness of response. Immediate awareness of correct response was looked upon by behavioral psychologists as a kind of reward that would "reinforce" what had been learned and would encourage further learning. ("Reinforcement theory" will be discussed more fully in Chapter 11.) Programmed instruction emphasizes the principle that human learning is an active process, not just reception of information. Communication is only the first step in learning.

The various other technologies of instruction developed more recently have also emphasized learning as a process requiring active participation by the student. But in the conventional group-based classroom, these functions are not always easy to carry out. How can each student be kept actively participating in the learning process? How can the busy instructor monitor each student's responses and administer appropriate rewards and corrections? Technologies of instruction aim to provide workable procedures for doing these things. A well-designed instructional simulation game, for example, employs rules that ensure that individual players spend time practicing some newly learned skill (response). A referee, other player, or some such device monitors the performance and points (reinforcers) are given on the basis of the performance.

It should not be inferred, however, that all current technologies of instruction are exclusively derived from reinforcement theory. Reinforcement theory sparked the movement and continues to provide new principles and techniques, but other organized bodies of knowledge, such as group dynamics, cognitive psychology, information theory, and developmental psychology, have provided bases for other and newer technologies of instruction.

Programmed instruction, for example, is based upon principles of human learning developed by behavioral psychologist B. F. Skinner and others in the 1950s. The teaching/learning arrangement worked out by these early instructional technologists consists essentially of printed informational material interspersed with blank spaces. The student fills in these spaces while reading along, the correct response being based in each case on information previously supplied. Filling in the blanks requires the learner to "process" the information rather than receive it passively. Most important, provision is made within the programmed material for

COMPUTER TECHNOLOGY AND INSTRUCTION

For the past decade or so, computers have been widely used for processing information, especially for administrative purposes. In schools, for example, they are commonly used to maintain up-to-date student records and to schedule classes.

The use of computers for instructional purposes is also growing rapidly. The computer, especially when combined with electronic transmission systems, can be used in an almost unlimited variety of ways in an almost unlimited variety of instructional situations and settings. The general concept of computer based education, however, is commonly considered to encompass two major categories: Computer Assisted Instruction (CAI) and Computer Managed Instruction (CMI).

CAI uses the computer directly as a medium of instruction and an information delivery system. The

Figure 1.15 With a television screen for displaying verbal and visual material, a keyboard for student responses, and a microprocessor to branch learners down different paths, the microcomputer brings new possibilities for individualizing instruction.

Figure 1.16 Educators are exploring ways to use computers to manage the data teachers need for sound decision making.

computer's ability to engage in instructional "dialogue" with the student while delivering information makes it adaptable to any number of instructional situations. CMI is basically a management technique for keeping track of instruction and supplying support services, such as materials appropriate to specific learning objectives, at specific stages of learner progress.

Flashback: Early Audiovisual Research Findings

As early as 1949, a summary of the research in media established the following advantages of using audiovisual materials in the classroom:

1. They supply a concrete basis for conceptual thinking and hence reduce meaningless word responses of students.
2. They have a high degree of interest for students.
3. They supply the necessary basis for developmental learning and hence make learning more permanent.
4. They offer a reality of experience which stimulates self-activity on the part of pupils.
5. They develop continuity of thought; this is especially true of motion pictures.

6. They contribute to growth of meaning, and hence vocabulary development.
7. They provide experiences not easily secured by other materials and contribute to the efficiency, depth, and variety of learning.*

Research since that time tends to confirm and expand these findings.

---

*Edgar Dale, Charles F. Hoban, Jr., and James D. Finn. "Research on Audio-visual Materials," in Nelson B. Henry (ed.), *Audio-Visual Materials in Instruction*. The Forty-Eighth Yearbook of the National Society for the Study of Education, Part I. Chicago: University of Chicago Press, 1949, p. 255.

Given the growing sophistication of computer technology and its increasing applicability to information delivery and instruction, we can be sure that the use of computers for instructional purposes at home, in school, and in other instructional settings, will continue to grow (see Chapter 13).

MEDIA/ TECHNOLOGY AND INSTRUCTIONAL STRATEGIES

Although instructional media may be used effectively in a wide variety of teaching/learning situations, they lend themselves particularly well to certain generalized educational purposes. Let us at this point briefly preview these purposes and suggest some basic strategies for their attainment, before fully discussing them in connection with specific media.

Support for Teacher-Based Instruction

The most common use of media in the instructional situation is for supplemental support of the instructor. Certainly there can be no doubt that properly designed instructional media can enhance and promote learning and support teacher-based instruction. But its effectiveness depends on the instructor (as will be made clear in the chapters that follow).

Research has long indicated the importance of the instructor's role in effective use of instructional media. For example, early studies showed that when teachers introduced films, relating them to

learning objectives, the amount of information students gained from films increased.* Later research confirmed and went beyond these original findings. Ausubel, for example, developed the concept of "advance organizers" as aids to effective instruction.† Advance organizers may take the form of an overview of or an introduction to lesson content, a statement of principles contained in the information to be presented, a statement of learning objectives, etc. In whatever form, they are intended to create a "mind set" for reception of instruction.

Advance organizers can be effective instruments for ensuring that media play their proper role as supplemental supporters of instruction. Many commercially produced instructional materials today have built-in advance organizers, which may be used as is or adapted by the instructor for specific educational purposes.

Student Drill and Practice

Certain media formats and delivery systems lend themselves particularly well to student drill and practice exercises. For example, learning laboratory instruction and programmed instruction are well suited to these purposes (Figure 1.18). Audio tapes can be used effectively for drill and practice exercises in spelling and arithmetic and in language instruction.

*Walter A. Wittich and J. G. Fowlkes. *Audio-visual Paths to Learning.* New York: Harper & Bros., 1946.
†David Ausubel. *Educational Psychology.* New York: Holt, Rinehart and Winston, 1968.

Figure 1.17 The instructor's skill in weaving audiovisual materials into the lesson is the single most important determinant of successful learning from media.

Figure 1.18 The listen-and-respond capabilities of the language laboratory support drill and practice in foreign languages and other similar subjects.

Discovery Learning

Instructional media can help promote the "discovery" or "inquiry" approach to learning and teaching. For example, 8-mm continuous loop films are frequently used for discovery teaching in the physical sciences. Students keep watching the loops until they perceive the relationships represented by the visuals and then they go on to "discover" the principles that explain these relationships. In the social sciences, various media formats can be used to present learners with visual and auditory experiences that provoke lesson-related inquiry. Media formats can also be used to confront professional and business trainees with "real-life" situations requiring inquiry into problems and discovery of their solutions. Films, simulations, and simulation games are often used to effect such "learning laboratory" situations.

Figure 1.19 In business/industry training, films are used to present realistic problems to be discussed in small groups.

Management of Instruction

Instructional media can permit a more productive relationship between instructor and student by allowing the teacher to become a manager of instruction rather than merely a dispenser of information. Media utilization allows teachers to spend more of their time diagnosing and correcting student problems, consulting with individual students, and teaching on a one-to-one and small-group basis (Figure 1.20).

How much time the teacher can spend on such activities will depend on the extent of the instructional role assigned to the media. Indeed, under certain circumstances, the entire instructional task may be left to the media. Experimental programs have demonstrated, for example, that an entire course in high-school physics can be successfully taught through use of films and workbooks without direct classroom intervention of the teacher. Successful programmed courses in calculus have been developed for use by able students whose high schools have no course in calculus.

This is not to say, of course, that instructional technology can or should replace the teacher, but rather, that media can help teachers become creative managers of the learning experience rather than merely monitors of instructional situations.

Figure 1.20 By putting task directions on audio cassette, teachers can use media to manage instruction more efficiently.

Individualized Instruction

Individualized instruction, wherein students use learning materials specifically designed or chosen to suit their individual interests, abilities, and experience, is now almost universally accepted as an important and productive instructional strategy. Interestingly, this comparatively recent educational innovation has developed more or less apace with the development of instructional media, with media contributing to the increasing growth (and, indeed, to the effectiveness) of individualized instruction and individualized instruction contributing to the increasing use of media in instruction.

Almost any instructional medium or media combination can be adapted for use in individualized instruction. Programmed instruction, for example, is specifically designed for individualized learning, as is the system of audio-tutorial instruction, which relies on audio recordings to individually guide student learning activities.

We will return to this point—the contribution of instructional media to the concept of individualized instruction—many times throughout this text, particularly in our discussions of the uses of individual media and media combinations in instructional situations.

Special Education

By now you may have inferred that instruction could be more individualized than it currently is. By individualized we do not necessarily mean that each student receives a separate instructional treatment, but that, at least, groups of students that exhibit certain common characteristics can be treated differently than groups of students with other characteristics. In this way we can best adjust instruction to the characteristics of the students. Handicapped children in

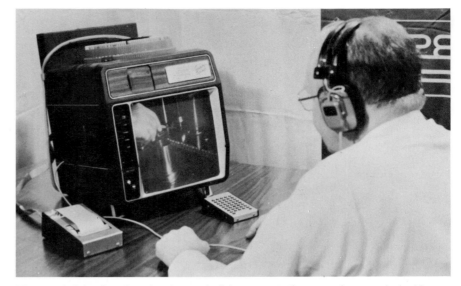

Figure 1.21 Synchronized sound-slide presentations can be coupled with programmed instruction techniques for effective individualized instruction.

particular need special instructional treatment. Mentally retarded children need highly structured learning situations because, referring back to our communication diagram, they lack the necessary field of experience and the ability to incorporate messages within their constructs. They need much more of the message placed within the context of their field of experience in order to expand that field of experience to any degree at all. Students who have impaired hearing or impaired vision require different kinds of learning materials; more emphasis should be placed on audio for visually impaired students than for normally-sighted individuals. Talking books, for example, are available to visually-impaired students to use in the institutional special education setting and in the home.

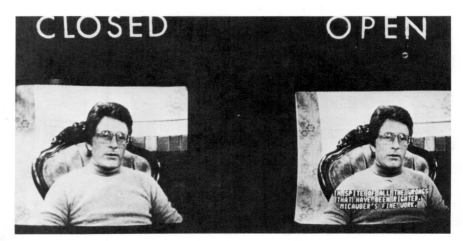

Figure 1.22 For the benefit of the hearing impaired, the Public Broadcasting Service transmits many of its programs with captions. The image on the left shows "closed" captions, visible only on television sets with special decoders. When it is fully implemented, this system will allow broadcasting of captions without disrupting the ordinary viewer's picture.

Adjusting instruction to all of these groups requires a heavy reliance on media and materials and the appropriate selection of those materials to fit specific purposes.

Although severely handicapped students need to be helped through special education classes and courses, the trend today is to "mainstream" students whose disabilities do not preclude them from profiting by exposure to regular classroom activities. Instructional media specifically designed for such students and/or classroom adaptation of media to compensate for physical and mental disabilities can contribute enormously to effective instruction of handicapped students and can help prevent their unwarranted (albeit unintentional) neglect by the busy regular-classroom teacher.

STRUCTURE AND FLEXIBILITY

Recent research lends considerable support to the principle that the amount of time students spend on the instructional task is directly and positively related to achievement.* Media directed instruction concentrates student time on a task. For example, television teachers have frequently commented that their televised instruction is more concentrated, has fewer diversions, than their classroom instruction. The learning laboratory has the effect of increasing the time spent directly on the task.

Students achieve more when instruction has some degree of structure, when they know what is expected of them, and the instructional environment is arranged to facilitate achievement of instructional objectives.† For example, if inquiry skills are the goal of instruction, then the obligation of the teacher is to be sure the environment is arranged to facilitate the necessary gathering of data from which inferences can be made by the student. Both the *kind* and *degree* of structure will vary with instructional objectives.

Structure, however, does not rule out flexibility. Even in a structured situation, accommodation should be made to individual needs and interests. Structured instruction need not be *excessively* task oriented. Nor does it rule out exploration, creativity, and self-direction.‡

The correct blend of structure and flexibility to best meet your instructional objectives will depend on a variety of factors, including the subject matter under study and the learning characteristics of your students—that is, their age and general level of intelligence and their specific knowledge about and attitude toward the topic at hand.

Drill and practice exercises are likely to be more structured than, say, a discovery lesson in geography. We would also expect a mathematics lesson on fractions to be more structured than a social science lesson in contemporary urban problems.

In general, younger children respond well to, and indeed need, a high degree of lesson structure. The Montessori method for teaching very young children, for example, is highly structured and its success depends on a carefully worked-out sequence of instruction and materials utilization. Yet the uninformed visitor to a Montessori type classroom may think the children are simply playing and having fun (Figure 1.23).

Figure 1.23 In Montessori schools, carefully structured activities stimulate and channel children's curiosity.

*N. L. Gage. *The Scientific Basis of the Art of Teaching.* New York: Teachers College Press, 1978, pp. 34-40.

†David L. Clark, Linda S. Lotto, and Martha M. McCarthy. "Factors Associated with Success in Urban Elementary Schools," *Phi Delta Kappan,* (March 1980), pp. 467-470. Also N.L. Gage, op. cit., pp. 31-33.

‡N. L. Gage, op. cit., p. 40.

Flashback: Media and Educational Innovation

In the last 25 years the introduction of a wide variety of new instructional methods, techniques, and curricula into North American education has contributed to the growing use of instructional media in the classroom. One could say it all started in 1954 with the School Mathematics Study Group (SMSG) at the University of Illinois, a group dedicated to revising elementary and secondary mathematics. Soon after, in 1957 Gerald Zakarias initiated the Physical Science Study Committee (PSSC), dedicated to wholesale revision of the teaching of physics in American high schools. Although both SMSG and PSSC had already been initiated before the dramatic launching of Sputnik by the Soviet Union in 1957, there is no doubt that Sputnik accelerated the interest of Congress and educators in revising and making more rigorous the curricula of the public schools.

After the success of the Physical Science Study Committee, a rapid succession of science curriculum projects were funded and brought to fruition. Very notable among these was the Biological Science Curriculum Study (BSCS), responsible for making drastic changes in high-school biology. According to a study made by the Educational Testing Service, BSCS was the curricular innovation that penetrated American high schools most quickly.

Along with curricular revisions came an emphasis on new instructional methods—or perhaps we should say reemphasis, since Dewey and other progressive educators had attempted to initiate many of the same innovations in the 1920s and 1930s. In the 1960s, Jerome Bruner emphasized the importance of "discovery" in instruction, insisting that children should experience the thrill of intellectual discovery in their school careers. Bruner was responsible for a widely respected innovation in elementary curriculum, a program he entitled *Man: A Course of Study*. Discovery was a basic part of the program and discovery elements were deliberately designed into the media accompanying the program. Bruner postulated three major modes of learning: the enactive or direct experience, the iconic or pictorial experience, and the symbolic, highly abstract experience. He suggested that, ideally, students should proceed from direct experience to iconic experience to symbolic experience, and

that students could not handle abstract experiences unless they had a rich background in the other two modes of learning. All of the curricular innovation projects sponsored by the academic disciplines relied heavily on the use of instructional media to achieve their objectives.

Concomitant with these innovations, were changes in organizational structures of the schools. For example, modular scheduling in secondary schools made a drastic change in the way students went through the school day. Team teaching was introduced, an approach which frequently used television as an integrating factor. The notion of grouping students according to factors other than simply grade level was brought to the fore. In the elementary schools, new organizational arrangements were introduced. The Individually Guided Education (IGE) program, developed at the University of Wisconsin, for example, organized instructional teams within the elementary school to focus on the most effective instructional arrangement for the individual child. The Individually Prescribed Instruction (IPI) program developed at the University of Pittsburgh successfully adapted programmed instruction for use at the elementary-school level. In IPI, students progress through a series of short modules individually and are evaluated by the teacher after completion of each module.

Instructional media have played a vital role in most of our recent educational innovations.[a] Without modern-day instructional technology, many, if not most, of them might have been impossible.

[a]Catherine Cornbleth. "Curriculum Materials and Learning," *Practical Applications of Research*. A Newsletter of *Phi Delta Kappa* (September 1979), p. 2.

In general, lower ability students prefer instruction to be fairly well structured, primarily because they do not have a high degree of confidence in their ability to work independently, nor in their ability to pull together what are to them unrelated strands of subject matter. Higher ability students respond well to a more flexible approach, since they have more confidence in their abilities, provided, of course, they are not students with high anxiety levels, or who prefer structured situations.

Motivation influences the tolerance students have toward a structured or flexible learning situation. Students who are highly motivated will be able to tolerate a very wide range of structure. Students with little motivation will prefer a learning situation that guides them to specific instructional ends. If given too much flexibility or too much independence in a learning situation, students with relatively low motivation will tend to lose direction along the way and not arrive at the specific goals that were set in the learning situation or may abandon the pursuit of those goals completely during the course of instruction.

Keep in mind that by structure we mean the extent to which the materials in the learning situation lead the student step by step to the specific objectives set by the program. Structure has nothing to do with difficulty. In the case of students with low motivation, we are not suggesting that the material be difficult or present difficult problems but that a structured learning situation can gently lead students toward instructional goals, and develop a degree of confidence they would not pick up in a situation that was extremely flexible or that placed a great deal of the responsibility to learn on their shoulders.

The role of media in allowing flexibility in learning is clear: materials—print and audiovisual—are attractive alternatives to the routine of the lecture. Materials that are relatively open-ended can be adapted to a variety of teaching/learning styles and situations. Self-instructional materials make possible such flexible arrangements as independent study and small-group work. Flexibility is enhanced when alternatives to teacher-talk are available.

Whatever blend of structure and flexibility you choose, instructional media can help you achieve your goals. Media and media systems can be structured toward specific learning objectives or they can easily be made open-ended and adapted to creative independent study and instructional flexibility.

Figure 1.24 An audiovisual learning station provides in-service training in nursing skills.

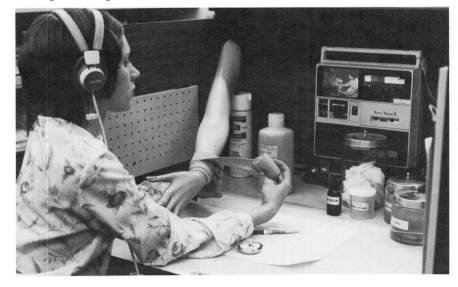

INSTRUCTIONAL MEDIA IN OUT-OF-SCHOOL SETTINGS

The development of sophisticated instructional media and our growing knowledge of how to use these media for effective learning have opened up instructional options not only for students in formal educational institutions but also for learners outside such institutions. Today, virtually any institutional setting can become a "classroom," with the aid of, and sometimes even near-total dependence upon, instructional technology.

Business, industrial, and financial institutions have today become major settings for instruction. No one knows exactly how much money United States corporations spend annually on "in-house" education and training of their employees (estimates range upward from $10 billion), but it is certain that the sum is tremendous and that it has begun to approach that spent on public school education. Many of the nation's labor unions operate extensive training programs for their members, and some have even included funding for membership education in their contract negotiations. Hospitals and other social welfare institutions have developed educational facilities to help keep their personnel abreast of current techniques and professional practices. Libraries, museums, and community centers of all types are likely to be organized centers of out-of-school education; and, of course, both national and local government agencies have contributed greatly to this overall trend toward instruction outside the formal educational setting.

The implications of this growing phenomenon are clear. In view of the increasing diffusion of instruction in our society, formal educational institutions must now be viewed as just one among many settings for education. As instruction moves more and more outside the school setting, more and more reliance will be placed on instructional media to meet diverse learning objectives. Significantly, formal educational institutions comprise the one setting in which the classroom teacher is still the dominant delivery system. Other settings—business, labor organizations, hospitals, community centers, government agencies, etc.—must rely much more heavily on instructional media specifically designed for specific learning objectives.

The fact remains, however, that the effectiveness of instructional media and media technology depends ultimately on the teacher, whatever the instructional setting. It is *how* the media are used that is instructionally important, not *where* they are used. Although this text is primarily centered on the specifics of classroom education, the principles and practicalities herein are as applicable to instruction outside the school setting as to instruction within it.

TECHNOLOGY AND "DEHUMANIZATION"

More than a few observers of the educational scene have argued that the widespread use of instructional technology in the classroom must lead to treating students as if they too are machines rather than individual human beings—that is, technology dehumanizes the teaching/learning process. It is, on the contrary, a major theme of this book that, properly used, modern instructional media can individualize and thus humanize the teaching/learning process to a degree hitherto undreamed of. The danger of dehumanization is not in the use of instructional media but in the way in which teachers perceive their students. If teachers perceive learners as machines, they will treat them as such with or without the use of instructional media. If teachers perceive their students as human beings with rights, privileges, and motivations of their own, they will treat them as such with or without instructional media. In other words, it is not technology that tends to mechanize people but the uses to which people put technology.

One of our most thoughtful observers of life in the classroom is Philip Jackson of the University of Chicago. He has been quite concerned about the quality of life in American classrooms and has found them somewhat impoverished. Perhaps you will see what a humanistic classroom is like if you see what a humanistic classroom is not like. In the book, *The Teacher and the Machine,* Jackson states that "the greatest intellectual challenge of our time is not how to design machines that behave more and more like humans, but rather, how to protect humans from being treated more and more like machines."* He

goes on to clarify what he means by human mechanization: "the process by which people are treated mechanically; that is, without giving thought to what is going on inside them." It is interesting that his illustrations of human mechanization in schools show how student attention, assignments, learning tasks, and discussion are mechanized with means as simple as the human voice and the teacher's right to turn students on and off. He lists six ways that human beings (students) are treated mechanically, as paraphrased by Lange:

1. *We turn them on and off whenever it suits our fancy.*
2. *It is unnecessary to offer an explanation of why they are working.*
3. *They are owned (no plans and future of their own; or unwillingly they relinquish their own plans and energies).*
4. *They are all work; idleness is waste (no play except as the owner may work them as part of his play).*
5. *A machine/human's worth is judged by the quality of its products.*
6. *There is absence of human empathy (no need to feel sorry for a machine that functions improperly).**

Jackson is disturbed to see that teachers in classrooms are treating many of their students mechanistically.

So we have seen that the question is not so much what is used in the classroom as how students are treated. A corollary of this statement is that it is not so much *what* a teacher teaches but *how* a teacher teaches. For example, many teachers, particularly in

---

*Philip W. Jackson. *The Teacher and the Machine.* Pittsburgh: University of Pittsburgh, 1968, p. 66.

*Phil C. Lange. "Review of *The Teacher and the Machine.*" *AV Communication Review.* (Spring 1969), p. 102.

English and social studies, consider themselves "humanists" but they may be anything but humanistic to their students. They may treat those students in the way in which Jackson said people can be treated mechanistically (Figure 1.25).

To reinforce this point, consider a case in which the introduction of machinery can make the instructional situation more humanistic. As research has indicated, students who have a high level of anxiety are prone to make mistakes and to learn less efficiently if under considerable pressure. Many teachers exert too much pressure on high anxiety students, thereby making the instructional situation not only disagreeable, but prone to error. Given the same sequence of instruction mediated through a machine that will continue only at the command of the student, the student can reduce the pressure from the machine simply by not responding. In other words, the machine patiently awaits for the command of the student to begin, whereas an overbearing teacher waits for no such command.

Contrary to what some educators believe, technology and humanism can work together or go their separate ways. Figure 1.26 suggests four basic mixes of techology and humanism.

Let's look at four examples of a mix of technology and humanism to see where each falls in Figure 1.26.

A. A college lecture with little or no interaction between professor and student.
B. A course consisting of a required series of modules, each composed of performance objectives, media to be used to complete objectives, and a self-evaluation test.

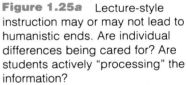

Figure 1.25a Lecture-style instruction may or may not lead to humanistic ends. Are individual differences being cared for? Are students actively "processing" the information?

Figure 1.25b Technology can help free the teacher for one-to-one interaction, doing what humans do best.

C. The same as B, except that students choose modules based on counseling sessions with an instructor, and they meet periodically to discuss the content of the modules.
D. A group that meets on a regular basis to discuss common reading assignments.

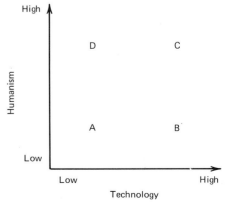

Figure 1.26

These examples are overly simplified and only illustrative, but they serve as a basis for analyzing the relationship between humanism and technology.

To reiterate, educational technology does not preclude a humane teaching/learning environment. On the contrary, instructional media can help provide a learning atmosphere in which students actively participate, as individual human beings, in the learning process. When instructional media are used properly and creatively in the classroom, it is machines that are turned on and off at will—not students.

REFERENCES

Print References

Asimov, Isaac. "His Own Particular Drummer." *Phi Delta Kappan,* September 1976, pp. 99–103.

* Barnouw, Eric. *Tube of Plenty* (New York: Oxford University Press, 1975).

Beard, R.M. *An Outline of Piaget's Developmental Psychology* (New York: Basic Books, 1969).

* Culkin, John. "A Schoolman's Guide to Marshall McLuhan." *Saturday Review,* March 18, 1967, pp. 51–53, 70–72.

Cunningham, William. "Technology: A New Era in Education." *Kappa Delta Pi Record,* October 1977, pp. 6–8.

* Fox, G.T., and DeVault, M.V. "Technology and Humanism in the Classroom: Frontiers of Educational Practice." *Educational Technology,* October 1974, pp. 7–13.

Gorman, Don A. "Instructional Management, A Meaningful Alternative." *Educational Technology,* June 1975, pp. 25–27.

Haney, John B., and Eldon J. Ullmer. *Educational Communications and Technology,* 2d ed. (Dubuque, IA: Wm. C. Brown Company, 1975).

Heinich, Robert (ed.). *Educating All Handicapped Children* (Englewood Cliffs, NJ: Educational Technology Publications, 1979).

* Hoban, Charles F. "Educational Technology and Human Values." *AV Communication Review,* Fall 1977, pp. 221–242.

Hooten, David E. "Educational Technology and the Adult Learner." *Educational Technology,* October 1976, pp. 20–25.

Kolesnik, W.B. *Humanism and/or Behaviorism in Education* (Boston: Allyn & Bacon, 1975).

Richardson, John, Jr. "The Mass Media and Cultural Exchange." *International Educational and Cultural Exchange,* Winter 1978, pp. 3–4.

Ruf, F. "Toward an Applied Science of Education: Some Key Questions and Directions." *Instructional Science.* January 1978, pp. 1–14.

* Schramm, Wilbur. *Men, Messages, and Media: A Look at Human Communication (New York: Harper & Row, 1973).*

Severin, Werner, and James W. Tankard, Jr. *Communication Theories: Origins, Methods, Uses* (New York: Hastings House, 1979).

Silberman, Harry F. "The Educational Potential of Technology." *Educational Horizons,* Winter 1974-75, pp. 85–91.

Srygley, Sara K. "Influence of Mass Media on Today's Young People." *Educational Leadership,* April 1978, pp. 526–529.

Stephens, Robert E. "The Role of Media in Minority-Related Education." *Negro Educational Review,* January 1978, pp. 33–41.

* Taggart, Dorothy T. *A Guide to Sources in Educational Media and Technology* (Metuchen, NJ: The Scarecrow Press, 1975).

Taylor, Kenneth I. "Media in the Context of Instruction." *School Media Quarterly,* Spring 1976, pp. 223–224, 237–241.

* Key references.

Audiovisual References

"The Child of the Future: how he might learn." (Montreal, Canada: National Film Board of Canada, 1965). (16-mm film, 60 minutes.)

"Communication Feedback." (Rockville, MD: BNA Film, 1965). (16-mm film, 21 minutes.)

"A Communication Model." (Bloomington, IN: Indiana University Audio-Visual Center, 1967). (16-mm film, 30 minutes.)

"Communications Primer." (Classroom Film Distributor, 1954). (16-mm film, 22 minutes, color.)

* "Media for Presentations." (Bloomington, IN: Indiana University, 1978). (16-mm film, 20 minutes, color.)

"Perception and Communication." (Columbus, OH: Ohio State University, 1967). (16-mm film, 32 minutes.)

* Schrank, Jeffrey. "The Electronic Classroom." (Chicago, IL: The Thomas More Association, 1974). (Three audio cassettes.)

* "This is Marshall McLuhan: The Medium is the Massage." (New York: McGraw-Hill, 1968). (16-mm film, 53 minutes.)

"To Help Them Learn." (Washington, DC: Association for Educational Communications and Technology, 1978). (16-mm film, 21 minutes, color.)

"Understanding Educational Technology." (Washington, DC: Association for Educational Communications and Technology, 1977). [Sound filmstrip (cassette).]

POSSIBLE PROJECTS

1-A. Read one of the books cited in the chapter or a book relating to a topic in the chapter and write or record on audio tape a book review/report. The report should be approximately 2½ double-spaced, typed pages or five minutes in length.

1-B. React to any of the topics or ideas presented in the chapter. Your reaction and comments may be written or recorded (approximately 5 double-spaced, typed pages or 10 minutes in length).

1-C. Analyze an instructional situation (either real or hypothetical) and identify the elements of the communication process and their interrelationship.

1-D. Prepare a "position paper" (approximately five double-spaced typed pages) on a topic such as: the role of humanism and/or instructional technology in education, or structure versus flexibility in teaching.

1-E. Describe an actual use of instructional media in an out-of-school setting based upon your experiences or readings.

CHAPTER 2

SYSTEMATIC PLANNING FOR THE USE OF MEDIA

OUTLINE

OBJECTIVES

After studying this chapter, you should be able to:

1. Describe six procedures (steps) in the systematic planning for the use of media (the ASSURE model).

2. List two general and two specific learner characteristics which could affect media selection.

3. Discuss the rationale for stating objectives for instruction. Your discussion should include three purposes or uses of objectives.

4. Write objectives which include performance terms, conditions (if necessary), and appropriate criteria.

5. Classify given objectives into cognitive, affective, and psychomotor domains; and rate them as "higher" or "lower" within each domain.

6. Describe the basic procedure for selecting, modifying, and designing materials, and indicate when each procedure is appropriate to use.

7. Explain how learner characteristics affect the selection of media.

8. State two examples of situational constraints on the selection of mediated materials.

9. Describe two examples of ways of modifying materials without actually altering the original materials.

10. Given a description of an instructional situation, utilize the Kemp charts to select the "best" media for that situation.

12. Identify general showmanship techniques in reference to strong and weak sectors of the classroom "stage," body positions, and movements.

13. Describe several methods for eliciting student response during and after using media.

14. Justify the need for requiring learner response when using media.

15. Compare and contrast the techniques for evaluating student achievement and the techniques for evaluating media and methods.

THE ASSURE MODEL

All effective instruction requires careful planning. Teaching with instructional media is certainly no exception to this educational truism. This chapter examines how you can systematically plan for the effective use of instructional media. We have constructed a procedural model to which we have given the acronym ASSURE, because it is intended *to ASSURE effective use of media in instruction.*

A Model to Help ASSURE Learning

A S S

Analyze Learner Characteristics

The first step in planning is to identify the learners. Your learners may be students, trainees, or members of an organization such as a Sunday school, civic club, youth group, or fraternal organization. You must know your students to select the "best" medium to meet the objectives. The audience can be identified by two types of characteristics: (1) general characteristics, and (2) specific entry characteristics—knowledge, skills, and attitudes about the topic.

State Objectives

The next step is to state the objectives as specifically as possible. The objectives may be derived from a course syllabus, stated in a textbook, taken from a curriculum guide, or developed by the teacher. Wherever they come from, they should be stated in terms of what the student will be able to do as a result of instruction. The conditions under which the student is going to perform and a statement of acceptable performance level should be included.

Select, Modify, or Design Materials

Once you have identified your audience and stated your objectives, you have established the beginning (audience's present knowledge, skills, and attitudes) and the ending points (objectives) of instruction. Your task now is to build a "bridge" between these two points. There are three options: (1) select available materials, (2) modify existing materials, or (3) design new materials.

ANALYZE LEARNER CHARACTERISTICS

If instructional media are to be used effectively, there must be a match between the characteristics of the learner and the content of the learning material and its presentation. The first step in the ASSURE model, therefore, should be analysis of your audience. Are your learners ready for the learning experience you wish to offer them? Is there a match between the learners' characteristics and your materials and methods?

For everyday purposes it is not feasible to analyze every psychological or educational trait of your audience. There are, however, several factors about your learners that are critical for making good media and method decisions. First, in the category of *general characteristics* are broad identifying descriptors such as age, gender, grade level, intellectual

U   R   E

Utilize Materials

Having either selected, modified, or designed your materials, you then must plan how the materials will be used and how much time will be spent using them. Next, prepare the class and ready the necessary equipment and facilities. Then present the material using the "showmanship" techniques and suggestions described in each of the chapters in this text. Finally, follow up with class discussion, small group activities, or individual projects and reports.

Require Learner Response

To assure learning, students must practice what they are expected to learn and should be reinforced for the correct response. The first time that the student is expected to perform the behavior called for in the objectives should *not* be on the examination. Instead there should be activities within the lesson that allow students to respond and to receive feedback on the appropriateness of their performances or responses.

Evaluate

After instruction, it is necessary to evaluate its impact and effectiveness. To get the total picture, you must evaluate the entire instructional process. Did the students meet the objectives? Did the media assist the students in reaching the objectives? Could all students use the materials properly? Was the environment comfortable (room temperature, comfortable seating, no distracting noises)? Did the teacher facilitate the students' learning by providing the necessary assistance for individual students?

aptitude, and cultural or socioeconomic factors. General characteristics are factors that are not related to the content of the lesson. These factors help you to determine the level of the lesson and to select examples that will be meaningful to the given audience.

Under the heading of *specific entry characteristics* you will think about content-related qualities that will more directly affect your decisions about media and methods: prerequisite skills (do learners have the knowledge base required to enter the lesson?), target skills (have learners already mastered the skills you are planning to teach?), study skills (do learners have the basic competencies in language, math, reading, reasoning and the like, needed to master the subject?), and attitudes (are there biases or misconceptions about the subject?).

Even a superficial analysis of learner characteristics can provide helpful leads in selecting instructional methods and media. For example, if your learners tend to be on the lower end of intellectual aptitude, they are more likely to need the special assists inherent in audiovisual presentations. By the same token, students with substandard reading skills may be reached more effectively with nonprint media. If you have a group strongly diverging in aptitudes, consider self-instructional materials to allow self-pacing and other aspects of individualization.

If you are dealing with a particular ethnic or cultural subgroup, you might want to give high priority to considerations of ethnic/cultural identity in selecting particular materials.

If learner apathy toward the subject matter is a particular problem, consider using a highly stimulating instructional approach, such as a dramatic film or a simulation game.

Learners entering a new conceptual area for the first time will need more direct, concrete kinds of experiences (e.g., field trips, role playing). The more advanced have a base for using audiovisual or even verbal materials. Heterogeneous groups, including learners varying widely in their conceptual sophistication or in their first-hand experience with the topic being discussed, can profit especially from an audiovisual experience like a videotape presentation. The videotape provides a common experience, one that is relatively concrete and shared by everyone in the same way. This common experiential base can serve as an important point of reference for subsequent group discussions and individual studies.

For instructors dealing with a familiar audience, analysis of general characteristics will be something of a given. Determining specific entry characteristics, though, may require some data gathering through means such as informal questioning or testing with standardized or teacher-made tests.

At times, however, audience analysis may be more difficult. Perhaps your students are new to you and you have had little time to observe and record their characteristics. Perhaps your learners are a more heterogeneous group than is ordinarily found in the classroom—business trainees, for example, or a civic club, a youth group, or fraternal organization—thus making it more difficult to ascertain if all or even a majority of your learners are ready for the media and method of instruction you are considering. In such cases, academic and other records may be helpful, as may direct questioning of and conversation with learners and group leaders. Pretesting, formal or informal, may be necessary to verify your assumptions.

In any case, you should make every effort to assess the characteristics and capabilities of your audience and to match your media and instructional methods to these characteristics and capabilities. Although you would not use ordinary audio media with a student handicapped by deafness or a filmstrip with a totally blind learner, you could fall into less obvious traps.

Suppose, for example, you intend your learners to observe cell division under a common laboratory microscope. Learner analysis leads you to believe, correctly, that your learners are able to identify visual representations of the parts of a cell—membrane, nucleus, mitochondrion, etc. Fine. They should, then, be able to identify these parts under a microscope. You proceed with your lesson, and then find to your chagrin that some of your learners do not know how to operate a laboratory microscope! Your lesson plan has failed, or at best enjoyed limited success, because of improper and incomplete assessment of learner characteristics.

STATE OBJECTIVES

The second step in the ASSURE model for using instructional media is to state the objectives of instruction. What learning goal is each student expected to reach? More precisely, what new *capability* should the learner possess at the completion of instruction? Thus, an objective is a statement *not* of what the instructor plans to *put into* the lesson, but of what the learner ought to *get out of* the lesson.

Your statement of objectives should be as specific as possible. For example, "my students will improve their mathematical skills" is far too general a statement to qualify as a specific lesson objective. It does, however, qualify as a "goal"—that is, a broad statement of purpose. A properly stated specific objective might be "The second-grade students will be able to solve single-digit addition problems, getting 8 out of 10 correct within one minute."

Why should you state instructional objectives? In the first place, you must know your objectives in order to make the correct selection of media and methods. Your objectives will, in a sense, dictate your choice of media and your sequence of learning activities. Knowing your objectives will also force you to create a learning environment in which the objectives *can* be reached. For example, if the objective of a unit of a drivers training course is "to be able to change a flat tire within 15 minutes," the learning environment must include a car with a flat tire. If, on the other hand, the unit objective is to be able "to name and describe the tools necessary to change a flat tire," a driver's manual or textbook would probably suffice.

Another basic reason for stating your instructional objectives is to help assure proper evaluation. You won't know if your students have achieved an objective unless you are absolutely sure what that objective is. Equally important, without an explicit objective your students won't know what is expected of them. If objectives are clearly and specifically stated, learning and teaching become objective-oriented. Indeed, a statement of objectives may be viewed as a kind of contract between teacher and students: "Here is the objective. Your responsiblity as a student is to achieve this objective. My responsibility as a teacher is to help you achieve it. Working together, we will carry out the terms of this contract and achieve our common goal."

Elements of Well-Stated Objectives

Most instructional developers include these three elements in a well-stated objective: (1) performance, (2) conditions, and (3) criterion.

© BRILLIANT ENTERPRISES, 1974   POT-SHOTS NO. 572

Ashleigh Brilliant

TO BE SURE OF HITTING THE TARGET, SHOOT FIRST AND, WHATEVER YOU HIT, CALL IT THE TARGET.

Performance. An objective should always include what the learner is expected to be able to do upon completion of instruction. Performance must be *observable*. Subjective terms such as "know," "understand," "appreciate," should not be the operative verbs in statements of objectives. Use verbs such as "measure," "discuss," "construct," which denote observable behavior (see the list of suggested performance verbs below).

Performance should be stated in terms of what the *learner* is expected to be able to do, not what the *teacher* is going to do.

"The teacher will describe five harmful consequences of excessive use of alcohol" is not an objective. It is merely an instructional activity. The objective would be: "You (the learner) will be able to describe five harmful consequences of excessive use of alcohol."

One useful format for stating multiple objectives for a given unit of instruction is to list each individual objective with its appropriate performance verb. For example: On completion of this unit, you should be able to:

1. Define *sociology*.
2. Describe three significant events in the development of sociology as an academic discipline.
3. Identify six misconceptions about sociology from a list of eight statements.
4. Analyze the results of a sociological study and state one appropriate conclusion from the study.
5. State and justify your position on the biological basis of socialization.
6. Evaluate the impact of the study of sociology on society.

The exact form of your statement of objectives is not critical. The important thing is that the statement be precise and tailored to your audience. In most instances using the informal "you" rather than the more formal "the student" is preferable if the objective is meant primarily to be read by the students. Using "you" helps to personalize the statement.

Conditions. A statement of objectives should include the conditions under which performance is to be observed, if such conditions are relevant. For example, may the student use notes in describing the consequences of excessive use of alcohol? If the objective of a particular lesson is to be able to identify birds, will identification be made from color representations or black/white photographs? What tools or equipment will the student be allowed to use in demonstrating mastery of the objective? What resources will the student *not* be allowed to use. One example is, "Given a political map of Europe, you will be able to mark the major coal producing areas." Another example is, "Without notes, textbook, or any library materials, you will be able to write an essay on the relationship of nutrition to learning."

The Helpful Hundred: Suggested Performance Verbs

Add	Defend	Kick	Reduce
Alphabetize	Define	Label	Remove
Analyze	Demonstrate	Locate	Revise
Apply	Derive	Make	Select
Arrange	Describe	Manipulate	Sketch
Assemble	Design	Match	Ski
Attend	Designate	Measure	Solve
Bisect	Develop	Modify	Sort
Build	Diagram	Multiply	Specify
Carve	Distinguish	Name	Square
Categorize	Drill	Operate	State
Choose	Estimate	Order	Subtract
Classify	Evaluate	Organize	Suggest
Color	Explain	Outline	Swing
Compare	Extrapolate	Pack	Tabulate
Complete	Fit	Paint	Throw
Compose	Generate	Plot	Time
Compute	Graph	Position	Translate
Conduct	Grasp (hold)	Predict	Type
Construct	Grind	Prepare	Underline
Contrast	Hit	Present	Verbalize
Convert	Hold	Produce	Verify
Correct	Identify	Pronounce	Weave
Cut	Illustrate	Read	Weigh
Deduce	Indicate	Reconstruct	Write

Check Yourself

Are the following statements written in *behavioral (performance) terms?* (Complete and then check your answers below.)

YES   NO

1. The student will grasp the true significance of the Taft-Hartley Law.
2. The students will learn the common tools in the woodworking shop.
3. The student will be able to name all bones in the hand.
4. The student will include 10 supporting facts in a written paragraph on the "Value of National Health Insurance."
5. The teacher will list on the chalkboard three major causes of the American Civil War.
6. The student will sit straight and quietly in his or her seat while the teacher is talking.
7. The student will show a favorable regard for volleyball by joining an intramural team.
8. The student will develop a sense of the cultural unity of mankind.
9. The student will like classical music.
10. The student will demonstrate a desire for a clean environment by voluntarily picking up litter in the classroom and on the playground.

Answers to "Check Yourself"

1. No, 2. No, 3. Yes, 4. Yes, 5. No, 6. Yes, 7. Yes, 8. No, 9. No, 10. Yes.

Criteria. A well-stated objective should include the criteria (or standards) by which acceptable performance will be judged. The criteria may describe quantity or quality or both. Ideally, the standards should be based on some real-world requirement. What level of skill is needed on the job? What degree of mastery is required to enter the next unit of study?

Time and accuracy are meaningful dimensions for many objectives. How quickly must the observable behavior be performed—for example, to solve five quadratic equations in five minutes, or to run a mile in less than eight minutes? How accurate must the results be—to the nearest whole number or within one sixteenth of an inch or plus or minus 1mm? If the learning activity is archery, criteria for performance acceptability might be stated, "The student will shoot ten arrows from 50 yards within five minutes and hit a three-foot-diameter target with at least seven of the arrows."

Quantitative criteria for judging acceptable performance may sometimes be difficult to arrive at. How, for example, can an industrial arts teacher specify how smoothly a piece of wood must be sanded? How can an English instructor state quantitative criteria for an essay or short story? Here performance is qualitative. Your task is more difficult in such cases, but not impossible. The industrial arts teacher, for example, might stipulate that the wood be comparable to a given example, or judged satisfactory by the teacher or a peer. The English instructor might stipulate that the student's work will be scored for development of theme, characterization, orginality, or the like. Again, a model story might be used as an exemplar. A quantitative criterion for the English instructor might be that more than five spelling and punctuation errors will be unacceptable. Whether quantitative or qualitative criteria are used, they should be as appropriate and as specific as you can possibly make them (see Appraisal Checklist, p. 41).

Classification of Objectives

Objectives may be classified according to the primary type of learning outcome they are intended to bring about. The most commonly used taxonomy of human learning sets out three major categories, referred to as the "domains" of learning: (1) cognitive learning, (2) affective learning, and (3) psychomotor learning.

Cognitive learning. This involves intellectual assimilation of information and knowledge. It ranges from simple recall, or memorization, to creation of new relationships.

Affective learning. This involves attitudes, feelings, and emotions. Affective learning skills range from simple awareness of a particular value to the internalization of clusters of feelings and values to form a well-integrated pattern of behavior ("character").

Check Yourself

Which of the following objectives include a *criterion of acceptable performance* properly stated? (Complete and then check your answers below.)

YES   NO

___ ___ 1. On the final exam, without references, the student will write an essay on the three themes in Shelley's poetry.

___ ___ 2. During a nature hike, the student will be able to identify correctly at least three different geological formations.

___ ___ 3. The student will sink 75 percent of his free throws in a single practice session.

___ ___ 4. The student will operate a potentiometer to determine the resistance of resistors.

___ ___ 5. In a ballet practice session, the student will display good form.

___ ___ 6. During the evaluation session, the student will demonstrate all the safety features listed on the chart at the front of the laboratory.

___ ___ 7. The student will be able to correctly name the football formations illustrated by each of 12 diagrams.

___ ___ 8. Given a list of authors, the students will match the names of each with the titles of their works.

___ ___ 9. On a questionnaire at the end of the course, the student will write at least two favorable comments about the course.

___ ___10. The student will properly operate model 63-9 metal lathe.

Answers to "Check Yourself"

1. No, 2. Yes, 3. Yes, 4. No, 5. No, 6. Yes, 7. Yes, 8. Yes, 9. Yes, 10. No.

Psychomotor learning. This involves muscular or motor skills. It ranges from simple imitative movements to physical skills requiring complex neuromuscular coordination.

Most learned capabilities contain elements of all three domains since we are urging the use of performance objectives that involve some observable behavior. Nevertheless, the primary emphasis can usually be classified as cognitive, affective, or psychomotor. For example, to achieve the objective of performing a somersault on a trampoline, the learner must have cognitive knowledge of the sequence of steps involved in the procedure. But the objective is primarily mastery of certain motor skills; hence it would be classified as a psychomotor objective.

Or let us say the objective of an elementary school lesson is to get the children to pick up classroom litter voluntarily. A certain amount of cognitive learning might be involved: learning, for example, how litter can contribute to acci-dents or why a clean classroom is easier to learn in than a cluttered one. The primary objective, however, is to change the children's behavior by changing their attitude toward littering and is, hence, an affective objective.

Taxonomy of the Domains of Learning

A knowledge of the taxonomy, or levels, of the domains of learning is useful as a guide to determine whether your objectives cover an appropriate range of skills and to decide the *sequence* of teaching those skills. It is very easy to fall into the habit of teaching only for low-level skills within a particular domain and to slight more advanced levels, since objectives which include high-level skills are likely to be more difficult to state and test.

Levels of Cognitive Learning*

The cognitive domain is based on a progression from *simple* to *complex* mental performance:

1. *Knowledge:* recalling specifics, remembering, defining, recognizing, repeating (e.g., You will state from memory *Paul Revere's Ride* by Longfellow.).

2. *Comprehension:* translating, interpreting, paraphrasing, summarizing, extrapolating (e.g., You will describe in your own words the story of *Paul Revere's Ride*.).

3. *Application:* using ideas and information (e.g., You will relate *Paul Revere's Ride* to modern communication techniques during a time of war.).

---

*Adapted from Benjamin S. Bloom (ed.). *Taxonomy of Educational Objectives, Handbook I: Cognitive Domain.* New York: David McKay Company, 1956.

APPRAISAL CHECKLIST: OBJECTIVES STATEMENTS

Performance

	High		Medium		Low
Specifies the learner(s) for whom the objective is intended	☐	☐	☐	☐	☐
Describes the *capability* expected of the learner following instruction	☐	☐	☐	☐	☐

—stated as a *learner* performance
—stated as *observable* behavior
—describes a real-world *skill* (versus mere test performance)

Conditions

Describes the *conditions* under which the performance is to be demonstrated	☐	☐	☐	☐	☐

—equipment, tools, aids, or references which the learner may or may not use
—special environmental conditions in which the learner has to perform

Criterion

States, where applicable, the *standard* for acceptable performance	☐	☐	☐	☐	☐

—time limit
—accuracy tolerances
—proportion of correct responses required
—qualitative standards

4. *Creation:* breaking down an example or system into its components; combining components to form results new to the student (e.g., You will compose an original poem following the rhyme scheme and imagery of *Paul Revere's Ride.*).

Levels of Affective Learning* The affective domain is organized according to the degree of internalization—the degree to which the attitude or value has become part of the individual.

1. *Receiving:* being aware of and willing to pay attention to a stimulus (listen or look) (e.g., The student will sit quietly while the teacher reads Longfellow's *Paul Revere's Ride.*).

2. *Responding:* actively participating, reacting in some way (e.g., The student will ask questions relating to *Paul Revere's Ride.*).

3. *Valuing:* voluntarily displaying of an attitude, showing an interest (e.g., The student will ask to read another story or poem about Paul Revere.).

4. *Characterization:* demonstrating an internally consistent value system, developing a characteristic "life style" based upon a value or value system (e.g., The student will devote a percentage of his or her free time to studying American history.).

*Adapted from David R. Krathwohl, et. al. *Taxonomy of Educational Objectives, Handbook II: Affective Domain.* New York: David McKay Company, 1964.

© 1971 United Feature Syndicate, Inc.

Check Yourself

Classify each of the following objectives into *one* of the domains according to its most prominent behavior. (C = cognitive, A = affective, and P = psychomotor). (Complete and then check your answers below.)

____ 1. You will be able to execute a tennis serve and receive a score of at least 85 points on a ten-item performance checklist.

____ 2. The student will voluntarily check out from the Instructional Resources Center media about insects following class discussion of the topic.

____ 3. Given a standard mechanic's tool box and the manufacturer's manual, you will be able to diagnose and correct within 15 minutes the cause(s) of an engine's misfiring.

____ 4. You will be able to copy a paragraph in cursive writing with 90 percent of the letters formed neatly and correctly according to the style taught.

____ 5. Given a table of reactivities, the student will predict the results of mixing phosphorus with sulfuric acid.

____ 6. The student will be able to type at a rate of 55 words per minute with fewer than one error per minute.

____ 7. Using the principles of plane geometry, a meter stick, and tape measure, you will determine the height of an actual building to within five feet of accuracy, on a sunny day.

____ 8. You will be able to write an essay of approximately 500 words contrasting the points of view of Lincoln and Douglas.

____ 9. After completing an introductory economics course, at least 50 percent of the students will enroll in an elective advanced economics course.

____ 10. You will be able to translate standard map symbols into verbal descriptions of topography without the use of a legend.

Levels of Psychomotor Learning*

The psychomotor domain may be seen as a progression in the degree of *coordination* required.

1. *Imitation:* repeating action which is shown (e.g., After viewing the film on the backhand tennis swing, you will demonstrate the swing with reasonable accuracy.).

2. *Manipulation:* performing independently (e.g., Following a practice period, you will demonstrate the backhand tennis swing scoring seven of the ten points on the performance checklist.).

3. *Precision:* performing with accuracy (e.g., You will demonstrate an acceptable backhand tennis swing, returning successfully at least 75 percent of practice serves to the backhand.).

4. *Articulation:* performing unconsciously, efficiently, and harmoniously, incorporating coordination of skills (e.g., During a tennis match, you will execute the backhand stroke effectively against your opponent returning nine out of ten of all types of shots hit to the backhand side.).

Objectives and Individual Differences

Objectives, whether in the cognitive, affective, or psychomotor domain may, of course, be tailored to individual learners. There is no rule that all students in a learning situation must reach objectives at the same time. In fact, if there were a rule on this matter, it should be that all students are *not* required or expected to do so.

Answers to "Check Yourself"

1. P, 2. A, 3. C, 4. P, 5. C, 6. P, 7. C, 8. C, 9. A, 10. C.

*Adaptation based upon published works of E. Simpson (University of Illinois) and R.H. Dave (National Institute of Education in New Delhi, India).

Flashback: Origins of Behavioral Objectives

Ralph Tyler, a professor at Ohio State University, is generally considered to be the "father" of behavioral objectives as we know them today. Tyler's original interest was in test-item construction. His main contribution was to point out the importance of constructing test items based on behaviorally stated objectives which could be determined by analyzing the curriculum content.[a]

However, it was the programmed instruction movement and particularly Robert Mager who popularized the use of objectives by educators. Mager was a research scientist at Fort Bliss, Texas, working on a study to compare an experimental version of a course with an ongoing Army course. He drafted the objectives for the course and insisted that they be signed by the proper authorities before instruction began. Later, while employed by Varian Associates in Palo Alto, California, he was involved in designing a one-day session on programmed instruction for school administrators. In order to teach them to discriminate between properly written and poorly written programmed instruction, Mager decided to write a branching program with a variety of instructional errors.

Robert F. Mager

But what topic to write on? I couldn't think of one. I stared at the typewriter, counted the leaves on the tree outside the window, and checked my fingernails. Nothing. Finally, while thinking about the nature of the target population (audience), I had a flash! I'll fix you, I said to myself. I'll write about a topic that will get you so emotionally aroused that you won't be able to see programming from the subject matter. And I began to type out a dogmatic (error-filled) branching program called "How to Write Objectives." In addition to such pedagogical niceties as branching the reader to pages that didn't exist, I berated them on the wrong answer pages with comments such as "How can you sit there and SAY a thing like that. You're lying and you know it." And "Now look here! I don't want to have any trouble with you. So read the little gem: 'How do YOU know? Have you ever tried seriously to specify exact objectives for an academic course? Or are you upset simply because what is being suggested sounds like work?'"[b]

Mager's initial program on writing objectives was duplicated and generated a great deal of discussion and provided practice in spotting good and bad characteristics in an instructional program. In Mager's words, "The day was a huge success."

Later Mager learned that at least two professors at local colleges were using his error-laden practice program as a textbook in their education courses, so he modified the original program and published *Preparing Objectives for Programmed Instruction*[c] in 1961. He and others quickly realized that his objectives could be applied to much more than just programmed learning, so the following year the book was re-released with the title *Preparing Instructional Objectives*.[d] The book is a classic in the field of education; now in its second edition, it has sold over one and a half million copies. As Mager says, "If you're not sure where you're going, you're liable to end up someplace else—and not even know it."

---

[a]Ralph Tyler. "The construction of examinations in botany and zoology." *Service Studies in High Education*. Bureau of Educational Research Monograph No. 15. Columbus: Ohio State University, 1932.
[b]Robert F. Mager. "Why I wrote..." *NSPI Journal*, October 1976, p. 4.
[c]Robert F. Mager. *Preparing Objectives for Programmed Instruction*. Palo Alto, CA: Fearon Publishers, 1961.
[d] See References at end of this chapter.

Nor is there a rule that the particulars of an objective be the same for all students. Again, if there were a rule it should state that they *not* be the same.

For example, the physical education teacher knows that not all the students in class will be physically able to run 200 yards in less than one minute after one week of practice and training. The specifics of the objective must be altered for particular individuals. Similarly, the teacher of math, or of English, or any subject, may alter specifics of an objective to accommodate slower than average learners. Or, on the other hand, the teacher may add "enrichment" tasks and objectives to accommodate gifted learners. Criteria will, of course, also be altered to accommodate changes in expected levels of achievement.

Objectives are not intended to *limit* what a student learns. They are intended only to provide a minimum level of expected achievement. Serendipitous or incidental learning should be expected to occur (and encouraged) as students progress toward an objective. Each learner has a different field of experience (as discussed in Chapter 1) and each has different learning characteristics (as discussed previously in this chapter). Because of these individual differences, incidental learning will take different forms with different students. Class discussions and other kinds of student involvement in the instructional situation, therefore, should rarely be rigidly limited to a specific objective. Student involvement should allow for incidental learning to be shared and reinforced. Indeed, in order to foster incidental learning and provide for individual differences, it is sometimes advisable to have the students specify some of their own objectives.

SELECT, MODIFY, OR DESIGN MATERIALS

The third step in the ASSURE model is selection, modification, or design of appropriate instructional materials. The pedagogical significance of choosing appropriate materials is magnified by the pervasive presence of instructional media in the classroom setting. Research has shown that, on the average, 90 to 95 percent of instructional class time is spent on activities based on the use of instructional materials.*

Obtaining appropriate materials will generally involve one of three alternatives: (1) selecting available materials, (2) modifying existing materials, or (3) designing new materials. Obviously, if materials are already available that will allow your students to meet your objectives, these materials should be used to save both time and money. When the media and materials available do not match your objectives or are not suitable for your audience, an alternate approach is to modify the materials. If this is not feasible the final alternative is to design your own materials. Even though this is a more expensive and time-consuming process, it does allow you to prepare materials to precisely serve your audience and meet your objectives.

Selecting Available Materials

The majority of instructional materials used by teachers are "off the shelf"—that is, ready-made and available from school or district collections or other easily accessi-

---

*P. Kenneth Komoski. "How Can the Evaluation of Instructional Materials Help Improve Classroom Instruction Received by Handicapped Learners?" in R. Heinich (ed.), *Educating All Handicapped Children.* Englewood Cliffs, NJ: Educational Technology Publications, 1979, pp. 189–191.

ble sources. How do you go about making an appropriate choice from among available materials? Your first step might well be a check of material catalogs and indexes to get a general idea of what is available. (See Appendix A and individual media chapters for lists of catalogs and indexes. See Appendix B for sources of free and inexpensive materials.) Your actual selection, however, will largely depend on the following factors:

1. The characteristics of the learners.
2. The nature of the objectives.
3. The instructional approach.
4. The constraints of the instructional situation.

Just as there must be a match between learner and objectives, there must also be a match between learner and materials. Is the vocabulary level of the material appropriate? Is the reading or listening level appropriate? Does the level of illustrative detail match the experience level of the students? If the material must be manipulated, do the learners possess the skills necessary to do so?

The selected materials must, of course, be relevant to your objectives. Does the material contain the information and activities necessary to achieve them? No matter how "good" it might be on other counts, of what benefit is it if it doesn't help you and your students attain your objectives?

Your choice of media may be influenced by the instructional approach involved in the lesson. Different media lend themselves to different instructional approaches and purposes. For example, filmstrips lend themselves better to individualized instruction than do multiscreen slide/tape presentations. One media form may fit an instructional situation stressing inquiry learning (e.g., silent loop film); another may be best suited for a lesson stressing open-ended discussion (e.g., videocassette). A format such as a film may be ideal for increasing motivation, but a simulation exercise might be better for introducing a new topic.

Your selection of instructional materials will also be influenced by the constraints of the instructional situation. Can sufficient classroom time be scheduled for proper use of the materials? Will all the necessary equipment be available to you (projectors, tape recorders, etc.)? If the materials require assistance of aides, are the necessary personnel available? Does the learning environment lend itself to use of your materials? For example, opaque projectors require a completely darkened room. Will your budget cover the cost of your materials? Some films and equipment, for example, may have high rental fees.

Media Appraisal Checklist.

We have now analyzed a number of media selection criteria related to learner characteristics, objectives, instructional approach, and situational constraints. If these criteria are to be *applied* to your own day-to-day selection decisions, they need to be summarized into a usable checklist. In the later chapters we provide suggested checklists for each of the specific classes of media. The form shown on page 46, "Appraisal Checklist: Generalized" suggests the general criteria you would look for regardless of the media format.

The Instructor's Personal File.

Every instructor should develop a file of media references and appraisals for personal use. The personal file card need not be as detailed as the appraisal form What you are primarily interested in recording are instructional

Title: _____ Format: _____

Length: _____ Source: _____ Technical data: _____

Synopsis:

Utilization pointers and problems (e.g., new vocabulary):

Figure 2.1 The instructor's personal file card should be an informal record of your own personal experience with particular audiovisual items.

strengths and weaknesses. Figure 2.1 illustrates a suggested personal file form that is relatively simple and will fit on a 4 in. by 6 in. card. Under "synopsis," you can note the overall content of the item. Under "utilization pointers and problems," you might note information about vocabulary used in the material, lack or inclusion of opportunities for student response, timeliness of the content, inclusion of sensitive topics, etc.

Modifying Available Materials

If you cannot locate entirely suitable materials and media off-the-shelf, you might be able to modify what is available. This alternative can be a challenging and creative task. In terms of time and cost, it is a more efficient procedure than designing your own, although type and extent of necessary modification will, of course, vary.

Perhaps the only visual available showing a piece of equipment being used in a junior-high woodworking class is from a repair manual and contains too much detail and complex terminology. A possible solution to the problem would be to use the picture but modify the caption and simplify or omit some of the names of the labelled parts.

Or perhaps there is just one film available which shows a needed visual sequence, but the audio portion of the film is inappropriate because it is at too high or too low a conceptual level or it discusses inappropriate points. In such a case, a simple solution would be to show the film with the sound turned off and provide the narration yourself. Another modification technique, which many instructors overlook, is to show just a portion of a film, stop the projector, discuss what has been presented, then continue with another short segment followed by additional discussion. A similar approach may be used for sound filmstrips with audio tape. You can re-record the narration and use the appropriate vocabulary level for your audience and even change the

APPRAISAL CHECKLIST: GENERALIZED

Title⎯⎯⎯⎯⎯⎯⎯⎯⎯⎯⎯⎯⎯⎯⎯⎯⎯⎯

Producer/distributor⎯⎯⎯⎯⎯⎯⎯⎯⎯⎯⎯⎯⎯⎯

Length⎯⎯⎯⎯minutes   Production date⎯⎯⎯⎯⎯⎯⎯

Audience/grade level⎯⎯⎯⎯⎯⎯

Cost⎯⎯⎯⎯   Subject area⎯⎯⎯⎯⎯⎯⎯

Format:

☐ audio tape/cassette
☐ slides
☐ filmstrip
☐ film
☐ videotape/cassette
☐ other⎯⎯⎯⎯

Objectives:

Brief description:

Entry capabilities required:

prior knowledge
reading ability
math ability
other

RATING

	High		Medium		Low
Likely to arouse student interest	☐	☐	☐	☐	☐
Accuracy of information	☐	☐	☐	☐	☐
Technical quality	☐	☐	☐	☐	☐
Provides meaningful student participation	☐	☐	☐	☐	☐
Evidence of effectiveness (e.g., field-test results)	☐	☐	☐	☐	☐
Provides guidance for discussion/follow-up	☐	☐	☐	☐	☐

Requirements:

equipment
facilities
personnel

Strong points:

Weak points:

Recommended action⎯⎯⎯⎯⎯⎯⎯⎯⎯⎯

Reviewer⎯⎯⎯⎯⎯⎯⎯⎯

Position⎯⎯⎯⎯⎯⎯⎯⎯

Date⎯⎯⎯⎯⎯⎯⎯⎯

Figure 2.2 The most basic way of modifying material such as a film is to show only a part of the material, or to show segments interspersed with group discussion.

emphasis of the visual material. If a transcript of the original narration is available, you will probably want to refer to it as you compose your own narration.

Modification can also be made in the audio portion of foreign language materials (or English language materials used in a bilingual classroom). Narrations can be changed from one language to another or from a more advanced rendition of a foreign language to a simpler one.

The availability of videocassette recorders now provides teachers with the opportunity to modify television programs which previously were available only as shown on the air. With video playback units available in most schools many producers now distribute programs having educational potential in videotape format. Programs may also be recorded off the air for replay on playback units.* Procedures and practices for modification of videotape are much the

same as noted above for film. Videocassette recorders also, of course, give the teacher much more flexibility in using television programs for instructional purposes. Programs can be shown at whatever time best suits the instructional situation and to whatever student group or groups that can best profit from viewing them.

One frequently modified media format is a set of slides with an audiotape. If the visuals are appropriate but the language is not, it is possible to change the language. It is also possible to change the *emphasis* of the narration. For example, an original audiotape might emphasize oceans as part of an ecosystem, whereas the teacher may want to use the slides to show various types of fish found in oceans. Rewriting the narration could adapt the material to the teacher's purpose while using the same slides. Redoing the tape can also change the *level* of the presentation. A slide-tape presentation produced for a high-school social studies class could

be modified for use at the junior-high or even elementary level. If some of the visuals are inappropriate or not in the desired sequence, the teacher might either add additional slides or change the order of the slides.

Instructional games can be readily modified to meet particular instructional needs. It is possible to use a given game format and change the rules of play in order to increase or decrease its level of sophistication. Many instructional games require the players to answer questions. It is relatively easy for the teacher to prepare a new set of questions at a different level of difficulty or even on a new topic.

If you try out modified materials while they are still in more or less rough form you can then make further modifications in response to student reaction until your materials meet your exact needs.

A word of caution about modifying commercially produced materials (and, indeed, about use of commercial products in general): Be sure your handling and use of such materials does not violate copyright laws and restrictions. If in doubt, check with your school administrator or legal advisor. (Copyright laws and guidelines are discussed in Appendix C.)

Designing New Materials

It is easier and less costly to use available materials, with or without modification, than to start from scratch. There is seldom justification for re-inventing the wheel. However, there may be times when your only recourse is to design your own materials. As with selecting from available materials, certain basic considerations must be taken into account when designing new materials. For example:

Objectives—what do you want your students to learn?

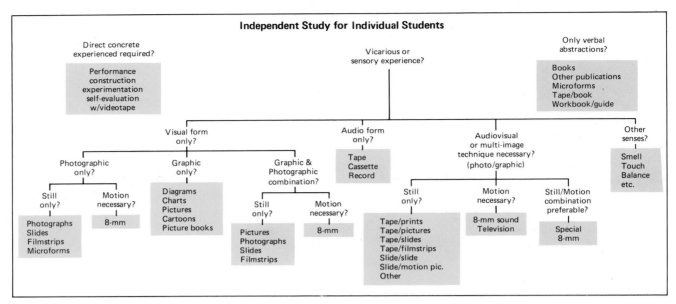

Figure 2.3

Audience—what are the characteristics of your learners? Do they have the requisite knowledge and skills to use and/or learn from the materials?

Cost—is sufficient money available in your budget to meet the cost of supplies (film, audio tapes, etc.) you will need to prepare the materials?

Technical Expertise—do you have the necessary expertise to design and produce the kind of materials you wish to use? If not, will the necessary technical assistance be available to you? (Try to keep your design within the range of your own capabilities. Don't waste time and money trying to produce slick professional materials when simple inexpensive products will get the job done.)

Equipment—do you have available the necessary equipment to produce and/or use the materials you intend to design?

Facilities—if your design calls for use of special facilities for preparation and/or use of your materials, are such facilities available?

Time—can you afford to spend whatever time may be necessary to design and produce the kind of materials you have in mind?

A useful scheme for determining which type of media to design has been developed by Jerrold Kemp in his book, *Planning and Producing Audiovisual Materials** (see Figure 2.3). Notice that Kemp presents a series of decision branches based on group size, the nature of the learning task, the attributes of the various media, if media are to be designed by the teacher, or if the teacher is drawing up specifications for media to be produced by the school or district media program. Kemp's chart can be extremely helpful in determining what media would give best results for what instructional situation. Specific techniques for the design of media materials are described in subsequent chapters of this book.

_____
*Jerrold E. Kemp. *Planning and Producing Audiovisual Materials*. 4th edition. New York: Harper & Row, 1980.

UTILIZE MATERIALS

The next step in the ASSURE model is the one that all the other steps lead up to and away from: the presentation itself. To get maximum learning impact from your presentation, formal research stretching back to U.S. military training in World War II and the practical experience of a couple of generations of teachers indicate that several utilization procedures must be followed. These can be summarized: preview, prepare the environment, prepare the audience, and present.

Preview

No instructional materials should be used blind. During the selection process you should have determined for yourself that the materials are appropriate for your audience and objectives. Published reviews, reports of field tests, distributors' blurbs, and colleagues' appraisals all add evidence. However, the prudent instructor will insist on previewing the materials. Only such detailed familiarity with the contents can

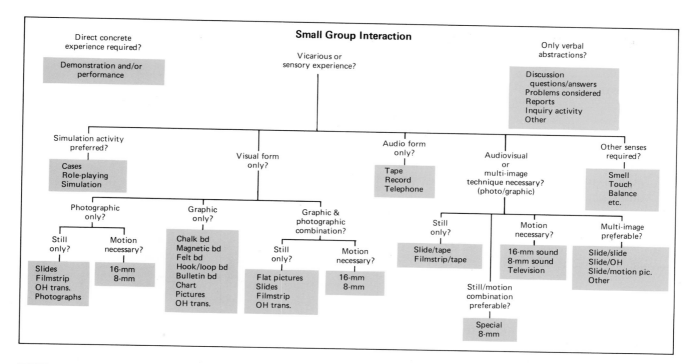

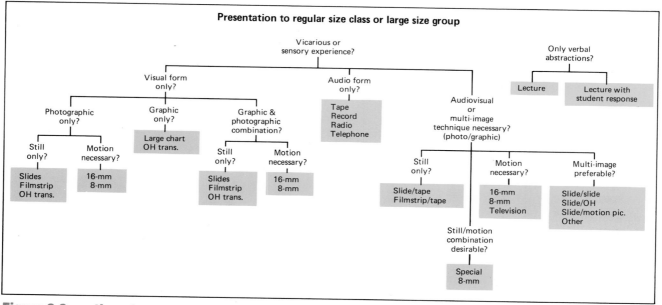

Figure 2.3 continued
"Media Selection Diagrams" p.46 from *Planning and Producing Audio-Visual Materials* by Jerrold E. Kemp. Copyright © 1980 by Harper & Row, Publishers, Inc. Reprinted by permission of the publisher.

enable you to properly wrap the lesson around the audiovisual material.

In addition, sensitive content may need to be eliminated or at least discussed prior to showing to prevent student embarrassment and/or impediment of learning. In one (admittedly extreme) case, an elementary teacher and her young students were horrified to find that an unpreviewed and ostensibly unobjectionable film on Alaska's fur seals contained a sequence showing baby seals being cold-bloodedly clubbed to death.

Prepare the Environment
Wherever the presentation is to take place—classroom, auditorium, meeting room, or whatever—the facilities will have to be put in order. Certain factors are taken for granted for any instructional situation—comfortable seating, adequate ventilation, climate control,

AV Showmanship—General Tips

• *You are a medium.*

Most audiovisual presentations include some sort of live performance by the instructor, perhaps as narrator or actor, perhaps as both. As a performer, you become an important component of the medium. Indeed, in a sense, you yourself, become a medium, a medium which must perform effectively if your presentation is to be successful.

Be natural. Your audience will quickly sense affectation. Do not try to be someone or something you are not. But, by all means be enthusiastic! Successful actors know that their "energy level" directly affects audience response.

Avoid distracting mannerisms. Do you have an annoying habitual mannerism—smoothing your hair, twisting your watch, clicking a ballpoint pen—or a "verbal tic" such as inserting "um" or "you know" at every pause? Such mannerisms can become very annoying to an audience. The listener stops hearing the message and begins concentrating on the mannerism. The first step toward controlling such distractors is to become aware of them. Videotaping yourself in action can be an effective aid to discovering and correcting them.

• *Your classroom is a stage.*

When you are making a presentation from the front of a classroom you are functioning like an actor on the stage. Your impact on the audience can be strengthened by observing a few of the basic principles of stagecraft.

Strong Areas. The front of the classroom, the "stage," can be divided into six sections, as shown in Figure 2.4. Note that the front (near the audience) is generally stronger than the back, and that the center is stronger than either

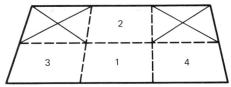

Figure 2.4 Ranking of the various sectors of the stage in terms of strength. Note that the left front is stronger than the right front and that both rear corners are "no-man's-land."

side. Of the two sides, the left (as seen by the audience) is stronger than the right.

The audiovisual presenter can use these strengths and weaknesses to good psychological advantage by using position to feature the dominant points of a presentation. See, for example, Figures 2.5, 2.6, and 2.7.

Figure 2.5 The screen, because of its placement in the center, has clear dominance over the presenter.

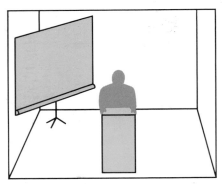

Figure 2.6 The presenter, situated in the front center, here has a stronger position than the screen.

Figure 2.7 Here the presenter is in a moderate position, but the display table, being at the front center, takes precedence.

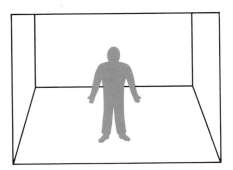

Figure 2.8 The full-front body position is the strongest one.

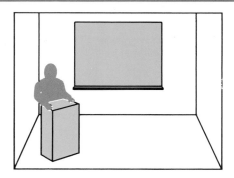

Figure 2.9 Three-quarters full-front is the second strongest body position.

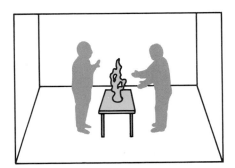

Figure 2.10 Standing in profile, these figures are in a rather weak body position.

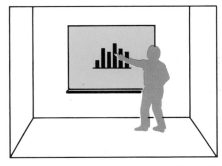

Figure 2.11 A one-quarter view body position is the very weakest.

Body Position. Facing the audience full-front is the strongest position. Three-quarters full-front is weaker; profile is weaker yet. Weakest is the one-quarter view, with the back nearly turned toward the audience. The use of chalkboards or charts will push you toward the weak position unless you consciously avoid it. (See Figures 2.8, 2.9, 2.10 and 2.11).

Movement. Given a static scene, any movement attracts the eye. This is one reason that nervous gestures are objectionable; they may distract attention from a point to be made. But movement can also be used positively to underscore important points. Experienced speakers often signal the beginning of a new topic by pausing and shifting their position, possibly walking to a different part of the room. But some movements are definitely stronger than others. As illustrated in Figure 2.12, the strongest movement is toward the front center of the "stage" from one of the weaker areas. Conversely, the weakest

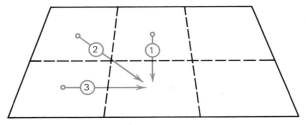

Figure 2.12 The three stage movements shown here give the greatest strength or emphasis to the presenter (numbers indicate the order of strength). The reverse of these would be the weakest movements.

movement is away from the front center, especially toward a corner.

In Figure 2.7, if the speaker leaves the lectern to approach the display table, he or she will be executing a very strong movement which will add dramatic emphasis to the presentation.

AV Showmanship—General Tips

● *Keep it light.*

A relaxed environment has been shown to increase suggestibility, a state conducive to rapid, effective learning. Humor can be very effective in establishing a relaxed environment, no matter what the age of the audience or the seriousness of the study. A joke, a humorous aside, poking fun at yourself, can help build receptiveness. Obviously, humor should flow naturally from the instructional situation and should never be forced. Negative humor, such as sarcasm or ethnic jokes, has a high likelihood of offending your audience and should not be used.

● *Keep a surprise in store.*

Don't be afraid to surprise your audience. Unexpected conclusions and surprising visuals can add dramatic emphasis to your presentation.

● *Control attention.*

Eye contact with your audience is extremely helpful in controlling attention. One of the great advantages of the overhead projector is that it allows you to maintain eye contact with your audience during presentation, since you are at the front of the room and the room is lighted.

Eye contact is more difficult with slides and filmstrips.

Keep in mind that attention naturally gravitates toward the brightest light in a given area. If you want your viewers to shift their attention from a lighted screen back to you, turn off the projector. Users of overhead projectors sometimes forget this simple rule. They leave a visual on the screen after they are finished with it or leave the projector on after the lesson segment is completed. When they then move on to a new topic, audience attention remains focused on the lighted screen rather than on the instructor.

● *Keep sight and sound synchronized.*

One sure way to confuse (and madden) your audience is to fail to synchronize sound and visuals. Careful scripting will help you avoid this serious pitfall. If a projectionist is advancing your visuals, provide a copy of the script containing clearly marked directions. If no such script is available, arrange ahead of time for signals which will alert the projectionist when to advance visuals. A nod of the head or an unobtrusive wave of the hand will suffice. A trumpeted "Next slide please!" is distracting and not at all necessary.

---

suitable lighting, and the like. Utilization of many media will require room darkening, convenient power supply, and access to light switches. At the least the instructor should check that the equipment is in working order and should arrange the facilities so that all the audience can see and hear properly. More specific details on audiovisual setups are found in Chapter 10.

Prepare the Audience

Research on learning tells us very clearly that what is learned from a presentation depends highly on how the learners are *prepared* for the presentation. In everyday life we notice that entertainers are obsessed with having the audience properly warmed up. Nobody wants to come after "a hard act to follow."

Proper *warm-up* from an instructional point of view will generally consist of an introduction including: a broad overview of the content of the presentation, a rationale of how it relates to the topic being studied, a motivation (creating a "need to know"—how the learner will profit from paying attention),

and cues directing attention to specific aspects of the presentation.

Several of these functions—directing attention, arousing motivation, providing a rationale—may be served simply by informing the viewers of the specific objectives.

In certain cases, other steps will be called for. For example, unfamiliar vocabulary may need to be introduced; or special visual effects, such as time-lapse photography, may need explanation. Other preparation steps relevant to particular media will be discussed in the later chapters.

Present the Material

This is what you've been preparing for so you will want to make the most of it! Our term for this is "showmanship." Just as an actor or actress must control the attention of an audience, so must an instructor be able to direct attention in the classroom. The later chapters on individual media point out "showmanship" techniques relevant to each specific media format. General showmanship tips for all types of presentations are given here.

REQUIRE LEARNER RESPONSE

The fifth step in the ASSURE model is encouraging student response to the instructional stimuli. Educators have long realized that participation in the learning process through opportunity to respond to instruction is a boon to learning. In the early 1900s, John Dewey urged reorganization of the nation's curriculum and instruction to make student participation a central part of the process. Later, behavioral psychologists such as B.F. Skinner demonstrated that instruction providing for constant reinforcement of desired behaviors is far more effective than instruction in which behaviors are not reinforced. The implications for the teacher are very clear. The most effective learning situations are those that provide for student response and for reinforcement of correct response.

Student response to an instructional situation may range from simple recitation of facts to completion of a product (a dress, a term paper). It might even consist of designing and producing instructional media suitable to a specific segment of classroom instruction. Building learner participation and opportunity for response into the instructional situation is highly desirable since it has been firmly established as an effective teaching technique.

Some media lend themselves to student participation more than others—at least on the surface. For example, student response to projected still pictures is easier to manage than response to a motion picture. Students can read or elaborate on captions in filmstrips, discuss what is on the screen, or refer to other materials while the image is held on the screen. (Substitution of sound filmstrips for silent tends to curtail this advantage.) However, students can also participate in and respond to the showing of a film. For example, May and Lumsdaine demonstrated that overt responses (vocalized verbal responses) during a film improved learning. The same authors cited research demonstrating that psychomotor skills are learned better if practiced while the skills are being performed in a film.* Overt written responses during the showing of a film (or any other fixed-pace medium) has been shown to facilitate learning, unless the responses are so involved that students are prevented from watching the film.

Materials may be designed to include covert or overt responses. A covert response might be silent repetition of key vocabulary at specified points in the lesson. An overt response might consist of vocalizing or writing out the key words. Manipulation of materials would also be an overt response. In general, covert responses are just as effective as overt responses for short learning sequences. Sequences of longer duration are learned better when students respond overtly.

Although delayed confirmation or rejection of response may be effective in certain situations, immediate feedback is generally better. Immediate confirmation of *correct* response is particularly important when working with students of lower than average abilities. For such students, evidence of immediate success can be a strong motivating force for further learning.

---

*Mark A. May and A.A. Lumsdaine. *Learning from Films*. New Haven: Yale University Press, 1958.

Discussions, short quizzes, and application exercises can provide opportunities for response and reinforcement during instruction. Follow-up activities can provide further opportunities. Teacher guides and manuals written to accompany instructional materials often contain suggested techniques and activities for eliciting and reinforcing student response.

Programmed instruction is a technology of instruction based on the premise that student response and reinforcement are essential to effective learning. One of the major contributions of the programmed instruction movement is that educators have been encouraged to design learner participation, response, and reinforcement into a wide variety of instructional situations and media combinations. Learning activities packages, audio-tutorial techniques, and computer-based instruction are just a few examples of incorporation of the programming principles of response and reinforcement into various media and technologies of instruction. As you study the chapters that follow, you will note how reinforcement principles can be incorporated into the design and utilization of specific instructional media.

EVALUATE

Evaluation of the Instructional Process

The final component of our ASSURE model for effective learning is evaluation. One major purpose of evaluation is, of course, assessment of student achievement. Its basic purpose, however, is assessment of the entire instructional process, including student achievement of objectives, the instructional media, the instructional approach, and even teacher effectiveness.

Although ultimate evaluation must await completion of the instructional unit, evaluation is an ongoing process. Evaluations are made before, during, and after instruction, For example, before instruction learner characteristics are measured to ensure that there is a fit between student skills and the methods and materials you intend to use. In addition, materials should be appraised prior to use, as noted earlier in this chapter. During instruction, evaluation may take the form of student practice of a desired skill, or it may consist of a short quiz or self-evaluation. Evaluation during instruction usually has a diagnostic purpose—that is, it is designed to detect and correct learning/teaching problems and difficulties in the instructional process which may threaten attainment of objectives.

Evaluation of Learner Achievement

The ultimate question in the instructional process is whether or not the students learned what they were supposed to learn. Can they display the capabilities specified in the original statement of objectives? The first step in answering this question was taken back near the beginning of the ASSURE process when you formulated your objectives, including in that statement of objectives a *criterion* of acceptable performance. You now want to assess whether the learner's new skill meets that criterion.

The method of evaluating achievement depends on the nature of the objective. Some objectives call for relatively simple cognitive skills, for example, recalling Ohm's law, distinguishing adjectives from adverbs, or summarizing the purposes of the European Common Market. Objectives such as these lend themselves to conventional paper-and-pencil tests or oral examinations. Other objectives may call for process-type behaviors (for example, conducting an orchestra, performing a forward roll on a balance beam, or solving quadratic equations), the creation of products (a sculpture, a written composition, or an account ledger), or the holding of attitudes (tolerating divergent political opinions, appreciating expressionist painting, or contrib-

Figure 2.13 A process- or performance-type skill should be judged according to the observation of the performance itself.

Figure 2.14 The ability to create a product should be judged according to the quality of the product itself; a rating checklist is helpful for calling attention to the most critical qualities of the product.

uting money to community charities).

Capabilities of the process, product, or attitude type could be assessed to some extent by means of written or oral tests. But test results would be indirect and weak evidence of how well the learner has mastered the objective. More direct and stronger evidence would be provided by observing the behavior *in action*. This implies setting up a situation in which the learner can demonstrate the new skill and the instructor can observe and judge it.

In the case of process skills, a performance checklist can be an effective, objective way of recording your observations. An example is shown below.

PERFORMANCE CHECKLIST: DRIVING SKILLS

Name_____   Class_____

Directions: Check yes or no with an X in the proper space.

Did the student:	Yes	No
1. Fasten seat belt before starting car?		
2. Use the 9 o'clock and 3 o'clock hand position on steering wheel?		
3. Drive with the flow of traffic yet stay within the speed limit?		
4. Come to full and complete stops at stop signs?		
5. Keep at least a two-second interval behind the vehicle ahead?		
6. Stay in the proper driving lane—not cross center line?		
7. Obey all traffic signs and signals?		
8. Negotiate all turns properly (according to driving manual)?		
9. Avoid excessive conversation with passengers?		
10. Display courtesy to other drivers?		

Instructor's name_____   Date_____

For product skills, a product rating checklist can guide your evaluation of critical subskills and objective qualitative judgments. An example is shown below.

Attitudes are admittedly difficult to evaluate. For some attitudinal objectives, long-term observation may be required to determine if the goal has really been attained. In day-to-day instruction we usually have to rely on what we can observe here and now, however limited that may be. A commonly used technique for making attitudes more visible is the attitude scale, an example of which is shown below. A number of other suggestions for attitude measurement can be found in Robert Mager's *Developing Attitude Toward Learning.**

---

*See References at end of this chapter.

PRODUCT RATING CHECKLIST: WELDING

Name_____ Date_____

Directions: Rate the welded product by checking the appropriate boxes. Add comments if you wish.

Base metal(s)_____ Filler metal(s)_____

	Excellent	Very Good	Good	Fair	Poor
Profile:					
Convexity (1/32 inch maximum)	☐	☐	☐	☐	☐
Fusion on toe	☐	☐	☐	☐	☐
Overlap	☐	☐	☐	☐	☐
Amount of fill	☐	☐	☐	☐	☐
Workmanship:					
uniform appearance	☐	☐	☐	☐	☐
arc strikes	☐	☐	☐	☐	☐
bead width	☐	☐	☐	☐	☐
bead start	☐	☐	☐	☐	☐
bead tie-in	☐	☐	☐	☐	☐
bead termination	☐	☐	☐	☐	☐
penetration	☐	☐	☐	☐	☐
amount of spatter	☐	☐	☐	☐	☐

Overall evaluation:

Evaluator comments:

ATTITUDE SCALE: BIOLOGY

Each of the statements below expresses a feeling toward biology. Please rate each statement on the extent to which you agree. For each, you may: (A) strongly agree, (B) agree, (C) be undecided, (D) disagree, or (E) strongly disagree.

A	B	C	D	E
strongly agree	agree	undecided	disagree	strongly disagree

_____ 1. Biology is very interesting to me.

_____ 2. I *don't* like biology, and it scares me to have to take it.

_____ 3. I am always under a terrible strain in a biology class.

_____ 4. Biology is fascinating and fun.

_____ 5. Biology makes me feel secure, and at the same time it is stimulating.

_____ 6. Biology makes me feel uncomfortable, restless, irritable, and impatient.

_____ 7. In general, I have a good feeling toward biology.

_____ 8. When I hear the word *biology*, I have a feeling of dislike.

_____ 9. I approach biology with a feeling of hesitation.

_____ 10. I really like biology.

_____ 11. I have always enjoyed studying biology in school.

_____ 12. It makes me nervous to even think about doing a biology experiment.

_____ 13. I feel at ease in biology and like it very much.

_____ 14. I feel a definite positive reaction to biology; it's enjoyable.

Evaluation of Media and Methods

Evaluation, as noted above, also includes assessment of instructional media and methods. Were your instructional materials effective? Could they be improved? Were they cost effective in terms of student achievement? Did your presentation take more time than it was really worth? Particularly after first use, instructional materials need to be evaluated to determine if future use, with or without modification, is warranted. The results of your evaluation should be entered on your personal file form.

Class discussions, individual interviews, and observation of student behavior should be used to sound out evaluation of instructional media and methods. Failure to attain objectives is, of course, a clear indication that something is wrong with the instruction. But student reaction to your instructional unit can be helpful in more subtle ways. Student–teacher discussion may indicate that your audience would have preferred independent study to your choice of group presentation. Or perhaps viewers didn't like your selection of overhead transparencies and feel they would have learned more if a film had been shown. Your students may let you know, subtly or not so subtly, that your own performance left something to be desired.

Evaluation is not the end of instruction. It is the starting point of the next and continuing cycle of our systematic ASSURE model for effective use of instructional media.

REFERENCES

Print References

Allen, Sylvia. *A Manager's Guide to Audiovisuals* (New York: McGraw-Hill, 1979).

Block, James H. (ed.). *Mastery Learning: Theory and Practice* (New York: Holt, Rinehart and Winston, 1971).

Block, James H. and Lorin Anderson. *Mastery Learning in Classroom Instruction* (New York: Macmillan, 1975).

* Bloom, Benjamin S. (ed.). *Taxonomy of Educational Objectives; Cognitive Domain* (New York: David McKay Company, Inc. 1956).

Brown, James W., Richard B. Lewis, and Fred F. Harcleroad. *AV Instruction: Technology, Media, and Methods,* 5th ed. (New York: McGraw-Hill, 1977).

The Center for Vocational Education. *Develop Student Performance Objectives* (Athens, GA: American Association for Vocational Instructional Materials, 1977).

* Davies, Ivor K. *Objectives in Curriculum Design* (Maidenhead, Berkshire, England: McGraw-Hill Limited, 1976).

Dewey, John. *Democracy and Education* (New York: Macmillan, 1916).

Eiss, A.F., and M.B. Harbeck. *Behavioral Objectives in the Affective Domain* (Washington, DC: National Science Supervisors Association, 1969).

Gerlach, Vernon S., and Donald P. Ely. *Teaching and Media: A Systematic Approach,* 2d ed. (Englewood Cliffs, NJ: Prentice-Hall, 1980).

* Gronlund, Norman E. *Stating Behavioral Objectives for Classroom Instruction* (New York: Macmillan, 1970).

* Kemp, Jerrold E. *Instructional Design: A Plan for Unit and Course Development,* 2d ed. (Belmont, CA: Fearon Publishers, 1977).

Krathwohl, D.R. et al. *Taxonomy of Educational Objectives; Affective Domain* (New York: David McKay Company, Inc., 1964).

Mager, Robert F. *Developing Attitude Toward Learning* (Palo Alto, CA: Fearon Publishers, 1968).

* ——*Preparing Instructional Objectives,* 2d ed. (Belmont, CA: Fearon-Pitman, 1975).

——"Why I wrote..." *NSPI Journal,* October 1976, p. 4.

* Romiszowski, A.J. *The Selection and Use of Instructional Media* (London, England: Kogan Page, 1974).

"Special Issue—Behavioral Objectives." *Educational Technology,* May 1977.

"Special Issue—Behavioral Objectives." *Educational Technology,* June 1977.

Tyler, Ralph. "The Construction of Examinations in Botany and Zoology," *Service Studies in Higher Education.* Bureau of Educational Research Monographs, No. 15 (Columbus, OH: The Ohio State University, 1932).

Wittich, Walter, and Charles F. Schuller. *Instructional Technology: Its Nature and Use,* 6th ed. (New York: Harper & Row, 1979).

Audiovisual References

"Behavioral Objectives in Education." (Englewood Cliffs, NJ: Educational Technology Publications, undated). (Twelve audio cassettes.)

* Edling, Jack V. "Individualized Instruction." (Washington, DC: Association for Educational Communications and Technology, 1970). (A kit of six sound filmstrips, case studies, and an administrator's handbook.)

"Instructional Objectives." (Portland, OR: Bel Mort Co., 1973). (Three filmstrips, color.)

Key references.

POSSIBLE PROJECTS

2-A. Plan a presentation using the procedures described in this chapter. Your description must include:

1. Description of learners.
   (a) General characterisitcs.
   (b) Specific knowledge, skills, and attitudes.
2. Objectives for the presentation.
3. Description of how you selected, modified, or designed instructional materials.
4. Procedures for the use of the materials.
5. Plans for learner involvement and reinforcement.
6. Statement about how you evaluated the lesson.

2-B. Classify a set of objectives into the cognitive, psychomotor, and/or affective domains.

2-C. Describe an instructional situation and then use the Kemp charts to select the most desirable media for that situation.

2-D. Use the Appraisal Checklist: Generalized to appraise sample audiovisual materials. Submit the materials and your completed checklist to your instructor.

CHAPTER 3

VISUAL LITERACY

OUTLINE

OBJECTIVES

After studying this chapter, you should
be able to:

1. Define or describe "visual literacy."

2. State a rationale justifying visual literacy training for all people.

3. Describe the function of a visual in the communication process.

4. Discuss the relationship between the degree of realism in a visual and the amount of learning from it.

5. Describe the relationship between people's preferences in visuals and the amount of learning from these preferred visuals.

6. List and describe *five* levels of decoding a visual.

7. State briefly the effect of developmental age and cultural background on visual literacy.

8. Identify three techniques for teaching visual literacy.

9. Explain the significance of eye-movement research for instruction.

10. Describe the proper use of arrangement, balance, and color in design of visuals.

11. Describe how the three types of objectives (cognitive, affective, and psychomotor) influence the selection and design of visuals.

THE CONCEPT OF VISUAL LITERACY

Until recently, the concept of literacy was applied almost exclusively to the ability to read and write. In the mid-1960s, however, we began to hear of a different kind of literacy, "visual literacy." This new concept of literacy came in response to the realization that specific skills are needed to "read" and "write" visual messages, just as they are needed to read and write printed ones.

Visual literacy is the learned ability to *interpret* visual messages accurately and to *create* such messages. Thus interpretation and creation in visual literacy may be said to parallel reading and writing in print literacy.

Visual literacy has also become a "movement" within the field of education. The movement now has its own professional association—the International Visual Literacy Association, and its own periodical, *The Visual Literacy Newsletter*. And educators see a growing number of courses and workshops devoted to visual literacy.

The upsurge of concern for visual literacy has accompanied the almost quantum leap in the production and distribution of visual messages in recent years. The seemingly ubiquitous television set comes immediately to mind, but the television set does not stand alone. New technologies of printing and reproduction have also contributed to this flood of visual messages. Illustrations (including graphics) now abound in books, periodicals, and newspapers as never before. We are surrounded by visual messages on billboards and posters. Advertising of all kinds has become increasingly visual. Even T-shirts have gotten into the act!

Obviously, this wealth of visual messages calls for a concerted effort to help people interpret accurately the flood of visual messages. They supply us with information (and misinformation). They influence our attitudes, our opinions, our lives. As recipients of communications, we need to become adept at "reading" visual messages. As managers of learning, we need to teach our students the skills of visual literacy so that they too can "read" visual messages correctly and use them to their educational advantage.

(a)

(b)

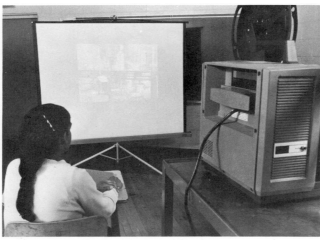

(c)

(d)

Figure 3.1 "Visual literacy"—the ability to interpret and create visual messages parallels traditional print literacy— the ability to interpret and create verbal messages in print form.

VISUALS AS REFERENTS TO MEANING

The essence of any communication activity is the transmission of signals intended to evoke meanings in the mind of the recipient. Effective verbal communication depends on the assumption that both sender and receiver have a field of mental concepts in common enough to ensure that the message is understood as intended. We all know, however, that effective verbal communication is a sometime thing. The process all too often fails due to language differences, variations in age and experience, cultural and social differences, etc.

The primary function of a visual as a communication device is to serve as a more concrete *referent* to meaning than the spoken or written word. Words are arbitrary symbols. They don't look or sound (usually) like the thing they represent. Visuals, however, are *iconic*. They normally resemble the thing they represent. As such, they serve as concrete clues to meaning. The more iconic, or pictorial, they are—that is, the closer they come to representing the thing (or concept) being referred to—the more likely they are to prevent breakdown in communication. It is a general principle of human communication that the likelihood of successful communication is increased when a concrete referent is present. Lacking the actual presence of the thing being discussed, the next best referent is a visual representation of it (Figure 3.2a and b).

Figure 3.2a We frequently miscommunicate when we rely on words alone.

Figure 3.2b The probability of communicating accurately increases when receivers can see a visual referent.

REALISM IN VISUALS

The various kinds of projected and nonprojected visuals discussed in the chapters that follow differ in many ways: size, composition, color, etc. One fundamental difference among them is their degree of realism. No media form, of course, is totally realistic. The real object or event will always have aspects that cannot be captured pictorially, even in a three-dimensional, color motion picture. The various visual media can, however, be arranged from highly abstract to relatively realistic as indicated in Figure 3.3.

One might naturally conclude that effective communication is always best served by the use of the most realistic visual available. After all, the more realistic a visual is, the closer it is to the original. This, however, is not necessarily so. There is ample research evidence that under certain circumstances realism can actually interfere with the communication and learning process. For example, the ability to sort out the relevant from the irrelevant in a pictorial representation grows with age and experience. So, for younger children, and for older learners who are encountering an idea for the first time, the wealth of detail found in a realistic visual may increase the likelihood of the learner's being distracted by irrelevant elements of the visual.

As Frank Dwyer notes in his review of visual research, "The arbitrary addition of stimuli in visuals makes it difficult for learners to identify the essential learning cues from among the more realistic background stimuli."* Dwyer con-

*Francis M. Dwyer. *Strategies for Improving Visual Learning.* State College, PA: Learning Services, 1978, p. 33.

Figure 3.3 The graphic symbol, cartoon, line drawing, and photograph represent a continuum of realism in visuals.

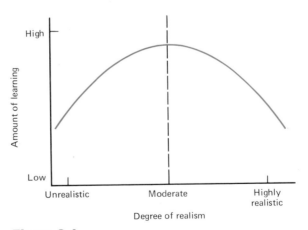

Figure 3.4

cludes that rather than being a simple yes-or-no issue, the amount of realism desired has a curvilinear relationship to learning. That is, either too much or too little realism may affect achievement adversely (Figure 3.4).

PICTURE PREFERENCES OF STUDENTS

We need to make a distinction between the pictures people *prefer* to look at and those from which they learn the most. People do not necessarily learn best from the kinds of pictures they prefer. For example, research on picture preferences indicates that children in upper elementary school tend to:*

1. prefer color to black and white.
2. choose photographs over drawings.
3. choose realism in form and color.
4. (younger children) prefer simple over complex illustrations.
5. (older children) prefer complex over simple illustrations.

Teachers have to make appropriate choices between *effective* illustrations and *preferred* illustrations.

---

*Barbara Myatt and Juliet Mason Carter. "Picture Preferences of Children and Young Adults," in *Educational Communication and Technology*, Spring 1979, p. 47.

TEACHING AND LEARNING THE SKILLS OF VISUAL LITERACY

As with verbal literacy, there is by no means unanimous agreement about what exactly are the skills and subskills of visual literacy, nor how they can be taught and acquired most effectively. We can, however, safely assume that visual skills mean abilities to decode and encode visuals.

Decoding includes "reading" visuals accurately, understanding and relating the elements of a visual, being able to translate from visual to verbal and vice versa, and appreciating the aesthetics of visuals.

Encoding includes using the tools of visual media to communicate effectively with others and to express one's self through visuals.

Decoding and Learning from Visuals

Decoding of visual stimuli and learning from them require practice. Seeing a visual does not automatically ensure learning from it. The student must be guided toward correct decoding of the visual. One effective technique is to guide your students to see and "read" the visual on various levels. Learning begins with differentiation: students identifying and analyzing the elements of an instructional unit. It then proceeds through integration: students putting the pieces together, relating the whole to their own experiences, drawing inferences, and creating new conceptualizations from what they have learned.

Learner Variables in Decoding

How a learner decodes a visual may be affected by many variables. We have already discussed individual differences and learner variables in Chapter 2. Two of these variables, however, are particularly germane to education for visual literacy: developmental age and cultural background.

Age. The findings of developmental psychology suggest that visual literacy is influenced by maturity. Prior to the age of 12, children tend to interpret visuals section by section rather than as a whole. In reporting what they "see" in a picture, they are likely to single out specific elements within the scene. Students who are older, however, tend to summarize the whole scene and report a conclusion about the "meaning" of the picture. Hence, abstract symbols or a series of still pictures whose relationship is not clearly spelled out may fail to communicate as intended with younger viewers.

We have already noted that realistic visuals may distract younger children. However, Dwyer notes, "As a child gets older, he becomes more capable of attending selectively to those features of an instructional presentation that have the greatest potential for enhancing his learning of desired information."*

Developmental age may also influence the interpretation of artistic conventions employed in line drawings: speed lines, foreshortening, size differences to connote distance, etc. For example, research indicates that motion cues are more likely to convey the idea of motion to children who have developed beyond the "pre-operational" stage as defined by Piaget (around age 7) than to younger children. It has also been found that an active posture, such as that of a running figure, communicates well with all ages, whereas arbitrary conventions,

---

*Dwyer, op cit., p. 229.

Here is how this approach might be used with Figure 3.5.

Figure 3.5 A domestic scene from another culture, in this case from France, can provide practice in "reading" a picture on different levels.

LEVEL OF LEARNING	EXAMPLE QUESTIONS

A. Differentiation
  1. Observe the basic elements depicted.
  2. Analyze the relevant details of the basic elements and how they are related.
	1. Identify the objects and people in the picture.
	2. How old is each person? What are they wearing? What are they doing? Etc.

B. Integration
  3. Relate to your experience.
 	
  4. Draw inferences.
	3. Is this how you bathe? Are the appliances like the ones in your home? Etc.
	4. Is this probably an American home? Is the bath water hot or cold? How did it get into the tub? What will probably happen next? Etc.

5. Create new constructs.	5. Write a story about living in a household like this with people such as these.

Figure 3.6 An active posture, as in the figure on the left, communicates movement more reliably than arbitrary graphic conventions such as speed lines, as in the figure on the right.

such as speed lines, do not (Figure 3.6).*

Cultural Background. In teaching visual literacy, we must keep in mind that decoding visuals may be affected by the viewer's cultural background. Different cultural groups may perceive visual materials in different ways. In a sense, this variable might be subsumed under prior learning experience, as discussed in Chapter 2. But these differences are more difficult to appraise. Cultural background has a strong influence on learning experience. For example, let us say your visual literacy instruction includes use of visuals depicting scenes typical of the home life and street life of inner-city children. It is almost certain that students who live in such an area will decode these visuals differently than will students whose cultural (and socioeconomic) backgrounds do not include firsthand knowledge of inner-city life styles. Similarly, scenes depicting life in the old West might be interpreted quite differently by an American Indian child than they would be by, say, a black, white, or a Mexican–American child (Figure 3.7).

*Ronald A. Saiet. "Children's Understanding of Implied Motion Cues," Indiana University, 1978 (unpublished dissertation).

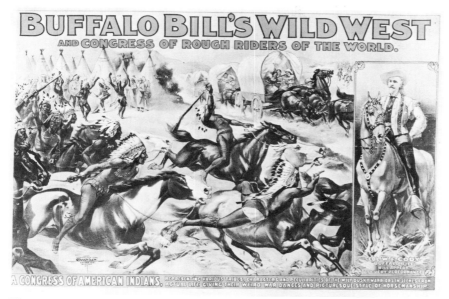

Figure 3.7 The cultural biases of a communicator, though unspoken, may be perceived vividly by viewers having a different cultural background.

Cultural differences as a factor in visual literacy may be even more pronounced if the decoder's cultural background is primarily foreign. In one research experiment, for example, a photograph of a bullfighter was seen through one lens of a stereoscopic viewer and a photograph of an American baseball player through the other. A Mexican looking quickly through the viewer reported seeing only a bullfighter. A native of the United States saw only the baseball player. Only after guidance by the researcher did each come to realize that the stereoscopic viewer contained two pictures.*

The iconic connotations of a visual may be affected by cultural differences. For example, a group of U.S. students and students from other countries were shown the two drawings (the Liberty Bell and Justice) as illustrated in Figure 3.8. Each student was asked to

state in one word what each drawing symbolized. United States students invariably responded "liberty" and "justice." Most foreign students, whose cultural backgrounds did not include the historical associations Americans attach to a particular cracked bell, saw no abstract connotation at all in the drawing at the left. To them it was merely "bell." Many foreign students also failed to find any symbolism in the drawing of the

robed woman on the right. Their response was merely "statue." Some, however, interpreted it as symbolizing "equality," a response that indicates a sharing, to some extent, of a common symbolic meaning. Others felt the drawing symbolized a religious concept, "angel," "God," and, in the case of some Islamic students, "pilgrimage" (to Mecca).

The symbolic connotations of color and color preference may also be culturally biased. Cultures vary widely as to how the color spectrum is perceived. Westerners see red, orange, yellow, green, blue, and violet as more or less distinct and equidistant points along a spectrum. But this kind of color perception is by no means universal. Even less universal are the symbolic values given to various colors. Black, for example, is generally accepted in Western countries as the color of mourning. In some Eastern countries, however, the color symbol of mourning is white.

Some years ago the federal government, in an attempt to ensure that all the Navahos of the Southwest who wished to vote in a tribal election could do so, color-coded the names of the two candidates on the ballot. This, they felt, would ensure participation in

*James W. Bagby. "A Cross-Cultural Study of Perceptual Predominance in Binocular Rivalry," *Journal of Abnormal and Social Psychology,* Vol. 54, 1957, pp. 331–334.

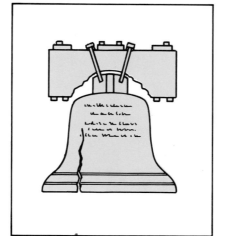

Figure 3.8 Symbolic images may be interpreted differently depending on cultural background.

the election by those Navahos who were nonliterate in English. Navahos who could not read the names of the candidates could be instructed beforehand which candidate was represented by which color. Unfortunately, the colors chosen by the government determined the outcome of the election. The loser happened to be assigned a color that to the Navahos symbolized bad luck!

Although you cannot eliminate all misconceptions in decoding arising out of differences in cultural background, you should always be cautious about using visuals that may without prior explanation cause confusion in some of your students.*

A Note on Photography

We assume that if you are concerned with visual education you will have access to a camera and sufficient skill in using it to make your own photographs and slides as aids to teaching visual literacy. However, you should be aware of some of the more recent innovations in camera technology brought about by advancements in electronics and optics. For example, the 35-mm camera has long been associated with professional photography and sophisticated equipment. However, since the late 1970s there are 35-mm cameras readily available that are as small and compact as the "Instamatics" of a few years ago. The model shown in Figure 3.9 is little bigger than the roll of 35-mm film and take-up spool it uses.

*A discussion of cultural differences in interpreting visuals and how to deal with them, is in James Mangan. "Cultural Conventions of Pictorial Representations," *Educational Communication and Technology,* Fall 1978, pp. 245–267.

In addition, recent advances in miniaturization of microprocessors (computers) have made possible the development of a camera that not only contains apparatus that sets the light controls automatically, but also includes a pair of sensors that measure the distance from your subject, analyze the information, and automatically set the focus (Figure 3.10).

Figure 3.9   Miniature 35-mm cameras are little larger than the roll of film and its take-up spool.

Figure 3.10   Automatic *focus,* as well as automatic exposure, is available on some 35-mm cameras. On this model the distance sensors are located on either side of the brand name.

Figure 3.11   The little type 110 camera, using cartridge film, has been upgraded by means of better lenses and through-the-lens focusing to produce higher quality pictures than before while maintaining subcompact size.

For strictly amateur picture taking, the type 110 camera has been the standard for a number of years. But in this domain, too, technical advances now ensure even higher quality while maintaining the ease of operation long associated with the 110. Figure 3.11 shows a 110 camera with automatic exposure and through-the-lens viewfinding ("single-lens reflex," like that found in the high-quality 35-mm family). It is comparable to a watchband in size.

For hints on planning your photographic project, see "How To... Develop a Sound-Slide Presentation" in Chapter 7. Further technical information on photography and suggestions for working with student photography will be found in the Eastman Kodak publications listed in the References at the end of this chapter.

Encoding: Learning from the Making of Visuals

Visual literacy, as we have noted, includes skill in "writing" as well as in "reading" visuals. Visual literacy programs employ a wide variety of techniques and activities to teach skills in encoding visuals. Some hint of this variety is illustrated in the "Close-up" (opposite).

One skill which is nearly always included in visual education curricula is that of *sequencing.* Reading specialists have long known that the ability to sequence—that is, to arrange ideas in logical order—is an extremely important factor in verbal literacy, especially in the ability to communicate in writing.

Excessive television viewing has often been cited as contributing to the decline of verbal literacy in today's children. Obviously, television takes away from time that might otherwise be spent in such activities as social play or reading.

CLOSE-UP: Visual Literacy Education.

A visual literacy project involving elementary school children in central Indiana began with the construction of zoetropes, a simple device to help understand how still pictures become moving images.

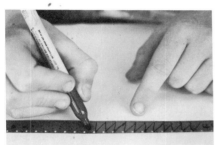

Students experimented with simple animation film techniques by drawing images on individual frames of 16-mm film. This was a good chance to put math skills to work.

Shooting and editing their own live action 8-mm film gave them an opportunity to put all of their new-found visual production skills into practice.

Specialists, however, are inclined to think the problem goes deeper. Television presents a predigested, orderly stream of imagery. Visual referents to meaning are prominent and are presented in logical order. The message (meaning) is easily grasped even by the passive viewer. In writing, the child practices sequencing skills in order to communicate effectively with others. Television viewing provides for no such incentive or practice.

Youngsters fed a steady diet of television must be made aware that visual sequencing is not always provided. It is a learned skill, just as it is in reading and writing. For this reason, many visual-literacy education programs, especially for primary school children, emphasize creative activities in arranging and making visuals. A popular set of instructional materials for this purpose is the *Photo-Story Discovery Kit* series developed in the 1960s by Eastman Kodak Company and now distributed by the Association for Educational Communications and

Technology (AECT). Some sample cards from one of these sets are shown in Figure 3.12.

One of the best ways to develop "encoding" skills is to encourage students to present their message through a pictorial medium. Most students have access to a camera that takes slides. They should be encouraged to present reports to the class by means of well-thought-through sets of slides. The 35-mm slide is also a medium for students to use to develop their

Figure 3.12 Shown are sample cards from *Photo-Story Discovery Set No.1.* The set contains 29 cards which can be arranged in different sequences to tell different stories.

aesthetic talents (Figure 3.13). Portable videotape equipment can be used by even elementary children and is an excellent way of giving students the opportunity to present ideas and events pictorially.

The importance of visual literacy in today's society can scarcely be overstressed. Teachers of young children have a special responsibility to see to it that students do not leave their classrooms visually illiterate. Visual literacy may even be seen as an essential survival skill. As one observer puts it:

> There is no easy way to develop visual literacy, but it is as vital to our teaching of the modern media as reading and writing was to print. It may, indeed, be the crucial component of all channels of communication now and in the future.*

*Donis A. Dondis. *A Primer of Visual Literacy.* Cambridge, MA: MIT Press, 1973.

Figure 3.13 The preparation of a slide presentation is an inexpensive and feasible way to develop visual sequencing skills.

RESEARCHING HOW PEOPLE LOOK AT VISUALS

All instructors ought to be concerned about *how* people look at pictorial and graphic materials and what they see in them, because these factors determine considerably what people will get out of the materials. There are basically two ways to determine what people notice: (1) make inferences based on what individuals have learned from pictorial material, (2) determine the pattern of eye movements as they look at the same pictorial material. The first is relied on most heavily by the behaviorists, who assume that, regardless of how people look at something, what they can recall is all we are interested in. Other psychologists, however, while not disputing the importance of response, maintain that if perception is not efficient or effective, communication is not as efficient or effective. Furthermore, if the ways in which people view and interpret pictures and graphics can be guided, then people will learn more because attention will be directed to relevant content and not misdirected by irrelevant cues.

As a corollary, we can also say that the more we know about perceptual "sets" of students, the better we will be able to design visuals to take advantage of those sets, or to overcome perceptual obstacles. For example, research on eye-movement of people looking at still photographs indicates that viewers tend to look first at the upper left-hand quadrant of a picture. The picture area in Figure 3.14 has been divided into quadrants. The percentage in each quadrant represents the frequency with which people first look at that part of the picture area. If upper and lower quadrants are combined, we see that observers tend to look first at the left-hand side of a picture two out of three times. It has been said that this is a culturally determined perceptual set because people from Western cultures learn to read and write from left to right. If so, then those people who learn to read from right to left, such as readers of Arabic and Hebrew, might be expected to look first at the upper right quadrant.

This information is relevant not only to your decision about where you should place important content in a picture area, but also in how people will interpret certain graphic representations. How you interpret Figure 3.15 may depend on your cultural background.

Do you see the graphic as many branches coming together to form a mainstream, or do you interpret the drawing as a mainstream being separated into many tributaries?

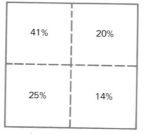

Figure 3.14 Research in the United States indicates a tendency for viewers to begin scanning a picture from the left side, particularly the upper left portion.

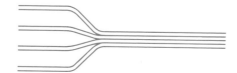

Figure 3.15 How does it look to you? Are the branches converging into one trunk or is a main stream diverging into smaller streams?

When designing visuals we can take advantage of this research by placing at least the start of our main message where the eye first strikes the area. The research does not mean that *all* important information should be located in the upper left quadrant or even in the left half of a picture. But it does indicate that if the message is required (by the nature of the content) to be in the lower right, the eye of the observer will have to be *led* there. This can be achieved by use of such pictorial elements as color, composition, texture, etc. The important point is that the tendency of people *not* to look first in the lower right must be compensated for if the message is located there.

How people look at moving as well as still images has been the subject of several research studies. Expensive and delicate apparatus is required to track the eye movements of film or television viewers. The apparatus used in a series of studies on eye movement is shown in Figure 3.16.

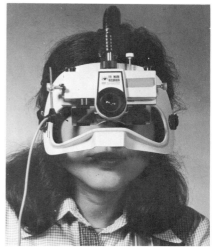

Figure 3.16 Current eye movement research is facilitated by automatic monitoring devices that record the movements of the pupils as they scan a picture.

APPRAISAL CHECKLIST: VISUAL LITERACY MATERIALS

Title_____ Format of materials:

Producer/Distributor_____

Publication Date_____

Audience/Grade Level_____

Objectives (stated or implied):

Brief Description:

RATING

	High		Medium		Low
I. Visual functions practiced:	☐	☐	☐	☐	☐
Perception	☐	☐	☐	☐	☐
Memory	☐	☐	☐	☐	☐
Logical reasoning					
II. Visual literacy skills practiced:	☐	☐	☐	☐	☐
Observing relevant details	☐	☐	☐	☐	☐
Relating visual elements to student's own experience	☐	☐	☐	☐	☐
Drawing inferences	☐	☐	☐	☐	☐
Making connections between pictures (e.g. time sequence, cause/effect, comparison/contrast)					
III. Design of material provides:	☐	☐	☐	☐	☐
High motivation	☐	☐	☐	☐	☐
Clear student and teacher instructions	☐	☐	☐	☐	☐
Meaningful practice/feedback activities	☐	☐	☐	☐	☐
Aesthetic appeal					

Strong Points:

Weak Points:

Reviewer_____

Position_____

Date_____

One of the most important of several findings of such studies concerns eye fixation on relevant cues.* For example, during a science telecast, the eyes of many of the students frequently strayed to an irrelevant microscope visible over a shoulder of the instructor. In another sequence, the eyes of the viewers watched the lips of the instructor rather than what he was demonstrating. When only his hands and the object were shown on the screen, the viewers fixated on the demonstration. The lesson to be learned here is that distractors must be kept out of the frame of the image.

Another important finding demonstrates the importance of movement. When the picture on the screen is static, viewers "tune out" after a while. When the image is changed by introducing motion or changing the picture, the viewers "tune in" again. Changes in the image help keep students' attention on the visual.

*Egon Guba, et al. "Eye Movements and TV–Viewing in Children," *AV Communication Review,* Vol. 12, No. 4, pp. 386–401.

Flashback: That Incomparable Moravian

One day in the late 1640s, Massachusetts's Cotton Mather, ever zealous to make Puritan New England the cultural center of the New World, noted in his journal his disappointment that a certain "incomparable Moravian" was not, after all, to become an American by accepting the presidency of Harvard College.

That brave old man, Johannes Amos Comenius, the fame of whose worth has been trumpeted as far as more than three languages could carry it, was indeed agreed...to come over to New England, and illuminate their Colledge and Country, in the quality of a President, which was now become vacant. But the solicitation of the Swedish Ambassador diverting him another way, that incomparable Moravian became not an American.

Who was this Johannes (John) Amos Comenius? Why had his fame as an educator spread all the way from Europe to Mather's Massachusetts Bay Colony?

Comenius was born in 1592 in Moravia (now part of Czechoslovakia). He was a clergyman of the United Brethren, an evangelical Protestant reform sect known popularly today as the Moravian Church. At the time of his consideration for the presidency of Harvard, he was living in exile in Sweden. Indeed, the religious persecutions of the Thirty Years War and its aftermath had forced Comenius to live most of his life away from his native Moravia.

Despite this and the deprivations of war, however, Comenius achieved fame throughout Europe as an educational reformer and writer of innovative textbooks and other educational works. He was, in addition, one of the earliest

IOHAN ~ AMOS COMENIVS, MORAUVS. Aº ÆTAT 50: 1642
Crols sculpsit

and certainly the most renowned champions of what we would today call "visual literacy" and "visual education." The last 14 years of his life were spent in Amsterdam. It was from his haven there that Comenius oversaw the publication in 1657 in Nurenberg of the work for which he is today best known and on which he had been working for years: *Orbis Sensualium Pictus* (The Visible World Pictured).

Flashback: That Incomparable Moravian

Orbis Sensualium Pictus was the first illustrated textbook specifically designed for use by children in an instructional setting. (It was not the first children's picture book. The English printer, Caxton, for example, had produced an illustrated edition of Aesop's *Fables* as early as 1484.) The design and illustrations of Comenius's text were expressly intended to enhance learning. The 150 woodcut drawings were learning and teaching devices, not mere decoration. The text embodied application of educational theories espoused by the author over a period of 40 years. It is interesting to note, for example, that Comenius chose Aristotle's observation, *Nihil est in intellectu, quod non prius fuit in sensu* (there is nothing in the mind which was not first in the senses), to adorn his title page.

Orbis Sensualium Pictus is truly remarkable for having incorporated, more than three hundred years ago, so many educational concepts that seem thoroughly modern. Underlying Comenius's use of visuals was a theory of perception based on the idea that we learn through our senses and that this learning "imprints" a mental image which leads to understanding. A real object is preferable for this process, but visuals may be used in the learning environment as substitutes for the real thing.

Many principles of modern day "message design" and "visual literacy" are embodied in Comenius's text, including the following principles currently considered to be well supported by empirical research.[a]

1. "Use of the concept name in contiguity with each presented example facilitates concept learning."

2. "An effective combination of iconic and digital signs appears to be a pictorial stimulus and a verbal response, e.g., label or description."

3. "The better organized or patterned a message is perceived to be, the more information we can receive (and process) at one time."

4. "We can perceive at a glance and hold in immediate memory up to about seven items."

5. "The more familiar the message to its audience, the more readily it is perceived."

6. "The more mature and/or the more motivated the learner, the greater can be the size of an instructional unit."

7. "...simplified examples such as line drawings, cartoons, charts, and diagrams have been found more effective than realistic pictures."

8. "Side-by-side arrangement...facilitates perception of differences."

9. "The sizes of unfamiliar objects are perceived as relative to that of familiar objects."

10. "Abstract concepts can be learned from a variety of verbal structures; e.g...sentence contexts, described examples,..."

---

[a]Malcolm Fleming and W. Howard Levie. *Instructional Message Design*. Englewood Cliffs, NJ: Educational Technology Publications, 1978, *passim*.

11. "The active form of sentence structure is easier to learn and use in solving problems than is the passive form."

Examine the sample pages from *Orbis Sensualium Pictus* carefully. Can you find Comenius's application of the above principles in the unit illustrated there?

Even beyond these message design innovations we find that other aspects of *Orbis Sensualium Pictus* foreshadowed techniques that today are closely identified with a "technology of instruction":

1. Instruction is broken down into small units, with attention paid to their proper sequencing. (In fact, the book was intended to be part of a series of texts, increasingly complex in language and treatment of topics.)

2. Vocabulary and conceptual level are purposely scaled down to be comprehensible at the primary-school age.

3. Each element in an illustration is numbered and keyed to a description in the text to maintain maximum order and clarity.

4. The typography is designed to provide visual emphasis to key words. The Latin text is set in roman type, with key words in italics. The English text (as with the German in the first edition) is set in black-letter type with roman type for key words. Such a use of multiple type faces was highly innovative at the time.

Although Comenius's work was based on scientific principles far in advance of his time, his philosophy of education was basically humanistic. His greatest hope was to make education a pleasure rather than a burdensome chore. For him, "instructional technology" had but one purpose: to serve the child.

The design and illustrations of *Orbis Sensualium Pictus,* he tells us in his preface, were intended "to entice witty children to it, that they may not conceit a torment to be in the school, but dainty fare. For it is apparent, that children (even from their infancy almost) are delighted with Pictures, and willingly please their eyes with these sights." His pedagogical aim, he tells us, was that children "may be furnished with the knowledge of the prime things that are in the world, by sport and merry pastime."

The idea that learning should be a "merry pastime" rather than a burdensome chore is startlingly modern. Indeed, centuries were to pass before this basic educational philosophy became what it is today—the common wisdom. Aptly called "that incomparable Moravian" in his own time, Johannes Amos Comenius may still be called so in ours.

(104)

LI.

Piscatio.

Fishing.

VISUAL DESIGN CONSIDERATIONS

Instructor-made visuals should exemplify, not contradict, the principles of visual literacy. Well-designed visuals—bulletin boards, posters, displays, and the like—not only help ASSURE learning of the subject matter but also provide good models for students' own creative projects.

When designing visuals, important general considerations are best faced by starting with a rough sketch or "layout" of the intended visual. The basic considerations to remember in planning your layout are summarized in the following mnemonic device:

| Select | **A**rrangement, **B**alance, and **C**olor |
| To maximize | **D**ynamism, **E**mphasis, **F**idelity, and **G**raphic Harmony. |

Arrangement

The visual and verbal elements of the display should be arranged in a pattern that *captures* the viewer's attention and *directs* it toward the relevant details. The manipulation of line, space, and mass are the designer's primary instruments. First, the elements should hang together in a unified whole (Graphic Harmony). Giving the display a recognizable overall shape assists in achieving this end. Basic geometric shapes and letters of the alphabet are convenient frameworks to build on (Figure 3.17).

Balance

The chosen shape or pattern, which provides Emphasis to the visual, should also occupy the space of the display in a way that connotes a sense of balance or equilibrium without being totally symmetrical. As shown in Figure 3.18, a formal balance with total symmetry tends to be static, but the informal balance contributes to a feeling of Dynamism. Imbalance creates an uncomfortable feeling in the viewer and should be avoided.

An important aspect of Arrangement and Balance that is difficult to put into a formula is the *feeling* that the visual is supposed to convey. Active or passive? Formal or informal? Serious or light? In Figure 3.19 either layout might be defended on purely mechanical grounds. But which one connotes

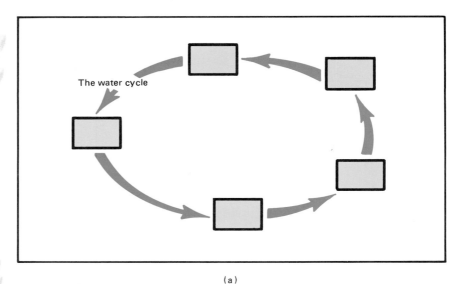

(a)

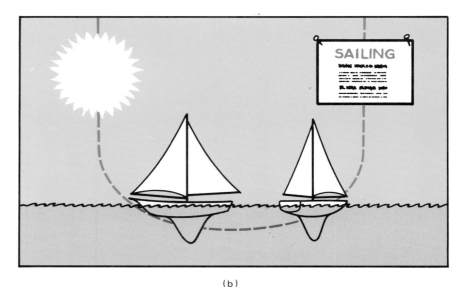

(b)

Figure 3.17 Arrangement should follow an overall pattern or shape. (*a*) Elliptical shape, (*b*) U-shape.

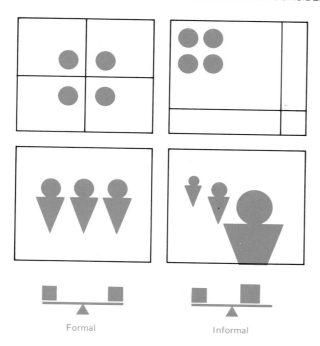

Figure 3.18 Formal versus informal balance: formal balance is simple symmetry; informal balance is achieved by manipulating mass and space as with weights on a fulcrum.

Figure 3.19 Which layout more vividly conveys the action and excitement of a class picnic?

the *feeling*—the spontaneity and liveliness—associated with a class picnic? The mixture of shapes, the clash of angles, the overlapping of elements in the right-hand example seem to communicate this sprightly theme more effectively.

Color

Several functions may be served by the colors selected for use in a visual: (1) to heighten the realism (Fidelity) of the image by depicting its actual colors, (2) to point out similarities and differences and to highlight important cues (Emphasis), and (3) to create a particular emotional response. The first two functions are quite self-explanatory, but the third one requires some elaboration.

Artists have long appreciated that blue, green, and violet are perceived as "cool" while red and orange are "hot." It is now understood that there is a physiological basis to this perception in the manner in which colors are focused in the human eye. The warmer colors appear to be approaching the viewer; the cooler colors seem to be receding from us. The designer can capitalize on this tendency by highlighting important cues in red and orange, helping them leap toward the viewer.

Contemporary research in the psychology of motivation reveals that different colors stimulate more than the visual senses. They have "taste": blue is sweet; orange is edible. They have "smell": pink, lavender, yellow, and green "smell" best. They have other psychological connotations: dark red and brown evoke masculine images of earth, wood, and leather; gold, silver, and black suggest the prestige and status associated with wealth.

So the designer needs to decide whether some emotional connotation will help advance the intended message. Are there some affective objectives consciously being aimed at? What mood should be associated with the idea? How can the sensory appeal of the message be improved with a judicious choice of color?

The key to achieving the desired emotional response is the term *judicious*. Graphic Harmony is lost if too many colors are used in the same display; so is Emphasis. One way to reduce the busyness of a color scheme is to choose analogous colors—colors that are next to each other on the color wheel, such as violet, red, and red-orange.

As a practical matter, there are certain color combinations which go well together when used for the background and foreground elements of a nonprojected display, such as a bulletin board. Figure 3.20 provides a handy guide to the color combinations that yield suitable background/foreground

Background Color	Lettering Color
White	Red, green, blue, black, brown, purple
Yellow	Red, blue, black, brown, green
Light blue	Yellow, brown, purple, black, dark blue, red
Dark blue	Red, green, yellow, white
Light green	Brown, red, black
Dark green	Black, white, yellow
Light red	Green, black, blue
Dark red	Green, white, yellow
Dark brown	Black, white, yellow, light green
Light brown	Green, dark blue, dark red, black
Light gray	Dark blue, red, black
Black	White, red, light blue, green

Figure 3.20 Color Combinations for Nonprojected visuals.

contrast. Which combination to choose, though, depends on factors concerning realism (Fidelity), highlighting different elements (Dynamism and Emphasis), and other psychological considerations.

In the case of projected visuals, legibility often becomes an overriding consideration. For slides or overhead transparencies that contain verbal material, the color combination of lettering and background is critical. Figure 3.21 indicates that the most legible combination is black lettering on a yellow background, followed by green, red, or blue on white (note that "white" means the color white, not clear or uncolored film).

Objectives

Clearly, what the student is expected to be able to *do* with the information presented in a visual will affect the design in a great many ways. For example, a message encouraging students to attend a class play or encouraging workers to use the proper

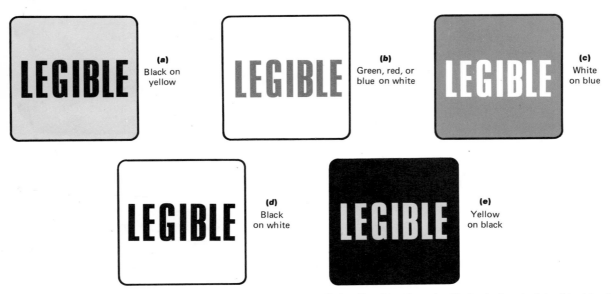

Figure 3.21 Color Combinations for Projected materials. Most legible is black on yellow (example a); (b), (c), (d), and (e) are in descending order of legibility.

safety equipment will be handled very differently from one instructing students how to form plurals in Spanish. The first two examples would probably take the format of a poster, using simple, bold words and images to capture the fleeting attention of passersby. The third example might be put into a display to be placed in a quiet corner for independent study; its layout could be quite detailed with various participation devices built in. The first question, then, in analyzing your objective is to decide whether the main learning task is primarily cognitive, affective, or psychomotor in nature.

Cognitive. For example, identifying, labelling, or memorizing of facts, discriminations, rules, concepts, etc. You should emphasize clarity, accuracy, and you should provide opportunities for practice of the mental skill being aimed at. Highlight relevant details. Sequence of elements might be important. Provide clear visual examples for any concepts to be mastered.

Affective. For example, motivating, persuading, developing appreciation. You should attract attention quickly and dramatize the benefits of adopting a new or altered attitude; you might call for specific action. Attractiveness and credibility are paramount. Address the values and needs of the receiver(s). Novelty, complexity, and exaggeration may contribute to gaining attention and making an impact.

Psychomotor. For example, performing, executing, manipulating. Emphasize clarity and highlight relevant details. Motion will frequently be required, although a series of still pictures may accomplish the goal as well or better. You should provide for practice of the pertinent skill. In many cases, this requires that a display be located in a particular place—near the machinery being referred to, close to the practice field, attached to an object such as a projector.

REFERENCES

Print References

Blagu, Jeffrey J. "Say Good-bye to Those Dumb Old Term Papers." *Audiovisual Instruction,* June/July 1977, pp. 16–18.

Bloomer, Carolyn M. *Principles of Visual Perception* (New York: Van Nostrand Reinhold, 1976).

* Debes, John. "Some Foundations for Visual Literacy." *Audiovisual Instruction,* November 1968, pp. 961–964.

* DeSantis, Lucille, and Dennis Pett (eds.). *Contributions to the Study of Visual Literacy* (Bloomington, IN: International Visual Literacy Association, 1981).

Dondis, Donis A. *A Primer of Visual Literacy* (Cambridge, MA: MIT Press, 1973).

Eastman Kodak Co. *Classroom Projects Using Photography. Part I: For the Elementary School Level* (Rochester, NY: Eastman Kodak, 1975).

Eastman Kodak Co. *Classroom Projects Using Photography. Part II: For the Secondary School Level* (Rochester, NY: Eastman Kodak, 1975).

Eastman Kodak Co. *Elements of Visual Literacy* (Rochester, NY: Eastman Kodak, 1968).

Eckhardt, Ned. "The Learning Potential of Picture Taking." *Media and Methods,* January 1977, pp. 48–50, 53.

Feldman, Edmund B. "Visual Literacy." *Journal of Aesthetic Education,* October 1976, pp. 195–200.

Fransecky, Roger B. "Visual Literacy and Teaching the Disadvantaged." *Audiovisual Instruction,* October 1969, pp. 28–31.

Gorman, Don A. "Simple Visual Formats." *Audiovisual Instruction,* May 1977, pp. 44–46.

Griffin, Paul F., and Ronald L. Chatham. "The Still Picture in Geography Instruction." *Journal of Geography,* May 1967, pp. 222–230.

Kaplan, Don. "Understanding Visual Continuity." *Media & Methods,* December 1976, pp. 48–50.

Kemp, Jerrold E. *Planning and Producing Audiovisual Materials,* 4th ed. (New York: Harper & Row, 1980).

*Key references.

Lesser, Michael L. "A Humanist Looks at Visual Literacy." *Audiovisual Instruction,* September 1975, pp. 31–32.

Logan, Ben, and Kate Moody (eds.). *Television Awareness Training,* 2nd ed. (New York: Media Action Research Center, 1979).

Midgley, Thomas K. "Graphics: Inexpensive, Creative Visuals." *Educational and Industrial Television,* April 1976, pp. 50–51.

Minor, Ed, and Harvey R. Frye. *Techniques for Producing Visual Instructional Media* 2d ed. (New York: McGraw-Hill, 1977).

Opdahl, Viola Woodruff. "Student-Made Audiovisual Productions." *Social Education,* May 1976, pp. 275–279.

Postman, Neil. "The New Literacy." *The Grade Teacher,* March 1971, pp. 26–27.

Richards, Betty. "Mapping: An Introduction to Symbols." *Young Children,* January 1976, pp. 145–156.

"Visual Literacy." *Audiovisual Instruction,* May 1972. (Special theme issue.)

Walker, David A. *Understanding Pictures: A Study in the Design of Appropriate Visual Materials for Education in Developing Countries* (David A. Walker, Publisher, 1979).

* Williams, Catherine. *Learning from Pictures,* 2nd ed. (Washington, DC: AECT, 1968).

* Wright, Andrew. *Designing for Visual Aids* (New York: Van Nostrand Reinhold, 1970).

Audiovisual References

"Experiencing Design," (Burbank, CA: Encore Visual Education, 1975). [Four sound filmstrips (cassette), 58 frames each, color.]

* "How Does a Picture Mean?" (Washington, DC: Association for Educational Communications and Technology, 1967). (Filmstrip, 76 frames, color.)

"Making Sense Visually," (Washington, DC: Association for Educational Communications and Technology, 1969). [Sound filmstrip (cassette), 76 frames, color.]

"The Simple Camera," (Washington, DC: Association for Educational Communications and Technology). (Twelve filmstrips, color.)

"A Visual Fable," (Washington, DC: Association for Educational Communications and Technology, 1973). [Sound filmstrip (record or cassette), 18 minutes, color.]

Organization

International Visual Literacy Association (IVLA), Dennis Pett, Executive Secretary, Audio Visual Center, Indiana University, Bloomington, IN 47405

IVLA publishes a monthly newsletter, *Visual Literacy Newsletter,* sponsors an annual conference, and publishes *The Proceedings of Annual Conferences.*

POSSIBLE PROJECTS

3-A. Obtain a visual (picture or photograph) and analyze it using the five response stages given in this chapter.

3-B. Use the "Appraisal Checklist: Visual Literacy Materials" of this chapter to evaluate some materials designed to teach visual literacy.

3-C. Design some instructional activities to teach or improve visual literacy with your students. Your description of the lesson should include the materials (or a description of the materials), the role/activities of the students, and the role of the teacher.

3-D. Obtain a visual and evaluate it in terms of intended audience, objectives, realism, arrangement, balance, and color.

3-E. Design a visual for your own use and evaluate it in terms of intended audience, objectives, realism, arrangement, balance, and color.

CHAPTER 4

NONPROJECTED VISUALS

OUTLINE

OBJECTIVES

After studying this chapter, you should be able to:

1. List five attributes (advantages and/or limitations) of nonprojected still pictures.

2. Describe at least three classroom applications of still pictures.

3. Identify five criteria for selecting still pictures and apply the "Appraisal Checklist: Still Pictures" to actual materials.

4. Suggest three techniques (showmanship tips) to enhance the use of still pictures with a group.

5. Define graphic material and describe three types of graphics.

6. Describe five applications for graphic materials in your teaching.

7. Apply the "Appraisal Checklist: Graphic Materials" to actual materials.

8. Define *realia.*

9. Identify three uses of models and/or realia for instruction.

10. Identify two methods of preserving nonprojected visuals and state three reasons for doing so.

11. Compare the advantages/limitations of rubber cement mounting with the advantages/limitations of dry mounting.

12. Describe five formats or devices for displaying visuals in the classroom.

13. Discuss eight techniques (showmanship tips) for improving your utilization of chalkboards.

14. State a major advantage that cloth boards and magnetic boards have over chalkboards.

15. Suggest five techniques (showmanship tips) to enhance the use of flip charts.

Nonprojected visuals are, simply, visuals that do not require projection for viewing. Because they are so abundant and easily obtainable, they are likely to be used more extensively in the classroom than any other visual medium of instruction. Indeed, nonprojected visuals are so common in our environment that educators are sometimes inclined to underestimate their importance in learning. But in some situations (e.g., due to lack of electricity, isolation, low budget, very small group size), they may be the *sole* source of audiovisual stimuli.

For the purpose of discussion, let us divide nonprojected visuals into three broad categories: (1) still pictures, (2) graphics, and (3) models and realia. After we have discussed still pictures, graphics, and models we will turn our attention to various ways of displaying them in the instructional setting.

STILL PICTURES

Still pictures are photographic (or photograph-like) representations of people, places, and things. The still pictures most commonly used in instruction are photographs, illustrations from books, periodicals, catalogs, etc., and study prints (oversized illustrations commercially prepared to accompany specific instructional units).

Advantages

- Nonprojected still pictures can translate abstract ideas into a more realistic format. They allow instruction to move from the level of verbal symbols in Dale's Cone of Experience (see page 12) to the more concrete level of still pictures.

Figure 4.1 Nonprojected visuals.

Figure 4.2 A study print and flash cards showing details of the larger picture.

Figure 4.3 A series of still pictures can approximate the impression of a motion picture sequence.

- They are readily available in books (including textbooks), magazines, newspapers, catalogs, and calendars. In addition, you may purchase large study prints for use with groups of students from educational supply companies or you may obtain them from your media center or library.
- Still pictures are easy to use since they do not require any equipment.
- Still pictures are relatively inexpensive. In fact, many can be obtained at little or no cost.
- Still pictures can be used in many ways at all levels of instruction and in all disciplines.

Limitations

- Some photographs are simply too small for use before a group. It is possible to enlarge any picture, but that can be an expensive process; however, the opaque projector (described in Chapter 5) can be used to project an enlarged image before a group.
- Still pictures are two-dimensional. The lack of three-dimensionality in a picture can be compensated for by providing a series of pictures of

the same object or scene from several different angles or positions.
- They do not show motion. However, a series of sequential still pictures can suggest motion (Figure 4.3).

Classroom Applications of Still Pictures

There are numerous applications of nonprojected still pictures. Photographs may be used in a variety of ways. Teacher-made and/or student-made photographs may be used to illustrate and to help teach specific lesson topics. Photographs of local architecture, for example, can illustrate a unit on architectural styles. (In this case, the students' skill in "reading" a visual could be reinforced by the instructor's pointing out that merely looking at the buildings in our environment is not the same as really "seeing" them.) Photographs taken on field trips can be excellent sources of information in classroom follow-up activities.

Students can and should understand that textbook pictures are not decorations, but are intended to be study aids and should be used as such. Students should be encouraged to "read" them as aids to learning. Skill in decoding textbook pictures may also be

included in instructional objectives to motivate the learners to use them for study purposes. The quality and quantity of illustrations are, of course, important factors in textbook choice. See "Appraisal Checklist: Still Pictures," p. 86. Pictures from newspapers and periodicals may be used in similar ways.

Study prints also have many applications in the instructional setting. They are especially helpful in the study of processes—the production of iron or paper, for example, or the principles of the internal combustion engine. They are also very useful in teaching the social sciences. In geography they may help illustrate relationships between peoples and their environments that, because of space limitations, could not easily be depicted in textbook pictures.

All types of nonprojected still pictures may be used in testing and evaluation. They are particularly helpful with objectives requiring identification of people, places, or things.

Nonprojected still pictures may also be used to stimulate creative expression such as the telling or writing of stories or the composing of poetry.

APPRAISAL CHECKLIST: STILL PICTURES

Title or content of picture(s)_____

Producer/distributor (if known)_____

Series (if applicable)_____

Date (if known)_____

Objectives (stated or implied):

Brief description:

Entry capabilities required:

Prior subject matter knowledge
Visual skills
Other

RATING

	High	Medium	Low
Relevance to your objectives	☐ ☐	☐ ☐	☐
Authenticity and accuracy of the picture	☐ ☐	☐ ☐	☐
Simplicity (uncluttered by irrelevant material, unnecessary objects, or distracting background)	☐ ☐	☐ ☐	☐
Timeliness (out-of-date hair styles or fashions can draw laughs and cause learners to miss intent of the picture)	☐ ☐	☐ ☐	☐
Scale (relative size of the object should be apparent from the picture. A familiar object can provide scale for unfamiliar objects)	☐ ☐	☐ ☐	☐
Technical quality (proper exposure, good contrast, in focus with good depth of field and clear detail, colors true and natural)	☐ ☐	☐ ☐	☐
Size (visibility adequate for viewing, large for group use, smaller if used by individuals)	☐ ☐	☐ ☐	☐

Strong points:

Weak points:

Reviewer_____

Position_____

Recommended action_____   Date_____

Close-up: Using Still Pictures

In a psychology course, for the unit on experimental methods, the students use the photographs in their textbook as study aids, since they are excellent illustrations of the mazes and other experimental apparatuses described in the text. During the class, the teacher draws attention to the photographs in the text and later asks various students to relate the pictures to the corresponding printed material. The teacher has also written the objectives for the course in a way that requires students to use the illustrations during their study.

Study prints are used by a fifth-grade teacher to show techniques for vegetable gardening. The teacher works with the children in small groups. While some of the students are working on other activities in the classroom and in the media center, the teacher gathers 10 to 12 students around her to discuss the study prints. Her objective is for the students to be able to "describe the proper method of spacing tomato plants." The students are shown the study prints and then describe what they see in terms of recommended procedures for measuring, planting, etc.

AV Showmanship —Still Pictures

Use large pictures that everyone can see simultaneously. To hold pictures steady when showing them to a group, rest them against a desk or table or put them on an easel. (If the pictures are not large enough for all to see, use one of the projection techniques described in Chapter 5.)

Limit the number of pictures used in a given period of time. It is better to use a few visuals well than to overwhelm your audience with an overabundance of underexplained pictures.

Except for purposes of comparison and contrast, use just one picture at a time. Lay one picture flat down on your desk or table before going on to the next. Don't keep them in view, on the chalk tray for example. If you do, your students' attention may be on Picture 1, 2, or 3 while you are vainly trying to get them to attend to your discussion of Picture 4.

Keep your audience's attention and help them learn from the picture by asking direct questions about it: "Why did the architect use brick in this part of the building?" "Why are the workers in this factory wearing protective clothing?"

When still pictures are displayed for nonsupervised perusal by the students, try to provide written cues to help highlight important information contained in the pictures. Another technique is display questions and answers pertaining to the pictures alongside each. Cover the answers with flaps of paper. Have each student immediately check his or her own response for accuracy.

GRAPHIC MATERIALS

Our second major category of nonprojected visuals is graphic materials, often referred to simply as "graphics." Graphics are non-photographic, two-dimensional materials designed specifically to communicate a message to the viewer. They often include verbal as well as symbolic visual cues.

As a group, graphics demand special caution in use by instructors. Because the images are visually symbolic rather than fully representational, they leave more room for viewers to misinterpret the intended meaning. This phenomenon is discussed in Chapter

3. As one example, research on newspaper readers' interpretations of editorial cartoons indicates that a large proportion of viewers may draw conclusions that are the *opposite* of what the artist intended. Psychologists find that people tend to "project" their own hopes, fears, and preconceptions into images or verbal messages that are ambiguous. This is the basis of the Rorschach or "ink-blot" diagnostic test (Figure 4.4). The younger or less visually literate the audience, the more guidance the instructor will have to provide to ensure that the intended message is conveyed.

Let us explore five types of graphics commonly found in the classroom situation: drawings (including sketches and diagrams), charts, graphs, posters, and cartoons.

Figure 4.4 Viewers tend to project subconsciously their own meanings into ambiguous images.

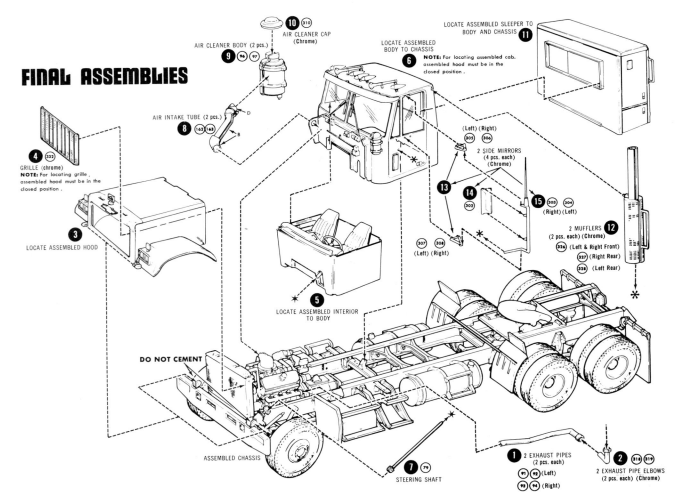

Figure 4.5 A diagram for assembling a scale-model plastic truck. Note that the actual assembly steps are communicated by means of visual symbols rather than words.

Drawings

Drawings, sketches, and diagrams employ graphic arrangement of lines to represent persons, places, things, and concepts. Drawings are, in general, more finished and representational than sketches, which are likely to lack detail. Stick figures, for example, may be said to be sketches. Diagrams are usually intended to show relationships or to help explain processes, such as how something works or how it is constructed (Figure 4.5).

Use of drawings may be similar to use of photographic still pictures. Drawings are readily found in textbooks and other classroom materials. They can be used in all phases of instruction, from introduction of the topic through evaluation. Because they are likely to be less detailed and more to the instructional point than photographic materials, they are easily understood by students of all ages.

Teacher-made drawings can be very effective teaching and learning devices. They can be drawn on the chalkboard (or some other appropriate surface) to coincide with specific aspects of the instructional unit. They can also be used as substitutes for or adjuncts to still pictures. For example, stick figures can be quickly and easily drawn to show motion in an otherwise static representation.

Charts

Charts frequently appear in textbooks and other classroom materials. Commercially published charts for specific instructional units are also available for school use. A chart should have a clear, well-defined instructional purpose. In general (especially for younger students), it should express only one major concept or configuration of concepts. If you are developing your own charts, be sure they contain the minimum of visual and verbal information needed for understanding. A cluttered chart is a confusing chart. If you have a lot of information to convey, develop a series of simple charts rather than a single complex one. The most important thing to keep in mind is "keep it simple."

A well-designed chart should communicate its message primarily through the visual channel. The verbal material should supplement the visual, not the reverse. For an example see Figure 4.6. This chart was developed for use by elementary school teachers in Arabic language speaking countries. Although you probably cannot translate the verbal descriptions you might want to imagine yourself trying to teach with this chart. How much do the visuals alone communicate?

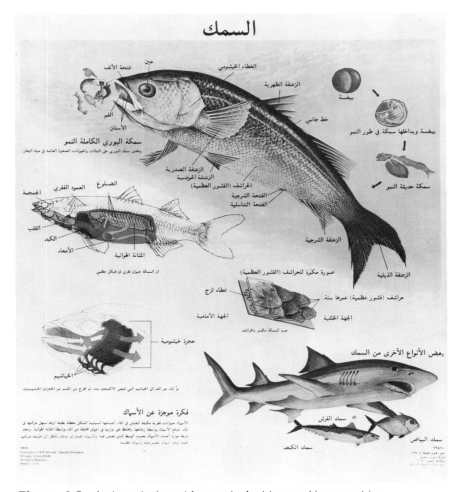

Figure 4.6 A chart designed for use in Arabic-speaking countries.

Types of Charts

Organization charts show the relationship or "chain of command" in an organization such as a company, corporation, civic group, or government department. Usually they deal with the interrelationship of personnel or departments.

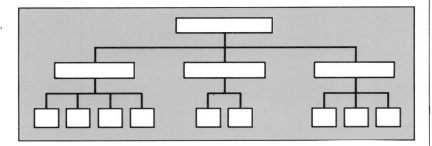

Classification charts are similar to organization charts, but are used chiefly to classify or categorize objects, events, or species. A common type of classification chart is one showing the taxonomy of animals and plants according to natural characteristics.

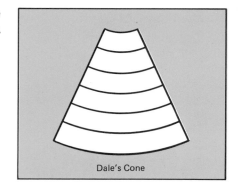

Dale's Cone

Time lines illustrate chronological relationships between events. They are most often used to show time relationships of historical events or the relationship of famous people and these events. Pictures or drawings can be added to the time line to illustrate important events. Time lines are very helpful for summarizing the time sequence of a series of events.

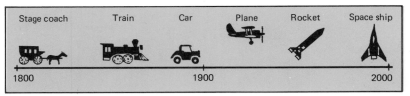

Tabular charts (or tables) contain numerical information or data. They are also convenient for showing time information when the data are presented in columns, as in time tables for railroads and airlines.

Import Percentages	Wheat	Cotton	Steel	Oil
USA	—%	—%	20%	35%
England	65	95	35	10
France	15	95	30	90
Japan	85	15	—	95
Brazil	—	—	20	70

Flowcharts (or process charts) show a sequence, a procedure, or, as the name implies, the "flow" of a process. Flowcharts are usually drawn horizontally and show how different activities, ingredients, or procedures merge into a whole.

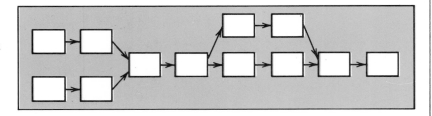

Graphs

Graphs provide a visual representation of numerical data. They also illustrate relationships between units of the data and trends in the data. Many tabular charts can be converted into graphs, as shown in Figure 4.7. Data can generally be interpreted more quickly in graph form than in tabular form. Graphs are also more visually interesting. There are four major types of graphs: bar, pictorial, circle, and line. The type you choose to use will largely depend on the complexity of the information you wish to present and the graph interpretation skills of your audience.

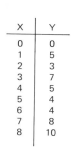

X	Y
0	0
1	5
2	3
3	7
4	5
5	4
6	4
7	8
8	10

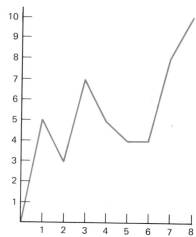

Figure 4.7 A line graph can make a table of data easier to interpret.

Posters

Posters incorporate a visual combination of lines, color, and words, and are intended to catch and hold attention at least long enough to communicate a brief message. To be effective, posters must be colorful and dynamic. They must grab attention and communicate their message quickly. One drawback in using posters is that their message is quickly blunted by familiarity. Consequently, they should not be left on display for too long a time. Commercial billboards are an example of posters on a very large scale.

Posters can be used effectively in numerous learning situations. They can stimulate interest in a new topic, a special class, or a school event. They may be employed for motivation—luring students to a school meeting, for example, or to the media center, or encouraging them to read more. In industrial education courses, science laboratories, and other situations where danger may be involved, posters can be used

to remind students of safety factors ("Always wear your safety glasses"). Posters can be used to promote good health practices ("Don't Smoke!"). A very effective

teaching and learning technique is to have students design posters as part of a class project—during fire prevention week, or dental health month, etc.

Figure 4.8 Posters provide a means for students to express their own messages.

Types of Graphs

Bar graphs are easy to read and can be used with elementary-age students. By convention they are usually constructed using vertical bars. The height of the bar is the measure of the quantity being represented. The width of all bars should be the same to avoid confusion. A single bar can be divided to show parts of a whole. It is best to limit the quantities being compared to eight or less, otherwise the graph becomes cluttered and confusing. The bar graph, a one-scale graph, is particularly appropriate for comparing similar items at different times or different items at the same time; for example, the height of one plant over time or the heights of several students at any given time. The bar graph shows variation in only one dimension.

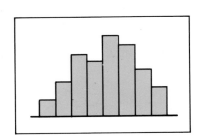

Pictorial graphs are an alternate form of the bar graph, in which a series of simple drawings is used to represent the value. Pictorial graphs are visually interesting and appeal to a wide audience, especially young students. However, they are slightly more difficult to read than bar graphs. Since pictorial symbols are used to represent a specific quantity, partial symbols are used to depict fractional quantities. To help avoid confusion in such cases, print values below or to the right of each line of figures.

Circle (or pie) graphs are relatively easy to interpret. In this type of graph, a circle or "pie" is divided into segments, each representing a part or percentage of the whole. One typical use of the circle graph is to depict tax-dollar allocations. The combined segments of a circle graph should, of course, equal 100 percent. Areas of special interest may be shown separate from the others, just as a piece of pie can be illustrated separately from a whole pie.

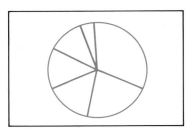

Line graphs are the most precise and complex of all graphs. Line graphs are based on two scales at right angles. Each point has a value on the vertical scale and a value on the horizontal scale. Lines (or curves) are drawn to connect the points. Line graphs show variations in *two* dimensions—how two or more groups of quantities changed over time. For example, a graph can show the relation between pressure and temperature when the volume of a gas is held constant. Since line graphs are precise, they are very useful in plotting trends. They can also help simplify a mass of complex information.

Posters may be obtained from a variety of sources. Commercial poster companies publish catalogs containing pictures of their wares. Other companies and advertising organizations have posters available without cost to teachers for use in their classrooms. Two of the most common sources of posters are airlines and travel agencies. Movie posters and political posters may also be available. Stores and supermarkets are often willing to give posters (and other display materials) to teachers when they are no longer needed in the store. And, of course, you can make your own posters.

Cartoons

Cartoons are perhaps the most popular and familiar graphic format. They appear in a wide variety

APPRAISAL CHECKLIST: GRAPHIC MATERIALS

Title or Content of Graphic:_____

Producer/Distributor (if known)_____

Series (if applicable)_____

Date (if known)_____

Objectives (stated or implied):

Format

☐ Drawing

☐ Chart

☐ Graph

☐ Poster

☐ Cartoon

Brief description

Entry capabilities required
Prior subject matter knowledge
Visual skills
Others

RATING

	High		Medium		Low
Simplicity (few elements or ideas to catch and hold the attention of the viewer)	☐	☐	☐	☐	☐
One main idea (to provide unity)	☐	☐	☐	☐	☐
Relevance to curricular objectives	☐	☐	☐	☐	☐
Color (attracts and holds attention)	☐	☐	☐	☐	☐
Verbal information (reinforces the ideas presented in the visual)	☐	☐	☐	☐	☐
Learner comprehension	☐	☐	☐	☐	☐
Legibility for classroom use	☐	☐	☐	☐	☐

Strong points:

Weak Points:

Reviewer_____

Position_____

Recommended Action_____

Date_____

of print media—newspapers, periodicals, textbooks, etc.—and range from comic strips intended primarily to entertain to drawings intended to make important social or political comments. Humor and satire are mainstays of the cartoonist's skill.

Cartoons are easily and quickly read and appeal to children and adults alike. The best of them contain wisdom as well as wit. As such, they can often be used by

Close-up: Getting Them Involved with Graphics

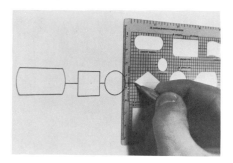

Use of Charts

As part of a training program for production supervisors, charts are used to graphically illustrate the various steps in the production process. The students develop charting skills as the program progresses. Each trainee creates a flowchart to represent production within a company. Charts are developed to represent raw material and manpower inputs and to compare them with plant outputs. Production outputs over time are graphed on line graphs. The data on individually prepared graphs are then compared with national averages over the same time period.

Use of Cartoons

A high-school social-studies class has its learning reinforced by political cartoons. The teacher has collected hundreds of such cartoons from various sources over the years and uses relevant cartoons to illustrate key points in the lessons. To get the students even more involved, the teacher has them draw their own cartoons relating to historical and political events being studied. The best of these student-drawn cartoons are saved for use with future classes.

the instructor to make or reinforce a point of instruction. As discussed earlier, appreciation and interpretation may depend on the experience and sophistication of the viewer. Research studies consistently have found that people tend to project their own feelings and prejudices into editorial cartoons. For example, a politician shown slinging mud at his opponent may be seen by supporters as a hero punishing the wicked. Further, since they usually refer to contemporary characters dealing with current issues and events,

editorial cartoons quickly become dated. Today's immediately recognized caricature becomes tomorrow's nonentity. Be sure that the cartoons you use for instructional purposes are within the experiential and intellectual range of your students.

MODELS AND REALIA

"Realia" (real models and objects such as coins, tools, artifacts, plants, animals, etc.) are not commonly thought of as visuals, since the term *visual* implies representation of an object rather than the object itself. Nevertheless, realia are the visual instructional aids most closely associated with a direct purposeful learning experience. (See Dale's Cone of Experience, Chapter 1.)

Models are *three-dimensional* representations of a real thing. A model may be larger, smaller, or the same size as the object it represents. It may be complete in detail or simplified for instructional purposes. Indeed, models may provide learning experiences real things cannot provide. Important details can, for example, be accented by color. Some models can be disassembled to provide interior views not possible with the real thing.

Models of almost anything, from insects to airplanes, can be purchased for classroom use. A wide variety of plastic-model kits are also available for assembly by you and/or your students. Assembly itself can be instructional. Classroom construction of plastic-model kits appeals to all ages of children (and, indeed, to adults) and can stimulate inquiry and discovery. Assembly activities help sharpen both cognitive and psychomotor skills.

Familiarize yourself with your model before using it in classroom instruction. Practice your presentation. If your model is a working one, be sure you know just how it works before class demonstration. Be sure your audience does not get the wrong impression of the size, shape, or color of the real object if the model differs from it in these respects. Whenever feasible, encourage your students to handle and manipulate the model. It is a good idea to store models out of sight when not being used for instruction. Left standing around, they are likely to take students' attention from other classroom activities.

PRESERVING NONPROJECTED VISUALS

One drawback in using nonprojected visuals in the classroom is that they are easily soiled or otherwise damaged as they are passed from student to student. Repeated display, storage, and retrieval can also add to wear and tear. Mounting and laminating are your two most effective preservation techniques and they can contribute to the instructional effectiveness of nonprojected visuals.

Mounting Nonprojected Visuals

Mount nonprojected visuals on construction paper, cardboard, or other such materials of sufficient durability. The color of the mounting material should not draw attention away from the visual. It is generally a good idea to use pastel or neutral tones rather than brilliant or primary colors. Using one of the minor colors in the visual as the color for the mounting can provide harmony. The total effect

Figure 4.9 An anatomical model, being three-dimensional, is a more concrete referent than a photograph, line drawing, or even a motion picture.

of your mounting should be neat and pleasing to the eye. Borders, for example, should be evenly cut, with side borders of equal width and the bottom border slightly wider than the top.

A variety of glues, cements, and pastes are available for mounting purposes. When used according to directions, almost all of them are effective. Some white glues, however, are likely to cause wrinkles in the picture when the adhesive dries, especially if used full strength. If you run into this problem, dilute the glue; for example, use four parts Elmer's glue to one part of water. Cover the entire back of the visual evenly with the adhesive before placing it on the mounting board. If excess adhesive seeps out around the edges, wipe it off with a damp cloth or sponge.

Glue sticks, marketed under names such as Stix-A-Lot and Pritt, may be used in place of liquid glues. They have the advantage of not running out around the edges of the material. More important, rubber cement can eventually damage and discolor photographs. Glue sticks are less likely to do so (Figure 4.10).

Figure 4.10 Glue sticks are convenient and effective for doing paste-ups and mounting pictures.

Rubber Cement Mounting. One of the most commonly used adhesives for mounting purposes is rubber cement. It is designed specifically for use with paper products. It is easy to use and less messy than many other liquid glues. Excess cement can easily be wiped away, and it is inexpensive. Rubber cement does, however, have two disadvantages. When the container is left uncovered for any length of time, the adhesive tends to dry out and thicken. Periodic doses of thinner (available commercially) may be necessary to keep the cement serviceable. A second disadvantage is that the adhesive quality of rubber cement tends to diminish over a period of time. Constant exposure to dry air may eventually cause it to lose its grip. This disadvantage may be compensated for with special precautions as noted for permanent

HOW TO... MOUNT PICTURES USING RUBBER CEMENT

- Cut picture to size. Edges should be straight and corners square.

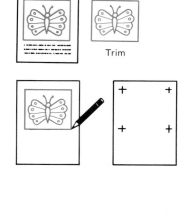

Trim

- Mark location of picture on mounting board with pencil to assist putting picture in correct position.

(Continued)

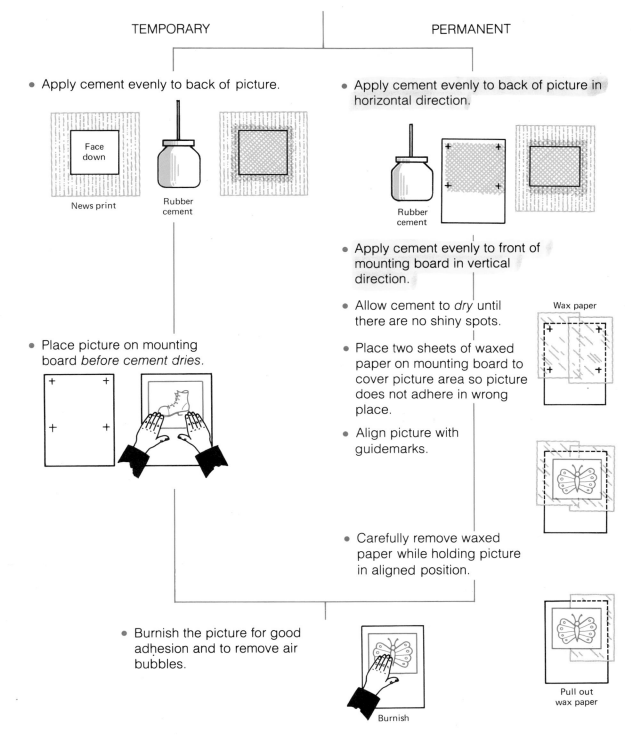

TEMPORARY

- Apply cement evenly to back of picture.

News print Rubber cement

- Place picture on mounting board *before cement dries*.

PERMANENT

- Apply cement evenly to back of picture in horizontal direction.

Rubber cement

- Apply cement evenly to front of mounting board in vertical direction.

- Allow cement to *dry* until there are no shiny spots.

Wax paper

- Place two sheets of waxed paper on mounting board to cover picture area so picture does not adhere in wrong place.

- Align picture with guidemarks.

- Carefully remove waxed paper while holding picture in aligned position.

Pull out wax paper

- Burnish the picture for good adhesion and to remove air bubbles.

Burnish

- Remove excess cement after it dries by rubbing with clean finger or ball of dried cement.

- Erase the guide marks.

Remove excess cement

rubber cement mountings. However, even these will not last indefinitely.

Dry Mounting. Dry mounting employs a specially prepared paper impregnated with heat-sensitive adhesive. The paper is available in sheets and in rolls and is marketed under such names as Fusion-4000 and MT-5. The dry-mounting tissue bonds the backing material to the back of the visual. A dry mount "press" is used to supply the heat and pressure necessary to activate the tissue's adhesive. The process is rapid and clean and results in permanent high quality mounting.

One disadvantage of dry mounting is that it is relatively expensive, requiring special paper and equipment. For example, the cost of mounting an 8-by-10-inch illustration with rubber cement is a few cents. Dry mounting the illustration could cost 10 times as much.

It is possible to dry mount visuals without a dry mount press by using an ordinary household iron instead of a press. Set the iron on "silk" or "rayon." If it is a steam iron, do *not* use the steam. Follow the procedure described in "How To...Dry Mount Pictures." The tip of the household iron can be used in place of a tacking iron. Tack the tissue to the picture and the tissue to the mounting board as described. Place a sheet of clean paper over the top of the picture, dry mounting tissue, and mounting board combination. Holding the materials (paper and picture, tissue and mounting board) in position, carefully and slowly move the iron over them while applying pressure (Figure 4.11). Remove the paper and allow the mounting to cool. If the picture is not completely adhered to the mounting board, cover again and apply more heat and pressure.

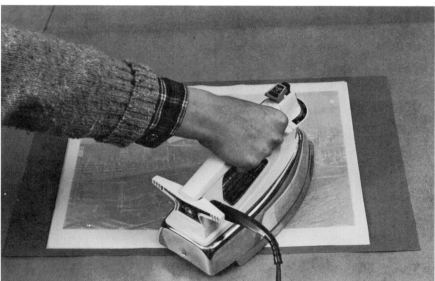

Figure 4.11 A picture can be attached to a mounting board by means of dry mounting tissue and an ordinary household iron.

Laminating
Nonprojected Visuals
Lamination provides visuals with protection from wear and tear by covering them with clear plastic or plastic-like surfaces. Lamination helps to protect your visuals against tears, scratches, and sticky fingers. Soiled surfaces can be wiped clean with a damp cloth.

Lamination also allows you to write on your visuals with a grease pencil or water-soluble ink for instructional purposes. The writing can be easily erased later with a damp cloth or sponge. A teacher of mathematics, for example, might write percentage figures on a laminated illustration of a pizza or a pie in order to help teach the concept of fractions. You can also have students write on laminated materials to facilitate learner responses. When the lesson is

HOW TO... **DRY MOUNT PICTURES**

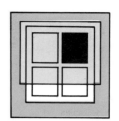

Dry the mounting board and picture before trimming picture by placing in dry mount press for about one minute at 225° F. Close press, but do *not* lock.

Place a sheet (either side up) of dry-mounting tissue over the *back* of the *untrimmed* picture with sheet overlapping edges.

Attach the tissue to the back center of the picture with tip of a tacking iron set on "medium."

Turn picture and tissue over and trim both simultaneously to desired size. (A paper cutter works best, but razor knife with metal straight edge or scissors may be used.)

Place the picture and dry-mounting tissue on the mounting board and align in proper position.

Tack the tissue to the mounting board at two *opposite* corners.

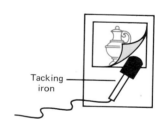

Tacking iron

Cover mounting board and picture with clean paper on both sides.

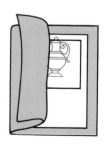

Place in dry-mount press preheated to 225° F for about one minute.

Remove from dry-mount press and allow the materials to cool. (Placing the cooling materials under a metal weight will help prevent curling.)

225° F
at least 1 min.

completed, the markings can be erased and the material made ready for further teaching. Classroom materials other than nonprojected visuals may also be laminated for extra durability and to allow for erasable writing by teacher and students—workbook pages, for example.

The simplest but also least effective technique for laminating visuals is to spray them with plastic from a can. More effective and durable procedures involve using specially prepared sheets of clear plastic cut to size. Rubber cement may be used for adhesion. Apply the rubber cement to the face of the visual and to one side of the plastic sheet. Allow the adhesives to dry and then carefully press the plastic over the surface of the visual.

Plastic sheets with built-in adhesive backing (such as Contact shelf paper) are also available for laminating purposes. Remove the backing cover to expose the adhesive and carefully press the clear plastic sheet on the visual. Any portions of the plastic sheet which extend beyond the edges of the visual can be cut off, or doubled back for additional protection.

Rolls of laminating film for use with a dry-mount press are available from commercial sources.

Filing and Storing Nonprojected Visuals

You will find it handy to have a system for filing, storing, and retrieving your nonprojected visuals. The nature of the filing system which you use will depend upon the number of nonprojected visuals in your collection and how you intend to use them. The simplest filing system usually involves grouping them according to the teaching units in which they are used. Elementary teachers often categorize them by subject or curriculum area (i.e., math, science, language arts, social studies, etc.) and then subdivide them (e.g., seasons, foreign countries, jobs, addition, subtraction, place value, telling time, etc.). Some instructors, especially those who teach just one subject, set up their filing system according to the chapters in their textbook, the topics they cover, or by objectives. Teachers who use just a few visuals may sometimes file them with their other teaching materials for each lesson.

Noting the size of the visuals will help you determine the most appropriate storage container. Many teachers store their pictures

---

HOW TO...LAMINATE PICTURES WITH A DRY MOUNT PRESS

The dry mount press should be heated to 225° F. If you live in an area with high humidity, you may get better results if you preheat the visual (to remove excess moisture) in the press for about 45 seconds. Close the press but do not lock it.

Cover the picture to be laminated with a piece of laminating film slightly larger than the picture. The inside of the roll (dull side) contains the heat sensitive adhesive and should be toward the visual. Press the film onto the picture with your hands. Static electricity should cause the film to stay in place.

Put the picture and laminating film in a cover of clean paper to protect the visual and to prevent the adhesive from getting onto the surfaces of the dry mount press.

Insert the material in press for one minute. Remove it; if the adhesion is not complete, put it back into the press for another minute. It may be helpful to put a magazine or a ¼-inch stack of paper on top of the picture to increase the pressure and improve adhesion between the picture and the laminating film.

Figure 4.12 Mounted pictures are stored conveniently in an artist's portfolio.

in file folders or large mailing envelopes. If the pictures are slightly larger than the mailing envelopes, you can open the envelopes on two adjacent sides, and the envelope will serve as a useful pocket. If the pictures are considerably larger than the 9-by-11-inch file folders or the envelopes which you have available, you can use artist's portfolios, which are available in various sizes up to 36 by 48 inches (Figure 4.12).

In addition to a workable filing system and proper size storage containers, you should have a clean, out-of-the-way place to store your visuals when they are not in use. The storage location can range from elaborate built-in drawers or filing cabinets to simple cardboard storage cartons. There is no problem in using cardboard cartons to store files of pictures and other visuals if you have a clean and dry location to place the cartons. Of course, the cartons should be readily accessible when you need them. Some teachers use the tops of closets in their classrooms or a corner of a supply room as storage spaces.

DISPLAY FORMATS

If you are going to use nonprojected visuals, such as photographs, drawings, charts, graphs, or posters, you need a way to display them. Nonprojected visuals may be displayed in the classroom in a wide variety of ways, ranging from simply holding up a single visual in your hand so the students can see it to constructing elaborate exhibits for permanent display. Classroom items commonly used for display of nonprojected visuals include chalkboards, multipurpose boards, peg boards, bulletin boards, cloth boards, and magnetic boards. Flip charts may also be used for display of visuals. Exhibits, a display format incorporating a variety of materials such as realia and models along with visuals, are also common. How you display your visuals will depend upon a number of factors, including the nature of your audience, the nature of your visuals, the instructional setting, your lesson objectives, and, of course, the availability of the various display formats.

Chalkboards

The most common display surface in the classroom is, of course, the chalkboard. Once called "blackboards," they, like chalk, now come in a variety of colors. Although the chalkboard is most commonly used as a medium of verbal communication, it can be used as a surface upon which to draw visuals (or pictures can be fastened to the molding above the chalkboard or placed in the chalk tray) to help illustrate instructional units and serve as adjuncts to verbal communication. Graphics, such as sketches and diagrams, charts and graphs, may be drawn on the chalkboard for display to the class.

A chalkboard is such a commonplace classroom item that instructors often neglect to give it the attention and respect it deserves as an instructional device. Using a chalkboard effectively requires conscious effort.

Figure 4.13 The chalkboard is universally recognized as a flexible and economical display format; however, *effective* use requires some sensitivity to the viewers' needs.

AV Showmanship—Chalkboard

- Put extensive drawing or writing on the chalkboard before class. Taking too much time to write or draw creates restlessness and may lead to discipline problems.

- Cover material such as a test or extensive lesson materials with wrapping paper, newspaper, or a pull-down map until you are ready to use it.

- Eye contact with students is important! Face the class when you are talking. Do not talk to the board. Do not turn your back to the class any more than absolutely necessary.

- Vary your presentation techniques. Do not overuse or rely entirely on the chalkboard. Use handouts, the overhead projector, flipcharts, and other media during instruction when appropriate.

- Print neatly rather than using script. For a 32 foot long classroom, the letters should be 2 to 2½ inches high and the lines forming the letters should be ¼ inch thick.

- Check visibility of chalkboard from several positions around the room to be sure there is no glare on the board. In case of glare, move the board (if portable), or pull window shades.

- If your printing normally runs uphill or downhill, use water soluble felt-tip pen markings as temporary guidelines for straighter printing. The guidelines will not be wiped off by a chalk eraser but may be washed off when no longer needed.

- Hold the chalk so that it does not make scratching noises.

- Use colored chalk for emphasis, but don't overuse it.

- Move around so you do not block what you have written on the chalkboard. Do not stand in front of what you have written.

- Use chalkboard drawing aids such as rulers, chalkboard stencils, and templates (patterns) to save time and improve the quality of your drawings.

- For frequently drawn shapes, use a template cut from wood or heavy cardboard. A dresser drawer knob or empty thread spool mounted on the template makes it easier to hold in position while tracing around it.

- Outline your drawings with barely visible lines before class and then fill them in with bold lines in front of the class. Your audience will think you are an artist!

Multipurpose Boards

Some newer classrooms are equipped with multipurpose boards instead of chalkboards. As the name implies, they can be used for more than one purpose. They have a smooth white plastic surface and use special marking pens rather than chalk. They are cleaned with a damp cloth. Sometimes called "visual aid panels," they usually have a steel backing and can be used as a magnetic board for display of visuals (Figure 4.14). The white nonglare surface is also suitable for projection of films, slides, and overhead transparencies. Materials (figures, letters, etc.) cut from thin plastic will adhere to the surface when rubbed in place.

Figure 4.14 The multipurpose board can serve as chalkboard, magnetic board, and projection screen.

Peg Boards

Another popular display surface is the peg board. It is particularly useful for displaying heavy objects and three-dimensional visuals.

Peg boards are made of tempered masonite with ⅛-inch holes drilled 1 inch apart. Peg board material is usually ⅛-inch thick and comes in 4-by-8 foot sheets which can be cut to any size. Special metal hooks and holders can be inserted into the peg board to hold books, papers, and other objects. A variety of these special hooks are available in most hardware stores. Golf tees can also be inserted into the holes for holding lightweight materials such as posters and visuals mounted on cardboard. For a background effect, the entire peg board surface can be covered with cloth or colored paper. Golf tees or the special hooks can then be inserted through the cloth or paper.

Bulletin Boards

The bulletin board is almost as common in the classroom as the chalkboard. The surface of the bulletin board is of a material designed to accept thumbtacks, pins, and other sharp fasteners without damage to the board. Boards come in a variety of sizes. They may be attached to a wall or kept portable for use on a table or easel.

Bulletin boards are frequently used to display visuals related to topics of classroom instruction. Bulletin-board visuals can also be used to stimulate discussion of special interests and current events, and to commemorate holidays and special occasions. Student-designed displays of visuals on the bulletin board can help stimulate creative expression and awareness of visual values.

Indeed, there are so many ways bulletin boards can be used to serve your instructional needs that your greatest concern is likely to be finding space on the board for all the visuals you would like to display there. One answer to this problem might be to construct additional boards for temporary use out of sturdy cardboard or some similar readily available material. Be careful though—too many boards may be distracting and lead to lack of focus on your objectives.

Take pains with your selection and arrangement of visuals for bulletin-board display. Some guidelines for this are given in Chapter 3. Do not overload the board. Use only those visuals which will contribute to attainment of your instructional objectives. Remove visuals that are no longer needed. Never pin new visuals over older ones. A cluttered, ill-kept bulletin board is not an inducement to learning—it is an eyesore. Be sure your bulletin board is what it is intended to be: a stimulation to learning and an aesthetically pleasing contribution to visual education.

Figure 4.15 How would you appraise these teacher-made bulletin boards in terms of arrangement?... balance?...dynamism?...emphasis?

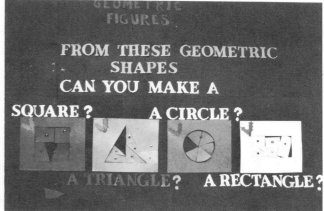

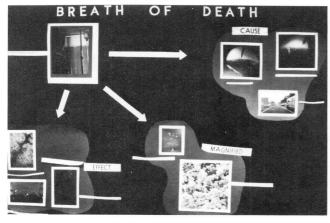

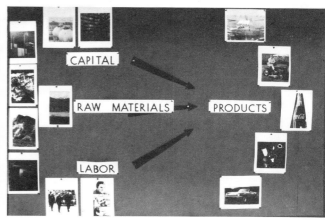

Cloth Boards

Cloth boards are constructed of cloth stretched over a sturdy backing material such as plywood, Masonite, or heavy cardboard. The cloth used for the board may be of various types, including flannel, felt, or hook-and-loop material.

Flannel is inexpensive and readily available. Pieces of flannel stick together when gentle pressure is applied. Visuals cut from flannel can be drawn on with felt-tip markers and put on the flannel board. You can also back still pictures and graphics with flannel. Coarse sandpaper sticks to flannel and can also be used to back visuals for attachment to the board. Pipe cleaners, available in a variety of colors, and fuzzy yarns stick to the flannel and can be used for drawing lines and letters. Felt, slightly more expensive than flannel, has the same properties. Durability of adhesion is less than could be desired with flannel and felt so slant the board slightly to help prevent materials from slipping or falling off.

The best cloth board, and the most expensive, is made from "hook-and-loop" materials (commercial names, Velcro and Teazlegraph). The hook-and-loop board has a fine but fuzzy surface composed of tiny, strong nylon loops. The material used for backing visuals and other items to be attached to the board has a coarse, hook-like texture. When pressed together, the two surfaces stick firmly. The hooklike material can be purchased in rolls or strips. One great advantage of the hook-and-loop board is that it can support large and heavy visuals, even entire books and three-dimensional models. One square inch of the cloth can support up to 10 pounds of properly backed visual material!

Cloth boards are particularly useful for instruction requiring that visuals be easily moved around to illustrate a process or sequence. They can also be easily removed from the board.

Teachers of reading and other creative activities often use the cloth board to illustrate stories, poems, and other reading materials. Visuals depicting characters and scenes in a story, for example, can be placed on the board and moved around as the story unfolds. Creativity may be further encouraged by allowing the children to manipulate cloth board materials. Shy children may particularly profit from this kind of activity. It encourages them to speak through the visual representations of story characters as they manipulate illustration on the board.

Be sure you have proper storage space for your cloth board and cloth board visuals when not in use. Proper storage will help keep them clean and prevent them from being bent or torn. If possible, store your materials on a flat surface rather than stacking them up against a wall. If you use sandpaper backing on your visuals, put paper between them during storage. Sandpaper will scratch the surface of visuals.

Figure 4.16 Cloth boards are often used to involve students in story telling.

HOW TO...MAKE A CLOTH BOARD

The base of the cloth board can be a piece of plywood, particle board, or heavy cardboard of whatever size you desire. Tan or gray colored materials make a good background. Cut the cloth material several inches larger than the board. Stretch the cloth tightly over the edges of the board and then fasten it with small nails, thumb tacks, staples, or tape. Covering the face of the board with white glue (Elmer's glue) before covering it will help the cloth to adhere to the board. Do not put the glue on too heavily or

it will soak through the cloth and appear unsightly even though it dries clear.

A two-sided cloth board can be made by sewing two pieces of cloth together in the form of a bag. Two different colors of cloth can be used and give you a choice of backgrounds. The wood base or heavy cardboard is then inserted into the bag and the open end can be sewn or pinned in place. Pinning it in place allows you to remove the board in order to clean the cloth.

Make a bag by sewing three sides of the cloth.

Turn it inside out and insert a stiff backing

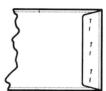

Pin the open end in place.

Magnetic Boards

Magnetic boards serve much the same purpose as cloth boards. With magnetic boards, however, adhesion is due to magnetism. Visuals are backed with a magnet and then placed on the metal surface of the board. Magnetic boards, magnets, and flexible strips of magnetic material for use in backing are available commercially. Plastic lettering with magnetic backing is available from supply stores and can be used for captioning visuals.

Any metal surface in the classroom that a magnet is attracted to can serve as a magnetic board. For example, some chalkboards are backed with steel and will thus attract magnet-backed visuals. Chalk can be used on such chalkboards for captioning or to depict lines of association between visuals. Steel cabinets and metal walls and doors can be used as magnetic boards.

You can make your own magnetic board from a thin sheet of galvanized iron, a cookie sheet, or any similar thin sheet of metal.

Figure 4.17 A portable magnetic board allows quick manipulation of items for arithmetic drill.

Paint the sheets in the color of your choice with paint designed for use on metal surfaces. Unpainted surfaces are likely to be unattractive and to cause glare. Another alternative is to fasten steel screening to a nonmetal surface (plywood, perhaps) and cover it with a piece of cloth.

The major advantage of magnetic boards is that they provide for easier and quicker maneuverability of visuals (and other instructional materials) than even cloth boards do. For example, magnetic boards are often used by physical education instructors to demonstrate rapid changes in player positions. Magnetic boards also provide greater adhesive quality. Visuals displayed on a magnetic board are not likely to slip or fall. They move only when you *want* to move them.

Flip Charts

A flip chart is a series of visuals mounted or drawn on large sheets of paper or newsprint fastened together at the top. Commercial flip charts to accompany specific instructional units are available for use in the classroom. Teachers of reading and science find them particularly useful. You may also construct your own flip chart and attach the visuals of your choice to its pages.

Flip charts can be an effective supplement to or even a substitute for board displays. They are especially useful for instruction involving sequential steps in a process. Each major point can be illustrated on a single sheet of the chart, along with printed cues. Each sheet can then be displayed to the students and discussed before flipping it over and moving on to the next page. The diagram and words can remind you of the next point in the presentation. Almost any type of nonprojected visual may be used for flip chart display—photographs, diagrams, stick figures, etc.

Figure 4.18 Unlike chalkboards, flip charts can be taken easily to where the learning group is and the images can be reused.

HOW TO...MAKE A PORTABLE FLIP CHART

Determine the number of pages you wish to use and stack them evenly.

Fasten them together with staples or by some other means to assure they will remain in position. If there is a likelihood you will want to change the sequence of the pages for instructional purposes use removable fastening pins.

Fasten a cover of heavy paper or light cardboard to the sheets. Two thicknesses of covering may be used for extra durability.

Hinge the cover and sheets together at the top.

For even more rigidity, the assembled flip chart may be mounted on light wood or heavy cardboard. The sheets can be held in place by placing a strip of cardboard or light wood on the face of the chart through which bolts can be inserted to make contact with the backing. Use wing nuts to fasten the bolts. If the backing is cardboard, heavy tape, such as duct tape or bookbinding tape, can be used to secure the sheets to the backing.

The inside covers of the flip chart may be treated with special "blackboard paint," thus giving you a small portable chalkboard to work with in your presentation. You can also convert the inside covers into miniature display boards by lining them with cloth or metal.

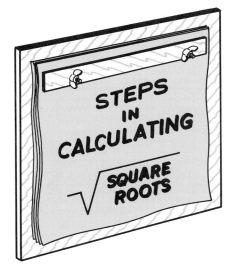

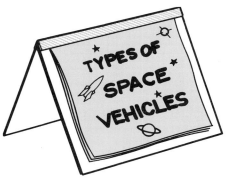

AV Showmanship—Flip Charts

- Keep the lettering and visuals simple, but large enough for everyone to see.
- Use marking pens that provide sharp contrast but will not bleed through to the next sheet.
- Talk to the audience, not to the flip chart.
- Avoid blocking student's view of the flip chart.
- Be sure your materials are in proper sequence.
- Reveal sheets only when you are ready to discuss them, not before.

- Print.
- Be sure the flip chart is securely fastened so it will not fall apart during your presentation. (The sudden collapse of your flip chart may get a laugh, but not the kind of laugh you may want.)
- Put summary points on a separate sheet rather than paging back as you make your summary.

Exhibits

Exhibits are displays of various types of nonprojected visuals designed to form an integrated whole for instructional purposes. (Projected visuals may also be included in the exhibit.) Any of the visuals discussed in this chapter, including models and realia, may be included in an exhibit. Any of the display methods discussed may be used to contribute to it. Exhibits may be used for much the same instructional purposes and in much the same ways as their individual components are used. Techniques for using them in the instructional situation are also similar.

Exhibit locations are readily available in most classrooms. Simple exhibits can be set up on a table, shelf, or desk. More complex exhibits may require considerable floor space and special

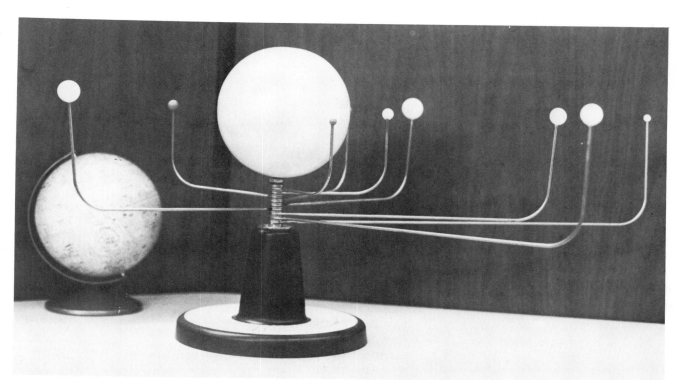

Figure 4.19 A solar system model can serve as the focus for a classroom exhibit on astronomy.

constructions (a booth, for example.)

Student assembly of an exhibit can be an excellent learning experience and can foster both retention of subject matter and sharpening of visual skills. For a lesson in transportation, one sixth-grade teacher had each student bring in a replica of a vehicle. Some students made their own vehicles from construction paper. Others brought in vehicle toys from home or contributed vehicles assembled from hobby kits (boats, cars, trucks, trains, space ships, etc.). The teacher placed tables and other classroom furniture along a wall to provide the children with a shelf on which to arrange and display their three-dimensional visuals. On the wall above this makeshift exhibit surface, the teacher placed a long sheet of paper containing a time line. The time line illustrated vehicles of transportation from early time (humans and beasts), through the present (trains, cars, planes, etc.), and on into the future (illustrations of space vehicles from *Star Wars* and *Star Trek*). The exhibit was a great success with the children, and with the teacher.

SELECTION OF NONPROJECTED VISUALS, UTILIZATION AND LEARNER RESPONSE

The ASSURE model discussed in Chapter 2 applies to nonprojected visuals as well as to all other media. However, because of the diversity of formats and countless uses of nonprojected visuals, it is difficult to provide a concise set of principles and procedures for them.

First, you must analyze your audience and determine their nature and characteristics. Find out what they already know about the topic. Then state your objectives in terms of what you want your audience to be able to do after viewing the presentation of visuals.

When selecting, modifying, or designing visuals, you should decide upon visuals which will best communicate your instructional message under the conditions in which you will be using them. Keep them simple! Be certain that all titles, lettering, figures, and the visuals themselves are large enough to be seen from the intended viewing distance.

Many utilization techniques are included in the showmanship tips presented in this chapter. Plan your presentation or display carefully. Start where the audience is (as determined from your audience analysis). Organize the presentation in a logical sequence. Practice your presentation before a mirror or colleague.

Build learner activity and response into the use of the visuals. Involve the viewers as much as possible. Repetition and emphasis will help your audience remember key points. Watch them to see if they are following the presentation. Use questions and dialogue to keep them interested and to provide opportunities for learner response.

Finally, as recommended in the ASSURE model, evaluate your visuals and associated presentation. Through formal and informal evaluation, determine if most of your audience were able to meet your objectives. Determine which parts of the presentation were received best, and worst. Solicit feedback from your audience, then make the necessary revisions.

REFERENCES

Print References: Nonprojected Visuals

* Bullough, Robert. *Creating Instructional Materials* (Columbus, OH: Charles E. Merrill, 1974).

The Center for Vocational Education. *Prepare Teacher-Made Instructional Materials* (Athens, GA: American Association for Vocational Instructional Materials, 1977).

The Center for Vocational Education. *Present Information with Models, Real Objects, and Flannel Boards* (Athens, GA: American Association for Vocational Instructional Materials, 1977).

Dwyer, Francis M. "Exploratory Studies in the Effectiveness of Visual Illustrations." *AV Communication Review*, Fall 1970, pp. 235–249.

Gropper, G., and Z. Glasgow. *Criteria for the Selection & Use of Visuals in Instruction* (Englewood Cliffs, NJ: Educational Technology Publications, 1971).

Holliday, William G. "What's in a Picture?" *Science Teacher*, December 1975, pp. 21–29.

Hollister, Bernard C. "Using Picture Books in the Classroom." *Media & Methods*, January 1977, pp. 22–25.

Jones, Colin. "Cartoons in the Classroom." *Visual Education*, November 1976, pp. 21–22.

* Kemp, Jerrold E. *Planning and Producing Audiovisual Materials*, 4th ed. (New York, NY: Harper & Row, 1980).

Krulek, Stephen, and Ann M. Welderman. "The Chalkboard—More Than Just for Chalk." *Audiovisual Instruction*, September 1976, p.41.

Marino, George. "A Do-It-Yourself 3-D Graph." *Mathematics Teacher*, May 1977, pp. 428–429.

* Minor, Ed. *Handbook for Preparing Visual Media*, 2nd ed. (New York: McGraw-Hill, 1978).

* Minor, Ed, and Harvey R. Frye. *Techniques for Producing Visual Instructional Media* 2d ed. (New York: McGraw-Hill, 1977).

Moore, Randall P. "Photographs as Instructional Tools." *American Biology Teacher*, October 1975, pp. 432–434.

Satterthwait, Les. *Graphics: Skills, Media and Materials*, 3d ed. (Dubuque, IA: Kendall-Hunt, 1977).

Trimblay, Roger. "Using Magazine Pictures in the Second-Language Classroom." *Canadian Modern Language Review*, October 1978, pp. 82–86.

Wagner, Betty Jane, and E. Arthur Stunard. *Making and Using Inexpensive Classroom Media* (Belmont, CA: Pitman Learning, 1976).

Wellesley, T. Corbett, and Robert T. Gasche. "Marking and Visual Display Surfaces for Classroom Use." *EPIE Report No. 79*, March/April 1977, pp. 1–21.

Wellesley, T. Corbett, and Robert T. Gasche. "The Forgotten Still Picture." *Audiovisual Instruction*, January 1978, pp. 24–25.

Print References: Bulletin Boards

Alsin, Mary Lou. "Bulletin Board Standouts." *Early Years*, September 1977, pp. 66–69.

Carney, Loretta J. "No Comment: Eloquent Dissent." *Social Education*, November 1976, pp. 586–587.

The Center for Vocational Education. *Prepare Bulletin Boards and Exhibits* (Athens, GA: American Association for Vocational Instructional Materials, 1977).

Kelley, Marjorie. *Classroom-Tested Bulletin Boards* (Belmont, CA: Fearon Publishers, 1961).

* Koskey, Thomas. *Baited Bulletin Boards* (Belmont, CA: Fearon Publishers, 1954).

* Prizzi, Elaine, and Jeanne Hoffman. *Teaching Off the Wall: Interactive Bulletin Boards That Teach With You* (Belmont, CA: Pitman Learning, 1981).

Ruby, Doris. *4-D Bulletin Boards That Teach* (Belmont, CA: Pitman Learning, 1960).

Ruby, Doris, and Grant Ruby. *Bulletin Boards for the Middle Grades* (Belmont, CA: Pitman Learning, 1964).

Audiovisual References

"Display and Presentation Boards." (Chicago, IL: International Film Bureau, 1971). (16-mm film or videocassette, 15 minutes, color.)

"Dry Mounting with Heat Press." (Salt Lake City, UT: Media Systems, Inc., 1975). (Filmstrip or slides, 40 frames, color.)

"Heat Laminating." (Salt Lake City, UT: Media Systems, Inc., 1975). (Filmstrip or slides, 40 frames, color.)

"Lettering: A Creative Approach to Basics." (Stamford, CT: Educational Dimensions Group, 1978). [Two sound filmstrips (cassette).]

"Production Techniques for Instructional Graphic Materials." (Columbus, OH: Charles E. Merrill, 1977). (27 filmstrips in basic series, 12 filmstrips in advanced series, 18 audio cassettes.)

"Three-Dimensional Displays." (Burbank, CA: Encore Visual Education, 1975). [Four sound filmstrips (cassette).]

*Key References.

Suppliers of Materials and Equipment

Graphics, Mounting, Laminating, Lettering

Dick Blick
Box 1267
Galesburg, Illinois 61401

Demco Educational Corp.
P.O. Box 1488
Madison, Wisconsin 53701

Chartpak
One River Road
Leeds, Massachusetts 01053

Seal, Inc.
251 Roosevelt Drive
Derby, Connecticut 06418

Cloth Boards

Ohio Flock-Cote Co.
14500 Industrial Avenue N.
Maple Heights, Ohio 44137

Instructo Corporation
1635 North 55th Street
Paoli, Pennsylvania

Charles Mayer Studios
168 East Market Street
Akron, Ohio 44308

Maharam Fabric Co.
420 New Orleans Street
Chicago, Illinois 60610

Bulletin Boards and Magnetic Boards

Bangor Cork Co.
William and D Streets
Pen Argyl, Pennsylvania 18072

Bulletin Boards and Directory
 Products
724 Broadway
New York, New York 10003

Charles Mayer Studios
168 East Market Street
Akron, Ohio 44308

Eberhard Faber, Inc.
Crestwood
Wilkes-Barre, Pennsylvania 18701

Magna Magnetics
777 Sunset Boulevard
Los Angeles, California 90046

Methods Research Corporation
Farmingdale, New Jersey 07727

Weber-Costello Company
1900 Narragansett Avenue
Chicago, Illinois 60639

POSSIBLE PROJECTS

4-A. Select four flat pictures and mount one with temporary rubber cement; one with permanent rubber cement, a third with dry mount tissue, and a fourth with any one of the additional techniques shown in class or discussed in the chapter.

4-B. Select several pictures that are approximately 8 1/2 by 11 inches and laminate them utilizing the cold or heat process.

4-C. Find a set of three flat pictures you might use in your teaching. Then apply a set of selection criteria from the textbook or of your own design to these pictures. Turn in pictures and evaluation forms for evaluation.

4-D. Plan a lesson in which you use a set of still pictures. Within this lesson show evidence that you have followed the utilization principles suggested. Submit pictures with lesson.

4-E. Devise for your subject field one graph (line, bar, circle, pictorial) and one chart (organization classification, time line, tabular chart, flowchart). Each of these should be prepared on a separate sheet. Final evaluation will include appropriateness of the visual with the subject content and the appropriate use of lettering and color on the visual.

4-F. Select a theme or subject in your teaching field and make one or two charts in which you use simple sketches. While one chart may use only stick figures, the other should be more detailed and representative of the real objects.

4-G. Make a list of 10 possible posters students could make to depict aspects of your teaching area. Prepare *one* yourself to serve as a motivational device. The poster should be at least 12 by 14 inches.

4-H. Examine books on bulletin board designs found in the library for bulletin board ideas. Develop and construct one of the ideas appropriate for your subject area. Finally, copy or make adaptations in sketch form on 8 1/2-by-11-inch paper the designs of two other bulletin boards that you could use.

4-I. Select a topic, identify your objectives, and construct a bulletin board or teaching display to support the topic and objectives. You may submit the components of the display with a sketch showing how to assemble it, you may present the actual bulletin board or display in a place agreeable to you and the instructor, or you may submit a photograph (polaroid, for example) of the assembled materials. Acceptable performance will be based on the degree to which you have incorporated good design principles in the final product.

4-J. Obtain an example of a real object or model that you could use for instruction. Submit the object or model and a description of how you would use it, including an objective.

4-K. Prepare a cloth board, magnetic board, flip chart *or* exhibit. Submit the material, a description of the intended audience, the objectives, how it will be used, and how it will be evaluated.

CHAPTER 5

PROJECTED VISUALS

OUTLINE

OBJECTIVES

After studying this chapter, you should be able to:

1. Define projected visuals.
2. Describe the characteristics and operation of opaque projection systems including two advantages and three limitations.
3. Discuss two applications of opaque projection in your teaching field.
4. Describe three utilization techniques to enhance the effectiveness of opaque projection in instructional situations.
5. Describe the characteristics and operation of overhead transparency projection systems including three advantages and three limitations.
6. Discuss two applications of the overhead in your teaching field.
7. Describe three utilization techniques to enhance your use of the overhead projector.
8. Describe the following techniques for overhead transparency production: write-on, thermal film method, electrostatic method, spirit duplication, and color lift.
9. Describe three utilization techniques to enhance the effectiveness of overhead transparencies in instructional situations.
10. Describe the characteristics of slides including three advantages and three limitations.
11. Synthesize an instructional situation in which you might use a series of locally produced slides.
12. Describe the basic operation of a Kodak Visualmaker.
13. Describe the characteristics of filmstrips including three advantages and three limitations.
14. Synthesize an instructional situation in which you might use a commercially produced filmstrip.
15. Describe two utilization techniques to enhance your use of filmstrips.

Because an illuminated screen in a darkened room tends to rivet the attention of viewers to itself, projected visuals have long been popular as a medium of instruction as well as of entertainment. The lighted screen is a silent shout—a shout likely to be heard and heeded even by the most reluctant learners.

It is not too fanciful to conjecture that some of this attraction is due to the aura of "magic" that seems to surround such presentations. The room lights are dimmed; the viewers grow quiet in expectation; a switch is thrown and (presto!) a large, bright image appears on the screen. You have their attention. They are ready to receive your message! Exploit this readiness by having selected materials that will maintain the viewers' attention and by using them in a way that *involves* viewers actively in the learning process.

Projected visuals refers to media formats in which still images are projected onto a screen. Such projection is usually achieved by passing a strong light through transparent film (overhead transparencies, slides, and filmstrips), magnifying the image through a series of lenses, and casting this image onto a reflective surface. Opaque projection is also included in this category. In opaque projection, light is cast onto an opaque image (one that does not allow light to pass through), such as a magazine picture or printed page. The light is reflected from the material onto mirrors which transmit the reflection through a series of lenses onto a screen.

This chapter will focus on the characteristics and applications of opaque projection, overhead projection, slides, and filmstrips—the most widely accepted means of providing projected visuals in education and training settings.

OPAQUE PROJECTION

Opaque projection, as noted above, is a method for projecting *opaque* visuals by reflecting light off the material rather than transmitting light through it. The opaque projector was among the first audiovisual devices to come into widespread use and is still used because of its unique ability to project a magnified image of two-dimensional materials and some three-dimensional objects.

The opaque projector works by directing a very strong incandescent light (typically about 1000 watts) down onto the material. This light is reflected upward to strike a mirror which aims the light beam through a series of lenses onto a screen (Figure 5.1).

The process of reflected, or indirect, projection is optically less efficient than the direct projection process used for showing slides, filmstrips, and overhead transparencies. Consequently, the image on the screen is dimmer and much more complete room darkening is required. Still, opaque projection makes such a wide range of visual materials available for group viewing that it should not be overlooked as a valuable tool.

Advantages
Opaque projection allows on-the-spot projection of readily available classroom materials, such as maps, newspapers, and illustrations from books and magazines (Figure 5.2).

It permits group viewing and discussion of student work, such as drawings, student compositions, solutions to math problems, and the like.

Three-dimensional objects, especially relatively flat ones such as coins, plant leaves, and insect specimens, can be magnified for close-up inspection.

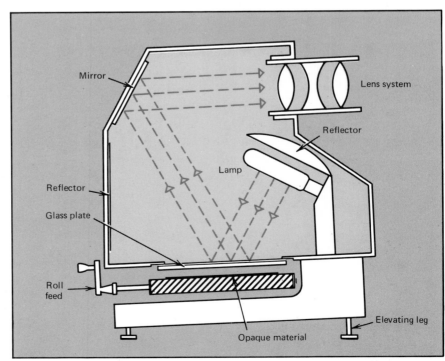

Figure 5.1 Opaque projector, cutaway view.

Figure 5.2 The opaque projector can be used to magnify small objects, such as coins, as well as print materials and pictures.

Limitations

The relative dimness of the reflected image demands rather complete room darkening if the visual is to be clear enough for instructional purposes. Areas which cannot be sufficiently darkened are unsuitable for opaque projection.

The opaque projector is bulky, heavy, and cumbersome to move. Also, it needs to be operated from a lower type of projection stand than other audiovisual equipment.

The high-wattage lamp generates a lot of heat, raising the room temperature and possibly even making parts of the projector unsafe to touch. The heat may also damage the materials being projected if they are exposed too long to the projector's light. If metal objects are being projected they may rapidly become too hot to handle.

Applications

The opaque projector is useful for many small groups or classroom size groups (up to about twenty) that need to view some printed or visual material together. Applications may be found in all curricular areas at all grade levels. Here are just a few typical examples:

Language arts—group examination of student compositions, picture books, or reference books.

Science—magnification of specimens; group study of the periodic table, tables of random numbers, and the like.

Social studies—map study; viewing of artifacts from other cultures, post cards, and atlas illustrations.

Art—group discussion of reproductions of paintings and architectural details; close-up views of fabrics and weaving styles; study of advertising layouts.

Music—group reading of musical scores.

Home economics—group viewing of sewing patterns, textiles, recipes, etc.

Business—group work on business and accounting forms, organization charts, sales territory maps, parts of a product, and the like.

All subjects—group critique of student work and review of test items.

One especially handy application of the opaque projector is to use it to copy or adapt illustrations for classroom display. You can make your own enlargement of any original picture that you might want to display on the chalkboard or as part of a bulletin board. The procedure is easy. Place the material to be copied in the projector and dim the room lights. Adjust the projector to enlarge (or reduce) the image to the size you want, and direct the projected image onto the surface on which

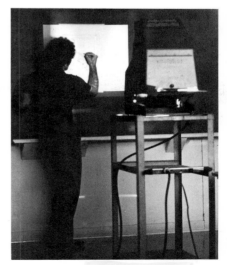

Figure 5.3 Copying visuals for classroom display is easy with the opaque projector.

AV Showmanship—Opaque Projection

In addition to the general principles of audiovisual utilization discussed in Chapter 2, there are several special techniques that apply particularly to opaque projection.

Since the opaque projector requires near total room darkening, be prepared to operate in the dark. A student should be stationed at the light switch to help you avoid tripping over students, cords, and other obstacles in getting to and from the projector in the dark. Although the projector does spill quite a bit of light around its sides, you may need to use a flashlight to follow any prepared notes or script.

Most opaque projectors are equipped with a built-in optical pointer—a bright arrow that can be aimed at any point on the screen. Experiment ahead of time so that you will be able to aim the pointer effectively during the presentation. It can be used to focus viewers' attention

to particular words on a printed page, details of an art work, and so on.

For some purposes (especially in teaching elementary-school language arts) it is useful to arrange pictures on a long strip or roll of paper. In this way you can put a series of illustrations into a fixed sequence to tell a story or show steps in a process. This simulates the action of a filmstrip.

The opaque projector will accept a wide range of picture sizes. When you are setting up the projector, be sure to use the *largest* of your illustrations to center the image on the screen. If you center with a smaller picture, the bigger one will extend beyond the edges of the screen when you get to it. This will force you to stop in the middle of the presentation (and thus distract your audience) to center the big picture.

---

your are working. Then trace over the projected image in whatever detail you wish. Every line of the original can be reproduced, or just the outlines for a more stylized effect. Your students will be impressed with your "artistic ability," and maybe you will be too.

OVERHEAD PROJECTION

Because of its many virtues, which will be discussed in detail later in this chapter, the overhead projection system has advanced rapidly in the past three decades to become the most ubiquitous audiovisual device in North American classrooms.

The typical overhead projector is a very simple device (Figure 5.4). Basically, it is a box with a large aperture or "stage" at the top. Light from a powerful lamp inside the box is condensed by a special type of lens, known as a fresnel lens, and passes through a transparency (usually approximately 8 by 10 inches) placed on the stage. A lens and mirror system mounted on a bracket above the box turns the light beam 90 degrees and projects the image back over the shoulder of the presenter.

Because of the widespread familiarity of overhead projection, the general term *transparency* has taken on, in the instructional setting, the specific meaning of the large-format 8-by-10 inch film used with the overhead projector. Transparencies may be composed of photographic type film, clear acetate, or any of a number of other transparent materials capable of being imprinted with an image by means of chemical or heat processes (for example, see thermal film, discussed below).

Transparencies may be used individually or they may be made into a series of images consisting of a base visual with one or more "overlays" attached to the base with hinges. Complex topics can be explained step by step by flipping on a series of overlays one at a time that add additional features to a diagram (Figure 5.5).

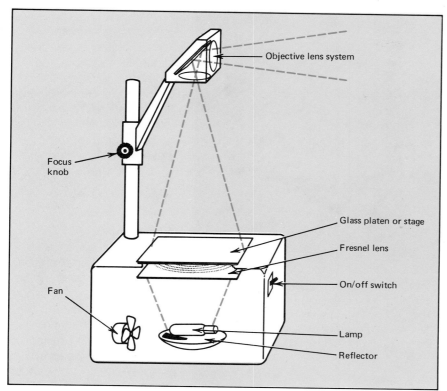

Figure 5.4 Overhead projector, cutaway view.

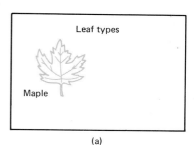

(a)

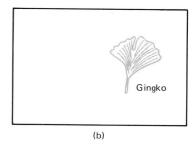

(b)

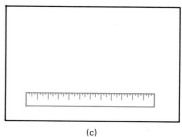

(c)

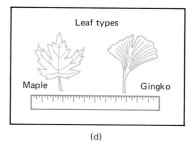

(d)

Figure 5.5 By means of overlays, complex visuals can be built up step-by-step.

Advantages

The overhead projection system has a number of unique features that give it the tremendous versatility for which it is rightly acclaimed by so many instructors.

Its bright lamp and efficient optical system generate so much light on the screen that the overhead can be used in *normal room lighting.*

The projector is operated from the front of the room with the presenter *facing the audience,* allowing direct eye contact to be maintained.

A variety of materials can be projected, including cutout silhouettes, small opaque objects, and many types of transparencies.

Projected materials can be *manipulated* by the presenter. You can point to important items, highlight them with colored pens, add details during the lesson (notes, diagrams, etc.) by marking on the transparency with a marking pen,

cover part of the message and progressively reveal information in a step-by-step procedure. As noted above, complex visuals can be presented in a series of overlays.

Commercially produced transparencies are available covering a broad range of curricular areas. A major directory of commercially available overhead transparencies is published by the National Information Center for Educational Media (NICEM)—*Index to Educational Overhead Transparencies.* See Appendix A for details and other sources.

Instructors can easily prepare their own transparencies (several common methods of production are explained later in this section).

Figure 5.6a The overhead projector has been adapted to many uses outside the classroom; here finalists in a national crossword puzzle contest perform before an audience.

Figure 5.6b With the overhead projector the presenter maintains eye contact with viewers.

Information that might otherwise have to be placed on a chalkboard during class session (lesson outlines, for example) may be prepared ahead for presentation at the proper time. Research indicates that retention of main points improves significantly when visual outlines are presented.

Most overhead projectors are light in weight and easily portable. All are simple to operate.

Limitations

The effectiveness of overhead projection presentations is heavily dependent on the presenter. The overhead projector cannot be programmed to display visual sequences by itself, nor is an audio accompaniment provided.

In general, the overhead system does not lend itself to independent study. The projection system is designed for large-group presentation. (Of course, an individual student could look at a transparency by holding it up to the light or laying it on a light table, but since captions or audio tracks are not a part of this format the material would ordinarily not be self-instructional.)

Printed materials and other nontransparent items, such as magazine illustrations, cannot be projected immediately, as is possible with the opaque projector. To use the overhead system such materials have to be made into transparencies by means of some sort of "production" process.

Distortion of images is more prevalent with the overhead than with other projection systems. It is commonly placed at desk-top level to facilitate the instructor's writing on transparencies. The screen, on the other hand, needs to be placed on a higher level for clear audience sight lines. This discrepancy in levels causes a distortion referred to as the "keystone effect." This problem and its solution are discussed in Chapter 10.

MEDIA FILE: "Ancient Egypt" Overhead Transparency

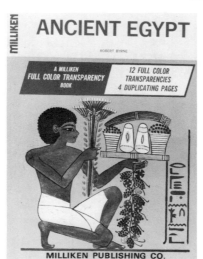

A book containing a dozen full-color, tear-out transparencies showing aspects of life in Ancient Egypt, mythological characters, and the like. Each transparency is accompanied by a teacher's guide providing a "script" to follow. Duplicating masters for quizzes included.

Source: Milliken Publishing Co.

AV Showmanship—Overhead

In addition to the general utilization practices, here are some hints specifically related to overhead projection.

Avoid diminishing the possible impact of over-head projection by using the projector as a doodle pad. For random notes or verbal cues, use the chalkboard.

Shift the audience attention back to *you* by switching off the projector during changes of transparencies and especially when you have finished referring to a particular transparency.

Plan ways to add meaningful details to the transparency during projection; this infuses an element of spontaneity. If the basic transparency is a valuable one which will be reused, cover it with a blank acetate before drawing.

Direct viewer attention to parts of the transparency by the following techniques:

Mask unwanted portions by covering them with a sheet of paper or using cardboard "windows" to reveal one section at a time.

Overlay new information one step at a time. Build up a complex idea by superimposing transparencies one at a time.

Point to specific portions, using a pencil as a pointer. Lay the pencil directly on the transparency because any elevation will put the pencil out of focus and any slight hand movement will be greatly exaggerated on the screen.

MEDIA FILE: "Map Reading" Overhead Transparency

A series of 27 full-color transparencies for use on the overhead projector designed for teaching basic geographic understanding. Divided into 13 lessons, packaged in a self-contained viewing stage book. Includes correlated notes next to every transparency. Topics included: location, scale, contour, projections, and map symbols.

Source: Denoyer-Geppert.

Applications

As indicated by its ubiquitous presence in the classroom, the overhead system has a myriad of group instruction applications, too numerous to list here.

One indication of the breadth of applications is that commercial distributors of transparencies have made available materials for virtually all curricular areas, from kindergarten through college levels.

These materials range from single simple transparencies to elaborate sets replete with multiple overlays, masking devices, and other teaching aids. Transparent plastic constructions such as clocks, engines, slide rules, and the like are available. These can be manipulated by the instructor to demonstrate how the parts interact as they are displayed on the screen.

Creating Overhead Transparencies

As previously noted, one of the major advantages of the overhead system is that instructors—and students—can easily prepare their own transparencies. Beginning with simple hand-drawing on clear acetate sheets, numerous other methods of preparing transparencies have evolved over the years. We will look closely at only the processes most commonly used at the classroom production level—direct drawing, thermal film process, electrostatic film process (xerography), and the color lift.

Direct Drawing Method. The most obvious way of quickly preparing a transparency is simply to draw directly on a transparent sheet with some sort of marking pen. Clear acetate of five to ten mils (.005–.010 inches) thickness is recommended. Other types of plastic can be used, including even household food wrap and dry cleaning bags. Although some of these alternatives may be a great deal cheaper than the thicker acetate, some of them impose limitations in terms of durability, ease of handling, and ability to accept different inks (including disintegrating completely under alcohol-based inks). If available, blue-tinted acetate is preferred because it reduces the glare of the projected image.

Although the glass platen or stage of the overhead projector generally measures about 10 by 10 inches, your drawing and lettering should be restricted to a rectangular "message area" of about 7½ by 9½ inches. This fits the dimensions of acetate sheets, which are commonly cut into rectangles of 8 by 10 inches or 8½ by 11 inches, the size of writing paper in the United States (Figure 5.7).

Some overhead projectors come equipped with a pair of roll attachments made to carry long rolls of plastic which can be advanced or reversed by a small hand crank. This assures a steady supply of transparency material for extemporaneous use. It also allows a series of images to be prepared in advance in proper sequence. Such rolls can be saved for later reuse.

In addition to the transparency, you will need a writing instrument. Felt-tipped marking pens are the handiest for this purpose. They come in two general types—*water-soluble* and *permanent* ink. Within these two types a wide variety of pens are available. Not all are suitable for overhead transparencies.

Here are some important cautions to keep in mind:

- Virtually all the permanent-ink felt-tipped pens will adhere to acetate, but only those labelled "for overhead marking" are sure to project *in color*. Otherwise the ink itself may be opaque and project only in black.
- Permanent inks really are permanent. They can be removed only with special plastic erasers.
- Markers with *water-soluble* ink generally will not adhere well to acetate; the ink tends to bead up and disappear as the water evaporates. A label stating "for overhead marking" means it *will adhere* to acetate and project in color. Such special pens can be erased readily with a damp cloth. This allows you to reuse the acetate sheet—a considerable advantage in view of the escalating cost of acetate, which is a petroleum product.

Less frequently used but very serviceable are *wax-based pencils*, often referred to as "grease pencils." Unless otherwise marked, they will project black. The great advantage of wax-based pencils is that they can be erased from acetate with any soft, dry cloth.

Finally, there are some specially treated ("frosted") acetate sheets made to be typed on directly by a typewriter or written on with a pencil. This option should be used with some caution, however. It may encourage the unwarranted use of a visual medium for purely verbal instruction. In addition, most typewriter-type sizes are too small to be legible when projected in a classroom. However, if a legible type is available (such as "Primary" typeface or IBM's "Orator" type) and the subject matter is necessarily verbal, typing on "frosted" sheets may be a useful alternative.

Thermal Film Process. In the thermal film process infrared light passes through a specially treated acetate film onto a prepared master underneath. The art work and lettering on the master are done with a heat-absorbing material such as India ink, ordinary lead pencil, or other substance containing *carbon*. An image is "burned into" the film wherever it contacts such carbonaceous marking.

Depending on the film used, a number of different color patterns are possible. The most common pattern is black print on a clear or pastel background analogous to positive film. Clear or colored lines can also be put on a black background analogous to negative film.

Another option is the use of printed, commercially prepared transparency masters. Thermal film producers and other audiovisual publishers offer a broad range of printed masters—many thousands of individual titles covering

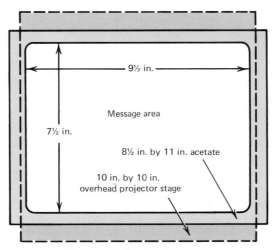

Figure 5.7 Overhead transparency dimensions.

HOW TO...MAKE THERMAL TRANSPARENCIES

First prepare the master. Any ordinary white paper may be used. Draw the artwork by hand or paste illustrations from other sources (magazine illustrations, photocopies, etc.) onto the master. Lettering, added by hand, by mechanical lettering guide, or by paste-up of existing lettering, must consist of a carbonaceous substance. An alternative is to create the visual using any types of materials and then electrostatically copy it and use the copy as the master. (Note some electrostatic copies work better than others. Experiment with what is available to you.)

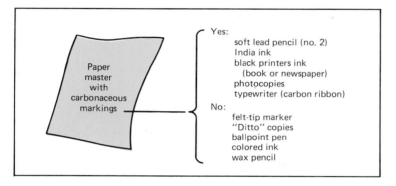

Second, place a sheet of thermal acetate over the master. Most brands of acetate have a notch in one corner of the film to ensure that it is put on correctly. The notch should always be placed at the upper right-hand corner of the master.

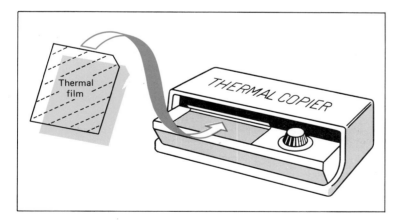

Third, feed the two sheets into a thermal copy machine, using the dial setting recommended by the manufacturer. Transfer of the image to the acetate requires only a few seconds. Then separate the two sheets. The film is ready for projection! The master is not affected in the production process and may be reused to make additional copies of the transparency.

virtually all curricular areas. Some publishers offer sets of masters specifically correlated with the leading textbooks in language arts, reading, math, social studies, and science.

To use commercially prepared thermal masters, simply remove one from the book or folder in which it is packaged, lay the thermal film on it, and run both through the copier. Commercial masters may, of course, be altered by the instructor to better suit the needs of a particular audience.

Electrostatic Film Process (Xerography). The rapidly evolving technology of xerography provides the newest method of producing transparencies. Xerox brand copy machines and other office copiers that operate by the electrostatic process can now be used to prepare black-and-white transparencies. (Some models, such as the Xerox 6500, can produce high quality full-color transparencies, but these costly machines are not widely available.)

Similar to the thermal process, this process requires a paper master and specially treated film. In this case the film is electrically charged and light sensitive (rather than heat sensitive). The steps outlined above for thermal film are essentially the same as those needed to produce an electrostatic film transparency. However, since the xerographic process responds to darkness of the image rather than carbon content, it is not necessary to confine the art work to carbonaceous images. Any substance which yields a good opaque mark can be used.

Spirit-Duplication Process.

If you are already planning to make a spirit-duplicator master (often referred to by the brand name, Ditto), it is just one simple extra step to make a transparency from that master.

After you have prepared a regular spirit-duplicator master and mounted it on the duplicating machine, feed in a sheet of frosted acetate with the etched side up. If greater permanence is desired, the resulting transparency can be sprayed with a clear plastic spray, such as Krylon, which will remove the matte effect and protect the ink image from smearing.

An advantage of this process is that it allows you to use a master you may have prepared for another purpose to produce a transparency. Your students may then refer to a hand-held copy of the visual while you project an image of it. A disadvantage is that the process requires some specialized materials—the frosted acetate and clearing spray.

Color Lift Process.

Full-color illustrations printed on coated paper (such as that found in "glossy" magazines, for example) can be transferred to transparencies. There are several ways this can be done, some of which require specialized equipment, others of which are laborious and not always reliable. The process described here is a compromise. With reasonable care it yields good results and most of the materials needed are relatively commonplace. However, it does require one specialized material—pressure-sensitive laminating acetate (a well-known brand in the United States is Con-Tact, in Canada Mac-Tac).

HOW TO...MAKE COLOR LIFT TRANSPARENCIES

Begin by gathering the needed materials: a magazine picture, a sheet of laminating acetate, a pan of soapy water, a comb or similar smoothing object, a sponge, plastic spray, and a sheet of clear acetate.

1. Test the picture to make sure it is printed on clay-coated paper. Wet your finger and rub a white portion of the page. It should pick up a whitish residue. If so, the picture is suitable for lifting.

2. Cut out the picture.
3. Remove the backing sheet from the laminating acetate.
4. With the sticky side of the laminating acetate down, bend it into a U-shape and lower it onto the picture, pressing down from the center outward.

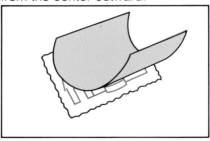

5. To smooth out any air bubbles and to get full adhesion of the laminate, rub the back of the picture with a comb or similar hard, smooth object. Rub from the center outward. Cover the picture with a protective sheet, such as the backing sheet from the acetate.

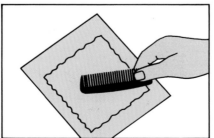

6. Place the visual in a pan of soapy water and let it soak for a few minutes.

7. Peel the soaked paper from the acetate.

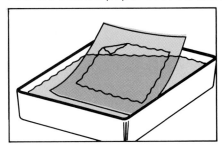

8. After the paper is removed, rub the visual with a sponge to remove the excess clay residue.

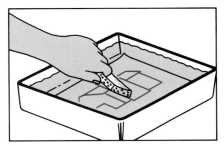

9. Hang the transparency up to dry.

10. When dry, spray the dull side of the transparency with a clear plastic spray. (Test a small spot first to make sure the spray will not damage the acetate.)

11. Cover the vulnerable side of the transparency with a sheet of clear acetate.

12. If desired, mount the completed transparency on a cardboard mount.

Whatever production process you may choose for preparing your transparencies, keep in mind these design guidelines based on research and considerable practical experience:

- *Horizontal* format covers projected viewing area best.
- The idea should be a *VISUAL* one; if not, consider using chalkboard or print to convey verbal information.
- Confine each transparency to a *single concept* expressed in simple, uncluttered visuals (in general, maximum of three to four images).
- Keep *verbiage* to a minimum.
- Observe *legibility* standards: at least $3/16$-inch high lettering.
- For more complex ideas, add information sequentially by preparing a base transparency plus *overlays*.
- It is often useful to summarize the main point of the transparency in a caption or title. If this is done, it usually will be most effective given as a "headline" at the top of the visual.

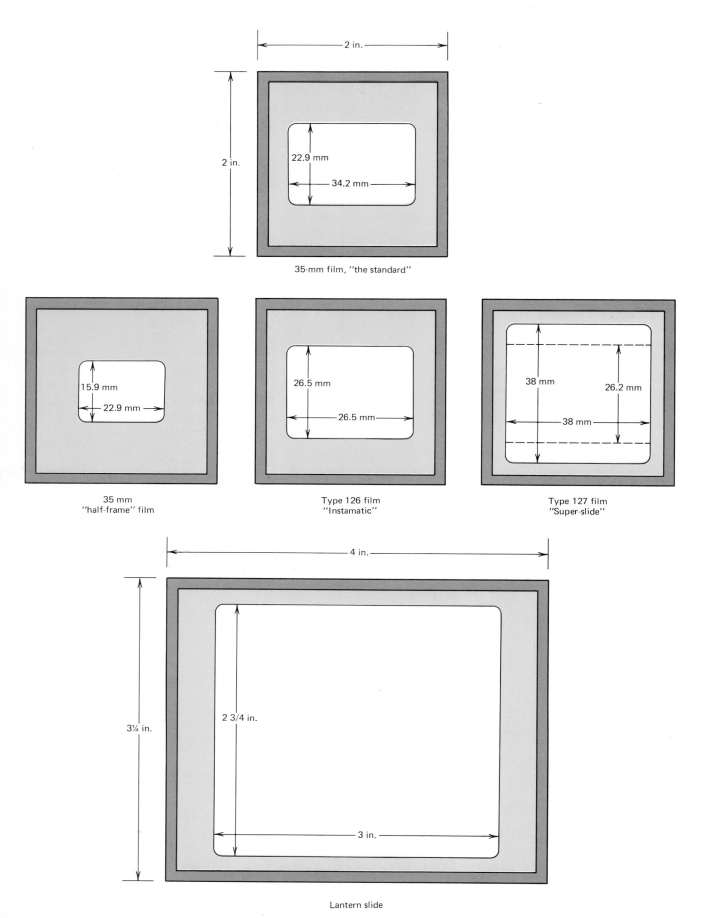

2 in.

2 in.

22.9 mm

34.2 mm

35-mm film, "the standard"

15.9 mm

22.9 mm

35 mm
"half-frame" film

26.5 mm

26.5 mm

Type 126 film
"Instamatic"

38 mm

26.2 mm

38 mm

Type 127 film
"Super-slide"

4 in.

3¼ in.

2 3/4 in.

3 in.

Lantern slide

Figure 5.8   Common 2 by 2 in. slide formats compared with the lantern-slide format.

SLIDES

The term *slide* refers to a small-format photographic transparency individually mounted for one-at-a-time projection.

The size of slide most frequently encountered in educational use is 2 by 2 in. (metric equivalency either 50 by 50 millimeters or 5 by 5 centimeters), measured by the outer dimensions of the slide mount. When 35-mm and other popular types of slide film are sent out to be processed they are usually returned mounted in 2-by-2-in. mounts. The actual dimensions of the *image* itself will vary with the type of film (Figure 5.8).

Another standard format still found in occasional use is the 3¼-by-4-inch slide, used with the projector known popularly as the lantern slide projector. It represents one of the oldest formats of image projection, being descended from the old "magic lantern" slides which were a popular entertainment medium back before the days of motion pictures.

The chief reason to use the lantern slide is that it is larger than 2-by-2-inch slides. Maps, charts, tables, and other detailed subjects can be presented more effectively since the larger film affords greater detail in the image. When the image is projected it can therefore fill a larger screen with less loss of definition and less room darkening required.

A second advantage of the larger size of the slide itself is that it allows slides to be hand-drawn. Various pencils and inks can be drawn directly onto frosted glass; silhouettes or thin specimens can be mounted between clear glass mounts; and photos, including the Polaroid instant type, can be shot on slide film in this format. The recent addition of the Polaroid option plus newer projectors featuring automatic advance and remote control have helped bring this older format more up-to-date.

Advantages

Since slides can be arranged and rearranged into an infinite variety of sequences they are more flexible than filmstrips or other fixed-sequence materials.

Figure 5.10 Originally, slides were fed into the projector one at a time, and manual feed projectors are still widely sold.

As photographic equipment is continually refined and simplified, more and more amateurs are able to produce their own slides. Automatic exposure controls, easy focusing, and high-speed color films have contributed to this trend. High-quality color pictures can be taken by any interested amateur photographer.

The assembly of slide programs is facilitated by today's automatic projectors which hold sets of slides in trays and feed them into place in sequence. Most automatic projectors also offer the convenience of remote-control advancing of slides, allowing the presenter to remain at the front of the room or off to a side while advancing the slides via a push-button unit connected by wire to the projector. Certain models can be preset to advance automatically every so many seconds. This feature allows continuous showing in exhibits, display cases, and other automated situations.

General availability and ease of handling make it relatively easy to build up permanent collections of slides for specific instructional purposes. Individual instructors may collect and store their own collections, or the slides may be compiled and kept in a learning resource center. Such collections enable users to assemble presentations partially or wholly from

Figure 5.9 The oldest of the slide formats, the lantern slide is still in use.

Figure 5.11 For most applications, the circular tray, automatic feeding projector is the standard.

Figure 5.12 The Ektagraphic III is Kodak's latest updating of the Carousel line of slide projectors.

existing pictures, thus reducing the expense required for new production.

Slides can be integrated into individualized instruction programs. Although developed primarily as a large-group medium, recent hardware innovations have made slides feasible for small-group and independent study as well. However, the complex nature of these new mechanisms makes them relatively expensive and fragile. Thus slide-tape viewers for individual use are more likely to be found in learning resource centers than in classrooms (Figure 5.13).

Figure 5.13   The slide-tape format has been adapted for individual viewers.

AV Showmanship—Slides

In addition to the general guidelines for audiovisual utilization discussed in Chapter 2, here are several specific practices that can add professionalism to your slide presentations.

Plan and rehearse your narration to accompany the slides if it is not already recorded on tape.

Use a remote control advance device; this will allow you to stand at the side of the room. From this position you can keep an eye on the slides while maintaining some eye contact with the audience.

Prepare a way to light up your script after the room lights are dimmed; a penlight or flashlight will serve this purpose.

Limit your discussion of each slide—even a minute of narration can seem long to your audience unless there is a complex visual to be examined at the same time.

Employ visual variety. Mix the types of slides, using verbal title slides to help break the presentation into segments.

If there is a "talky" section in the middle of your presentation, put a black slide on rather than holding an irrelevant slide on the screen. (Actually, gray slides, which can be produced locally or purchased from commercial sources, are preferable. They let through enough light to allow the presenter to be seen, avoiding total darkening of the room during the "blackout.")

Consider adding a musical accompaniment to your live or recorded narration. This can help to establish the desired mood and keep your audience attentive. But do not have music playing in the background when providing narration.

Begin and end with a black slide. A white flash on the screen at the beginning and end is irritating to the eye and appears amateurish.

Make *very* certain your slides are in sequential order and right-side up. Disarrangement can be an embarrassment to you and an annoyance to your audience. Refer to the section below, "How to...Thumb Spot Slides," to find a fool-proof method of avoiding this embarrassment.

Limitations

Since slides, unlike filmstrips, come as individual units, they can easily become disorganized: out of sequence, upside down, sideways, backwards, etc. Even when stored in trays, if the locking ring is loosened the slides can come spilling out (usually just as the tray is being placed on the projector for the beginning of a showing!).

Slide mounts come in cardboard, plastic, and glass of varying thicknesses. This lack of standardization can lead to jamming of slides in the slide-changing mechanism: cardboard becomes "dog-eared" with the frayed edges getting caught in the mechanism; plastic mounts swell or warp in the heat of the lamp; glass mounts thicker than the aperture chamber fail to drop into showing position.

Slides which are not enclosed in glass covers are susceptible to accumulation of dust and fingerprints. Careless storage or handling can easily lead to permanent damage.

A final limitation of slides is their cost in comparison to filmstrips. The cost *per frame* of a commercially produced slide set may be two to three times the cost per frame of a filmstrip of equal length.

Applications

Like other forms of projected visuals, slides may be used at all grade levels and for instruction in all curricular areas. A good many high quality slides are available commercially, individually and in sets. In general, the fine arts, geography, and the sciences are especially well represented with commercially distributed slides.

The examples shown below give some idea of the types of slide materials available through commercial channels. A major directory of commercially available slides is published by the National Information Center for Educational Media (NICEM)—*Index to Educational Slides*. See Appendix A for details and other sources.

As noted earlier, a major attraction of slides as an instructional device is the ease with which they can be produced by instructors—and students. Modern cameras are so automatic and simple to operate that even the most amateur of photographers can expect usable results. As with all locally produced materials, instructor- and student-made slides are likely to have an immediacy and a specificity lacking in commercially produced instructional materials.

MEDIA FILE: Harbrace "Science 700" Slides

"Science 700" consists of three sets of slide programs: Life Science, Earth Science, and Physical Science. All the slides are developed with dark backgrounds to allow projection on chalkboards in normal room lighting.
Source: Harcourt, Brace, Jovanovich.

MEDIA FILE: "Contemporary Painting and Sculpture" Slides

A set of 358 slides illustrates contemporary works of painting and sculpture, including landscapes, figurative, still life, new realism, pop art, and surrealism.
Source: Art Now, Inc.

HOW TO..."THUMB SPOT" SLIDES

There are eight possible ways a slide can be placed in a projector. *Seven of them are wrong* (e.g., upside-down, backwards, sideways, etc.). To avoid all seven mistakes a standardized procedure is recommended for placing a reminder spot on the slide.

First, your slides should be arranged and numbered in the order in which they are to be shown.

Then take each slide and hold it the way it is supposed to be seen on the screen, that is, right-side up with any lettering running left to right—just as it would be read. (If the slide lacks lettering or other orienting information, hold it so that the *emulsion* side is toward the screen.)

Then simply place a spot on the bottom, left-hand corner.

Use each of the slides below for thumb spot practice. On each slide indicate where you would place the thumb spot. Check below for correct answers.

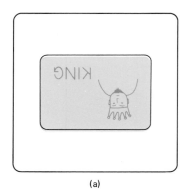

(a)

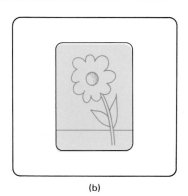

(b)

(c)

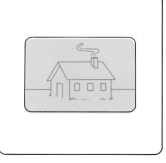

(d)

Here are the correct answers to the thumb spot practice problems:

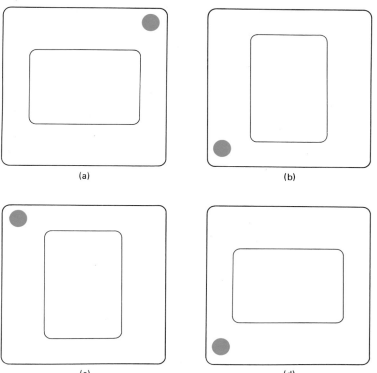

(a) (b)

(c) (d)

This spot is referred to as a "thumb spot" because when the slide is turned upside-down to be placed in the projector your thumb will grip the slide at the point of the thumb spot, as shown below.

After all the slides are in the tray in proper order, some users like to run a felt-tip pen across the tops of the slide mounts in a diagonal line. This way, if some slides later get out of order they can be replaced just by following the line.

Further, such locally produced efforts gain credibility by depicting local people and conditions.

Among the myriad possibilities, here are some "starter" ideas as typical subjects for slide presentations:

- Documenting student activities, products of student work, community problems (e.g. crime and pollution).
- Simulating a field trip.
- Making a visual history of your community, school, or organization.
- Showing people at work in various jobs, for career awareness.
- Promoting public understanding of your school or organization.
- Teaching a step-by-step process with close-ups of each operation.

Along with modern camera technology, a further boon to teacher/student production of slides has been a device called the Kodak Visualmaker. This device permits reproduction of flat visual materials—such as magazine illustrations, maps, charts, photographs, business forms, and the like, without the need for specialized photography skills. The secret is in the Visualmaker hardware itself: a copystand containing a built-in supplementary lens that is positioned and focused to allow easy picture taking with a Kodak Instamatic camera. This preset mechanism eliminates the need for extra lenses and specialized skills in proper framing of the picture (Figures 5.14 and 5.15).

Figures 5.14 and 5.15 The Visualmaker is equipped with two copystands—3 by 3 in. and 8 by 8 in.—to allow easy copying of different size art work.

HOW TO...**MAKE SLIDES WITH THE VISUALMAKER**

The basic steps for making slides from your original visuals are simple and fool-proof:

1. Attach the Instamatic camera to one of the two copystands included in the Visualmaker kit.
2. Insert a Magicube in the camera (unless you are using one of the new Visualmakers with electronic flash).
3. Place the copystand on top of your visual, aligning the picture within the frame formed by the copystand legs.
4. Hold the camera down firmly with one hand while squeezing the shutter release with the other hand. Snap! It's done.

Further Hints for Using the Visualmaker. To get the most benefit from your Visualmaker kit you will need to take some care with certain steps, especially in preparing the original visual material.

Select a suitable visual. Keep in mind that the flash unit is going to flood a lot of light onto the picture. If the picture is shiny, that light is going to reflect back in the form of glare. So avoid glossy photos, glass, acetate, and such surfaces. White backgrounds, too, should be avoided.

Photographs, drawings, and tables from books, magazines, and other printed media generally reproduce well. (Remember, though, that published materials including illustrations are protected by the copyright laws. For an extensive discussion of educators' rights and responsibilities refer to Appendix C.)

Choose one of the two available copystands. The Visualmaker kit is equipped with a copystand having an 8-by-8-in. frame and a smaller one having a 3-by-3-in. frame. Choose the one which frames your artwork best.

Figures 5.16 and 5.17 Artwork that contains unwanted information can be masked by means of two L-shaped pieces of construction paper.

Three-dimensional objects will photograph well if they are not too thick. In the large Visualmaker copystand, the sharp-focus area extends up to about 1½ inches above the table top. In the smaller copystand, ½ inch is approximately the thickness limit.

Compose the shot. If your visual is equal to or *larger* than the frame, keep in mind that the outer edges of the visual will be lost, so make sure that important visual information is no more than 7½ inches square (for the large copystand) or 2¾ inches square (for the small copystand). Keep critical information out of the "bleed" area around the border.

If your visual is *smaller* than the frame, mask the leftover space with dark colored construction paper or other such matte material, as illustrated below. Textured fabrics also make attractive backgrounds. Again, avoid white or shiny materials, to reduce possible glare.

Adding lettering. Lettering can be added to your visual with a typewriter if you are using the small copystand. Size and specifications are shown in the illustration below. However, if you are using the large copystand, you will need to use transfer letters, cutouts, a "primary" or "bulletin board" typewriter, or some other special lettering method. Your typewriter letters should be at least ⅜ inch high in order to be legible when projected on the screen (Figure 5.18).

```
TYPEWRITTEN LETTERING

FOR THE VISUALMAKER

SHOULD BE ALL CAPITALS,

DOUBLE-SPACED,

NO MORE THAN SEVEN

LINES LONG.
```

Figure 5.18 Legibility standards for typewritten information on slides.

Lighting the shot. The Visualmaker system is designed to provide adequate, even lighting by means of the flash unit supplied with the kit. Use this artificial lighting system even if you are shooting outdoors, or indoors in a well-lighted area. The type of flash unit you use is determined by what vintage of Visualmaker you are using. Two models are in common use: the Kodak Ektagraphic Visualmaker and the Kodak Ektagraphic *EF* Visualmaker. The former is the older model, distributed prior to 1979; it uses Magicubes as the lighting source. The *EF* model comes equipped with a special electronic flash unit, thereby doing away with the need to keep a stock of Magicubes on hand.*

---

*For more complete and detailed information on using the Visualmaker, see the Kodak publication, *Simple Copying Techniques with a Kodak Ektagraphic Visualmaker* (publication #S-40), available from audiovisual dealers or the Eastman Kodak Company, Rochester, NY 14650.

FILMSTRIPS

A filmstrip is a roll of 35-mm transparent film containing a series of related still pictures intended for showing one at a time.

Various filmstrip formats have evolved since their advent over a half century ago. Formats most widely seen today are the single frame and the double frame filmstrips. The difference between the two types is illustrated below. Note that in the single frame format the images are printed *perpendicular* to the length of the film, whereas in the double frame format the images are *parallel* to the length of the film. A second major distinction is that the double frame image has twice the area of the single frame image. It is, in fact, the same size and configuration as the 35-mm slide before the slide is cut apart and mounted. (In North America the single frame format is standard; in Europe the double frame is more common.)

Commercially produced filmstrips typically contain about 20 to 60 images or "frames" and are stored rolled up in small plastic canisters.

Until the 1960s most filmstrips were "silent"; that is, there was no audio accompaniment. Narrative information was printed at the bottom of each frame. Since that time there has been a growing trend toward having recorded sound tracks accompany the filmstrip. Initially the narration, music, sound effects, and so on were recorded on phonograph records and were played on record players either separate from the projector or built into it. Currently audio cassette tapes are becoming the standard means for giving *sound filmstrips* their "voice." It should be noted, though, that the sound track is *not* recorded on the filmstrip itself; rather, it comes on a separate cassette tape which is played back on a regular cassette recorder or on one which is built into the filmstrip projector unit.

For most sound filmstrips, the record or tape contains, besides the sound track, a second track carrying inaudible signals which automatically trigger the projector to advance to the next frame. Users generally have a choice of manually advancing the filmstrip according to audible beeps or setting the projector to run automatically according to the inaudible synchronization pulses.

Advantages

The filmstrip has gained considerable popularity because of its compactness, ease of handling, and relatively low cost. A filmstrip of 60 frames will fit comfortably in the palm of a hand and weighs only a few ounces. It is inserted easily into a simple projector. A commercially distributed filmstrip costs substantially less *per frame* than a set of slides or overhead transparencies purchased from commercial sources.

The sequential order of the frames can often be a teaching and learning advantage. A chronological or step-by-step process can be presented exactly in order, without any fear of having any of the pictures out of sequence or upside-down, as can sometimes happen with slides.

In contrast with audio and motion media, the pace of viewing filmstrips can be controlled by the user. This capability is especially relevant for independent study, but is also important for teacher-controlled group showings. A slow, deliberate examination of each frame might be suitable for the body of a lesson, while a quick

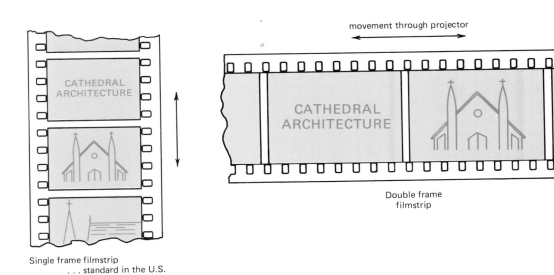

Single frame filmstrip
. . . standard in the U.S.

Double frame
filmstrip

movement through projector

Figure 5.19 Comparison of a single frame filmstrip and 35-mm slide formats.

Figure 5.20 The filmstrip and its container make a small, light package.

Figure 5.21a Most manual feed slide projectors can be adapted to show filmstrips also.

Figure 5.21b New style silent filmstrip projectors feature easy threading and remote-control advance.

Figure 5.22 Sound filmstrip projectors combine cassette and filmstrip functions in one machine.

run-through might suffice for purposes of advance overview and review. Not only the pace, but also the level of instruction can be controlled. Particularly with silent filmstrips, the vocabulary and/or level of narration supplied by the presenter can be adapted to audience abilities.

Filmstrips lend themselves well to independent study. Many types of table-top viewers are made especially for individual or small-group use. Young children have no difficulty loading light, compact filmstrips into these viewers. The fixed sequence of the frames structures the learner's progress through the material; the captions or recorded narration add a verbal

Figure 5.23a and b Compact tabletop viewers for silent filmstrips.

component to the visuals, creating a convenient self-contained learning "package." And because the user controls the rate of presentation, the filmstrip allows self-pacing when used for independent study.

Limitations
Having the frames permanently fixed in a certain sequence has disadvantages as well as advantages. The main drawback is that it is not possible to alter the sequence of pictures without destroying the filmstrip. Backtracking to an earlier picture or skipping over frames is cumbersome.

Since the filmstrip is pulled through its projector by means of toothed sprocket wheels, there is the constant possibility of tearing the sprocket holes and/or damag-

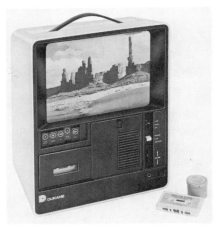

Figure 5.24a and b Sound filmstrip viewers for individual or small-group use; they can be viewed in fully lighted rooms.

ing the film. Improper threading or rough use can cause tears which are very difficult for you to repair, although, if you have a 35-mm splicing block, filmstrips are not impossible to repair. (In cases where damage to the sprocket holes is extensive, the frames can be cut apart and mounted individually to be used as slides.)

Applications

Because they are simply packaged and easy to handle, filmstrips are well suited to independent-study use. They are popular items in learning stations and media centers. Students enjoy using filmstrips on their own to help prepare research reports or in the presentation of reports to their classmates.

The major difference in application between slides and filmstrips is that slides lend themselves to teacher-made presentations while filmstrips are better suited to mass production and distribution. Further, slide sets tend to be used in a more open-ended fashion than filmstrips. Nowadays filmstrips are usually packaged as self-contained kits. That is, the narration to accompany the pictures is provided either in the form of captions on the filmstrip, a printed teacher's script, or a recorded sound track on record or cassette. Other teacher support material is integrated into the kit.

As with the other sorts of projected visuals discussed in this chapter, filmstrips find appropriate applications in a wide variety of subjects and grade levels. Their broad appeal is attested to by the constantly growing volume of commercial materials available. Tens of thousands of titles are already in distribution. Indeed, it would be difficult to identify an audiovisual medium offering a larger number of different titles in commercial distribution.

A small sample of the broad range of filmstrips on the market is illustrated by the examples below. A major directory of commercially available filmstrips is published by the National Information Center for Educational Media (NICEM)— *Index to 35mm Filmstrips.* See Appendix A for details and other sources.

MEDIA FILE: **"Caring" Filmstrip**

These filmstrips discuss the people and things a child cares about. They examine the responsiblities that caring implies—caring for a bicycle or your own health, caring for relationships with friends or classmates, caring for parents or siblings. Each strip presents episodes familiar to children, in which various aspects of responsibility are explored.
Source: Paramount Communications.

MEDIA FILE: **"Myths of Greece and Rome" Filmstrip**

And so, in many ways, the ancient gods and their stories live with us today.

Dramatic filmstrip stories introduce some of the great myths and dominant themes in mythology. Carefully detailed and researched artwork with captions illustrates how these ancient characters still play a role in our language, culture, science, and symbolism.
Source: Society for Visual Education, Inc.

MEDIA FILE: **"The American Revolution: Who Was Right?" Filmstrip**

TEACHER'S GUIDE

The American Revolution: Who Was Right?

The American Revolution would never have occurred if there had not been disagreement between England and her colonies. Both sides of the issues are revealed through visuals and spoken dialogue. One recording discusses the topic from the English point of view and the other recording gives the American interpretation using the same visuals. The categories have been carefully selected in order to present material that was not only relevant in 1776, but is still discussed and pertinent today.
Source: Denoyer-Geppert.

APPRAISAL CHECKLIST: PROJECTED VISUALS

Series title (if applicable)_____

Individual title_____

_____

Producer/distributor_____

Length_____frames

Intended audience/grade level_____

Date_____

_____minutes (sound track)

Subject area_____

FORMAT:

☐ Overhead

☐ Slides

☐ Filmstrip

Objectives (stated or implied):

Brief description:

Entry capabilities required

—prior subject matter knowledge
—reading ability
—math ability (or other)

RATING

	High		Medium		Low
Likely to arouse student interest	☐	☐	☐	☐	☐
Technical quality	☐	☐	☐	☐	☐
Provides relevant viewer practice/participation	☐	☐	☐	☐	☐
Relevance to curricular needs	☐	☐	☐	☐	☐
Focusses clearly on its objectives	☐	☐	☐	☐	☐
Evidence of effectiveness (e.g., field test results)	☐	☐	☐	☐	☐
Provides guide for follow-up, discussion	☐	☐	☐	☐	☐
Free from race, gender, other bias	☐	☐	☐	☐	☐

Strong points:

Weak points:

Recommended action:

Reviewer_____

Position_____

Date_____

AV Showmanship—Filmstrip

The general utilization guidelines discussed in Chapter 2 apply comprehensively to filmstrip use. There are several additional points, though, that pertain especially to filmstrips.

Do not feel compelled to run the filmstrip all the way through without stopping. You can do this as a kind of overview and then go back and reshow it, pausing for discussion at key frames.

Encourage *participation* by asking relevant questions during the presentation.

Use filmstrips to test visually the mastery of visual concepts. This can be done, for instance, by projecting individual frames without the caption or sound track and asking students to make an identification or discrimination.

SELECTION CRITERIA FOR PROJECTED VISUALS

This chapter has attempted to survey broadly the many similarities and differences among several major formats of projected visuals—opaque projection, overhead projection, slides, and filmstrips. You might have noticed that the differences are mainly logistical ones—small technical differences that lead to trade-offs in cost, portability, flexibility, and so on. Basically, projected visuals look very much alike on the screen. For the viewer/learner there is, in most cases, "no significant difference" among these formats in terms of learning impact. So it is appropriate that the chapter close by emphasizing the commonalities among the various types of projected visuals. The "Appraisal Checklist: Projected Visuals" is designed to apply equally to the various formats.

REFERENCES

Print References

Brainard, Alan J. "Preparing Effective Slides for Classroom Use." *Engineering Education,* February 1976, pp. 412–414.

* The Center for Vocational Education. *Present Information with Overhead and Opaque Materials* (Athens, GA: American Association for Vocational Instructional Materials [AAVIM], 1977).

* ———. *Present Information with Filmstrips and Slides* (Athens, GA: AAVIM, 1977).

Dayton, Deane K. "How to Make Title Slides with High Contrast Film, Part I." *Audiovisual Instruction,* April 1977, pp. 33–36.

———. "Inserted Post-Questions and Learning from Slide-Tape Presentations—Implications of the Mathemagenic Hypothesis." *AV Communication Review,* Summer 1977, pp. 125–146.

* Eastman Kodak Co. *Effective Visual Presentations* (Rochester, NY: Eastman Kodak, 1979).

* Elliot, Floyd. *The Filmstrip—A Useful Teaching Aid* (Montreal, Canada: National Film Board of Canada, 1963).

Gardener, C. Hugh. "Shortcuts to Better Slides." *Audiovisual Instruction,* September 1978, pp. 33–36.

Gibson, Stephanie S. "Teaching Basic Concepts with Slides." *Arithmetic Teacher,* October 1977, pp. 47–48.

Gorvine, George. "Using the Overhead to Train Perception." *The Instructor,* January 1974, p. 146.

Howard, William L. "Visual Response System." *Exceptional Children,* March 1978, pp. 466–468.

Jenkins, David M. "Multiple Image Slides." *Audiovisual Instruction,* January 1977, pp. 40–43.

Johnson, Roger. "Overhead Projectors: Basic Media for a Community College." *Audiovisual Instruction,* March 1978, pp. 21–22.

Jones, J. Rhodri. "Getting the Most Out of an Overhead Projector." *English Language Teaching Journal,* April 1978, pp. 194–201.

Locker, Kitty. "Teaching with Transparencies." *ABCA Bulletin,* September 1977, pp. 21–27.

Miller, Doris P. "The Case for Filmstrips: Producing Filmstrips in the Classroom." *English Journal,* October 1977, pp. 70–72.

Patterson, Adele. "First-Class Filmstrips." *Media & Methods,* April 1977, pp. 56–63.

Perez, Fred. "Using Slides to Promote Intramurals." *Journal of Physical Education and Recreation,* May 1978, pp. 63 ff.

Publications Index (S-4). (Rochester, NY: Eastman Kodak Co., annual).

Rees, Alan L. "Cartoon Slides for the Language Class." *English Language Teaching Journal,* July 1978, pp. 274–281.

Ring, Arthur. *Planning and Producing Handmade Slides and Filmstrips for the Classroom* (Belmont, CA: Pitman Learning, 1974).

Runte, Roseann. "Focusing in on the Slide—Its Practical Applications." *Canadian Modern Language Review,* March 1977, pp. 547–551.

Sanders, Freddie. "Pupil Participation with the Overhead Projector." *Visual Education,* March 1976, pp. 17–19.

Sheard, B.V. "They Love to Read Aloud from Filmstrips." *Teacher,* May 1973, pp. 66 ff.

Slawson, Wilbur S. "Making Home-made Filmstrips." *Language Arts,* February 1976, pp. 125–127.

Smith, Judson. "How to Choose and Use Slide Projectors." *Training,* November 1978, pp. 44–52.

Steele, Kenneth F., and James A. Wisman. "Diazochrome Transparencies for Education and Professional Meetings." *Journal of Geological Education,* November 1977, pp. 149–150.

Tildin, Scott W. "Design Your Organization's Own Slide-Tape Show." *Journal of Educational Communication,* September-October 1975, pp. 26–34.

Walther, R.E. "Mind-Bending Visuals." *Training,* April 1978, pp. 34–35.

Winters, Harold A. "Some Unconventional Uses of the Overhead Projector in Teaching Geography." *Journal of Geography,* November 1976, pp. 467–469.

Wyman, Raymond. "Overhead Projection with Dry-and-Wipe Markers." *Audiovisual Instruction,* February 1977, pp. 48–50.

Audiovisual References

"'Color Lift' Transparencies." (Salt Lake City, UT: Media Systems, 1975). (Filmstrip or slides, 40 frames, captioned.)

"I Like the Overhead Projector Because..." (Washington, DC: National Audiovisual Center, 1977). [Sound filmstrip (cassette), 12 minutes, color.]

POSSIBLE PROJECTS

5-A. Take a series of slides for use in your teaching. Describe your objectives, the intended audience, and how the slides will be used.

5-B. Design a lesson around a commercially available filmstrip. Describe your objectives, the intended audience, how the filmstrip will be used, and how the lesson will be evaluated. (If possible submit the filmstrip with the project.)

5-C. Prepare transparencies using *each* of the following techniques: write-on, thermal method, and color lift.

5-D. Prepare a set of visuals for use with an opaque projector.

5-E. Preview a set of slides or a filmstrip. Complete an appraisal sheet (from the text or one of your own design) on the materials.

5-F. Examine *two* of the selection sources for slides, filmstrips, or overheads and report on the kinds of materials you believe would be appropriate for your teaching situation.

CHAPTER 6

AUDIO MEDIA

OBJECTIVES

After studying this chapter, you should be able to:

1. Distinguish between "hearing" and "listening."

2. Identify four areas of breakdown in audio communication and specify the causes of such breakdowns.

3. Describe four techniques for improving listening skills.

4. Discuss 10 attributes of audio media including five advantages and five limitations.

5. Describe the four types of audio media most often used for instruction. Include in your description the distinguishing characteristics and limitations.

6. Describe one possible use of audio media in your teaching field. Include the subject area, the audience, objective(s), role of the student, and the evaluation techniques to be used.

7. Identify five criteria for appraising/ selecting audio materials.

8. Discuss the techniques for making your own audio tapes including guidelines for the recorder controls, the acoustics, microphone placement, tape content, and audio presentation.

9. Distinguish among the four common types of microphones classified by construction.

10. Describe three procedures for duplicating audio tapes.

11. Describe two procedures for editing audio tapes.

12. Identify the advantages of "rate-controlled audio playback."

13. Describe a situation in which a telelecture would provide enhancement of an instructional activity.

14. Select the best audio medium for a given instructional situation and justify the selection of that medium stating advantages and/or disadvantages.

If you were asked which learning activities consume the major portion of a student's classroom time, would you say reading instructional materials, answering questions, reciting what one has learned, or taking tests? Actually, typical elementary and secondary students spend about 50 percent of their school time just listening (or at least "hearing," which, as we shall see, is not the same as "listening"). College students are likely to spend nearly 90 percent of their time in class listening to lectures and seminar discussions. The importance, then, of audio media in the classroom should not be underestimated. By *audio media* we mean the various means of recording and transmitting the human voice and other sounds for instructional purposes. The audio devices most commonly found in the classroom are the phonograph or record player, the open-reel tape recorder, the cassette tape recorder, and the audio card reader.

Before going on to discuss these audio formats in particular and audio media in general, let us examine the hearing/listening process itself, as it pertains to the communication of ideas and information and to the development of listening skills.

THE HEARING/ LISTENING PROCESS

Hearing and listening are not the same thing, although they are, of course, interrelated. At the risk of some oversimplification, we might say that hearing is a *physiological* process, whereas listening is a *psychological* process.

Physiologically, *hearing* is a process in which sound waves entering the outer ear are transmitted to the ear drum, converted into mechanical vibrations in the middle ear, and then changed in the middle ear into nerve impulses which travel to the brain (Figure 6.2).

The psychological process of *listening* begins with someone's awareness of and attention to sounds or speech patterns, proceeds through identification and recognition of specific auditory signals, and ends in comprehension.

The hearing/listening process is also a communication/learning process. As with visual communication and learning, a message is encoded by a sender and decoded by a receiver. The quality of the encoded message is

affected by the skill of the sender to express the message clearly and logically. The quality of the decoded message is affected by the skill of the receiver to comprehend the message.

The efficiency of communication is also affected by the hearing/listening process as the message passes from sender to receiver. The message can be affected by physical problems such as an impaired hearing mechanism. It can also be affected by auditory fatigue. The brain has a remarkable capacity for filtering out sounds it doesn't want or need to hear. We have all had the experience of "tuning out" a boring conversationalist, or gradually losing cognizance of noises (the ticking of a clock, traffic outside a window, etc.) that seemed very obtrusive when we first encountered them. Nevertheless, in the classroom extraneous noise can cause auditory fatigue and make communication difficult. A monotonous tone or a droning voice can also reduce communication efficiency by contributing to auditory fatigue.

The message can also be affected by the receiver's listening skills or lack of them. The receiver must be able to direct and sustain concentration on a given series of sounds (the message). He or she must have the skill to "think

Figure 6.1 Elementary/secondary students spend about half of their in-school time listening to others; at the college level closer to 90 percent of class time is spent listening.

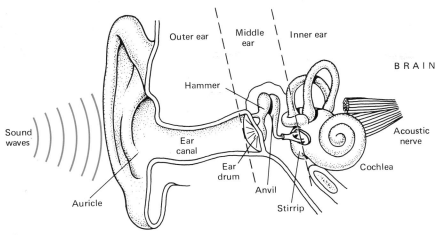

Figure 6.2 The mechanisms of human hearing.

DEVELOPING LISTENING SKILLS

In formal education much attention is given to reading, a little to speaking, and essentially none to listening. Listening is a skill, and like all skills, it can be improved with practice. You should first determine that your students can hear normally. Most school systems regularly request the services of speech and hearing therapists who administer audiometric hearing tests which provide the data you need. There are also standardized tests that measure students' listening abilities. These tests are often administered by the school district so you

ahead" as the message is being received (we think faster than we hear, just as we think faster than we read or write) and use this time differential to organize and internalize the information so that it can be comprehended.

Breakdowns in audio communication, then, can occur at any point in the process: encoding, hearing, or decoding, as illustrated in Figure 6.3. Proper encoding of the message depends upon the sender's skill in organizing and presenting it. For example, the vocabulary level of the message must be within the vocabulary range of the receiver. And, of course, the message itself must be presented in such a way that it is within the receiver's experiential range. The transmission process can be affected if the sender speaks too loudly or too softly or if the receiver has hearing difficulties or auditory fatigue. Communication can be reduced by the listener's lack of attentiveness or lack of skill in auditory analysis. Finally, communication may break down because the receiver lacks the experiential background to internalize, and thus comprehend, the message.

Figure 6.3 The hearing/listening process: impediments at each step act like sieves, reducing the perceived meaning to a small fraction of the original intended meaning.

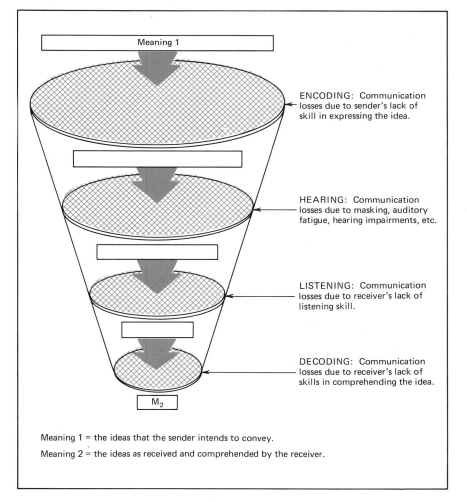

Meaning 1

ENCODING: Communication losses due to sender's lack of skill in expressing the idea.

HEARING: Communication losses due to masking, auditory fatigue, hearing impairments, etc.

LISTENING: Communication losses due to receiver's lack of listening skill.

DECODING: Communication losses due to receiver's lack of skills in comprehending the idea.

M_2

Meaning 1 = the ideas that the sender intends to convey.
Meaning 2 = the ideas as received and comprehended by the receiver.

should check to see if listening test scores are available.

There are a number of techniques which the teacher can use to improve student listening abilities:

1. *Directed listening.* Before orally presenting a story or lesson, give the students some objectives or questions to guide their listening. Start with short passages and one or two objectives, then gradually increase the length of the passage and the number and complexity level of the objectives or questions.

2. *Following directions.* Give the students directions individually or as a group on audio tape and ask them to follow these instructions. The teacher can evaluate the students' abilities to follow the audio instructions by examining worksheets or products of the activity. When giving directions orally, the "say it only once" rule should be observed so that a value is placed on both the teacher's and student's time and the incentive to listen is reinforced.

3. *Listening for main ideas, details or inferences.* Keeping the age level of the students in mind, you can present an oral passage and ask the students to listen for the main idea and then write it down. A similar technique can be used with details of and inferences to be drawn from the passage.

4. *Using context in listening.* Younger students can learn to distinguish meanings in an auditory context by listening to sentences with words missing and then supplying the appropriate missing words.

5. *Analyzing the structure of a presentation.* The students can be asked to outline (analyze and organize) an oral presentation. The teacher can then determine how well they were able to discern the main ideas and to identify the subtopics.

6. *Distinguishing between relevant and irrelevant information.* After listening to an oral presentation of information, the student can be asked to identify the main idea and then rate (from most to least relevant) all other ideas that are presented. A simpler technique for elementary students is to have them identify irrelevant words in sentences or irrelevant sentences in paragraphs.

CHARACTERISTICS OF AUDIO MEDIA

Audio media have many desirable attributes. First and foremost, they tend to be inexpensive forms of instruction. In the case of audio tape, once the tapes and equipment have been purchased there is no additional cost, since the audio tape can be erased after use and a new message recorded if desired. Audio materials are readily available and very simple to use. They can be adapted easily to any vocabulary level and can be used for group or individual instruction. Students who can not read due to blindness or illiteracy can learn from audio media. For young and nonreading students, audio can provide early language experiences. Audio can present stimulating verbal messages more dramatically than print can. With a little imagination on the part of the teacher, audio can be very versatile. Audio cassette tape recorders are very portable and can even be used "in the field" with battery power. Cassette tape recorders are ideal for home study. Many students already have their own cassette machines. Audio tapes are easily duplicated in whatever quantities are needed.

As with all media, audio instructional devices have limitations. Audio tends to fix the sequence of a presentation even though it is possible to rewind the tape and hear a recorded segment again or advance the tape to the upcoming portion. Without someone standing over them or speaking with them face-to-face, some students do not pay attention to the presentation. They may "hear" the presentation but not "listen" to and comprehend it. The initial expense of playback and recording equipment may be a problem. Development of audio materials by the instructor is time-consuming.

Determining the appropriate pace for presenting information can be difficult if your listeners have a wide range of listening skills and experiential backgrounds. Storage and retrieval of audio tapes and phonograph records can also be problems.

AUDIO FORMATS

Let's examine the comparative strengths and weaknesses of the audio formats most often used for instructional purposes—phonograph records (disc recordings), the open reel tape, the cassette tape, and the audio card, plus two formats more suited to home and office use, microcassettes and cartridges.

Phonograph Records

The phonograph record (disc recording) has a number of attributes which help make it an excellent instructional medium. Its frequency response is such that it can reproduce the audio spectrum even beyond the limits of human hearing. All types of "communication," from the spoken word, through the sounds of a hurricane or the mating call of the yellow-billed cuckoo, to Beethoven's Ninth Symphony are recorded on phonograph records. A major directory of commercially available records is published by the National Information Center for Educational Media (NICEM)—*Index to Educational Records.* See Appendix A for details and other sources.

Selections are separated by a "band" thereby making cuing of segments easier. The location or "band" of various segments of the recording is usually indicated on the label of the record and on its sleeve or "dust cover." Because phonograph records are stamped from a master in a fairly high-speed process, they are relatively inexpensive.

Despite all the advantageous features of phonograph records, they are not without their serious limitations from an instructional point of view. The most limiting is that you cannot economically prepare your own records. The record is easily damaged if some-one drops the stylus (needle) on the disc or otherwise scratches the surface. Excess heat and improper storage may cause the disc to warp and make it difficult, if not impossible, to play. Storage can pose another problem in that records take up more space than either open reel or cassette tapes with the same amount of information recorded on them.

Audio Tapes

The major advantage of magnetic audio tape over discs is that you can record your own tapes easily and economically, and when the material becomes outdated or no longer useful you can erase the magnetic signal on the tape and reuse it. Tapes are not as easily damaged as discs and they are easily stored. Unlike discs, broken tapes can be repaired.

Of course, there are some limitations to magnetic tape recordings. In the recording process certain undesirable sounds are sometimes recorded along with the intended material. Even a relatively low level noise can ruin an otherwise good recording. The

Figure 6.4 A vast diversity of audio material is easily accessible on phonograph record. At the elementary school level, records are the most used audiovisual materials.

AUDIO FORMATS

		SPEEDS	ADVANTAGES	LIMITATIONS	USES
Phonograph record (disc recording)	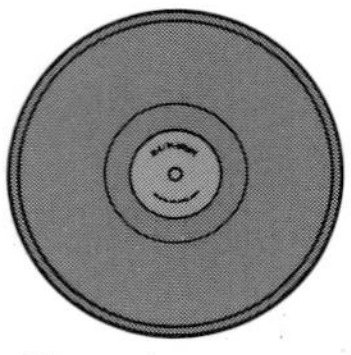 Diameters: 7, 10, 12 in.	78 rpm[a] 45 rpm $33\frac{1}{3}$ rpm $16\frac{2}{3}$ rpm	• Excellent frequency response • Compatibility of records and phonographs • Selection easily cued • Wide variety of selections • Inexpensive	• Impractical to prepare locally • Easily scratched • Can warp • Requires much storage space	• Music • Long narrations • Classroom listening • Historical speeches • Drama, poetry
Open Reel audio tape (reel-to-reel)	Reel sizes: 3, 5, 7 in. 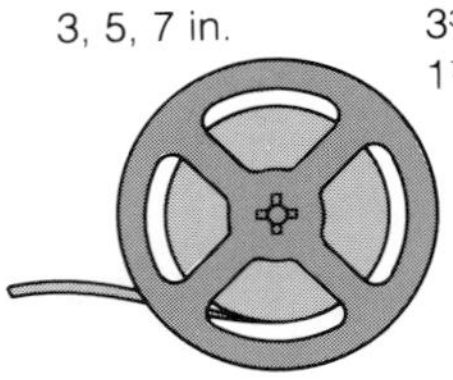 Tape $\frac{1}{4}$ in. wide	$7\frac{1}{2}$ ips[b] $3\frac{3}{4}$ ips $1\frac{7}{8}$ ips	• Can be prepared locally • Can be erased and used again • Not easily damaged • Easily stored • Broken tapes easily repaired • Excellent frequency response • Easily edited	• Accidental erasure • Difficult to use (threading) • Unlabelled or mislabelled tapes • Selection difficult to locate and cue	• Teacher-made recordings • Group listening • Self-evaluation
Cassette tape	Size: $2\frac{1}{2}$ by 4 by $\frac{1}{2}$ in. 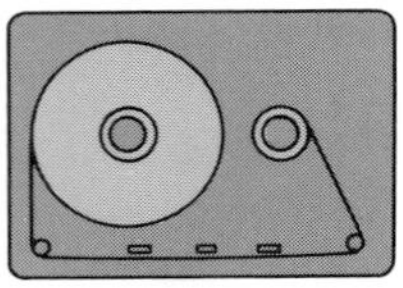 Tape $\frac{1}{8}$ in. wide	$1\frac{7}{8}$ ips	• Very portable (small and light) • Durable • Easy to use (no threading) • Can prevent accidental erasing • Requires little storage space	• Tape sometimes sticks or tangles • Noise and hiss • Poor fidelity (inexpensive models) • Broken tapes *not* easy to repair • Difficult to edit	• Listening "in the field" using battery power • Student-made recordings • Extended discussions • Individual listening
Microcassette	Size: $1\frac{5}{16}$ by $1\frac{3}{32}$ by $\frac{21}{64}$ in. 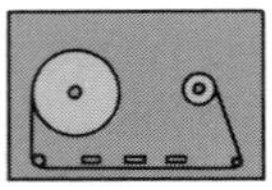 Tape $\frac{1}{8}$ in. wide	$\frac{15}{16}$ ips	• Very compact • Portable • Fits in pocket	• Not compatible with other cassettes • Poor fidelity	• Dictation by business executives • Amateur recording • LIMITED EDUCATIONAL USE
Audio cartridge (eight-track tape)	Size: $5\frac{1}{2}$ by $3\frac{7}{8}$ by $\frac{7}{8}$ in. 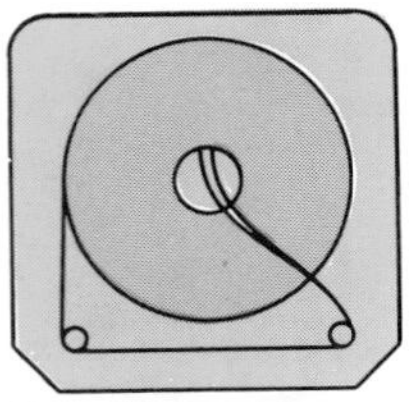 Tape $\frac{1}{4}$ in. wide	$3\frac{3}{4}$ ips	• Continuous loop on one reel • Minimum tape breakage • Automatically switches from one track to another • Easy loading	• Cannot rewind • Cannot record economically • Not high-quality sound reproduction	• Continuous play • Playback only • Entertainment (music) with home and auto systems • Radio station use • LIMITED EDUCATIONAL USE
Audio card	$3\frac{1}{2}$ by 9 in. or $5\frac{1}{2}$ by 11 in. 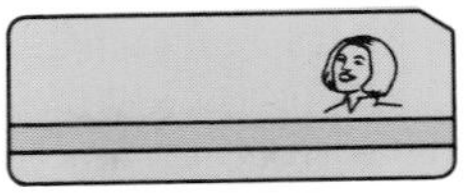 $\frac{1}{4}$ in. magnetic stripe	$2\frac{1}{4}$ ips $1\frac{1}{2}$ ips $\frac{2}{3}$ ips	• Sound with visual • Student can record response and compare with original • Designed for individual use • Participation; involvement	• Most cards less than 15 seconds • Time-consuming to prepare	• Vocabulary building • Identification • Associating sounds with visuals • Technical vocabulary

[a] rpm = revolutions per minute.
[b] ips = inches per second.

fact that audio tapes can be erased easily can pose a problem as well. Just as you can quickly and easily erase tapes you no longer need, you can accidentally and just as quickly erase tapes you want to save. It is difficult to locate a specific segment on an audio tape. Counters on the recorder assist retrieval, but they are not very accurate. Audio tapes also tend to deteriorate in quality when stored for a long period of time.

Open Reel Tapes. Open reel tapes are, as their name implies, tapes which wind from one exposed reel to another exposed reel. This accessibility of the tape makes it easier to alter (edit) its message, either by "dubbing" (as described later in this chapter) or by splicing (as described later in this chapter).

Open reel tapes have the disadvantage of having to be threaded manually. For example, let's say you wish to use only part of one open reel tape and continue your lesson with part or all of another. When you come to the end of the wanted portion of the first tape, you must wind the tape back on the supply reel before removing it from the recorder.

Cassette Tapes. The cassette tape is in essence a self-contained reel-to-reel system with the two reels permanently installed in a rugged plastic case (Figure 6.6). The ⅛-inch-wide tape is permanently fastened to each of the reels. Cassette tapes are identified according to the amount of recording time they contain. For example, a C–60 cassette can record 60 minutes of sound using both sides (that is, 30 minutes on each side). A C–90 can record 45 minutes on each side for a total of 90 minutes on the cassette. Cassettes are available in C–15, C–30, C–60, C–90, and C–120 lengths, plus other lengths can be

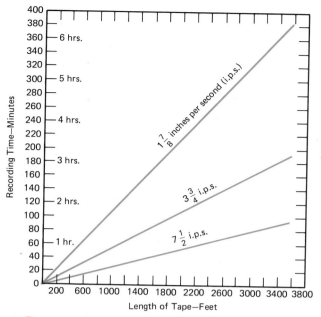

Figure 6.5 Tape running times. The slower the recording speed, the more the material that can be fitted onto a tape of a given length. Some guidelines for recording speeds: 7½ ips speed is best for high fidelity music and for recordings you plan to edit; 3¾ ips speed is adequate for other music and all narration; 1⅞ ips speed can be used for extended discussions and when quality of reproduction is not critical.

To determine how long a given reel of tape will play, locate the length of the tape on the horizontal axis of this chart; then go straight up to the line indicating recording speed (e.g., 7½ ips) to find where that line intersects with the length of tape. Finally, follow across to the left and read the recording time shown on the vertical axis. To find the number of feet of tape required for a fixed recording time, just reverse the process.

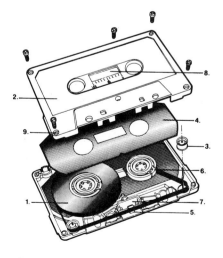

Figure 6.6 "Exploded" view of an audio cassette. (1) The ⅛-in. tape. (2) Styrene Housing. (3) Idler rollers. (4) Lubricated liner. (5) Pressure pad. (6) Hub and clip. (7) Metal shield. (8) Clear styrene index window. (9) Screw or other closure.

specially ordered. The size of the plastic cassette containing the tape is the same in all cases and they all can be played on any cassette machine. The cassette is

durable—virtually immune to shock and abrasion. It is the easiest of the tape formats to use since it requires no manual threading of the tape. It can be snapped into and out of a recorder in seconds. It is *not* necessary to rewind the tape before removing it from the machine. You just stop the tape and push the eject button. Accidental erasures can be avoided by breaking out the small plastic tabs on the rear of the cassette. Storage is another convenient feature. A cassette collection can be stored in about one-third the space required for discs or open reel tapes with the same amount of program material on them.

With all of these attributes you might wonder if there are any drawbacks. Unfortunately, cassette tapes, particularly C–120s, sometimes become stuck or tangled in the recorder. If this happens, and unless the content on the tape is one of a kind and of considerable value to you, you are best advised to throw the tape away. If it sticks or gets tangled in the machine once, it is likely to do so again. If a cassette tape breaks, its smaller size and difficult access make it much more difficult to splice than the open reel tape. However, there are special cassette splicers that make the job easier. The frequency response and overall quality (fidelity) of cassette playback units are not as good as those of reel-to-reel machines or record players due to the small speakers in most portable cassette playback units. However, for most instructional uses the quality is more than adequate.

A major directory of commercially available audio tapes is published by the National Information Center for Educational Media (NICEM)—*Index to Educational Audio Tapes*. See Appendix A for details and other sources.

Audio Cards
Another widely used audio instructional format is the audio card (Figure 6.7). An audio card is similar in appearance to a computer card. It contains a strip of magnetic recording tape near the bottom edge. The audio card is essentially a flashcard with sound. The card is inserted into a slot on a machine, such as the Bell and

HOW TO...**PREVENT ACCIDENTAL ERASURE OF CASSETTE TAPES**

Cassette tapes provide protection against accidental erasure. At the rear corners of each cassette are small tabs which can be broken out. The tab on the left controls the top side of the tape. The tab on the right controls the bottom side. No machine will record a new sound on a side of a tape for which the appropriate tab has been broken out.

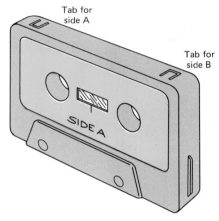

If you want to reuse the tape, carefully place some cellophane tape over the hole where the tab was removed. The tape can then be used for a new recording. Most prerecorded tapes come with both tabs already removed to prevent accidental erasure.

Figure 6.7 The audio card reader allows individual or small-group practice of skills that can be broken into small steps. At 2.25 ips, about a dozen words can be recorded on a 10-in. card.

Howell Language Master, (Figure 6.8) or the Audiotronics Tutorette (Figure 6.9), and a transport mechanism moves the card through the slot. Up to 15 seconds of sound can be played through the speaker (or headset for individual use). The audio card has a dual-track tape that allows the student to record his or her own response on the card and then play it back for comparison with the prerecorded response. If the student's response is incorrect, it can be erased and re-recorded correctly by simply running the audio card through the machine again while depressing the record lever. Both the student's and the prerecorded response can be replayed as often as desired by just flipping a lever. The prerecorded message is protected from erasure by a switch on the back of the machine. The teacher can use the switch to change the prerecorded message.

A similar device which can be attached to a *standard cassette* recorder is the VOXCOM Audible Graphics System (Figure 6.10). The device, as its promotional copy asserts, "makes paper talk and teach." The VOXCOM system uses adhesive-backed audio magnetic tape that allows the teacher to add sound to any piece of paper, thin cardboard, or plastic. The sound tape can be affixed to the back of textbook pages or photographs. Transparent plastic sleeves are available to accommodate newspaper clippings and materials up to 3½-by-5-in. in size. VOXCOM is a slow-speed card reader (.4 ips*), so the 3½-by-5-in. plastic sleeve will provide up to 12½ seconds of sound. A standard 8½-by-11-in. sheet of paper with an 11-in. strip of magnetic tape on the back will provide nearly 30 seconds of recording

*The abbreviation ips means inches per second.

Figure 6.8 Bell & Howell's "Language Master" audio card reader.

Figure 6.9 Audiotronics' "Tutorette" audio card reader.

Figure 6.10 VOXCOM's "Card Reader Adapter" fits onto a regular cassette recorder; its adhesive-backed magnetic tape can be attached to any paper materials to add teacher-made narrations to existing visuals.

time. Some prepared materials are available in this format, but the system is such that the teacher can easily create a wide variety of "talking" materials to fit specific instructional purposes.

APPLICATIONS OF AUDIO MEDIA

The uses of audio media are limited only by the imagination of teachers and students. They can be used in all phases of instruction from introduction of a topic to evaluation of student learning. Perhaps the most rapidly growing general use of audio media today is in the area of self-paced instruction and in "mastery learning." The slow student can go back and repeat segments of instruction as often as necessary since the recorder-playback machine can serve as a *very* patient tutor. The accelerated student can skip ahead or increase the pace of his or her instruction.

Prerecorded audio materials are available in a wide variety of subjects. For music classes, records and tapes can be used to introduce new material or to provide musical accompaniment that might otherwise not be available. The sounds of various musical instruments can be presented individually or in combinations. In preschool and primary grades, tapes and records can be used for rhythm development, storytelling, playing games, and acting out stories, songs, etc. In social studies, the tape recorder can bring the voices of persons who have made history into the classroom. The sounds of current events can also be presented.

One special application of prerecorded audio media is "talking books" for blind or visually impaired students. A "Talking Books Program" has been set up by The American Printing House for the Blind to make as much material as possible available to the visually impaired. At present over 11,000 book titles are available, along with recordings of several current periodicals. The

Figure 6.11 A "Talking Books" record player and disc recording.

service is a cooperative effort of the Library of Congress and 56 regional libraries in the United States. The materials are provided on 8⅓-rpm records which require special record players.

Audio tapes can easily be prepared by teachers for specific instructional purposes. For example, in industrial arts, audio tapes can describe the process of or steps in operating a machine or making a product. Recordings of class presentations by the teacher can be used for student make-up and review. One of the most common uses of audio materials is for drill work. For example, the student can practice spelling vocabulary words recorded by the teacher on tape, can practice multiplication tables, can practice taking dictation or typing from a prerecorded tape, and can practice pronunciation of foreign-language vocabulary.

Tape recorders can be used to record information gleaned from a field trip. Upon return to the classroom, the students can play back the tape for discussion and review. Many museums, observatories, and other public exhibit areas now supply visitors with prerecorded messages about various items on display which may (with permis-

---

MEDIA FILE: "I Can Hear it Now" Record Series

The *I Can Hear It Now* series featuring Edward R. Murrow (Columbia Records, D3L 366) brings the voices of people who made history into the social studies classroom. The three-record set is a compendium of sounds from 30 years of American history (1919-1949). A portion of the recording traces the career of President Harding, and includes excerpts from speeches before he came into office and 6 months, 12 months, 18 months, and 26 months after he was in office. Statements by Senator Fall and others connected with the famous Teapot Dome oil scandal are presented. The story of the Second World War is told in the authentic sounds of the war and in the voices of the people who were involved in it. The record includes the announcement of the invasion of Poland by the Germans and excerpts from several speeches by Winston Churchill. Franklin D. Roosevelt's speech asking Congress to declare a state of war after the attack on Pearl Harbor, General Eisenhower's message on D-Day, and General MacArthur's acceptance of the Japanese surrender are also heard.

MEDIA FILE: "A Cat in the Hat" Audio Tape

A second-grade teacher uses the prerecorded audio tape entitled *The Cat in the Hat* (RCA NO. DEK 1-0003) to teach her students novelty songs such as "My Uncle Terwilliger Waltzes with Bears," "The No-Laugh Race," and "The Left-Sock Thievers." (The tape is based on *The Cat in the Hat Song Book* by Dr. Seuss). First the children listen to the tape, then the teacher displays the words on a screen, using an overhead projector. The children discuss the words and their meanings to learn new vocabulary as well as to conceptualize some of Dr. Seuss' nonsense words. The teacher plays the tape again. As the students sing along, the teacher points to the words on the screen. An accompanying musical-score songbook allows the teacher to play the notes on a piano if one is available. The tape allows the teacher to integrate vocabulary building, phonetics, and music in an entertaining educational activity.

sion) be re-recorded for playback in the classroom.

Students can also record themselves reciting, presenting a speech, performing music, etc. They can then listen to the tape in private or have the performance critiqued by the teacher and/or other students. Initial efforts can be kept for comparison with later performances and for reinforcement of learning. Many small-group projects can include recorded reports that can be presented to the rest of the class. Individual students can prepare oral book reports and term papers on tape for presentation to the class as a whole or one student at a time. One high-school literature teacher maintains a file of taped book reports which students listen to before selecting books for their own reading. It is also possible for the students and teacher to bring interviews with local people or recordings of discussion of local events and concerns into the classroom.

An often overlooked use of audio materials is evaluation of student attainment of lesson objectives. For example, test questions may be prerecorded for members of the class to use individually. Students may be asked to identify sounds in a recording (to name the solo instrument being played in a particular musical movement, or to identify the composer of a particular piece of music). Students in social studies classes could be asked to identify the historical person most likely to have made excerpted passages from famous speeches, or they could be asked to identify the time period of excerpted passages from their content. Testing and evaluating in the audio mode is especially appropriate when teaching and learning has also been in that particular mode.

Close-up: Audio Applications

Prerecorded Audio Cards (Vocabulary Practice)

In an elementary classroom, the teacher uses a set of audio cards for vocabulary building. They are used on an individual basis with children who are having difficulty grasping the meaning of words because they cannot attach the appropriate spoken word to the printed form of the word or to the object it represents. The audio cards provide simultaneous visual and auditory stimuli designed to increase a child's spoken vocabulary by developing the ability to attach the correct word to the appropriate visual stimulus. The teacher shows the student how to use the machine and the cards, then lets the child work alone. Later, the teacher uses the same cards without the machine, holding them up one at a time and asking the child to say the word. Audio cards help children identify likenesses and distinguish differences among similar words.

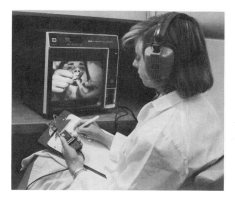

Teacher-Prepared Audio Tapes (Direct Instruction)

In a vocational–technical school, dental-laboratory-technology students are instructed on the procedures for constructing prosthetic devices such as partial plates and bridges by listening to an audio tape prepared by their instructor. To be efficient and effective in their work, these students must have both hands free and their eyes must be on their work, not on a textbook or manual. Audio tapes allow the students to move at their own pace, and the instructor is free to circulate around the laboratory and discuss each student's work individually.

Close-up: Audio Applications

Teacher-Prepared Audio Tapes (Student Practice)

In a high-school business-education class, the students practice taking dictation by listening to audio tapes prepared by the teacher and other individuals in the school, such as the principal, guidance counselor, and shop instructor. The variety of voices on the tapes allows the students to practice dealing with different voices, different accents, and a variety of dictation speeds. The business teacher categorizes the tapes according to difficulty of transcription and word speed. The students begin with the easy tapes and then move to more difficult ones. The teacher is also experimenting with a variable-speed tape recorder, which will allow the teacher to present the same tape to the students at a variety of speeds. Individually, the students use the variable-speed recorder to determine how fast they can take dictation and still maintain accuracy.

Teacher-Prepared Audio Tapes (Evaluation)

A teacher of ninth-grade students with learning difficulties (but normal intelligence) provides instruction on how to listen to lectures, speeches, and other oral presentations. The students practice their listening skills with tapes of recorded stories, poetry, and instructions. Commercially available tapes of speeches and narration are also used. After the students have practiced their listening skills under teacher direction, they are evaluated using a tape they have not heard before. The students listen to the five-minute tape without taking notes and then are given a series of questions dealing with important content of the passage.

Student-Prepared Audio Tape (Gathering Oral History)

One of the most exciting projects in a twelfth-grade social studies class is the oral history project. The students interview local senior citizens regarding the history of their community. Only one student interviews each senior citizen, but the interviewing task is rotated among the students, and the entire class assists in determining which questions should be asked. In preparation for this project, the students study both the national and local history of that time. All the tapes prepared during the interviews are kept in the school media center. Excerpts are duplicated and edited into programs for use with other social studies classes and for broadcast by the local radio station. This audio tape project serves the dual purpose of informing students and local residents about local history and collecting and preserving information which might otherwise be lost.

Student-Prepared Audio Tapes (Oral Book Report)

The tape recorder can be used for presenting book reports. Students may record their book reports during study time in the media center or at home. The reports are evaluated by the teacher and the best ones are kept on file in the media center. Other students are encouraged to listen to them before selecting books for leisure reading. Since the reports are limited to three minutes, the students are required to extract the main ideas from the book and to organize their thoughts carefully. During the taping, they practice their speaking skills and are encouraged to make the report as exciting as possible in order to get other students to read the same book.

Student-Prepared Audio Tapes (Self-Evaluation)

As part of a sales training program in a large insurance company, trainees learn sales presentation principles through taped examples and associated programmed booklets. They are then asked to prepare a series of their own sales presentations for different types of clients and for selling different types of insurance. The trainees outline their presentation, practice, and then record them on audio tape. For example, they role-play making a presentation on group health insurance to the board of directors of a large corporation. After the simulated presentation they listen to the recording and evaluate their performance using a checklist provided in the teaching materials. If they are not satisfied with their performance, they can redo the tape. Since no instructor is present, the inexperienced salesperson is not embarrassed by mistakes made during a training period. Later the instructor will listen to and critique the tape for the individual trainee. The final step in the training program is a "live" presentation, with the other trainees role-playing the clients.

SELECTING AUDIO MATERIALS

In selecting audio materials to use in your classroom, first determine what materials are available locally. If appropriate materials are not available, refer to the various directories of audio materials (see Appendix A). Materials both commercially and locally produced which seem appropriate should be previewed before introducing them to your students. The checklist on p. 152 can serve as a model for the sort of form you can use to guide your selection decisions.

MAKING YOUR OWN AUDIO TAPES

As previously noted, a major advantage of audio tapes as instructional media is the ease with which they can be prepared by teacher and students. All that is needed is a blank audio tape, a tape recorder, and bit of know-how.

The first order of business in making an audio tape is to familiarize yourself with the operation of the particular tape recorder you

APPRAISAL CHECKLIST: AUDIO MATERIALS

Title_____

Format   *Speed*   *Time*

Producer/distributor_____

__Record   __rpm   __min.

Series (if applicable)_____

__Reel-to-reel   __ips

Date (if known)_____ Price_____

__Cassette

Objectives (stated or implied):

Brief description:

Entry capabilities required:

–Prior subject matter knowledge
–Audio skills
–Other

RATING	High	Medium	Low
Accuracy	☐ ☐	☐	☐ ☐
Sound quality	☐ ☐	☐	☐ ☐
Student involvement	☐ ☐	☐	☐ ☐
Interest level	☐ ☐	☐	☐ ☐
Vocabulary level	☐ ☐	☐	☐ ☐
Overall value	☐ ☐	☐	☐ ☐

Strong points:

Weak points:

Reviewer_____

Position_____

Recommended action_____

Date_____

intend to use. Find out how it works. If there is no manual available, ask a colleague who has used the machine for directions.

Recorder Controls

Most recorders have clearly marked knobs, dials, or levers for control of the recorder's mechanism: on, off, play back, tone, volume, etc. (Figure 6.12). Experiment a bit. For volume control, try a moderate setting. A high setting expands the pickup range of the recorder's microphone, increasing its ability to pick up extraneous sounds and unwanted noises. A high setting also tends to distort the sounds you do wish the microphone to pick up. Many newer recorders have automatic volume control, thus making it unnecessary for you to adjust volume while recording. While playing back the tape, experiment with the tone control until you find the tone level that will give you the most lifelike quality. A high treble setting is generally more conducive to fidelity of human-voice recording.

Acoustics and Microphone Placement

Wherever you record—in the classroom, at home, on a field-trip—you need to consider the area's acoustics. Sparsely furnished rooms with plaster walls and ceilings and bare cement or tile floors are likely to be excessively "live," with distracting sound reverberations interfering with the fidelity of the recording. Such areas can, of course, be improved by installation of acoustic tiles and floor carpeting. However, you will probably have to make do with more makeshift improvements— place throw rugs, for example, or even heavy blankets or sheets of cardboard on the floor. Cardboard and blankets may also be used to cut down on bare wall reverbera-

Figure 6.12 Making your own recordings is simplified when the recorder's controls are clearly labeled.

tions. Fabric-covered movable screens and drawn window shades and draperies may help. (The latter will also help eliminate unwanted noise from outside.)

Many recording problems can be traced to the microphone's inability to ignore sounds. Unlike the brain, which can concentrate on only meaningful sounds (your quiet conversation with a friend in a restaurant, for example) and ignore extraneous ones (the clink of dishes, doors opening and closing, the air conditioner, other conversations), the microphone picks up every sound within its range and transmits them faithfully to the recording device. Thus microphone placement becomes an artful compromise between maximum pickup of desired

sounds and minimal pickup of extraneous ones.

Avoid placing the microphone close to any hard surface that might act as a sounding board. In a classroom, for instance, the recording setup should be at least six feet from the chalkboard, windows, or hard walls. Since many tape recorders themselves generate unwanted clicking, whirring, and humming noises, keep the microphone as far as possible from the recorder. Correct positioning will often require a bit of trial-and-error testing. As a rule of thumb, you should remain about a foot away from the microphone. If you are much closer, "popping" of

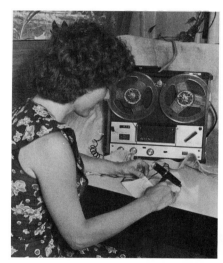

Figure 6.13 A good setup for amateur recording.

Figure 6.14 The absence of nearby walls and the separation between microphone and recorder help reduce extraneous sounds.

p's and b's and other "breathy" sounds may become annoying. Placing the microphone on a cloth or some other sound-absorbing material or on a stand will decrease the possibility of noise being transferred to the microphone from the desk or table. Do not speak directly into the microphone, but rather, talk over it. Avoid handling sheets of paper near the microphone. If possible, use index cards or some such materials and handle them quietly. For recording multiple sound-source performances (such as musical shows) other variables must also be taken into consideration. For instance, a greater sound-to-microphone distance might be needed in order to pick up the entire range and scope of sounds emanating from a musical ensemble.

Tape Content and Audio Presentation Techniques

Introduce the subject of the audio tape and other appropriate introductory material. ("This is Biology 101, Lesson 2, on Plant Function...") at the outset of your recording. Identifying the tape is particularly important if it is to be used for individual instruction.

Try to use conversational rather than pedantic or "textbook" diction. Of course, the normal rules of grammar and clarity of expression must be followed. Talk to the tape recorder as you would normally talk to a friend. Explore your subject with your listener. Do not lecture on it. In general, your presentation will come across as more natural if you work from informal notes. If you do feel you must work with a more formal script, remember that a good script requires special writing skills and skill in script reading.

Keep the tape short even if it is to be used only by adult students—20 to 25 minutes for

adults and even less for younger students.

Whenever appropriate for your learning objectives, involve your listener(s) in meaningful learning activities. You might, for example, supply a study guide or worksheet for use along with the tape. Such materials may contain lesson objectives, key information, diagrams or other visuals, questions to be answered, or practice exercises. Try, also, to provide ample

space for students to take notes while listening to the tape. These ancillary materials can also be used for review purposes after the lesson has been completed (Figure 6.15).

Note, however, that if you include student activities you may have to allow time on the tape for the listener to complete an activity. In addition, different students will take various amounts of time to complete these activities. Rather than trying to guess how much quiet time to leave on the tape, you can provide a brief musical interlude (approximately 10 sec-

---

OBJECTIVE 3: Compute depreciation using the "straight-line method."

"Straight-Line" Method Summarized

Formula $\dfrac{\text{Cost of the Asset - Estimated Salvage Value}}{\text{Number of Accounting Periods in Productive Life}}$

Application $\dfrac{\$1250\ \text{COST} - \$250\ \text{SALVAGE}}{5\ \text{Years of Productive Life}}$ = $200 to be DEPRECIATED Each Year

TURN OFF TAPE AND COMPLETE ACTIVITY NO. 4.

Activity # 4

A machine costs $2600 and was estimated to have a four-year service life and a $200 salvage value. Calculate the yearly depreciation using the straight-line method.

ANSWER_____

TURN ON TAPE AND COMPLETE ACTIVITY NO. 5 WHILE LISTENING.

Activity # 5

Advantages of the "units-of-production" method are:
1. _____
2. _____
3. _____
4. _____

Disadvantages of the "units-of-production" method are:
1. _____
2. _____

Figure 6.15 Sample Page from study guide to accompany an audio tape.

onds) as a signal for the student to turn off the tape and perform the activity or exercise. The student can then return to the tape, hear the music again, and know that nothing has been missed.

If your listeners are to use slides with your audio presentation, a nonvocal signal should be used to indicate when to advance the slides rather than continually repeating "Change to the next slide." There are electronic tone devices available for this purpose or a door chime can be used. A simple technique for producing your own signal is to tap a spoon on a glass partially filled with water.

When you are finished with the recording, give it a critical evaluation. As a guide, you might use a checklist such as the one shown below. It may also be helpful to have a colleague and/or students listen to the tape and give you their reactions to it.

CHECKLIST FOR TEACHER-PREPARED AUDIO TAPES

- minimum extraneous background noise
- constant volume level
- voice quality and clarity
- clarity of expression
- conversational tone
- listener involvement
- coordination with worksheet or study guide, if used
- content clear
- length not too long or too short

MICROPHONES

A wide variety of microphones are available; they vary in the type of generating element used in their construction, their sensitivity, their directionality, and in other technical features.

The basic function of any microphone is to convert sound waves into electrical energy. The major components of all microphones are basically similar. Sound waves enter the "mike" to strike the diaphragm, which vibrates from the pressure of the sound waves.

Connected to the diaphragm is a generating element which converts these vibrations into electrical impulses (Figure 6.16).

As noted, microphones differ with regard to their directionality, that is, the pattern of the area from which they can efficiently pick up the signal or "pickup pattern." The

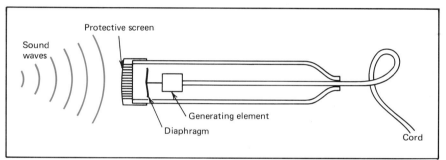

Figure 6.16 Cutaway view of the main components of microphones.

MICROPHONE TYPES	ATTRIBUTES
Crystal	• Simplest construction • Least expensive • Fragile • Sensitive to temperature and humidity • Can be used for speech
Ceramic	• Simple construction • Moderately expensive • Produces weak signal • More rugged than crystal • Not sensitive to temperature and humidity
Dynamic (moving coil)	• High quality • Good fidelity • Very rugged • Very reliable • Expensive
Condenser or electret	• Good frequency response • Sensitive to physical shock • Sensitive sound pickup • Not sensitive to mechanical vibration

microphones most commonly found in educational use these days are of two basic directional types—unidirectional and omnidirectional. The differences in their pickup patterns are illustrated in Figure 6.17.

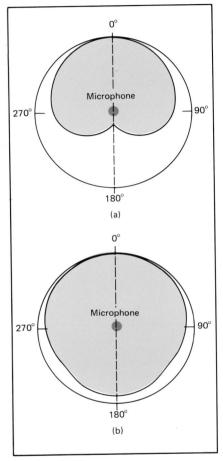

Figure 6.17 Pickup patterns of two common types of microphones: (a) the unidirectional or "cardiod" microphone; (b) the omnidirectional microphone.

DUPLICATING AUDIO TAPES

It is a relatively simple procedure to duplicate (or "dub") an audio tape. You can duplicate your tapes by one of three methods: the direct method, the patch cord method, and the high-speed duplicator method.

The *direct* method does not require any special equipment, just two recorders (either cassette, reel-to-reel, or one of each). One recorder plays the original tape, the sound of which is transferred via a microphone to blank tape on the other recorder. The drawback to this method is that fidelity is lessened as the sound travels through the air to the microphone, and the microphone itself may pick up unwanted noise from the environment (Figure 6.18).

The *patch cord* method avoids this problem. Sound travels from the original tape to the dubbing recorder via an inexpensive patch cord. The cord is attached to the output of the first machine and the "line" or auxiliary input of the second. It picks up the signals of the original tape and transfers them electronically to the duplicating tape (Figure 6.19).

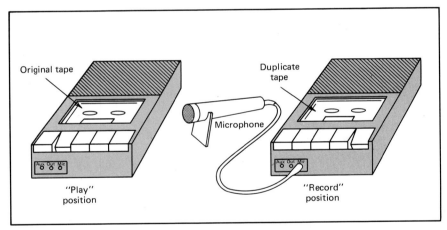

Figure 6.18 Configuration for duplicating with the *direct* method.

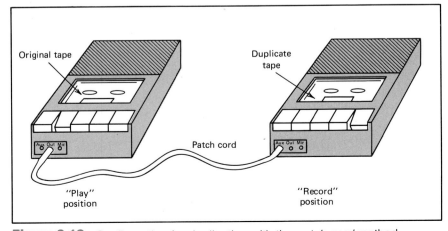

Figure 6.19 Configuration for duplicating with the *patch cord* method.

If you use reel-to-reel recorders for both playing and recording, you can save half the normal duplicating time by playing 3¾-ips tapes at 7½ ips. The speed of the machine doing the recording must also be set at 7½ ips. The duplicated tape can then be played back at the 3¾-ips rate of the original tape.

The *high-speed duplicator* method requires a special machine. Master playback machines have a series of up to 10 "slave units," each of which can record a copy of the original tape at 15 times its normal speed. Since the master machines are connected by a patch cord, fidelity is likely to be very good, and there is no danger of picking up background noise. This method is excellent for producing multiple copies of audio tape recordings. Ten copies of a 30-minute cassette tape can be duplicated in about two minutes (Figure 6.20).

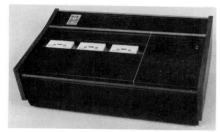

Figure 6.20 A machine for high-speed duplicating of multiple cassette tapes.

EDITING AUDIO TAPES

You may wish to edit your audio tapes, either to remove errors or imperfections or to adapt a tape to a specific learning situation. There are two general methods for editing tapes: mechanical editing and electronic editing.

Mechanical editing (splicing) involves physically removing unwanted portions of the tape or changing the sequence of materials by reordering sections of the tape. If you plan to do mechanical editing, record your original tape on only one side and at the fastest speed possible. Open reel tapes can be mechanically edited more easily than cassette tapes because they are wider and more accessible. A general rule, then, is to use open reel tape recorded at the fastest speed possible if you plan to do mechanical editing. Splicing tape and splicing blocks are available for open reel as well as cassette tape. Follow the specific instructions given for the equipment you are using. The general procedures for splicing are shown below.

HOW TO...SPLICE AUDIO TAPE

1. Overlap two ends of broken tape and cut diagonally.

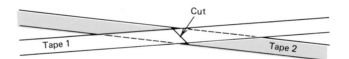

2. Align ends with shiny side up.

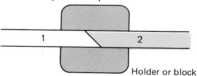

3. Place splicing tape over ends. (Do not use cellophane tape. Cellophane tape can get "gum" on the play/record head and damage the tape recorder.)

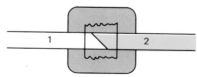

4. Trim excess tape, cutting slightly into recording tape.

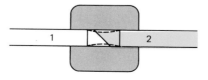

For *Electronic Editing,* set up two recorders as described for tape duplication and then record just the portion of the original tape that you want on a second tape. You can accomplish the same effects (deleting and resequencing) as with mechanical editing, but the results may not be as precise.

RATE-CONTROLLED AUDIO PLAYBACK

A relatively recent and promising innovation in audio instructional technology has been the introduction of equipment that can play back recorded speech either at a faster or slower rate than the rate at which it was recorded—without loss of intelligibility. Previous to this technological breakthrough, playing a tape back at a higher speed resulted in high-pitched distortion, as if the speaker were a chattering chipmunk. Slowing down the playback resulted in a low-pitched, unintelligible garble.

The pedagogical significance of this innovation lies in the fact that although the average person speaks at 100 to 150 words per minute, most of us can comprehend spoken information at the rate of 250 to 300 words per minute. In fact, research has shown that most students learn as quickly and retain as much when spoken

instruction is speeded up. On the other hand, slowing down recorded instruction also has instructional advantages, especially in working with slow learners or in special-education situations and in foreign-language instruction. It is also useful in ordinary circumstances for emphasizing a specific instructional point or for explaining a particularly difficult one.

Early speech compressors (technically, speeding up recorded speech is called "compressing") were costly and their technology not very refined. The machine could only be set at certain fixed speeds, such as 200 words per minute. The entire recording had to be made and played back at this rate.

Newer compressors provide for variable speed rates. Recorders can now be equipped with rate control devices which, using a

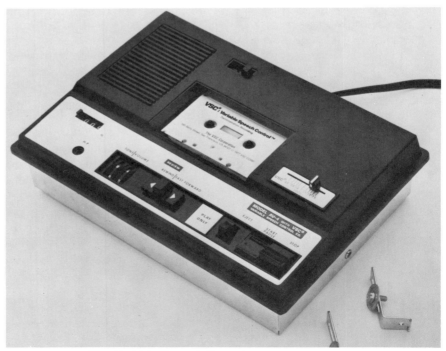

Figure 6.21 The Variable Speech Control recorder allows playback of any recording at slower or faster than the normal rate, as preferred by the listener (note the rate control lever).

tape recorded at normal speaking speed, are capable of providing variable rates of speech at the discretion of the listener, from half the normal speed to 2½ times normal speed. Changing the rate during playback allows the listener to listen at his or her own pace, skimming over familiar material at a high rate, slowing down for material that may require more time for comprehension.

Research has shown that learning time can be cut (as much as 50 percent and an average of 32 percent) and comprehension increased (as much as 9.3 percent and an average of 4.2 percent) through use of compressed and variable-speed audio tapes.* One reason that comprehension increases with accelerated listening rate may be that the listener is forced to increase his or her concentration on the material and is also freed from the distractions which often accompany normal speech, such as pauses, throat-clearing, and other extraneous sounds.

Research also indicates that variable-speed audio tapes can be very effective in increasing reading speed. One junior-high-school teacher prepared variable-speed tapes of printed material for his students to listen to as they read the material. The students' reading rate gradually increased with increase in their listening rate. The ear, it seems, helps train the eye.

---

*See the listings under Olsen, Hughes, and Short in the References.

TELELECTURES

The telephone has only recently come into its own as an instrument of educational technology. "Telelecture" systems are now in use in a growing number of schools and educational systems. The telelecture system utilizes a special amplifier and microphone(s) to enable a class or other student group to listen in on ordinary telephone conversation. It can bring into the classroom the expertise of resource persons from all over the nation—at a fraction of the cost of the expert's actually visiting the classroom. The special equipment can be rented from most local telephone companies. Some larger schools own their own telelecture equipment (Figure 6.22).

The system allows for two-way communication. Individual students can question the resource person, and the entire learning group can hear the response. Students can discuss politics and current issues with their elected representatives (or candidates for political office). They can talk with great writers about literature. They can discuss or critique their current textbooks with the authors of the texts. They can discuss the current economic situation with expert economists, art with well-known artists, science with prominent scientists, etc. The possibilities are almost endless.

Planning is very important for a successful telelecture. Arrangements may have to be made with the telephone company to have the telelecture equipment available in the classroom or conference room. The resource person must be arranged for in advance and a mutually convenient time must be settled upon for the telelecture. The speaker should be briefed by the teacher as to the purposes and objectives of the telelecture call and the types of questions that the students are likely to ask. The students should

Figure 6.22 The portable conference telephone set allows group listening to and student participation in telephone conversations.

prepare for the call by deciding what kinds of questions to ask, perhaps, even who will ask which questions.

When the call has been put through, the teacher should briefly introduce the speaker (a more lengthy description of the speaker's background and the objectives of the telelecture will have been presented during preparation of the class for the telelecture). Usually the speaker will make some introductory statement and then call for a question-and-answer period. A predetermined time limit should be set for the length of the call. After the telelecture, the students can discuss it, write reports, make evaluations, and suggest future activities. As a courtesy, a personal thank-you note from the class might be sent to the resource person.

If the telelecture presentation requires visuals to supplement the audio, the speaker can send slides or overhead transparencies in advance. He or she can direct the instructor when to project a transparency or to advance the slides during the call. A more sophisticated technique is to use

Flashback: The Bee Who Came in From the Cold

The time was summer, 1915. World War I had already begun and America was poised for her own entry into the conflict. Talk of Allied and Axis espionage activities in America was in the air—and so was a persistent and peculiar noise which could be heard nightly on the radio airwaves up and down the East Coast.

The strange noise perplexed radio ham operators, not to mention the United States Secret Service. It began promptly each night at eleven o'clock and continued into the wee hours of the morning. One ham operator described it as "a musical note, like the buzzing of a titanic bumblebee" speeding through space. Was it a secret signal being sent to one of the warring parties? Very likely. But what kind of code was it being sent in? How could anyone decode a bumblebee's buzz?

The sinister noise and the question of how an intelligible message could be encoded in it so disturbed one New Jersey ham operator that he recorded excerpts from it on his own home-made wax cylinder recorder. He did so faithfully for two weeks but was still unable to solve the mystery.

Then one night he forgot to fully wind his recording machine. As the machine slowed down it began to play back the buzzing more slowly. The operator found that the buzzing did indeed contain an encoded message, a message encoded not in some fiendishly clever code, but in the simple, universally known Morse code of dots and dashes!

The station transmitting the messages was later found by United States authorities and shut down. The messages had been recorded in simple Morse code at standard speed. The recording was then compressed (played at high speed) and transmitted in this form to Germany. There it was re-recorded and played back at its original speed. There was no code to be broken at all. It was merely a matter of ingenuity in using the then-current technology of "rate-controlled audio recording." Incidentally, the ingenuity may have been German but the technology was American. The recorders used in the operation had been developed and manufactured by the American Telegraphone Company. Six machines had been sold unknowingly to the German Navy on an order from Denmark.

Source: Adapted from Robert Angus, "75 Years of Magnetic Recording," *High Fidelity Magazine,* March 1973, pp. 42–50.

---

a "telewriting" device. With this device, the speaker can write on a special stage and the message will be transmitted via telephone lines and can then be projected on a screen at the listeners' location. The speaker can thus add diagrams, drawings, equations, or any hand-drawn figures to the audio portion of the telelecture.

REFERENCES

Print References

Banerjee, Sumanta. *Audio Cassettes: The User Medium* (Paris: UNESCO, 1977).

* The Center for Vocational Education. *Present Information with Audio Recordings* (Athens, GA: American Association for Vocational Instructional Materials, 1977).

Clifford, Martin. *Microphones: How They Work and How to Use Them* (Blue Ridge Summit, PA: TAB Books, 1977).

Cuker, S. *Time Compressed Speech: An Anthology and Bibliography* (Metuchen, NJ: The Scarecrow Press, 1974).

Gates, Ward M. "Recording Tips for Teachers." *Clearing House,* January 1976, pp. 229–230.

Gerlach, Gail J. "Tape It! Using Audio Tapes as an Integral Part of a Multi-Media, Multi-Material Approach to Social Studies in the Intermediate Grades." *Social Studies Journal,* Spring 1977, pp. 18–22.

Harnishfeger, L. *Basic Practice in Listening* (Denver, CO: Love Publishing, 1977).

* Hughes, Lawson H. "Developments in Rate-Controlled Speech." *NSPI Journal,* September 1976, pp. 10–11.

Jacobson, Thomas, and Joyce Hardin. "Education by Telephone." *Phi Delta Kappan,* June 1977, pp. 769–771.

Jacobson, Thomas, and Joyce Hardin. "A Phonograph Album." *Music Educator's Journal,* December 1977, pp. 52–59.

Olsen, Linda. "Technology Humanized—the Rate Controlled Tape Recorder." *Media & Methods,* January 1979, p. 67.

Postlethwait, S.N. "Audio Technology: Audio Tape for Programming Instruction." *Educational Broadcasting,* July-August 1976, pp. 17–19.

Schribert, Delwyn. "Your Teaching Twin—The Tape Recorder." *Reading Improvement,* Spring 1978, pp. 78–80.

Short, Sarah H. "A Comparison of Variable Time-Compressed Speech and Normal Rate Speech Based on Time Spent and Performance in a Course Taught by Self-Instructional Methods." *British Journal of Educational Technology,* May 1977, pp. 146–156.

Short, Sarah H. "The Use of Rate Controlled Speech to Save Time and Increase Learning in Self-Paced Instruction." *NSPI Journal,* May 1978, pp. 13–14.

Smith, Judson. "How to Buy Headsets and Listening Centers." *Training,* September 1977, pp. 92–95.

Spencer, Margie. "Personalized Teaching Aids: Tape Recorder as an Instructional Tool." *Pointer,* Winter 1975, pp. 61–62.

Spencer, Margie. "The Use of Audio Tape-Cards in Auditory Training for Hearing Impaired Children." *Volta Review,* September 1976, pp. 209–218.

Audiovisual References

"Basic Audio." (Alexandria, VA: Smith-Mattingly Productions, 1979). (Videocassette, 30 minutes, color.)

"Learning About Sound." (Chicago, IL: Encyclopedia Brittannica Educational Corporation, 1975). (16-mm sound film, 17 minutes, color.)

"Sound Recording and Reproduction." (Salt Lake City, UT: Media Systems, Inc., 1978). [Six sound filmstrips (cassette), color.]

"Tape Recorders." (Salt Lake City, UT: Media Systems, Inc., 1978). [Sound filmstrip (cassette), color.]

"Tips on Tapes for Teachers." (Boulder, CO: National Center for Audio Tapes, 1972). (Audio cassette.)

"Utilizing the Tape Recorder in Teaching." (Salt Lake City, UT: Media Systems, Inc., 1975). [Two sound filmstrips (cassette), color.]

POSSIBLE PROJECTS

6-A. Prepare an audio tape including *your* voice and some music. It will be evaluated using the criteria in the "Checklist for Teacher-Prepared Audio Tapes" (page 00). Include a description of *how* the tape will be used along with its objective(s).

6-B. Obtain any commercially prepared audio materials and appraise them using a given set of criteria, such as "Appraisal Checklist: Audio Materials," (page 00), or using your own criteria.

CHAPTER 7

MULTIMEDIA SYSTEMS

OUTLINE

Sound–Slide Combinations
  Applications
  Storyboarding
Multi-Image Systems
  Planning a Multi-Image Presentation
  Dissolve Units
  Programmers
  Applications of Multi-Image Systems
Eight-Millimeter Film–Audio Cassette
    Systems
  Applications
Multimedia Kits
  Commercial Multimedia Kits
  Teacher-made Multimedia Kits
  Applications
Classroom Learning Centers
  Carrels
  Applications
  Advantages and Limitations of
    Learning Centers
  Learning Center Management
  Designing Your Own Learning Cen-
    ter Materials (ASSURE Model)

OBJECTIVES

After studying this chapter, you should be able to:

1. Define *multimedia systems* and state a rationale for the use of multimedia systems.
2. Identify three advantages of sound–slide programs.
3. Describe four combinations of projected visuals and audio materials including three procedures for synchronizing them.
4. Design an instructional situation in which you could use an audio plus projected visual presentation. Your description should include the topic, the audience, the objectives, and a rationale for using this media format.
5. Apply and/or describe the basic steps involved in the planning of a slide–tape presentation.
6. Discuss instructional applications of dissolve units and programmers.
7. Describe an instructional situation in which you could use a multi-image presentation. Your description should include the topic, the audience, the objectives, and a rationale for using this media format.
8. Describe the characteristics and applications of 8-mm film–audio cassette systems.
9. List five considerations when preparing, purchasing, and/or selecting multimedia kits.
10. Describe a multimedia kit that you could use in your teaching field. Your description should identify the topic, the audience, the overall objectives, and the contents of the kit.
11. Identify five types of classroom learning centers.

12. Describe the characteristics, advantages, limitations, and components of classroom learning centers.
13. Discuss the teacher's role in learning-center management.
14. Identify three methods of providing learner feedback in a classroom learning center.
15. Design a learning center for your discipline. Your description should include the audience, objective(s), how materials will be obtained and used, the types of learner response, and how it will be evaluated.

We have previously considered various basic modes of audio and visual instructional media. We will now explore various combinations of these media and how these combinations can be used for instructional purposes. Media combinations are generally referred to as *multimedia systems*.

The multimedia concept involves more than using multiple media for a given instructional purpose. It involves integrating each medium and medium format into a structured, systematic presentation. Each instructional medium in a multimedia system is designed to complement the others, so that, ideally, the whole multimedia system becomes greater than the sum of its parts.

The use of multimedia systems in the classroom has received considerable impetus from the general trends toward individualization of learning and encouragement of active student participation in the learning process. Multimedia systems are especially adaptable to these current educational concepts.

Multimedia systems are also multisensory and thus stimulate learning as it takes place in the world outside the classroom. Learning in the real world is indeed multimedia and multisen-

Figure 7.2 Like any other instructional approach, multimedia presentations can be overdone. © 1979 King Features Syndicate, Inc.

Figure 7.1 A multimedia kit for basic reading skills.

sory learning. We are constantly learning via all our senses and via a multitude of stimuli—newspapers, books, radio, television, pictures, etc.

In this chapter we will discuss the major multimedia systems commonly used in the classroom: sound–slide combinations, multi-image systems, the 8-mm film–audio cassette system, multimedia kits, and classroom learning centers.

SOUND–SLIDE COMBINATIONS

Combining 2-by-2-in. slides with audio tape is the easiest multimedia system to produce locally, which is one reason for the increasing popularity of its use in the instructional setting. The system is also versatile, easy to use, and effective both for group instruction and independent study.

Figure 7.3 The sound-slide set is a familiar example of a multimedia system.

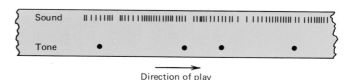

SOUND		Slides	Filmstrip
		VISUALS	
	Audio Tape	Local production	Commercial
	Phonograph record	Commercial	Commercial

Sound | ‖‖‖‖‖‖ ‖‖‖‖‖‖‖‖‖‖‖‖ ‖‖‖‖‖‖‖‖‖ ‖ ‖‖‖‖‖‖‖‖‖ ‖‖ ‖‖‖‖‖

Tone | ● ● ● ●

Direction of play

Figure 7.4 Synchronized sound-slide programs are controlled by inaudible tones put on one track of the tape.

A well done sound–slide presentation can have significant dramatic impact, thus further enhancing the learning process. Filmstrips may also be combined with audio tape, to the same general educational purposes as sound–slide tape presentations.

Sound–slide programs can be developed locally by teachers or students. In terms of emotional impact and instructional effectiveness they may rival film or television productions, yet they can be produced for a fraction of the cost and effort. Indeed, sound-slide sets are produced frequently as prototypes of more elaborate film or video projects, since they allow the presentation to be tried out and revised in its formative stages.

Sound-slide sets are available from commercial sources. However, mass distribution programs of this sort usually are converted to a filmstrip/audio tape format, since filmstrips require less storage space than slides and are less expensive. Some commercial programs are available with phonograph records instead of audio tapes. Major guides to identifying the many thousands of sound-slide and filmstrip sets available commercially are the National Information Center for Educational Media (NICEM) publications,— *Index to Educational Slides* and *Index to 35mm Filmstrips*. See

Appendix A for details and other sources.

The visuals in sound–slide programs may be advanced manually or automatically. In manual operation, the visual and audio components are usually on two separate machines. You begin by projecting the title slide or frame on the screen and then starting the sound track. An audible beep on the sound track signals you to advance the slides or filmstrip to the next visual. In manual operation, it is important that you test out at least the beginning of the program to make certain that you have sound and visuals in proper synchronization. Note also that some soundtracks do not contain a beep signal, in which case a script containing instructions for advancing visuals must be used.

In automatic advancing of visuals with an audio tape, two sound tracks are used, one for the audible narration and one with inaudible tones which activate the advance mechanism on the slide or filmstrip projector, as shown in Figure 7.4.

Applications

Sound–slide presentations may be used in almost any instructional

setting and for instructional objectives involving the presentation of visual images to inform or to evoke an emotional response. They may be used to excellent effect in group instruction, and they can be adapted to independent study in the classroom and in the media or learning center. This comparatively simple multimedia system is especially versatile as a learning/teaching tool in that more than one narration can be prepared for a given set of visuals.

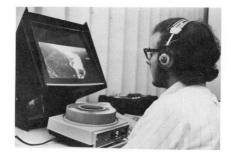

Figure 7.5 Sound-slide presentations are readily adapted to individual use.

HOW TO... **DEVELOP A SOUND—SLIDE PRESENTATION**

Here is a simple approach to developing your own sound-slide presentation:

Step 1. Analyze your audience both in terms of general characteristics and specific entry characteristics (as described in Chapter 2).
- Why are they viewing the presentation?
- What is their motivation toward your topic?
- How much do they already know about the subject?

Step 2. Specify your objectives (as described in Chapter 2).
- What do you want to accomplish with the presentation?
  —learning to be achieved
  —attitudes to be formed or changed
  —skills to be developed
- What should the viewers be able to *do* after the presentation?
  —activity or performance?
  —under what conditions?
  —with what degree of skill?

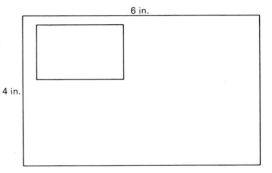

Step 3. Having completed your audience analysis and stated your objectives, you now have a much clearer idea of how your presentation will fit into your overall lesson plan, including what might precede it and follow it. Perhaps you will decide at this point that a slide—tape presentation is *not* really what you need to do after all.

If it is what you need to do, get a pack of planning cards (use index cards or cut some sheets of paper into 4-by-6-in. rectangles). Draw a large box in the upper left-hand corner of each card.

Step 4. Take a planning card. In the box draw a rough sketch of whatever image comes to your mind when you think about one of your major points.[a] You don't have to start with the *first* point, just whatever comes into your mind first. Your sketch may be a symbol, a diagram, a graph, a cartoon, or a photo of a person place or thing, for example:

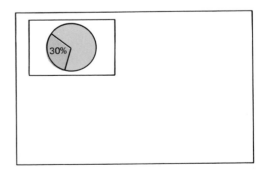

Step 5. Below your sketch, write a brief statement that captures the essence of the point you are trying to make. State it in as few words as needed to cue yourself to the thought, for example:

Some developers prefer to start with the visuals and then write the narration. Others prefer to do the narration first. Actually developing a sound-slide presentation is likely to be a dynamic process, with visual and narration evolving one from the other, separately and simultaneously. In some cases, of course, your narration will be already at hand— printed information, for example, or a story or poem—and all that remains is to develop the proper visuals to fit it. Or, the visuals may already be in hand—slides from a field trip,

nearly one-third begin smoking in high school.

for example—and all you have to do is organize them and then develop your script to accompany the visuals.

Step 6. Now make a card for the thought that *leads into* the point you have just sketched. Then do another one about the thought that *follows* your first one. Continue like this, building a chain of ideas as you go along.

Step 7. When you run out of ideas in the chain, switch to one of the other major points that hasn't fallen into sequence yet.

Step 8. Arrange the cards in sequential and logical order. (This technqiue is called "storyboarding" and is described in more detail in the next section.)

Would some other arrangement liven up the beginning and the end of your presentation? Keep in mind the "psychology" of the situation as you thought it through in your audience analysis. The *beginning* and the *end* are generally the best places to make major points. Have you grabbed the viewer's attention right from the beginning?

How about pacing? Are any complicated ideas skimmed over too lightly? Do sections get bogged down in unnecessary detail? Add or subtract cards as needed.

Step 9. Edit your planning cards in terms of practicality. Be sure you have ready access to the artistic talent and/or photographic equipment needed to turn your sketches into slides.

Step 10. Use your notes to prepare an audio script. Consider using two different voices for the narration, perhaps one male and one female for variety. Would sound effects add impact to your presentation? How about actuality sounds from the place where you will be shooting the pictures? You can take along a recorder and pick up background sounds and personal interviews while doing the photography. Consider, too, adding music, especially as a finishing touch to the beginning and end. Be careful to keep it unobtrusive. Avoid highly recognizable tunes, trendy songs that will "date" your presentation, and music aimed at very specialized tastes.

Step 11. Rehearse your presentation, pretending that your cards are slides on the screen. Time your presentation and see if you need to shorten or lengthen it. To keep your audience's attention, limit your show to 15 minutes. If you need more time than that, break it into two or more parts interspersed with audience activity.

Now you are ready to turn your sketches into slides! And to record your tape see Chapter 6.

For example, a simple set of visuals might have one audio narrative suitable for introduction of and preliminary instruction in a study unit and another narrative for more detailed study. The narration could be on two or more vocabulary levels—one for regular students and another for educationally handicapped students. For foreign language instruction, one audio tape might be narrated in the student's native language and a matching narration recorded on another tape in the foreign language being taught. This technique can also be used in bilingual situations.

Storyboarding

As previously noted, storyboarding is one important step in the development of audiovisual presentations. Storyboarding, an idea borrowed from film and television production, is a technique for helping you generate and organize your audiovisual materials. A sketch or some other simple representation of the visual you plan to use is put on a card or piece of paper along with production notes pertaining to production of the visual and verbal cues to its accompanying narration. After a series of such cards have been developed, they are placed in rough sequence on a flat surface or on a storyboard designed to keep them in place.

Index cards are commonly used for storyboarding because they are durable, inexpensive, and available in a variety of colors and sizes (3 by 5 in., 4 by 6 in., 5 by 8 in., etc.) Small pieces of paper can also be used.

---

aThe visual organization hints given here are adapted from *How to Give a Better Than Offhand Talk...*, Rochester, N.Y.: Eastman Kodak.

Figure 7.6 The storyboard helps in visualizing the total presentation and rearranging parts within it.

6 in.

Visual

Production notes

4 in.

Narration

Figure 7.7 A sample storyboard card.

The individual storyboard cards can be divided into areas to accommodate the visual, the narration, and the production notes (Figure 7.7). The exact format of the storyboard card should fit your needs and purposes. Design a card that facilitates your working rather than constraining yourself to an existing or recommended format.

You can make a simple sketch or write a short description of the desired visual on the card. Polaroid pictures or visuals cut from magazines can also be used.

Some people like to use different color cards for different topics within the program, or various colors for objectives, content, and types of media (visuals, audio, films, etc.) Each component (slide, overhead, film sequence) should be on a separate card.

When a series of cards has been developed, the cards can be laid out on a table or placed on a storyboard. The cards are sequenced in tentative order, thus giving you an overview of the production. The storyboarding technique facilitates addition, deletion, replacement, revision, and refinement of the sequence, since the cards can easily be discarded, added to, or rearranged. The display of cards also allows others (teachers, students, production assistants) to look at the presenta-

HOW TO...MAKE A STORYBOARD

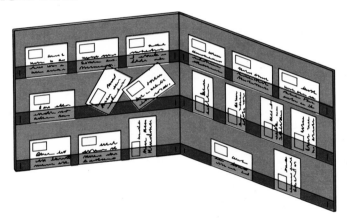

You can construct an inexpensive storyboard from cardboard and strips of clear plastic. Obtain one or two pieces of cardboard about the size that you need to accommodate the number of cards which you will be using. About 18 by 24 in. is a convenient size if you plan to carry the storyboard with you.

If you use two pieces, they can be hinged in the middle (as shown above) with bookbinding tape or wide masking tape, giving you a usable surface measuring 36 by 24 in. when unfolded. If you do not plan to move the storyboard frequently, you could use a larger piece of cardboard (perhaps from a large appliance box such as a refrigerator carton) which could give you up to 6 by 4 ft. of usable surface.

Staple or tape 1-in.-wide strips of clear plastic on the cardboard to hold the cards. If you are planning to use 3-by-5-in. index cards, the strips should be attached about 4 in. apart. One-in. strips of paper or light cardboard can be used to keep the card in place instead of the clear plastic, but this has the disadvantage of not allowing you to read the portion of the cards that is behind the strip.

tion in its planning stage. Number the cards in pencil—you may wish to erase and change numbers as your planning progresses.

Several cards in sequence on a page can be photocopied for use with the final script, thus avoiding duplication of effort and providing a convenient assemblage of visuals, narration, and production notes.

Your narration can be written from the notes on your storyboard cards. It is a good idea to triple space the typing of the final script for easy reading and last-minute changes. Marking pauses on the script with slash (/) and underlining key words will help you record your narration effectively.

MULTI-IMAGE SYSTEMS

The multi-image presentation is another very popular multimedia system. Whether you call the system "multi-image" or "multi-screen" depends primarily upon the way you design it. *Multi-image* refers to the use of two or more separate *images,* usually projected simultaneously in a presentation. (It does not usually refer to two images from a single source.) *Multi-screen* refers to the use of more than one *screen* in a single presentation. The two concepts usually go hand in hand, since the multiple images are often projected on adjacent multiple screens. Most often the images are projected from slides, but

overhead transparencies, filmstrips, or motion pictures may also be used.

Planning a Multi-Image Presentation

Having learned how to develop a single-screen presentation, your next project could be a two-screen or even a three-screen presentation—although it should be pointed out that multiple-image presentations require even more planning and attention to detail. A two-screen presentation may require more than twice the time and effort needed to produce a single-screen one, and a three-screen display may require more than four times as much time.

Figure 7.8 Showing a broad panorama is a typical application of multi-image systems.

Left screen	Right screen	Narration

Left screen	Middle screen	Right screen	Narration

Figure 7.9 Sample development charts for multi-image or multi-screen presentations.

A "development chart" can help ease your extra burden. After you have storyboarded the sequence of your material, use the development chart for your production notes on the images to appear on each screen and for your notes on accompanying narration (see Figure 7.9).

Multi-image presentations must be carefully planned to fit your audience (multiple-images may confuse younger students) and to meet your objectives. You should do a complete practice run-through prior to classroom presentation to be sure that the sequencing is correct and that equipment is operating the way you want it to operate.

Multi-image productions can incorporate film clips, overhead transparencies, slides, or a series of slides to simulate movement. They can also incorporate dissolve units.

Dissolve Units

You can achieve dramatic effects in your slide/tape presentations by using a fade/dissolve unit and two slide projectors. A fade/dissolve unit has a mechanism for slowly turning one projector bulb off, causing one picture to fade out, while the other picture slowly appears on the same screen. The screen does not go black between

Figure 7.10 Adding a dissolve unit allows you to make smooth transitions between images.

pictures, but rather, one picture fades into the next. With a dissolve system you can gradually overlap images, fade or change directly from one visual to another, or fade one image into the other while the level of screen illumination remains constant. This provides a smooth visual presentation without any intervals of darkness on the screen between slides.

All dissolve units require two projectors focused to a single point on the screen so that the images will overlap. The projectors may be placed along side each other or stacked one above the other (as shown in Figure 7.11).

You can achieve some very interesting and dramatic effects by superimposing images from

the two projectors. You can add elements to a particular visual or eliminate unneeded ones. You can make an object appear to rotate, or make a head turn or a facial expression change in apparent response to a comment on the audio tape.

With the push of a button, you can control the speed and type of dissolve. A fast dissolve provides an instantaneous change from one visual to the next. A medium dissolve, lasting a couple of seconds, provides a visual blend between the slides. A slow dissolve allows one image to change more gradually into the next. The modes of changes available on most fade/dissolve units include:

Cut mode—the slide presentation switches from one projector to the other with instantaneous image change.

Dissolve mode—the first slide gradually fades in intensity as another slide from the second projector increases in intensity, creating a fading and overlapping effect as slides are changed.

Fade-out/fade-in mode—the slide gradually fades as light is reduced until there is total darkness on the screen; then a new image appears as light is gradually increased.

Programmers

There is a limit to the number of pieces of equipment you (with or without helpers) can operate and control directly. Fortunately, *automatic programmers* are available that can control a number of projectors. They can also be programmed to stop during your presentation for discussion or questions from the audience and then resume at the touch of a button.

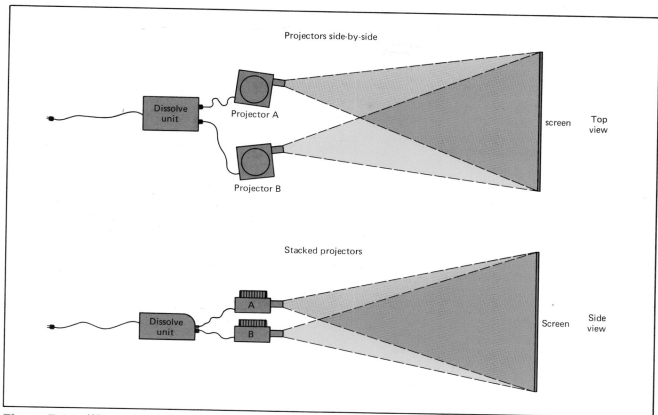

Figure 7.11 When using a dissolve unit, the projectors may be aligned side-by-side or stacked one above the other.

There are three common types of programmers—punch tape, magnetic tape, and microcomputers. Punch-tape programmers use a strip of paper or mylar plastic about 3/4 in. wide with holes punched in it. The programmer will automatically change the slides on the basis of the preset signals punched on the tape. Magnetic-tape programmers are increasing in popularity and use and at the same time decreasing in cost. The newer microcomputers can also be used to control multi-image presentations. Microcomputers are very versatile and relatively easy to program for this function.

Automatic programmers enable motion pictures, filmstrips, and slide projectors to be operated together, separately, or in any combination with synchronized

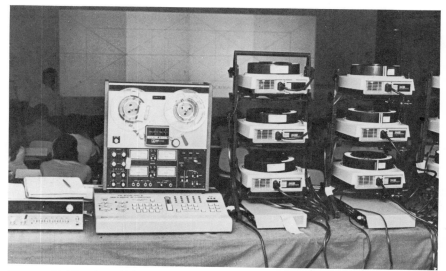

Figure 7.12 A multi-image presentation controlled by an automatic programmer using magnetic tape.

sound from an audio tape. A typical three-screen setup with dissolve control for each projector is shown in Figure 7-13.

Applications of Multi-Image Systems

Multi-image presentations can be used creatively in a variety of instructional situations. For example, one screen could be used to present an overview or long-range view of a visual while another presents a close-up view or a detail of it. This technique might be used to show the relationship of a component of a system or process to its entirety, or to show a detail of a work of art in relationship to the complete piece. Two or more images could be projected side-by-side for students to compare and contrast different art forms, or

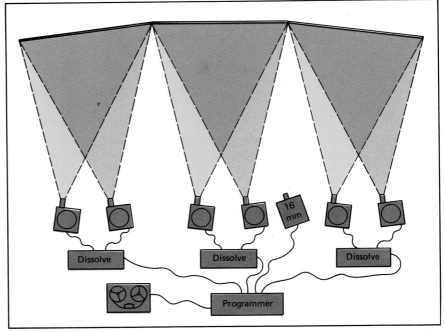

Figure 7.13 Setup for a three-screen presentation using dissolve units and an automatic programmer.

Figures 7.14 and 7.15 A typical instructional application of multiple images is to show a significant detail alongside a larger view.

art and architectural forms in different periods of history.

"Before and after" shots could be used in industrial arts classes, for example, to show the final results of a furniture refinishing project; or they could be used in a social studies class to show the inroads of industrialization on an ecological system. In electronics instruction, schematic codes of circuit components could be shown next to visuals of the actual components. Similarly, line drawings of an object can be exhibited adjacent to its photograph, or a photograph could be displayed on one screen and data or questions about the picture presented on another. A map of an area might be shown on one screen, and a photograph or aerial view of the area presented in another.

Two or more screens may also be used to present wide-angle or panoramic views of a visual that might be impossible to present on a single screen. Multiple-screen images can also be used to show physical activities in more detailed sequence, activities such as swimming, diving, swinging a tennis racquet or hitting a golf ball. They can also be used to present several views of the same object to achieve a three-dimensional effect or to allow an object to be viewed from different distances and angles.

Multi-image presentations can also be used very effectively for learning in the affective domain and for establishment of mood. For example, one could provide a visually dramatic background for listening to musical and choral works, plays and readings.

EIGHT-MILLIMETER FILM–AUDIO CASSETTE SYSTEMS

One of the most versatile multimedia systems utilizes an 8-mm film and an audio cassette. Unlike standard motion picture presentations, the sound and the picture in the 8-mm film–audio cassette system are separated into two individual packages. The audio tape moves at a constant speed, but the film can be programmed to move at variable speeds from still (stop action) up to 24 frames per second. The film cartridge contains 50 feet of Super-8-mm film and includes 3600 frames (visuals) which can be shown individually or in rapid succession to simulate motion. The film and sound are synchronized by inaudible pulses recorded on the audio cassette. The systems provide "variable motion sound filmstrips" with the impact of motion pictures and the teaching effectiveness of still pictures.

The most commonly available of these systems are Norelco's PIP (Programmed Individual Presentation), Beseler's Cue/See, and the RCS Retention II. All three systems can intermix the equivalent of slides, filmstrips, and motion pictures along with narration or sound effects. Separate audio cassettes allow the user to choose which narration to use with a given film. The projection mechanism is essentially a variable speed projector with a built-in tape player and synchronization device. The machinery is light, weighing about 20 pounds, and is thus readily portable.

The speed at which the image changes on the screen can be determined by the nature of the material being presented. Separation of "soundtrack" from the film permits the film to be moved at variable speeds while the tape is moving at a constant speed. Just as pulses advance the frames of a filmstrip, pulses in this system advance the frames of the film slowly to illustrate specific lesson points or very rapidly to create motion.

All of the machines have a built-in rear projection screen as well as a mirror and lens system for projecting the image on a screen, so the machine is suitable for individual or small group use. It can show slow motion, time-lapse, or stop-action. The machines also incorporate a "skipped" frame mechanism which allows two, three, or even five frames at a time

Figure 7.16 Beseler "Cue/See" combines cartridged Super-8-mm film and audio cassette programmed to show a mixtures of still and motion pictures.

Figure 7.17 The RCS "Retention II" uses Super-8-mm film and audio cassette enclosed in a single cartridge.

to be advanced at high speed without detection by the viewer, since each new frame is advanced in less than a hundredth of a second. This feature is particularly valuable when the same film is used with separate audio tapes for two different types of audiences.

The major disadvantages of the system are initial cost of the equipment, the lack of commercially available materials, and the time and expense required for local production. The cost of production goes up very rapidly as you move beyond simple presentations. Also, in order to produce your own materials, you must have a device called a "Frame Pulse Generator" to put the sound frequency pulses on the audio cassette.

Applications

The 8-mm film–audio cassette system is especially useful in learning situations that lend themselves to integration of still visuals and moving pictures. As noted above, since the audio cassette is separate from the film cassette, you can use different sound tracks with the visual component of the system. For example, in a foreign language class, the audio could be in English on one cassette tape and in a foreign language on the other. A demonstration in an industrial arts class or in a home economics class could use one film cassette with separate audio tapes geared to beginning, intermediate, and advanced students. Tapes can also be geared to different ability levels.

When the same instruction is needed for a large number of students in widely scattered locations, the 8-mm film–audio cassette system becomes cost effective. For example, the U.S. Army uses the Beseler Cue/See to provide individual or small-group instruction on standard military procedures and the use of common pieces of equipment. Industries sometimes use one film with separate narrations for training of personnel and for product promotion.

MULTIMEDIA KITS

A multimedia kit is a collection of teaching/learning materials involving more than one type of medium and organized around a single topic. The kits may include filmstrips, slides, audio tapes, records, still pictures, study prints, overhead transparencies, single-concept films, maps, worksheets, charts, graphs, booklets, real objects, and models.

Some multimedia kits are designed for use by the teacher in classroom presentations. Others are designed for use by individual students or by small groups. The variety and wide range of the instructional purposes to which such kits may be put is indicated below in our discussion of commercially available and teacher-made multimedia kits.

Commercial Multimedia Kits

Commercial multimedia kits are available for a variety of educational subjects. For example, the Society for Visual Education markets a series of multimedia kits ("learning modules") with titles such as *Beginning Math Concepts, Metric System, Communities in Nature* (an ecology unit), *Planning the Human Community, Initial Consonant, Vowel Sounds* and *Threshold to Reading*.

These learning modules include sound filmstrips, cassette tapes floor games, board games, posters, full-color photographs, activity cards, lotto cards, murals, wall charts, geometric shapes, flash cards, student workbooks, and a teacher's manual. They stimulate active participation, encourage individualized, multi-sensory learning, and help make learning exciting and enjoyable. Clearly defined objectives are stated and supported with suggested teaching strategies for using the materials in the kit. The kits are versatile in that they may be used in traditional or open classrooms. In short, they provide a systematic approach to the use of multimedia materials for instructional purposes.

Many other multimedia kits on a wide variety of topics are available from commercial sources, some of which contain, among other instructional materials, transparencies, laboratory materials for science experiments, and even puppets to act out story concepts.

Teacher-made Multimedia Kits

Multimedia kits can also be prepared by teachers. First of all, you must, of course, decide if the kit is to be used by the students. Obviously, this decision will affect your choice of materials. Obviously, too, you will have to decide if you are going to prepare only one kit for student use or if you are going to duplicate the kit so that more than one student can have access to it at any given time. Another alternative might be to make a variety of kits and have the students take turns using them.

Availability and cost of materials will also affect your choice of media materials to be included in the kit. Cost is particularly important if duplicate kits are to be pro-

Figure 7.18 Multimedia kit, "Language Experiences in Early Childhood."

vided and if purchased materials are not reusable. Remember too, that if the kits are to be taken home for unsupervised individual use, allowance should probably be made for loss or accidental damage to some items. Nevertheless, cost need not be an insurmountable problem. Many simple but satisfactory resource materials are free. Multimedia kits need not be expensive to be effective.

It is important that the components of the kit be integrated—that

is, that each component contribute to attainment of your lesson objective. Multimedia activities should also, of course, be correlated with other relevant learning activities in the classroom.

The availability of equipment will also affect your selection of materials. If filmstrips or other projected visuals are included, for example, you will need a projector for group use. A hand-held viewer, however, might suffice for individual use. Audio materials will require playback machines.

Multimedia kits should be designed to teach specific knowledge and skills. They should involve the student in the learning process as he or she handles and manipulates the resource materials.

Your multimedia kit should include some sort of introduction to its topic and instructions on or suggestions about how the various components of the kit are to be used. If the kit is to be used only under your direct supervision,

---

MEDIA FILE: **"Using the Telephone Book" Multimedia Kit**

Interpretative Education markets multimedia kit for educable mentally retarded (EMR) students entitled *Using the Telephone Book*. The materials explain in a simple step-by-step manner how to use the white and yellow pages of a telephone book. Practice in using the telephone book is provided for.

verbal introduction and instructions may suffice. In most cases, however, a printed study guide should be included with your kit. The guide should introduce the topic of the kit and relate its components to the learning objective. It should give instructions for using the media included in the kit and include directions for the learning activities involved. Questions and space for responses may also be contained in the guide. The study guide should be as simple as possible, containing just the essential facts, explanations, and relevant information, without unnecessary embellishment.

Some teachers prefer to put their study guide materials on audio tape. This procedure can be helpful for slow readers and may be essential for very poor readers and nonreaders.

It is important for the teacher to monitor each student's progress in order to reward successes and to alleviate frustrations. At the conclusion of each kit's use, the student should discuss the activity with the teacher individually or in a small group. The teacher and the student(s) can go over the nature of the problem presented in the kit, compare answers (if appropriate), and discuss the concepts learned from the multimedia kit. The follow-up discussion can be used as an evaluative device in addition to or instead of a paper and pencil quiz.

Shoe boxes or similar size containers make handy containers for teacher-made multimedia kits. Each box should have a label indicating its topic and perhaps its learning objective. A list of materials included in the kit may be pasted on the inside of the box lid as an aid to use and as a check to make certain that all the materials have been returned.

Figure 7.19 Multimedia kits frequently provide raw materials for student inquiry into the phenomena of nature.

Applications

The instructional uses of teacher-made multimedia kits are limited only by teacher ingenuity. Here are a few examples.

A multimedia kit on magnetic fields might include (among other materials) several types of magnets, such as permanent and electromagnets, and an assortment of metal objects which may or may not be attracted to them. For older students, iron filings might also be provided. A kit on aerodynamics might include paper or balsa along with patterns and instructions for constructing various types of aircraft. If proper safety precautions are taken, you might allow the students to fly their models and award prizes for the longest or highest flight.

Mathematical topics are especially suitable for multimedia kits. Such kits could include a statement of the problem(s) the student must solve, suggestions for procedures to use, and materials needed. A kit on metric measurement, for example, could include a metric ruler or meter stick, various objects to be measured, and suggestions for taking metric measurements of various objects in the classroom.

Close up: Teacher-made Multimedia Kit

An elementary teacher developed a series of separate multimedia kits on science topics for use with her third-grade class. She incorporated real objects, such as magnets, small motors, rocks, harmless chemicals, and insect specimens in the kits. She also gathered pictures from magazines and old textbooks associated with the topic. A study guide, prepared for each unit, required the student to inquire into the topic, make hypotheses, and conduct investigations. Audio tapes were prepared for use at school and at home for those students who had access to a cassette player.

The students enjoyed taking the kits home to work on the "experiments." The response from parents was very positive. Several parents reported that they too learned by working through the activities with their children. Students often preferred to stay in at recess and work on the multimedia kits in the science corner.

Flashback: The MATCH Program

Multimedia kits were an integral part of the Materials and Activities for Teachers and Children (MATCH) program[a] developed by the Children's Museum in Boston during the late 1960s. The program incorporated learning materials and activities in the form of a series of multimedia kits designed to be used by students and teachers in the elementary grades. The focus was on nonverbal learning and the acquisition of skills not unique to any one subject matter area. The program emphasized the development of thinking, feeling, and learning skills through direct experience with authentic materials.

The long-range goal of the MATCH project was to explore the ways of communicating nonverbally through the use of a variety of media. The developers combined various materials with classroom activities in the form of kits designed to teach specific objectives. Sixteen such kits were developed. The kits, designed to be used for two or three weeks, supplemented regular classroom instruction in the elementary grades. Each MATCH multimedia kit was independent of the other kits and could be used in any order or combination. The 16 titles were:

Grouping Birds
The City
The Algonquins
Seeds
A House of Ancient
  Greece
Houses
Animal Camouflage
Netsilik Eskimos

Musical Shapes and
  Sounds
Rocks
Japanese Family
Medieval People
Waterplay
Imagination Unlimited
"Paddle-to-the-Sea"
The MATCH Box
  Press

For example, the MATCH multimedia kit on the Netsilik Eskimos was designed especially for third and fourth graders. Its purpose was to put children in touch with the traditions of the Netsilik Eskimos by focusing on their lives during the seal-hunting season. The kit materials illustrated Netsilik hunting technology, spiritual beliefs, social relations, and leisure activities as they related to seal hunting. The media in the kit included authentic Eskimo artifacts and materials, such as seal-hunting tools, boots, a seal skin, a drum, Eskimo amulet, three films showing seal hunting and Eskimos setting up camp, a model igloo, figures, a book, and a record. Kit activities included simulating a seal hunt,

[a]Materials and Activities for Teachers and Children—The MATCH Program, B.A. Sanderson, and D.W. Kratochvel, Palo Alto, Calif.: American Institutes of Research, 1972.

Flashback: The MATCH Program

"Japanese Family" MATCH curriculum kit.

concentration on limited objectives, and integration of learning activities. Provision for motivating student participation and learning was built into each unit, as were opportunities for providing feedback to the learners. All units were designed to be used for 1 hr. or 1 1/2 hrs. a day, over a period of two to three weeks.

Each kit was tried out in some 15 to 22 classrooms involving a total of 330 teachers and over 10,000 children. The director of the MATCH Project summarized the results of the field test as follows:

Teachers and children were overwhelmingly enthusiastic about the units and this form of teaching. Teachers judged class interest, attention, participation, and learning to be greater than usual. They delighted in having such rich material to work with. Children who were previously unresponsive participated, often for the first time. Many children surprised their teachers with what they could do. The units altered the relationship between teacher and children, making it more collaborative rather than teacher-directed. Teachers said they could see what the children were learning and therefore didn't need special tests.[b]

recreating everyday activities of Netsilik life, hearing the story of the sea spirit, Nuliajuk, and performing the Netsilik drum dance.

Learning activities throughout the entire series were designed to be relevant to the children's interests while keeping the objectives of the unit in mind. Most of the activities were designed for small-group participation, with four to six children taking part in the activity. The most important characteristic of these activities was that they were intended to place responsibility for learning in the hands of the child and thus to make the child the agent of his or her own learning.

The teacher's manual for each kit stressed reliance on real objects and other visual media,

[b]F. H. Kresse, *Materials and Activities for Teachers and Children: A Project to Develop and Evaluate Multi-Media Kits for Elementary Schools. Final Report, Volume I,* Boston: The Children's Museum, 1968, p.7.

CLASSROOM LEARNING CENTERS

The development of multimedia instructional technology and the growing interest in small-group and individualized instruction have led to the establishment of special learning environments generally called *classroom learning centers.* A learning center is an individualized environment designed to encourage the student to use a variety of instructional media, to engage in diversified learning activities, and to assume major responsibility for his or her own learning.

Learning centers may be set up in any suitable and available classroom space. Or they may be set up outside the classroom, in a laboratory, for example, or even in a school corridor.

Learning center materials may include practically any or all of the media and multimedia formats discussed or mentioned in this text. Center materials may be purchased from commercial producers or may be teacher made.

Carrels

Although simple learning-center activities might be carried out at a student's desk or some other open space, it is advisable that learning centers be confined to a clearly identifiable area and that they be at least partially enclosed to aid concentration and avoid distraction. Learning carrels (booths), which may be purchased from commercial sources or made locally, will provide a clearly identifiable enclosure.

Carrels may be made by placing simple cardboard dividers on classroom tables, or free-standing commercially constructed carrels complete with electrical connections and rear projection screens may be purchased.

Carrels are often referred to as being either "wet" or "dry." A dry carrel provides private space for study or other learning activities but contains no electrial equipment. The typical library carrel is a dry carrel. A wet carrel, on the other hand, is equipped with or has outlets for audiovisual mechanisms such as cassette recorder, a projection screen, television monitor, or computer terminal.

Figure 7.20 A "wet" carrel provides facilities for audiovisual media.

Applications

Learning centers can be used for a number of basic instructional purposes and, indeed, are often categorized according to their primary purpose.

As *Teaching Centers* they can be used to introduce new content or skills and to provide an environment for individual or small-group instruction in lieu of whole-class instruction. Teaching the basics of the "three R's" lends itself quite

Figure 7.21 As a *skill center*, this learning center provides motivating practice in language skills.

well to the learning-center instructional approach.

As *Skill Centers* they can provide the student with an opportunity to do additional practice or can reinforce a lesson that has previously been taught through other media or teaching techniques. For example, a skill center might be designed to reinforce skill in using prefixes to be used by students who are learning to read.

As *Interest Centers* they can promote present interests or stimulate new interests and encourage creativity. For example, a get-acquainted center on insect life might be set up in the classroom before actually beginning a unit on specific insects.

As *Remedial Centers* they can be used to provide students who need additional assistance with a particular concept or skill. A student who has difficulty determining the least common denominator of a group of fractions, for example, could be given the needed help in a remedial learning center.

As *Enrichment Centers* they can provide stimulating additional

Close-up: "Indy 500" Learning Center

A fifth-grade teacher in Indianapolis capitalizes on local enthusiasm for the "Indianapolis 500" car race by designing a math learning center based upon car numbers and speeds. Center material includes a variety of questions. "What is the difference in speed between Car 20 and Car 14?" "How many cars have even numbers?" "If an Indianapolis race car gets 1.8 miles per gallon, how many miles can it go on one tank of fuel (40 gallons)?" The center has colorful pictures and souvenir post cards of the cars and drivers. Each student draws, colors, and numbers his or her own race car, which goes in the "Victory Circle" when the lesson is completed. The students complete worksheets, for which they are awarded "completed laps" rather than numerical points. When they have completed their "500 miles," they have "finished the race" and receive a miniature checkered flag. The center is designed so that all students can eventually master its content and be rewarded by receiving a flag.

learning experiences for those students who have completed other center or classroom activities. Students who have completed their assigned math activities, for example, may be allowed to go to a center, "How Computers Work."

Advantages and Limitations of Learning Centers

Aside from exposing students to a variety of multimedia learning experiences, the advantages of learning centers are chiefly those that generally accrue to individualized learning and teaching. Learning centers force the teacher to move around the classroom and provide individual help to students when they need it. Centers encourage students to take responsibility for their own learning and allow them to learn at their own pace (thus minimizing the possibility of failure and maximizing the likelihood of success). They provide for student participation in the learning experience, for student response, and for immediate feedback to student response. Students tend to spend more time on the task of learning.

On the other hand, learning centers do have some drawbacks. They can be costly. A great deal of time must be spent in planning and setting up centers and in collecting and arranging for center materials. The teacher who manages the learning center must be a very good classroom manager and organizer—and must avoid the temptation to let the learning center replace the teacher.

Learning Center Management

There are a variety of learning center management strategies. A block of time can be set aside for use of each center and students can be assigned to it for certain periods. The length of the time block should be determined by the age of the students and the content of the center. The alternative of having the students move from center to center on their own is acceptable as long as they are held accountable for getting the "job" done. (See film "Classroom Learning Centers" cited in Audiovisual References.)

As a teacher using learning centers, your role is not to teach one subject or to control the students from the front of the room. Instead, it is to move around and deal with the students on an individual or small-group basis. While circulating about the classroom, you can assist students who are having difficulty, while becoming actively involved in the learning process with the students and assessing the progress of each student.

Within an hour class-period, it is helpful to have 10 to 15 minutes at the end of the period for group discussion and wrap-up. Of course, follow-up activities may be available for the students when the learning center project is completed.

Designing Your Own Learning Center Materials (ASSURE Model)

As noted above, more or less elaborate learning centers may be purchased from commercial sources. You may, however, wish to design your own somewhat less elaborate center. Let us consider how you might go about planning for and designing your own center according to the ASSURE model discussed in Chapter 2. The ASSURE model lends itself to the structuring of any learning environment.

Analyze Learner Characteristics. Diagnosis of student characteristics is the key to placing your students in the learning center that best suits their abilities, need, and interests.

State Objectives. Determine the learning objective(s) you wish your students to attain in the center. State these objectives in terms of student behavior. Be sure the content of the center includes a statement of the objectives for user reference. A statement of objectives might be included in the center's printed material, or it might be recorded on tape.

Select, Modify, or Design Materials. Your selection of materials, of course, should be dictated by the abilities and instructional needs of your students and by the availability of slides, filmstrips, audio tapes, realia, multimedia kits, printed materials (worksheets and instruction sheets), etc. Ideas for materials to include in your center, either as is or adapted for your own specific purposes, may be gleaned from descriptions of commercially produced learning centers and from audiovisual periodicals and reference books. A list of the materials contained in your center should be included in the center for user reference.

Utilize Materials. Learning centers are designed for use by individual students or small groups. Grouping has the advantage of allowing the students to interact as they utilize center materials, thus learning from one another's efforts and mistakes and reinforcing correct responses. In either case, instructions for using center materials should be included in your center. They should be concise and as clear as possible, and may be in print format or on audio tape.

The exact nature and order of learning activities within the center may be strictly controlled by the teacher, or may be left in whole or in part to the student. In most cases it is advisable to control activities at the outset and gradually increase students' freedom to choose activities as they demonstrate ability to assume responsibity for self-direction. Similarly, assignment to specific centers may be strictly controlled or left in whole or in part to the students.

Be available to your students when they are utilizing center materials. Many students, particularly younger children, need or can profit by frequent teacher contact as they use the materials and carry out the activities of the learning center. Circumstances may also warrant scheduling short one-to-one conferences with center users at periodic intervals.

Require Learner Response.

Learning centers should be designed to include opportunities for learners to respond to center materials and receive feedback to their reponses. There are various ways of providing such opportunities. You might, for example, provide an answer key to printed or audiotaped questions. The key might be included within the center or placed outside it, perhaps on a bulletin board. The latter procedure allows the student to get up and move around a bit, thus alleviating the sense of confinement some children may feel with prolonged center use. Answers might also be put on the back of an activity card. Puzzle pieces may also be used to provide for student responses and feedback. This device entails putting questions and answers on a piece of paper or cardboard and then separating questions from answers by zig-zag cuts. Only the correct answer portion of the paper will fit

Figure 7.22 Learning centers offer opportunities for informal teacher-student interaction.

a given question as shown in Figure 7.23. It is advisable to use a variety of techniques for providing feedback to learner response. In all cases, feedback to learner response should be as immediate as possible. Instant feedback has the distinct advantage of reinforcing correct responses and correcting wrong ones while material is fresh in the student's mind.

Evaluate.

Attention to student response and providing some feedback will have given you some opportunity to evaluate student progress toward attainment of your center's learning objectives. Further evaluations can be made through periodic testing while work is in progress and through individual conferences. When the learning center project is completed, student mastery of

the center's objectives can be tested by traditional end of lesson pencil and paper tests, performance tests, or other appropriate techniques.

Now is the time, also, to evaluate the learning center itself. Did most of its users attain its learning objectives? If not, why not? Were your materials well chosen? Were they too difficult for your students to work with or manipulate, or too easy? Did your center provide the right learning environment? Was it too dark? Too bright? Too noisy? Were your objectives clearly understood? Were your instructions clear? Your own careful observations and solicitations of student comments and suggestions will help you evaluate your center.

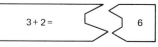

Figure 7.23 Examples of self-checking puzzles for math drills.

REFERENCES

Print References: Multi-Media Systems

* Benedict, Joel A., and Douglas A. Crane. *Producing Multi-Image Presentations* (Tempe, AZ: Arizona State University, 1976).

Cromer, Nancy. "Why Should We Teach Multi-Media?" *English Journal,* December 1975, pp. 68–71.

Dunn, Rita, and Kenneth Dunn. "Seeing, Hearing, Moving, Touching, Learning Packages." *Teacher,* May/June 1977, pp. 48–5l.

Eastman Kodak Co. *Effective Visual Presentations* (Rochester, NY: Eastman Kodak, 1979).

"A Few More Images Can Mean a Lot More Learning." *Training,* March 1976, pp. 28–31.

Goldstein, E. Bruce. "The Perception of Multiple Images." *AV Communication Review,* Spring 1975, pp. 34–68.

A Guide to Effective Presentations for Teaching, Training and Selling Multi-Image Productions (St. Paul, MN: Wollensak/3M, 1977).

Hitchens, Howard B. "The Production of Multi-media Kits." *Educational Media International,* March 1977, pp. 6–13.

* *Images, Images, Images—The Book of Programmed Multi-Image Production* (Rochester, NY: Eastman Kodak, 1980).

Perrin, Donald G. "A Theory of Multi-image Communication." *AV Communication Review,* Winter 1969, pp. 368–82.

* *Planning and Producing Slide Programs* (Rochester, NY: Eastman Kodak, 1975).

Print References: Classroom Learning Centers

Beach, Don M. *Reaching Teenagers: Learning Centers for the Secondary Classroom* (Santa Monica, CA: Goodyear Publishing, 1977).

Blake, Howard E. *Creating a Learning-Centered Classroom* (New York: A & W Visual Library, 1977).

Godfrey, Lorraine L. *Individualizing through Learning Stations* (Menlo Park, CA: Individualized Books Publishing Co., 1972).

Marshall, Kim. *Opening Your Class with Learning Stations* (Palo Alto, CA: Learning Handbooks, 1975).

Maxim, George W. *Learning Centers for Young Children* (New York: Hart Publishing Co., 1977).

* Nations, Jimmy E. (ed.). *Learning Centers in the Classroom* (Washington, DC: National Education Association, 1976).

Audiovisual References

* "Classroom Learning Centers." (Birmingham, AL: Promethean Films, 1976). (16-mm film, color.)

* "Creating Slide-Tape Programs." (Washington, DC: Association for Educational Communications and Technology, 1980). [Sound filmstrip (cassette), color.]

* "Effective Visual Presentations." (Rochester, NY: Eastman Kodak, 1978). [Sound slide set (cassette) and 16-mm film, color.]

"Planning a Presentation." (Bloomington, IN: Agency for Instructional Television, 1980). (16-mm film or videocassette.)

"Synchronizing a Slide/Tape Program." (Rochester, NY: Eastman Kodak, Co., 1976). (Sound slide set, 12 minutes, color.)

Suppliers of Materials and Equipment

Multimedia Kits

Interpretive Education
400 Bryant Street
Kalamazoo, Michigan 49001

Society for Visual Education
1345 Diversey Parkway
Chicago, Illinois 60614

Dissolve Units and Programmers

Eastman Kodak Co.
1187 Ridge Road West
Rochester, NY 14650

Multi Image Systems
Wollensak/3M
2501 Hudson Road
St. Paul, Minnesota 55119

Spindler and Sauppe
13034 Saticoy Street
North Hollywood, California 91605

Film/Cassette Systems

Charles Beseler Co.
8 Fernwood Road
Florham Park, New Jersey 07932

Norelco
Training & Education
100 East 42nd Street
New York, New York 10017

Retention Communications Systems
5 Paul Kohner Place
Elmwood Park, New York 07407

Learning Carrels

LEM Carrel System
Synsor Corporation
2927 112th S.W.
Everett, Washington 98204

Monroe Industries, Inc.
2955 S. Kansas
Wichita, Kansas 67216

*Key references.

POSSIBLE PROJECTS

7-A. Plan a lesson in which you use a sound-slide or sound filmstrip. With this lesson show evidence that you have followed the utilization principles suggested in Chapter 2 as well as other pertinent suggestions from this chapter. Include a brief description of the audience and your objectives.

7-B. Plan a sound-slide presentation including a description of the visuals and a script or tape.

7-C. Locate and examine a multimedia kit in your field of interest. Prepare a written or oral report on the possible applications and relative merits of the kit (appraisal).

7-D. Locate and examine one of the media combination machines, such as film loop and audio-cassette devices. Prepare a written or oral report on the possible applications and relative merits of the equipment (appraisal).

7-E. Design a classroom learning center. Describe the audience, the objective, and the materials/media to be incorporated. Explain the roles of the students and the teacher in using the center. Evaluate its actual effectiveness if used and potential effectiveness if not used.

CHAPTER 8

FILM

OUTLINE

OBJECTIVES

After studying this chapter, you should
be able to:

1. Describe how a movie presents
motion.

2. Describe two techniques by which
sound can be added to motion picture
film.

3. Discuss three different film formats.

4. Describe five attributes of film.

5. Identify two film conventions which
must be learned.

6. List seven instructional values
(advantages) of film.

7. List three limitations of films.

8. Identify five criteria useful in
appraising films.

9. Discuss why caution must be used
in the use of sponsored films.

10. Relate the ASSURE model to
effective film presentation including
specific examples.

11. Explain the use of film as an "aesthetic experience" and include three
examples with your explanation.

12. Describe a situation in your teaching field in which students might produce their own film or video tape.

13. Discuss the possible future of film
as an instructional medium.

14. Identify two *specific* sources
where you can get information about
films.

In a previous chapter we spoke of the aura of "magic" surrounding the projection of visuals, of how the brilliant illumination of a screened image in a darkened room tends to grab the attention of viewers, and of how this attribute can contribute to effective learning. We come now to an instructional medium in which the power to hold attention greatly contributes to a mind-set conducive to learning—the film, which adds the magic of motion to the projected visual image.

Before discussing film as an instructional medium, however, let us briefly consider the basic mechanics of motion picture projection and some basic characteristics of motion picture film.

WHY A MOVIE MOVES

Essentially, movie movement is an illusion. A movie moves because our sensory apparatus tricks us into thinking it moves. At the bottom of the next page is the first of a series of still pictures which ends on page 211. If you flip these pages at a fast enough rate of speed, you will create the illusion of movement. Each individual's optical system retains an image for a brief moment after it has been viewed. If the next image is exposed to view before this trace of the previous image fades, the images blend together creating the impression of actual movement. The basic function of all the "hardware" connected with the recorded moving image— camera, projector, etc.—is to take advantage of this "persistence of vision" sensory phenomenon.

Because the camera photographs a scene as a series of separate, discrete images, motion picture film consists of a sequence of slightly different still pictures called frames. When these frames are projected on a screen at a certain speed (at least 12 frames per second), the images appear to be in continuous motion.

Each still picture (frame) is allowed to remain stationary at the film aperture (1), as seen on the left side of Figure 8.1. While it is stationary, the shutter (2) is open, permitting the light from the projection lamp to pick up the image, go through a focusing lens system (3), and display the picture on the screen. Then the shutter closes and a device like a claw (4) engages the sprocket holes and pulls the film down so that the next frame is in position, shown in detail on the right side of Figure 8.1. (Ironically, the film "moves" only when the audience doesn't see the image.) The claw with-

Figure 8.1 The basic mechanics of motion picture film projection. From Wyman, Raymond, *Mediaware: Selection, Operation, and Maintenance,* 2nd. ed., Copyright © 1969, 1976. Wm. C. Brown Co., Publishers, Dubuque, Iowa. Reprinted by permission.

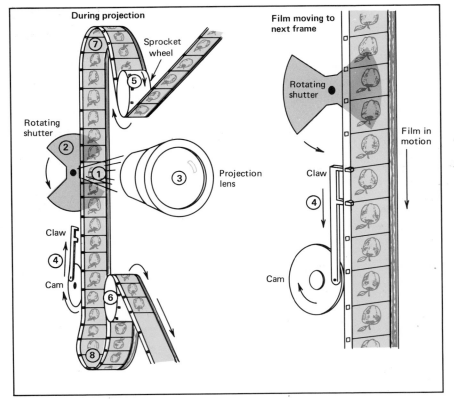

This is the last frame in a film sequence that begins on page 210. If you flip the pages from back to front you will see about ½ second of screen action.

draws, the shutter opens, and the next picture is projected on the screen.

Although the film moves past the aperture intermittently, the top sprocket wheel (5) pulls the film into the projector at a steady 24 frames per second (sound speed), and the bottom sprocket wheel (6) pulls the film out of the projector at the same steady rate of speed. If no slack were put into the film at upper and lower loops (7) and (8), the film would be torn apart. These two loops compensate for the two different motions the film must have. Because sound cannot be accurately recorded or reproduced on a film that is not moving smoothly, the intermittent movement of the film must be smoothed out by the bottom sprocket and an idler system before the film reaches the sound drum.

SOUND ON MOTION-PICTURE FILM

The sound that accompanies a film is contained in a *track* that runs down one side of the film (Figure 8.2). The track may be *optical* or *magnetic*. An optical sound track is actually a photographic image of sound recorded at one edge of the film in variable shades of dark and light. A magnetic sound track is one in which sound is recorded on magnetic tape bonded to one edge of the film.

Projectors that will handle only one or both types of sound tracks are available. However, in projectors built to handle both types, the separate mechanisms required to pick up the sound in each format must be positioned one behind the other. Consequently, the sound that accompanies a specific image (or frame) is recorded at a slightly different distance from that frame for each of the formats.

Figure 8.2 Comparison of optical and magnetic sound tracks. In the 16-mm optical sound track system, the sound accompanying a specific image (frame) is recorded on the film 26 frames ahead of that frame. Note that the displacement (separation between image and sound) differs for each of the other film formats. The proper setting of the lower loop on all film projectors is critical for keeping the picture and sound synchronized.

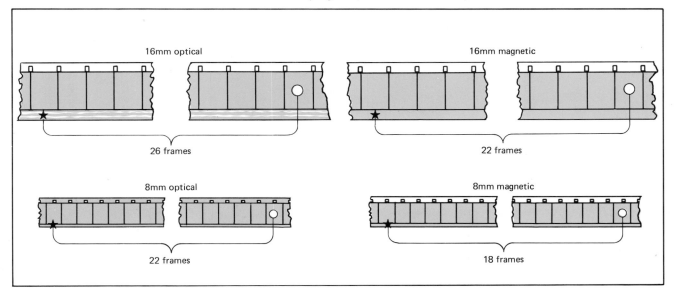

Flip the pages of the text from here to page 211. If you flip them fast enough, the stills will appear to move, approximating ½ second of screen action.

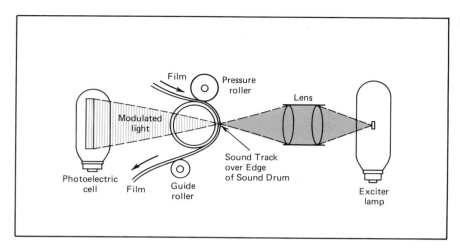

Figure 8.3 Playback of optical sound tracks. The steady light from the exciter lamp passes through the sound track, picking up the image of the recorded sound. This image is then focused on a photoelectric cell. The varying light pattern of the optical sound track is converted into correspondingly varying electrical impulses by the photoelectric cell. These very weak signals are amplified and then converted back into sound waves by the speaker. From Wyman, Raymond, *Mediaware: Selection, Operation and Maintenance,* 2nd. ed., Copyright © 1969, 1976. Wm. C. Brown Co., Publishers, Dubuque, Iowa. Reprinted by permission.

FILM FORMATS

Motion-picture film comes in various widths and image sizes. For theatrical films 35-mm film is most commonly used. The size most commonly used for instructional films and entertainment films shown in schools is 16-mm film.

The most common formats of motion picture film are illustrated in Figure 8.4. Note how the physical characteristics of the film changed with the addition of sound, and how the sprocket hole size and image area of 8-mm film changed in the evolution from the original 8-mm to Super-8-mm size.

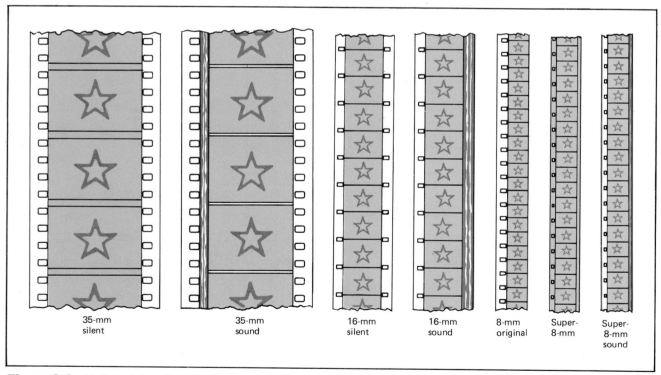

| 35-mm silent | 35-mm sound | 16-mm silent | 16-mm sound | 8-mm original | Super-8-mm | Super-8-mm sound |

Figure 8.4 Motion picture film formats.

Flashback: Mr. Edison's Dream

Thomas A. Edison, whose work in developing the kinetograph (a camera that used film rolls) and the kinetoscope (a peep-show device) contributed greatly to the development of motion pictures, had high hopes for the instructional value of this by then popular medium. As depicted in the cartoon from *The Chicago Tribune* of 1923, he fully expected the motion picture to revolutionize education and even perhaps to "take the place of books in the schools." He anticipated that the most important and widespread use of film would be in schools, where it would give new life to curricular content and provide students with new motivation for learning.

We all know that the history of the motion picture took a turn quite different from that anticipated by Edison. "Movies" were quickly and eagerly adopted as an entertainment medium but in education the progress of film utilization

was extremely slow. Part of the problem was technical. The standard size for film quickly became set at 35 mm, which meant that equipment for projection was extremely bulky and expensive. Also, the film base that was used for many years, cellulose nitrate, was extremely flammable and many state regulations required a film to be projected only from an enclosed booth and by a licensed projectionist. Thus, films were too expensive for schools to use for other than special occasions. There was also resistance on the part of the educational establishment to acknowledge the educational value of this "frivolous" new invention. Its very success as an entertainment medium automatically made it suspect as an educational tool.

The first extensive use of film as an educational medium occurred during World War I, outside the classroom, when psychologists

Thomas A. Edison.

Flashback: Mr. Edison's Dream

working with the U.S. Army produced a series of training films on venereal disease. The research techniques used to determine the effectiveness of those films set the pattern for research in film evaluation for several decades.

After World War I, several prestigious organizations combined forces to produce a series of American history films that became known as the *Yale Chronicles of America Photoplays*. This series of films was also the subject of extensive research and documented for the first time the effectiveness of films in direct instruction, even though the films were considerably handicapped because they were made in the "silent" era.

When sound on film finally did become a reality, many educators resisted its use in educational films. They felt that by putting a sound track on a film the producer was imposing external standards on every class in the country. They insisted that teachers should be free to narrate their own films according to principles and practices prescribed locally. Teacher narration of films was a notion favored by theorists and administrators but not by practitioners. (Anyone who has ever attempted to narrate a film knows what a difficult task it can be.) Some administrators also resisted the use of sound films in the classroom because this newer technology made existing inventories of silent film projectors and silent films obsolete. Eventually, of course, films incorporating sound were to become commonplace in the instructional setting.

World War II gave an even greater impetus to the educational use of films than had World War I. In a crash program to train Americans in the skills necessary to produce weapons of war, the Office of Education engaged in an extensive program of film production under the leadership of Floyde Brooker. Most of the films produced by the Office of Education were technical. (A typical title was *Turning Between Centers on the Metal Lathe*.) Although educational quality was uppermost in the minds of the production teams

under Brooker, there was no opportunity to do any extensive formative evaluation. The armed forces, however, also produced films during this period for training purposes and their research indicated that films (and other audiovisual media) contributed significantly to the success of their training programs.

The success of instructional technology, including film, in achieving war-related instructional objectives created sentiment among educators and lay-people alike for more widespread use of this technology in the nation's schools. *(Reader's Digest,* for example, asked rhetorically, "Can Our Schools Teach the GI Way?" and strongly urged that they do so.)

While the publishing industry in general was reluctant to get into the unfamiliar territory of motion pictures, Albert Rosenberg, who had worked with Floyde Brooker in the Office of Education, convinced the McGraw–Hill Book Company that it should create what was to become known as its Text–Film Division. McGraw–Hill quickly developed an impressive catalog of instructional films for colleges and universities as well as for public schools. Slowly other companies joined McGraw–Hill and Ency-

Floyde Brooker directing one of the wartime training films of the U.S. Office of Education.

clopaedia Britannica Films (which had been formed in 1938 through purchase of ERPI[a], the first company to produce educational films in quantity) in producing films for the school and college market. Coronet Films, for example, became one of the largest producers of educational films, along with Young America Films, later purchased by McGraw–Hill.

The late 1950s witnessed the introduction of 8-mm film into education. Cartridged, looped 8-mm films were introduced by Technicolor Incorporated. These cartridged films quickly acquired the title "single concept films" because they concentrated on presenting a single event or process for student study. Because 8-mm cartridges are easily inserted in their projectors and the projectors are small, portable, and simple to use, they lent themselves particularly well to individual and small-group study and to incorporation into programs of individualized instruction.

The introduction of 8-mm film also gave considerable impetus to the movement toward student-produced films. Although some school districts, Denver, for example, had previously been active in film production, 16-mm film was not, by and large, a very satisfactory medium for school production of films. With 8-mm however, film, camera, and projector became easier to handle and less expensive. Once 8-mm film was introduced into the schools, school —

---

[a]Education Research Products, Inc. Maurice Mitchell, when president of EBF, was fond of commenting that he was not sure if ERPI was a company or a condition.

produced motion pictures became much more common. Soon student film festivals were being held on a regular basis at local, state, and national levels.

In the meantime, as sales of 16-mm educational films increased, commercial publishers were encouraged to produce film "packages." Along with the individual film for a specific learning objective, companies began to market series of films to be incorporated as major components of various courses. This trend led in the late 1950s to the introduction of complete courses on film. Encyclopædia Britannica Films, for example, produced a complete course in high-school physics, consisting of 162 half-hour films in color.

Educational television soon became the primary source of most filmed courses used in the instructional setting, and, with the rise of videotape technology, television itself, both educational and commercial, became a major force in the growing use of recorded moving images for instructional purposes.

Mr. Edison's dream of the immediate and overwhelming impact of the film on education may have been a little fuzzy around the edges—as dreams sometimes are—but it was not, after all, so far off the mark. It took a quarter century longer than the Wizard of Menlo Park had anticipated for the film to become an important factor in education and another quarter century for it to reach its present state of instructional prominence. His dream did come true, in its own time and in its more realistic way—as dreams sometimes do.

ATTRIBUTES OF FILM

Because most of us are inclined to think of the film as a medium designed primarily to produce a "realistic" image of the world around us, we tend to forget that a basic attribute of the moving image (whether recorded photographically on film or electronically on videotape) is its ability to *manipulate* temporal and spatial

perspectives. Filmic manipulation of time and space not only serves dramatic and creative ends, it also has important implications for instruction.

Manipulation of Space

Film permits us to view phenomena in microcosm and macrocosm—that is, at extremely close range or from a vast distance.

Charles and Ray Eames made a film called *Powers of Ten* that within a few minutes takes us from a close-in observation of a man lying on a beach to a view of the man as observed from distances

expressed as increasing powers of ten until he disappears from sight. Perspective then changes quickly in the reverse direction and the film ends with a microscopic view of the man's skin. A similar effect can be seen in a National Film Board of Canada film titled *Cosmic Zoom*. This film starts with a microscopic examination of the skin of someone in a rowboat and then moves farther and farther away until we lose track of the individual entirely and, from some vantage point far from earth, we see only the world of which he is a part. Both films are extremely effective examples of how film can manipulate spatial perspective.

Alteration of Time

Film permits us to move through space in what might be called altered time. The *Cosmic Zoom* film shows movement through space in continuous time and far faster than we could possibly move in reality. But we can also take out pieces of time, so to speak, as we move through space. For example, we are all familiar with the type of film sequence in which two automobiles approach each other at high speed and the film is suddenly cut to a scene showing the wreckage of both cars. Time has been taken out of that sequence but we all accept the fact that the two cars did come together in real continuous time. In other words, film convinces us that we have witnessed an event even when we have not seen it in its entirety. This is an important convention for educational as well as entertainment films. For example, it would take an impossibly long time for students actually to witness a high-

Figure 8.5 *Cosmic Zoom.*

way being constructed, but a carefully edited film of the different activities that go into building a highway can recreate the essentials of such an event in a few minutes.

Compression of Time: Time-lapse

Film can compress the time that it takes for an event to occur. We have all seen films of flowers slowly opening before our eyes. Simple arithmetic indicates that if a process normally takes four hours and we want to be able to see that process in one minute on the screen, then a single picture must be taken of that process every 10 seconds. When projected at normal sound speed, the process will be shown in one minute. This technique has important instructional uses. For example, the process of a chrysalis turning

into a butterfly is too slow for classroom observation. However, through time-lapse cinematography, the butterfly can emerge from the chrysalis in a matter of minutes on the screen. (Renowned British composer Sir Michael Tippett attributes the inspiration for his fourth symphony to seeing a time-lapse film of the growth of a single cell into a baby—an interesting instance of one medium triggering creativity in another.)

Expansion of Time: Slow Motion

Time can also be expanded by film. Some events are too fast to be seen by the naked eye. By photographing these events at extremely high speeds and then projecting the film at normal speed we are able to observe what is happening. For example, when a lightbulb is struck with a hammer, it is impossible to determine with the naked eye whether an explosion or an implosion has taken place. But by high-speed cinematography we can see the precise sequence of events. A chameleon catches an insect too rapidly for the naked eye to observe. High-speed cinematography can slow down the motion so that the process can be observed.

Figure 8.6 *The Monarch Butterfly.*

Figure 8.7 Slow motion: attained by exposing more than 24 frames (up to several thousand) frames of film per second.

Revealing the Unseen World

Films can help us observe operation of objects we normally cannot see. For example, X-ray cinematography can show how bones move during certain bodily motions or how the valves of the heart work.

Arrested Motion: Freeze Framing

Films permit us to isolate components of an event for detailed study. For example, the film maker can select any image in a motion sequence and print that image over and over again so that one moment is held frozen on the screen. We are all familiar with this technique in television and in feature films. It is also extremely useful in instructional films; for example, freezing a pole vaulter to allow study of the athlete's technique at various stages of the vault.

Moving the Motionless: Animation

Time and space can also be manipulated in animated films. Animation is a technique in which the film maker gives motion to otherwise inanimate objects. If such an object is photographed, then moved a very short distance and photographed on one frame of film, moved again, then photographed again, and so on, the object when projected will look as though it has been continuously moving through space. There are various and sophisticated techniques for achieving animation, but basically animation is made up of a series of photographs of small displacements in space of objects or images. The film *Frame by Frame* (Figure 8.9) illustrates various animation techniques. Animation, however, can even be achieved without the use of a camera. As popularized by Canadian film maker Norman McLaren,

Figure 8.8 Action is "frozen" by repeated printing of the same image over an extended series of frames.

Figure 8.9 *Frame by Frame*.

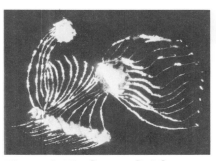

Figure 8.10 *Begone Dull Care*.

images may be drawn directly on film, which, when projected sequentially, will give the illusion of movement. (Flip the pages of this chapter backwards from p. 210 to the beginning of Chapter 8.)

Computer-Generated Animation

Animation can also be achieved by the use of computers. The animated images generated by the computer can be displayed on a cathode-ray tube and then photographed by a motion picture camera, or they can be electronically imprinted directly on videotape. While computer-generated images have generally been of interest primarily for aesthetic reasons, a number of instructional films have used computer animation techniques. One such effort is a very effective film in the mathematics of topology titled *Turning a Sphere Inside Out*.

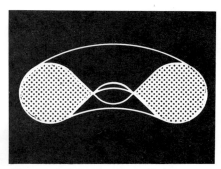

Figure 8.11 *Turning a Sphere Inside Out*.

UNDERSTANDING FILM CONVENTIONS

The devices and techniques used in film making to manipulate time and space are for almost all of us readily accepted conventions. We understand that the athlete whose jump is stopped in mid-air is not actually frozen in space, that the flashback is not an actual reversal of our normal time continuum, that the light bulb does not really disintegrate slowly enough for us to see that it implodes rather than explodes. As instructors, however, we must keep in mind that our ability to make sense out of film conventions is an acquired skill. When do children learn to handle flashbacks, dissolves, jump cuts, etc? Unfortunately, we know very little about when and how children learn to make sense of filmic manipulation of reality, and much research on the matter remains to be done.

Some insight into the kind of difficulties that may be encountered in the instructional situation because of student inability to handle film conventions can be gleaned from the experiences of film makers involved with adults unfamiliar with standard film conventions.

After World War II, film crews from the United States were sent to various parts of the world to make instructional films designed to help the people better their skills in farming, housing, sanitation, etc. One crew member working in rural Iran noted that in the United States moviemakers could have a man walk out a door in lower Manhattan and immediately pick him up in another shot at Times Square. In Iran this technique was not possible. Viewers there would insist that the man be shown making the journey to Times Square. In other words, rural Iranians, because they were at that time unfamiliar with the conventions of time–space manipulations, could not accept this filmic view of reality.

John Wilson, another American film producer of the period, commented:

We found that the film is, as produced in the West, a very highly conventionalized piece of symbolism, although it looks very real. For instance, we found that if you were telling a story about two men to an African audience and one had finished his business and he went off the edge of the screen, they wanted to know what happened to him; they didn't accept that this was just the end of him and that he was of no more interest to the story....We had to follow him along a street until he took a natural turn.... It was quite understandable that he could disappear around the turn. The action had to follow a natural course of events.... *

The film is not, of course, alone among media in its reliance upon accepted conventions for interpretation and appreciation. Flashback techniques are regularly used in literature and usually accepted by readers. The theatrical convention of the "aside" is readily accepted by playgoers. The following anecdote about Picasso illustrates how a new artistic convention may seem to the uninitiated to be merely a distortion of reality rather than, as intended, a particular and valid view of reality. It also illustrates how a convention (in this case a convention of photography) can become so readily accepted and commonplace that we are amusingly surprised at being reminded it exists.

Picasso showed an American soldier through his villa one day, and on completion of the tour the young man felt compelled to confess that he didn't dig Picasso's weird way of painting, because nothing on the canvas looked the way it really is. Picasso turned the conversation to more acceptable matters by asking the soldier if he had a girl back in the States. The boy proudly pulled out a wallet photograph. As Picasso handed it back, he said "She's an attractive girl, but isn't she awfully small?" *

A word should also be said here about the bearing of experiential and cultural background on interpretation of films and film conventions. As with all other media, what the viewer brings to the film determines what he or she takes from it. In *American Time Capsule*, a Charles Braverman film about the history of the United States, for example, even if the student were able to handle the film convention of rapid projection of briefly glimpsed images on a screen, the film would be virtually meaningless if the viewer had no experiential background in American history.

As to the importance of cultural determination of filmic interpretation, perhaps it will suffice to note that in Thailand, each episode of television's *Laverne and Shirley* begins with the following announcement in Thai: "These women are from an insane asylum." Apparently, this is the only context in which the Thai culture can accept the antics of these two United States culture heroines.

---

*Joan Rosengren Forsdale and Louis Forsdale. "Film Literacy," *The Teachers College Record,* May 1966, p. 612.

---

*Ibid, p. 609.

SOME INSTRUCTIONAL ADVANTAGES OF FILM

The film's ability to manipulate time and space has, as noted earlier, important instructional implications. Let us now consider several other related characteristics of film and look at just a few of the ways they can be turned to instructional advantage.

1. The most obvious instructional characteristic of film is its ability to show *motion*. This characteristic gives the film a distinct advantage over all other media for use in instructional situations in which the concept or depiction of motion can contribute to the learning process.

2. Film can present a *process* more effectively than other media. For example, industrial operations (manufacturing processes, assembly-line operations, etc.) can be observed and studied through use of film, with the

Figure 8.12 On-the-job operational processes can be depicted realistically on film.

camera offering manipulated views of such processes unobtainable with other media. Difficult-to-observe scientific experiments, such as measuring the speed of light, can be shown easily by means of film.

3. Film permits *safe observation* of phenomena that might be hazardous to view directly, for example, total eclipse of the sun or hazardous scientific experiments and demonstrations. Violent or disruptive events can also be safely presented on film—natural disasters, such as a volcanic eruption, or violence stemming from human activities.

4. Research has shown that films are particularly useful in teaching *skills*. Learning a skill is likely to require repetition of observation and effort before the skill is mastered. Film can present the skill over and over again for observation and emulation (8-mm-loop films are particularly good for this purpose).

Figure 8.14 Discrete skills can be observed close-up and repeatedly via film.

Figure 8.13 The eruption of Mt. St. Helens: destructive in real life, instructive on film.

Figure 8.15 Problems in human relations can be dramatized, as in *Leadership: Style or Substance.*

Figure 8.16 *Roots.*

5. The ability of film *to dramatize* events and situations makes it particularly suitable for instruction in the social sciences and humanities. Dramatizations can bring historical personages and events to life. It can deepen the student's understanding and appreciation of the creative merit of literary works. Students can learn to deal with human relations problems by observing problem situations (particularly helpful in business and industrial programs designed to train personnel to handle difficult human relationship situations expeditiously and graciously).

6. Because of their great *emotional impact*, films are very useful for teaching and learning within the affective domain. Personal and social attitudes can be changed by films designed to do so. A film on oral hygiene, for example, can lead a child to develop better dental care habits. Documentaries and commercial "message-films," such as *Roots,* (Figure 8.16) can change social, cultural,

and political attitudes, for adults as well as children. The Payne Fund Studies in the early 1930s demonstrated that children's attitudes toward minority groups can be influenced by the films that they see.

7. Open-ended filmic episodes can be used effectively in *problem-solving* instructional situations. For example, a problem situation can be

Figure 8.17 *Face to Face.*

dramatized on film and its resolution left to the class to discover through group discussion, or through individual written assignments if ability to express ideas in writing is part of the learning objective.

8. The subtleties of *unfamiliar cultures* and their relation to our own can be effectively captured on film for observation and discussion. A film on Eskimo life, for example, will help students understand the influence of physical environment on lifestyle. A film depicting life in a developing nation will help students appreciate the impact of modernization on traditional cultures. A film on the marriage rites of an exotic people will lead to better understanding of the relationship between culture and sexual mores. In recent years, ethnographers have

Figure 8.18 Although not a true ethnographic film in itself, *Nanook of the North* vividly portrayed the impact of modernization on traditional life-styles.

become prolific producers of films, an effective way to document indigenous lifestyles, particularly those of primitive cultures. Some examples of excellent feature-length ethnographic films* are: *The Hunters, The Tribe that Hides from Man, The Nuer, River of Sand.* Examples of shorter ethnographic films are: *Gravel Springs Fife and Drum, Mosori Monika,* and the series of films by Julien Bryan on the *Indians of South America.*

9. Films *command attention* in the instructional situation. Eye movement studies, for example, show that when a student has lost interest in

Figure 8.19 Through dramatization, film can simplify the complexity of management problems, as in *Performance Appraisal.*

the image on the screen, his attention can be immediately regained by altering the rhythm of the images on the screen.

10. The *cuing power* of the film in the instructional situation is likely to be greater than that of other media. Techniques such as close-ups and image-freezing can direct the attention of the student to specific aspects of instruc-

tion and isolate key components of the situation to be understood or the problem to be solved, thereby minimizing irrelevant cues. Irrelevant cues may also be minimized by filming only the essential elements of a process or situation. Training films often use this technique, especially for novices in the program.

11. Films, of course, are ideal media for instruction of *heterogeneous groups with common interests* and/or learning objectives. They can be shown to large or small audiences, with a minimum of instructor intervention, within the formal educational setting (a film on how a bill becomes law shown to students of government, for example) or outside such a setting (a film on company operations shown to management trainees).

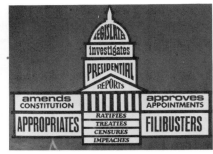

Figure 8.20 *U. S. Congress.*

*Producer and distributor sources of all films in this chapter can be found in the NICEM *Index to 16mm Films,* and rental sources are in *The Educational Film Locator of the Consortium of University Film Centers.* See Appendix A for details.

This list of instructional values shows that films are useful in many ways in all areas of the curriculum. Social studies benefits especially from the ability of film to recreate the past and to document how people live. The film's dramatic and expressive powers are of particular value to the language arts and literature. Science makes extensive use of film's ability to make processes and relationships clear. Better mathematics films use the graphic ability of film to represent mathematical functions and relationships. The capability of films to present real life situations is extremely useful in training supervisory personnel.

Because of the power of films, teachers need to be very careful about the possibility of creating misinterpretations or of reinforcing socially undesirable attitudes. For example, students who have not yet mastered understanding of film conventions may not interpret a film the way in which the film maker intended. The film *Phoebe* uses a stream-of-consciousness approach as the protagonist fantasizes about what the reactions of parents and boyfriend (Paul) to her announcement of her pregnancy will be, and as she recalls details of her relationship with Paul. A number of students (and parents) have misinterpreted the speculations and memories of a tortured mind as being the attitude of the film maker toward all involved in the story. Teachers have used the film *Toys* (Figure 8.21) with upper elementary students, partly because that age group is featured in the film. However, fourth and fifth graders are so absorbed with the virtuoso animation of toys engaged in hectic battle that they never get past the surface excitement to see the antiwar message that impresses the adult viewer. Many guidance films use dramatized situations to provoke discussion of the problems explored. Some of the role models portrayed, however, may be very appealing to students. For example, in *I Dare You* from the *Inside/Out* series, the characters are very likeable and the pranks they play are appealingly daring. Improperly handled, the film could easily be a lesson in imitation—the last thing the producer or teacher wants! A teacher must continually check not only to be sure that the desired outcomes from film showings are being achieved, but also that undesirable side effects are not being produced.

Figure 8.21 *Toys*.

LIMITATIONS OF FILM

As with all other instructional media there are, of course, limitations to the instructional effectiveness and value of film. The film is not the best medium for all instructional purposes and in all instructional situations. For example, although a film may be stopped and one frame held on the screen for detailed study or discussion, a filmstrip or set of slides would be better for study of a sequence of still phenomena, such as a series of maps. Remember, too, that not every student's mind runs at 24 frames per second.

Film is exceedingly expensive, and rapidly becoming more so because of the increasing cost of raw film stock (the price of silver has made black-and-white film nearly as costly as color film). Although video tapes are less expensive than films, they are still considerably more expensive than filmstrips or slides.

Partly because of the high cost, most instructional films are purchased through district, regional, or state agencies and kept in more or less centrally located collections rather than in individual schools. This means that films must usually be ordered well in advance of their scheduled class use. Careful planning is required to ensure proper correlation between film arrival and its scheduled use. Without such planning, an expensive, albeit valuable, instructional medium could well be wasted.

LOCATING AND APPRAISING FILMS

As mentioned above, because of the high cost of 16-mm films and the impracticality of local production, an individual school or small organization is unlikely to have its own film collection. So most instructors must acquire films on loan from an outside agency—the school district, state library, or university rental library, for instance. A basic resource for you, then, is a collection of catalogs of those rental agencies you are most likely to turn to for films. To be more thorough in your searching you will want *The Educational Film Locator*, a comprehensive listing of the films that are available in various rental collections. If you are just beginning your search you should consult the *Index to 16mm Educational Films* or the *Index to 8mm Motion Cartridges* published by the National Information Center for Educational Media (NICEM), as a means of finding out just what films are currently available overall; it provides listings according to subject to aid your search. Details on these and other directories are found in Appendix A.

After a film has been identified, located, and acquired, you will want to preview and appraise it carefully.

Official appraisal forms for films used in schools vary considerably among school districts and regional agencies. Some are meticulously drawn up to cover almost all conceivable criteria for rating a film as to its usefulness in a given teaching/learning situation. Others rate films in a much more perfunctory manner. A good appraisal form should not only help agencies choose films that will be most useful in future instructional situations, but also should provide a public record that can be used to justify the purchase of specific titles. Comparative cost effectiveness of instructional methods is always on the minds of training directors and school and college administrators. Purchase of expensive materials such as films must be justified by carefully planned selection procedures. (See accountability section in Chapter 14.) The appraisal form included on page 200 is one that has proved useful for selecting films that will contribute to the instructional program.

As mentioned in Chapter 2, you should also construct and keep a card file of film notes for your personal use. Your specific instructional purposes may be somewhat different or even quite different from the general instructional needs catered to on an official form. Included here is an example of a card form that can help you make best use of the films available to you. Fill out the card form after using the film and add or modify entries after each use of the film.

PERSONAL FILM RECORD

Title_____ Format [16 mm, 8 mm, video?][a]_____
Length___Source [where you got it]___B/W___Color___Sound___
Synopsis:_____
_____
_____
_____
_____

Style of production [documentary, animation, narration, open-ended]_____

Utilization pointers and problems: [vocabulary, controversial topic or treatment, introduction needed, supplementary materials needed, etc.]_____
_____
_____

Follow-up activities:_____
_____

---

[a]Notations in brackets would not appear on form. They indicate the kind and character of the information to be entered on form.

APPRAISAL CHECKLIST: FILM

Title_____ Format __16 mm

Producer/distributor_____ __8 mm

Date (if known)_____ Length_____ __other

Audience/grade level_____ _____

Subject area(s)_____ __color

__black/white

Objectives (stated or implied):

Brief description (include presentation style: animated, dramatic, etc.):

Entry capabilities required:

—language ability
—prior subject matter knowledge

RATING

	High	Medium	Low
Likely to arouse student interest	☐ ☐	☐ ☐	☐
Technical quality	☐ ☐	☐ ☐	☐
Opportunity for viewer participation	☐ ☐	☐ ☐	☐
Relevance to curriculum (or learning task)	☐ ☐	☐ ☐	☐
Accuracy of information	☐ ☐	☐ ☐	☐
Scope of content	☐ ☐	☐ ☐	☐
Organization of content	☐ ☐	☐ ☐	☐
Student comprehension	☐ ☐	☐ ☐	☐

Strong points:

Weak points:

Reviewer_____

Position_____

Recommended action_____ Date_____

SPONSORED FILMS

Private companies, associations, and government agencies sponsor films for a variety of reasons. Private companies may make films to promote products or to enhance their public image. Associations and government agencies sponsor films to promote causes: better health habits, conservation of natural resources, proper use of park and recreation areas. Many of these sponsored films make worthwhile instructional materials. They also have the considerable advantage of being free.

A certain amount of caution, however, is called for in using sponsored films for instructional purposes. Some private-company films may be too flagrantly self-serving. Or they may deal with products not very suitable for certain instructional settings: the making of alcoholic beverages, the production of cigarettes. Some association and government films may contain a sizable dose of propaganda or special pleading for pet causes along with their content. Ralph Nader's Center for the Study of Responsive Law has issued a report highly critical of instructional materials distributed free by industry.* It claims that many sponsored materials subtly influence the curriculum in socially undesirable ways. Certainly you must preview sponsored films.

Properly selected, many sponsored films can be valuable additions to classroom instruction. The best single source of information on sponsored films is the *Educator's Guide to Free Films*. Details on this and similar "free and inexpensive" sources are given in Appendix B.

DOCUMENTARIES: FROM NEWSREEL AND TRAVELOGUE TO CINÉMA VÉRITÉ AND DOCUDRAMA

Broadly speaking, the *documentary* deals with fact, not fiction or fictionalized versions of fact. As such, it has long held a special place in the use of films for instructional purposes. Through the work of film makers such as Robert Flaherty in the United States and John Grierson in England, the documentary has also acquired a reputation for artistic merit.

Grierson defined the documentary as "a creative treatment of actuality." He believed that the documentary should have a point of view, that it should be a vehicle for presenting and interpreting "human problems and their solutions in the spheres of economics, culture, and human relations." Thus, Grierson, Flaherty, and other like-minded film makers inaugurated the concept of the documentary as a socially significant film form rather than merely a

Figure 8.22   John Grierson.

Figure 8.23   Robert Flaherty and crew on location.

---

*Sheila Harty. *Hucksters in the Classroom: A Review of Industry Propaganda in the Schools*. Washington D.C.: Center for Study of Responsive Law, 1980.

Figure 8.24 The making of *Nanook of the North*.

Figure 8.25 *The River*.

vehicle for presentation of news-reel footage and "travelogue" material. Flaherty's film on the Eskimos of Hudson Bay, *Nanook of the North,* is generally credited with generating world-wide recognition of the documentary as a distinct film genre. (Figure 8.24).

The advent of sound on film gave further impetus to the growth and development of the documentary. By the late 1930s many countries had inaugurated documentary film units or were commissioning documentaries from independent producers. In the United States important and classic documentaries were produced both by government film units (e.g., *The River, Power and the Land*) and by independent film units (e.g., *The City, Valleytown, And So They Live*). In Great Britain, government units produced documentary classics such as *Night Mail* and *Song of Ceylon* (Figure 8.26). In Spain renowned feature-film director Luis Buñuel made the striking film, *Las Hurdes* (released in the United States as *Land Without Bread*). In Belgium Henri Storck directed what is regarded by many as the classic film on slums and slum clearance, *Les Maisons de la Misére* (1937). In the Soviet Union the work of

Figure 8.26 The making of *Song of Ceylon*.

Figure 8.27 *Olympia*.

Dziga Vertov culminated in the technical and conceptual tour de force, *Man with a Movie Camera* (1929). In Germany, the two controversial but classic films by Leni Riefenstahl, *Triumph of the Will* (a film of the Nazy Party Congress of 1934) and *Olympia* (the 1936 Olympic games in Berlin) were prominent among a number of other powerful documentaries.

Newsreels were a standard part of commercial movie programs in the 1930s and 1940s. Presented before the showing of the feature film, newsreels were little more than illustrated headlines depicting current news in segmented and superficial form. *The March of Time* (1934) took a different approach—a documentary approach. For an average length

Figure 8.28 Over the years *The March of Time* documented such events as World War II war bond rallies led by show business celebrities.

of 18 minutes, *The March of Time* examined one topic in reasonable depth and often with a point of view (Figure 8.28). Today, many of *The March of Time* films are still

valuable because they are historical perspectives of critical events and issues. For example, the *March of Time* film, *Palestine*, made before the state of Israel was formed, gives students an opportunity to examine a current issue from a unique historical point of view.

In World War II, the documentary was widely used by all combatants in training programs and for propaganda purposes. More than a few "propaganda" documentaries, however, also had lasting artistic and historical merit and many still serve instructional purposes—John Huston's *Battle of San Pietro*, for example, and Humphrey Jennings's *The Silent Village* and *Diary for Timothy*.

The documentary has always been an important training ground for directors and cinematographers, and the post World War II period saw a number of documentaries made by people who later became well known for their work in feature films: Alain Resnais's *Night and Fog*, Tony Richardson's

Figure 8.29 *Battle of San Pietro.*

Figure 8.30 *The Selling of the Pentagon.*

Momma Don't Allow, Lindsay Anderson's *Every Day but Christmas*, etc.

Today television has become the prime influence on the continuing development of documentary films. The commercial networks, primarily through their news departments, and the Public Broadcasting System regularly produce and broadcast significant documentaries that are later released in 16-mm-film form. Programs such as *Sixteen in Webster Groves*, *The Selling of the Pentagon, Yo Soy Chicano*, and the Jacques Cousteau and National Geographic specials are examples of outstanding TV documentaries that have wide use in education as 16-mm films.

The term *cinéma vérité* is the French translation of the Russian term *kino pravda* (film truth), coined by Russian director Dziga Vertov. In recent years, the term has come to be identified with a film-making technique in which the camera becomes either an *intimate observer* of or a *direct participant* in the events being documented.

The advocates of *cinéma vérité* as an observer technique thrust their cameras and sound equipment into the action, following it wherever it may lead. Films such as *Lonely Boy* (on the early career of pop singer Paul Anka), *Primary* (about the 1960 primary contest between John Kennedy and Hubert Humphrey in Wisconsin), and *Warrendale* (about a home for disturbed children) are examples of this type of *cinéma vérité*.

Camera and microphone may also become part of the action in *cinéma vérité*—that is a "provoca-

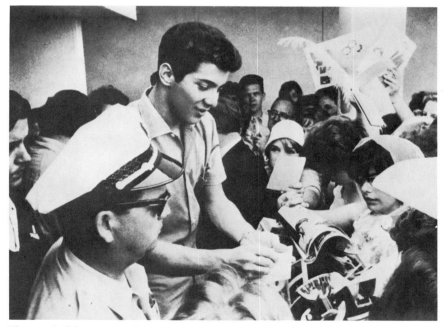

Figure 8.31 *Lonely Boy.*

Figure 8.32 *The Sorrow and the Pity.*

teur" of events or theme development. The penetrating but unobtrusive interview in which participants often seem to be interviewing themselves is a hallmark of this technique. Outstanding examples of this approach are the films of Marcel Ophuls such as *The Sorrow and the Pity* (about French resistance to and collaboration with the Nazi conquerors of France in World War II).

Documentaries such as those noted above, as well as films such as Frederick Wiseman's *High School, Hospital*, and *Law and Order*, which combine the *cinéma vérité* techniques of camera and microphone as intimate observer *and* participant, are provocative discussion and learning materials, especially for students involved in or being trained to become involved in the institutions portrayed in the documentaries and for students with special interest in sociopolitical themes.

Documentaries have also become an important historical record and source of information about cultural lifestyles fast disappearing from the American scene. The Foxfire program, for example, which began in Rabun Gap–Nacoochee School in Georgia with student publication of *Foxfire*, a magazine devoted to document-

ing disappearing local skills such as how to make soap or how to make an ox cart, also resulted in several films, including *Foxfire* and *Aunt Arie*. Films such as *Tinker, The Last Pony Mine, Gravel Springs Fife and Drum*, and *The Bakery* (Canada) document and record disappearing trades and sociocultural mores.

Almost all present-day documentaries contain a social or political message, stated or implied, and evaluation of this message is, of course, part of the teaching/learning process. Normally, the documentary's point of view is not too difficult to ascertain and evaluate. A relatively new development,

Figure 8.33 *The Last Pony Mine.*

however, the "docudrama," has complicated the process. In general, the docudrama is a dramatization (with actors) of current newsworthy events and trends, rather than creative reportage. Although the makers of docudramas insist their films are dramatizations of fact, not fiction, the line between "docu" and "drama" may sometimes be difficult for the viewer to draw. Evaluation of point of view may, hence, also be comparatively difficult.

The 1980 film *Death of a Princess* (Figure 8.34), which dramatized the search of an English journalist for the truth behind published reports that a young Saudi Arabian princess and her lover had recently been publicly executed for adultery at the instigation of her royal father, is a prime example of the docudrama genre. Shown on PBS, the film generated considerable controversy. Did it document Saudi-Arabian ruling-class mores and Islamic legal principles? Or did it dramatize them in such a way that fiction prevailed over fact?

Figure 8.34 *Death of a Princess.*

EFFECTIVE FILM USE: THE ASSURE MODEL

Six basic procedures are essential to the effective use of film in the instructional setting, and, indeed, the effective use of all instructional media, as noted in our discussion of the ASSURE model of learning in Chapter 2. Let us see how the use of film fits the ASSURE model.

Analyze Learners

Your first step is to assess your audience. Obviously a docudrama such as *Death of a Princess* would not be appropriate material for a fifth-grade class studying foreign cultures. The limited experiential background of the class would negate the film's instructional value as a portrayal of culture clash.

State Objectives

Your next step is to define and state the learning objectives you wish to achieve by using the film. Only then will you be in a position to select the right film to reach those objectives.

Select Materials

Ideally you should preview your film selection before showing it to the class to be sure it meets your teaching/learning criteria. Unfortunately, preview is not always pos-

sible. You may have to rely on official appraisal forms and/or teacher-guide materials that accompany the film, or, if you have used the film before, on your personal appraisal form. Once you have selected your film, you may wish to tailor its use to meet your instructional needs. To use only part of the film you will have to cue parts of the film separately for showing. You may wish to stop the film at various points for class or teacher discussion. Perhaps you will decide you need to use supplementary materials in order to reach your objectives. You may, for example, note that the film you have chosen for a geography lesson does not contain a map of the area under discussion. You will, then, want to make sure that such a map is available in the viewing area for student reference.

Utilize Materials

Do not present the film cold. Effective utilization of the film as an instructional medium requires that it be effectively introduced. Students should be given some idea of the content of the film you are about to present and informed how the content relates to the learning objectives involved. You may wish to alert them to particular features of the film that relate to these objectives. Include special instructions in your introductory "advance organizer." Perhaps new

Figure 8.37

vocabulary words contained in the film need to be explained prior to its showing. Discuss any concepts not likely to have been previously encountered by the students.

Require Learner Response

Follow-up activities for reinforcement of learning should include class discussion of the film's content, particularly points of the film that directly relate to your learning objectives. They may also include individual and small-group discussion of the film, library work, writing assignments, or other similar activities. Films are powerful motivators. Be prepared to take advantage of this film attribute with effective and diverse follow-up activities designed to reinforce and encourage new or increased interests.

Figure 8.38

Figure 8.35

Figure 8.36

AV Showmanship—Film Projection

General guides to projection practice are in Chapter 10. Some additional advice is necessary for film projection.

Many classrooms have a wall-mounted screen in the front of the room. In many of these classrooms, unfortunately, the door is also near the front of the room and often has a large window in it or a window area beside it. If light from the hall interferes with the brightness of the projected image, you may have to cover part or all of the window area with poster board or butcher paper. If this is not possible, move the projector closer to the screen to get a brighter picture. Remember that a smaller, brighter image is better than a larger, dimmer one.

You should always set the focus and note the correct sound level before the class assembles; then turn the volume knob back down to zero and run the film back to the beginning. Some films have focus and sound level adjustment footage before the start of the film. If so, you can properly set focus and sound before you reach the beginning of the film.

It is *not* good showmanship to project the academy leader (the strip of film with the number sequence on it). The first image the audience should see is the title or opening scene of the film.

When ready, start the projector, turn on the lamp, and turn the volume knob to the predetermined level (this is particularly important when the film has no introductory music). Fine adjust the focus and sound after you start the projector.

Most projectors must run a few seconds before the sound system stabilizes. Therefore, if you stop the film to discuss a particular sequence, the viewers may miss the first few seconds of narration or dialogue when you start the projector. If so, turn the volume knob down, back up the film a few feet, start the projector, turn on the lamp, and then turn up the sound.

When the film is over, turn off the lamp, turn down the sound, and stop the projector. Run the rest of the film footage through after class. Rewind the film after class if you are going to show it again. If you are not showing it again, and if you used the same size reel the film came on, you need not rewind the film. The agency you got it from will rewind the film during routine inspection. Before putting the film back in the container, fasten down the end of the film with a piece of tape. The film normally arrives with the film held down with tape. Peel it off and stick it on the projection cart so that you can use it later to hold the end down. The film is better protected when this is done.

Evaluate

Your evaluation of the film as an effective or ineffective instructional instrument will be at least partly based on class discussion of the film and your observation of student response to its content. Tests based on learning objectives will contribute further, and perhaps more reliable, data on which to base your evaluation. When your evaluation is completed, enter the results on your personal appraisal form.

THE FILM AS AN ART FORM

Although we are primarily concerned with the film as an instructional medium, we should keep in mind that the film is also an art form and can be studied and appreciated as an aesthetic experience in much the same manner as literature and the fine arts. Marshall McLuhan once commented that introduction of a new technology tends to make an art form out of the preceding one, and, indeed, it was only after the introduction of television that film

achieved general and widespread acknowledgement as an art form.

Today, schools have come to accept the film (and film making) as an aesthetic experience worthy of study as such. In elementary schools, film as an aesthetic experience is widely regarded as a logical extension of language arts. In many high schools, film study is now incorporated as a unit in literature courses. Most colleges and universities have courses devoted to the study of film and many offer at least a minor in film study. The University of Southern California,

Figure 8.39

which, incidentally, established the first cinema department in an American university, offers a freshman course in film as an option in its required humanities sequence.

Both in high schools and in colleges, belonging to a film club and going to film showings as extracurricular activities have grown rapidly in recent years. Outside the educational setting, film societies dedicated to the aesthetic appreciation of films have sprung up in many communities. The availability of fine commercial films in 16-mm format and the establishment of collections of noteworthy film, foreign and domestic, in many public libraries have given considerable impetus to such activities.

The *Media File* included here presents some exemplary films representative of scores of films available for study and appreciation of the film as an art form (as well as for instruction, given the proper instructional situation). For lists of other films of this kind see Gaffney, *Films Kids Like*, and Parlato, *Super Films*, in the References at the end of this chapter.

MEDIA FILE: "The Loon's Necklace"

A classic film, *The Loon's Necklace*, uses the telling of a folk legend to reveal the social and cultural life of the Indians of the Pacific Northwest. The unique masks made by the Indians and shown to us on film tell us much about how they perceived themselves in relation to the forces of nature and to the supernatural.
Source: Encyclopædia Britannica Education Corporation.

MEDIA FILE: "The Hunter"

The Hunter portrays the excitement of a pre-teenage boy upon receiving a BB gun as a birthday present. After imagining himself as a soldier and then as a defender of an encircled wagon train, he sees a cardinal and kills it. As he reaches down to pick it up, the enormity of his act dawns upon him. The film ends with the boy slowly walking away from the dead bird. The low-key style of the film is very effective in rivetting attention on the main point of the film—that guns are not toys.
Source: ACI Films.

MEDIA FILE: "Pigs"

Another film classic, *Pigs!*, gives us a pig's eye view of pigs. Non-narrated, this film is an outstanding testimonial to the ability of film to transmit experience from one level of existence to another.
Source: Churchill Films.

MEDIA FILE: "Omega"

This is perhaps the most widely acclaimed film made by a student. *Omega*, a film by Donald Fox, is a tour de force of filmic and film-lab technique. The rather obscure storyline is concerned with death and rebirth. But the special effects, painstakingly executed by Fox under difficult conditions, are masterpieces of film art.
Source: Pyramid Films.

MEDIA FILE: "The Fat and the Lean"

Another film commentary on the human condition, this one by the controversial Polish director Roman Polanski, *The Fat and the Lean* is allegorical in form. It is probably the most political of a group of short films made by Polanski when he was a student.
Source: Pyramid Films.

MEDIA FILE: "The Adventures of *"

John Hubley started his film career with Disney, then became one of the founders of United Productions of America (UPA), innovators in animation. He and his wife, Faith, formed one of the most creative animation teams in the history of film, their films testing the limits of film conventions. *The Adventures of** *** is representative of their work and is a fascinating comment on the care and feeding of creativity.
Source: Story Board Films.

STUDENT-MADE FILMS

The introduction of 8-mm film as a replacement for the less easily handled and more expensive 16-mm film gave considerable impetus to the now relatively widespread production of student-made films in schools and colleges.

Considerable versatility was added to this format with the introduction of a method to record sound directly on the film while it is being exposed. The use of videotape and portable videotape equipment has also contributed to simplification of production of student-made films and has thus further stimulated this growing activity.

Many student-made films are produced in connection with secondary-school English programs, a natural extension of the English program's normal concern with literary communication and self-expression. A 16-mm film called *The Moving Image—8-mm* demonstrates vividly how one secondary school teacher, inexperienced in film production, organized and conducted her English class to produce films. Many very fine films have come out of such classes, and a few student-made films have even been accepted for commercial distribution.

Figure 8.40 Even elementary school-age students have produced their own 8-mm films successfully.

Figure 8.41 Ready to screen the final product.

THE FUTURE OF FILM

Recorded moving images will always have a firm place in instruction. Motion pictures and videotape have proved their usefulness in just about every kind of instructional situation. The main question is in what format will the moving image be displayed in the classroom of tomorrow. As of now videotapes have not made a significant impact on the use of commercially produced films. Surveys conducted at Indiana University* indicate that videotape is used primarily to distribute locally produced or recorded program material. However, the cost of videotape in comparison with film is making it more attractive as a substitute for film. If manufacturers of video equipment can perfect video projection to the point where large screen images are sharp and faithful in color rendition, the last obstacle to overtaking film as *the* medium for moving images will have been overcome.

By the time that has happened, however, videodisc may have replaced videotape as the most popular format. Because they can be mass produced like phonograph records, videodiscs will be considerably cheaper than video tape. Videodiscs are also a more versatile format for instructional purposes, as Chapter 9 points out. It could well be that in the future, film will be a "Flashback" in the chapter on video!

Report of Second Annual Survey of the Circulation of Educational Media in the Public Schools. Office of Media Studies, Audio-Visual Center, Indiana University, Bloomington, Indiana, 1978.

REFERENCES

Print References

Arwady, Joseph W. "The Oral Introduction to the Instructional Film: A Closer Look." *Educational Technology,* July 1980, pp. 18–22.

Blackowicz, Camille. "Media Techniques for the Reading Teacher." *Reading Horizons,* Spring 1977, pp. 181–182.

The Center for Vocational Education. *Present Information with Films* (Athens, GA: American Association for Vocational Instructional Materials, 1977).

Cox, Carole. "Films Children Like—and Dislike." *Language Arts,* March 1978, pp. 334–338.

———"Film Is Like Your Grandma's Preserved Pears." *Elementary English,* April 1975, pp. 515–519.

Epple, Ron. "Animation: Alive and Well." *Media & Methods,* April 1977, pp. 42–46.

Ferguson, Robert. *How to Make Movies* (New York: The Viking Press, 1969).

Finley, Otis E. "Using Super 8 As a Video Display Training Medium." *Training and Development Journal,* December 1975, pp. 36–38.

* Gaffney, Maureen (ed.). *Films Kids Like* (Chicago, IL: American Library Association, 1973).

* Gaffney, Maureen (ed.). *More Films Kids Like* (Chicago, IL: American Library Association, 1977).

Johnson, Stephen C. "Films for the Social Studies: Pedagogical Tools and Works of Art." *Social Education,* May 1976, pp. 264, 270–272.

* Marcus, Fred N. *Short Story/Short Film* (Englewood Cliffs, NJ: Prentice-Hall, 1977).

Mercer, John. *The Informational Film* (Champaign, IL: Stipes Publishing, 1981).

*Key references.

Parlato, Salvatore J., Jr. *Films Too Good For Words: A Directory of Non-Narrated 16-mm Films* (New York: Bowker, 1973).

* Parlato, Salvatore, J., Jr. *Superfilms: An International Guide to Award Winning Films* (Metuchen, NJ: The Scarecrow Press, 1976).

Parlato, Salvatore, J., Jr. "Those Other Captioned Films." *American Annals of the Deaf,* February 1977, pp. 33–37.

Rice, Susan. "Is Film Basic?" *Teacher,* May/June 1976, pp. 14–16.

Struck, H.R. "Twenty Well-Tested Films for Freshman Writing Courses." *College Composition and Communication,* February 1976, pp. 47–50.

Tortora, Vincent R., and Peter Schillaci. "The Educational Film Industry," *Preview,* October 1975, pp. 10–11.

Audiovisual References

"The American Super 8 Revolution." (New York: International Film Foundation, 1975). (16-mm film, 31 minutes, color.)

* "Basic Film Terms: A Visual Dictionary," (Santa Monica, CA: Pyramid Films, 1970). (16-mm film or videocassette, 15 minutes, color.)

"Basic Movie Making," (Rochester, NY: Eastman Kodak Co., 1973). (16-mm film, 14 minutes, color.)

* "Claymation," (Santa Monica, CA: Pyramid Films, 1980). (16-mm film, 18 minutes, color.)

* The Eye Hears and the Ear Sees," (Montreal, Canada: National Film Board of Canada, 1970). (16-mm film, 59 minutes, color.)

"Facts About Film," 2d ed. (Chicago, IL: International Film Bureau, 1975). (16-mm film or videocassette, 10 minutes, color.)

'Facts About Projection," 2d ed. (Chicago, IL: International Film Bureau, 1975). (16-mm film or videocassette, 14 minutes, color.)

"Frame by Frame: The Art of Animation." (Santa Monica, CA: Pyramid Films, 1973). (16-mm film or videocassette, 13 minutes, color.)

* "The Moving Image—8mm," (Bloomington, IN: Indiana University, 1976). (16-mm film, 27 minutes, color.)

"Odette's Ordeal." (Wilmette, IL: Films Incorporated, 1976). (16-mm film, 38 minutes, color.)

* "Project the Right Image," (Lincoln, NB: Great Plains ITV Library, 1976). (16-mm film or videocassette, 14 minutes, color.)

"So You Wanna Make a Film," (Lawrence, KS: Centron Films, 1980). (16-mm film or videocassette, 9 minutes, color.)

Organizations

American Film Institute
John F. Kennedy Center for the Performing Arts
Washington, DC 20566

American Library Association
50 E. Huron Street
Chicago, Illinois 60611

Association for Educational Communications and Technology
1126 Sixteenth Street, N.W.
Washington, DC 20036

Educational Film Library Association, Inc.
43 W. 61st Street
New York, New York 10023

University Film Association
School of Communications
University of Houston
Houston, Texas 77004

Periodicals

American Cinematographer
American Society of Cinematographers Corp.
1782 N. Orange Drive
Los Angeles, California 90028

American Film Magazine
American Film Institute
John F. Kennedy Center for the Performing Arts
Washington, D.C. 20566

Booklist
American Library Association
50 E. Huron Street
Chicago, Illinois 60611

Film News
250 West 57th Street
Suite 1527
New York, New York 10019

Instructional Innovator
Association for Educational Communications and Technology
1126 16th Street, N.W.
Washington, D.C. 20036

Instructor
Instructor Publications, Inc.
7 Bank Street
Dansville, New York 14437

Landers Film Reviews
Landers Associates
Box 69760
Los Angeles, California 90069

Learning
Thomas O. Ryder
530 University Avenue
Palo Alto, California 94301

Media & Methods
American Society of Educators
1511 Walnut Street
Philadelphia, Pennsylvania 19102

Media Index
343 Manville Road
Pleasantville, New York 10570

Sight and Sound
111 Eighth Avenue
New York, New York 10011

Sightlines
Educational Film Library Association, Inc.
43 W. 61st Street
New York, New York 10023

Super-8 Filmmaker
Sheptow Publishing
3161 Fillmore Street
San Francisco, California 94123

Teacher (formerly *Grade Teacher*)
Macmillan Professional Magazines, Inc.
262 Mason Street
Greenwich, Connecticut 06830

From the opening sequence of an Indiana University television series, animated by William Orisich.

POSSIBLE PROJECTS

8-A. Preview a film and critique it with a film appraisal form.

8-B. Observe a teacher using a film in a classroom situation and evaluate the teacher's use of the film, pointing out good and bad techniques.

8-C. Examine one or more of the film locators included in Appendix A, and submit a report on the kinds of materials you might want to use in your teaching.

8-D. Plan a lesson in your subject field in which you will use a specific film. Secure and preview this film from an appropriate source. Then make a specific lesson plan showing how you would implement the principles of utilization suggested for this medium.

8-E. Review a documentary (or *cinéma vérité*) film. Your review may be written (approximately 700 words) or recorded on tape (approximately five minutes). Briefly summarize the content of the film and describe your reactions to it.

From "Movement in Classical Dance," Indiana University Audio-Visual Center.

CHAPTER 9

TELEVISION

OUTLINE

OBJECTIVES

After studying this chapter, you should be able to:

1. Identify four advantages and three limitations of television as an instructional medium.

2. Characterize the current status of ITV in (a) elementary and secondary schools, (b) higher education, and (c) nonformal education. Indicate the number of teachers, students, and organizations using it, types of programs and applications, typical usage patterns, and growth rate.

3. Describe the following instructional television delivery systems: (a) broadcast via commercial station, (b) broadcast via noncommercial station, (c) closed-circuit system, (d) cable TV system, (e) microwave, and (f) portable video.

4. Identify an educational application of *each* of the delivery systems included in Objective 3.

5. Differentiate between the role of public television in home and in-school viewing.

6. Diagram the components of a basic, an intermediate, and a complex closed-circuit television system.

7. Discuss three educational potentials of CATV not available with standard broadcast television delivery systems.

8. Describe ITFS and characterize its current role in American education.

9. Identify four different storage/playback formats for portable video.

10. List six important selection criteria that apply to instructional television programs.

11. Describe three educational situations in which instructional television (ITV) programs might be locally produced.

12. Describe the necessary components for a portable video recording system, indicating not only the components but how they should be arranged for good recording quality.

13. Apply the basic steps of media utilization specifically to instructional television.

14. Describe the "ideal" physical arrangements for class viewing of television. Your description must include the factors of lighting, seating, and acoustics, with the minimum and maximum distances and angles.

ATTRIBUTES OF TELEVISION

In the early 1980s, as television entered its second generation as a mass medium, it had blossomed from a remote, expensive, restricted business to what some referred to as the "television of abundance." Television is now easily accessible for use in education not only via over-the-air broadcasts but also by means of closed-circuit and cable TV systems, all of which may be linked by satellite relays. Vast libraries of programs are now available on videocassette and videodisc, making TV materials nearly as available as audio tapes and records. Further, portable video recorders enable instructors—and their students—to create their own materials.

Clearly TV now represents many things, and is a rich resource for instruction and training.

Advantages

Like film, TV can present color moving pictures with sound. As such it shares many of the instructional advantages of film. But a major difference is that, being an electronic rather than a mechanical process, television can be transmitted long distances and its signals can be recorded and played back instantly.

By means of broadcasting, large audiences can be reached at a low cost per person. Viewers dispersed over vast geographic areas can experience a live event simultaneously. Learners can be reached at home, making "open learning" a reality.

At the same time, this mass medium is becoming an individual medium. The development of small, inexpensive home video recorders makes it feasible for students to view video materials on an individually prescribed basis.

Limitations

The complex electronic technology which affords television so many of its advantages is also, in a sense, its Achilles' heel. The complexity of the technology allows many possibilities for disruption of the communication flow. Programs may be poorly produced, even in sophisticated studio surroundings. Atmospheric conditions may disturb broadcast signals or satellite reception. Classroom receivers may malfunction. There is, in short, always the possibility that technical difficulties over which the instructor has little or no control will intervene between the lesson and the learner.

Figure 9.1 Broadcasting educational programs for at-home viewing brings the concept of open learning to life.

Cost may be another limiting factor. Even basic equipment (color TV receivers, for example) can be expensive. Sophisticated equipment (cable distribution systems, satellite reception setups) can cost a great deal of money. Hardware costs are only the most visible expenses. In the long run, the human labor involved in production, distribution, maintenance, and utilization usually overshadow the original equipment costs. So, unless large numbers of learners are being served or unless TV is performing a vital reaching function that cannot be performed efficiently and effectively by less expensive means, these costs may be difficult to justify.

In typical use the TV image is displayed on a rather small surface. This means that for ordinary classroom purposes one TV receiver is needed for approximately every 30 viewers, a cumbersome arrangement for large-group situations. This limitation can be overcome by using the newer large-screen TV projection systems but their cost is still prohibitive for most educational applications.

Perhaps television's most serious limitation as an instructional tool is that under typical conditions it is a one-way channel of communication. A feedback loop can be provided of means of push-button student-response systems or even "talk-back" arrangements. Such systems have been in use since the earliest days of instructional television experimentation and are employed in numerous special cases. But in normal practice one-way communication is still the rule.

TELEVISION IN TODAY'S INSTRUCTIONAL SETTINGS

We all know how television has permeated North American popular culture since it first leaped into existence a scant 25 years ago. How has it fared as an instructional tool in this relatively short period of time—in the schools, in higher education, and in nonformal education?

We will use the term *instructional TV* or *ITV* to refer to any planned use of video programs to meet specific instructional goals regardless of the source of the programs (including commercial broadcasts) or the setting in which they are used (including business/industry training).

Instructional TV in the Schools

According to a 1979 report of a large-scale survey conducted by the Corporation for Public Broadcasting, television is now being widely used in the classroom for instructional purposes.*

- 72 percent of all U.S. elementary and secondary school teachers had access to facilities for using ITV in their classrooms, either through over-the-air telecasts or through video recordings.
- 42 percent of the teachers surveyed had made some use of ITV during the school year, and 32 percent had used it "regularly"—that is, they had used at least three-quarters of the programs of at least one series. All in all, some 15 million students (35 percent of the total number

*Peter J. Dirr and Ronald J. Pedone. *Uses of Television for Instruction 1976–77: Final Report of the School TV Utilization Study.* Washington, D.C.: Corporation for Public Broadcasting, 1979.

Figure 9.2 Series most widely used for ITV.

RANK	SERIES	INTENDED GRADE LEVEL	TOTAL TEACHERS USING
1	The Electric Company	Primary, intermediate	174,000
2	Cover to Cover I	Intermediate	72,000
3	All About You	Primary	67,000
4	Inside/Out	Intermediate	55,000
5	Sesame Street	Preschool, primary	51,000
6	Ripples	Primary	33,000
7	Bread & Butterflies	Intermediate, Junior high school	26,000
8	Villa Allegre	Preschool, primary	21,000
9	Matter of Fiction	Intermediate	17,000
10	Mulligan Stew	Intermediate	17,000
11	Measuremetrics	Intermediate, junior high school	16,000
12	Word Shop	Primary, intermediate	15,000
13	Cover to Cover II	Intermediate	15,000
14	Nova	High school	15,000
15	Art (general)[a]	N.A.	15,000
16	Let's All Sing	Primary, intermediate	14,000
17	Wordsmith	Intermediate	13,000
18	Ascent of Man	High school	12,000
19	Music (general)[a]	N.A.	12,000
20	America	High school	11,000
21	Letter People	Primary	10,000
22	Draw Man	Intermediate	10,000
23	Adams Chronicles	High school	10,000
24	Infinity Factory	Intermediate	9,000
25	National Geographic Series	High school	9,000

Source: Peter J. Dirr and Ronald J. Pedone. *Uses of Television for Instruction 1976–1977: Final Report of the School TV Utilization Study.* Washington, D.C.: Corporation for Public Broadcasting, 1979.

[a] Some teachers listed Art or Music as the "title" of the series they used. They may have been referring to some local production or any of several nationally distributed series.

of students in U.S. classrooms) had been exposed to ITV in the classroom.

The survey also indicated that ITV usage is more prevalent in the elementary grades than in junior or senior high schools, as shown by the report's ranking of the 25 series most widely used in the classroom. All of the 10 top-ranked programs are intended for use in elementary or preschool instruction, and, in fact, only 5 of the top 25 series are intended for high school use.

Teacher attitudes toward ITV appear to be predominantly positive. For instance, in the survey 59 percent agreed that "ITV shows great possibilities for stimulating teacher creativity," while only 10 percent felt that "The possible relationship between student and teacher is lost when ITV is used."

Although nearly all users of ITV reported spending some time in preparing their classes for ITV program viewing and in follow-up activities, half of them reported spending less than 5 minutes on the former and 10 minutes or less on the latter. This rather scant

CLOSE-UP: Instructional Television in Broward County, Florida.

This county-wide school district provides ITV to its classrooms in a number of forms, including a 4-channel microwave system reaching all 147 schools and a telephone hookup allowing teachers to call in requests for transmissions. Furthermore, programs can be duplicated for later playback on the school's own videocassette recorder, and tapes can be borrowed from the loan library for up to five days. A monthly program guide describes dozens of programs available each month.

attention to preparation and follow-up activities would seem to indicate a need for more teacher training in ITV utilization: Only 17 percent of the teachers surveyed had received any pre-service or in-service training in this area.

Instructional ITV in Higher Education

In higher education the use of television for instruction appears to be widespread but quite conservative. According to a Corporation for Public Broadcasting survey in 1979, 71 percent of all colleges

*Peter J. Dirr and Ronald J. Pedone. "Television Use in Higher Education," *Educational and Industrial Television,* (December, 1979), 39–47.

and universities in the United States were making some use of television; 61 percent reported specifically instructional use. The proportions varied considerably with the type of institution; only 50 percent of private four-year colleges made instructional applications, whereas 64 percent of the community colleges and 86 percent of the public four-year universities did.

Although some institutions serve sizable enrollments of students in many different courses, the typical pattern is very limited. In the most common case only a few courses are offered via television, enrolling a total of only about a hundred students. Further, despite television's potential for extending the university's reach beyond the

campus, only about 14 percent of the total college TV effort is devoted to off-campus course work.

There are, however, some major exceptions to this general neglect of off-campus activities. The TAGER network in Dallas, for example, shares the resources of nine local colleges in telecasting courses, and transmits graduate engineering classes to workers at nearby industrial plants. The University of Mid-America offers course credit via off-campus television to viewers in seven mid-American states, and the University of Maryland has enrolled some 13,500 credit-earning students in its off-campus television program since its inception in 1972.

CLOSE-UP: Off-Campus Study at the University of Mid-America.

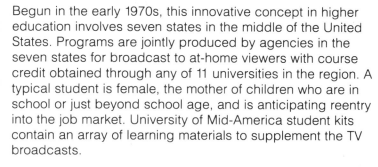

Begun in the early 1970s, this innovative concept in higher education involves seven states in the middle of the United States. Programs are jointly produced by agencies in the seven states for broadcast to at-home viewers with course credit obtained through any of 11 universities in the region. A typical student is female, the mother of children who are in school or just beyond school age, and is anticipating reentry into the job market. University of Mid-America student kits contain an array of learning materials to supplement the TV broadcasts.

In 1980 the National University Consortium, a nonprofit consortium of 7 colleges and universities, ranging from New England to California, and 11 television stations, inaugurated the nation's first coast-to-coast network of television courses leading to a bachelor's degree. More than 30 colleges and television stations applied to join the consortium, but, for reasons of quality control, this pilot program was limited in size to 7 institutions, with provisions made for later additions to the consortium as the program develops.

Instructional ITV in Nonformal Education

The extent to which business and industrial organizations rely on television for job training and basic skill instruction is revealed by a 1980 survey* indicating that over 700 such organizations were using instructional television programs. Indeed, the vast majority of user organizations operate television "networks," sending their programs to seven or more viewing locations. Hundreds of corporations, among them IBM, Ford Motor Company, Coca-Cola, John Deere, Equitable Life Assurance, Norwich Laboratories, and Burlington Industries, operate "corporate video networks" with more than 50 outlets. Most organizations produce their own programs, about 18 a year on the average. The total annual program output of corporate video is far greater than the combined output of the major commercial television networks, and total usage has increased each year that this survey has been conducted.

_____

*Judith M. and Douglas Brush. _Private Television Communications: 1980 and Beyond_. Berkeley Heights, NJ: International Television Association, 1980.

Government agencies and some of the nation's larger private institutions (labor unions, public interest groups, foundations, etc.) produce instructional television programs for distribution within their organizations.

Smaller organizations and businesess have generally been inhibited in their use of ITV because of the high costs involved. The advent of videocassettes and portable field production equipment, however, will probably spur use of instructional television in these sectors.

INSTRUCTIONAL ITV DELIVERY SYSTEMS

There are literally thousands of institutions and agencies, public and private, using video communications for instruction within formal and nonformal education settings. The overall impression is one of tremendous diversity. One way to organize a closer look at this panorama is to consider one-by-one each of the major ITV "delivery systems," that is, the physical methods used to package and transmit programs to users: commercial and noncommercial broadcasting, closed-circuit TV, cable systems, microwave transmission, and portable video.

Broadcasting by Commercial Stations

Both entertainment and instructional TV trace their roots to the commercially licensed stations which began to make their impact as instruments of mass communication in the early 1950s. Early attempts to reach mass audiences with educational programming were made using commercial channels, including such pioneering efforts as NBC's "Continental Classroom" (described in the accompanying Flashback).

Although the commercial networks soon dropped the idea of becoming major vehicles for instructional television, commercial broadcasting still plays a major role in ITV in the United States. In fact, about one-quarter of the television programs used today in schools originate with *commercial* stations. Most of these programs are not designed with educational intents (although in some areas educational programs such as *Sesame Street* and *The Electric Company* are carried by commercial stations). They are, instead, programs intended to

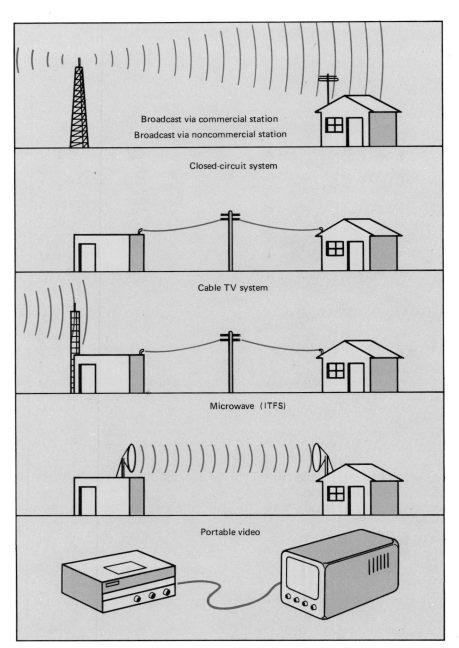

Broadcast via commercial station
Broadcast via noncommercial station

Closed-circuit system

Cable TV system

Microwave (ITFS)

Portable video

Figure 9.3 The major delivery systems by which ITV programs reach viewers.

Flashback: Continental Classroom

All things considered, Sputnik I has to get the credit for breathing life into this project, the NBC-TV series which had a five-year run from 1958 to 1963. Sometime after Sputnik spurted aloft on October 4, 1957, NBC's Director of Public Affairs and Education, Edward Stanley, was coming back from Europe. He read that New York State's Commissioner of Education, the late James Allen, was planning a refresher course for science teachers in the state. Probable cost: $600,000. Stanley thought that "for not a great deal more than that you could reach every science teacher in the country." And, he thought further, "we could do the whole damn thing."

While Sputnik may have catalyzed "Continental Classroom," two people, more than any others, made it work. Ed Stanley had the institutional punch and the moxie to argue and lead, at a level essential for a venture of this scope. Then, the late Mrs. Dorothy Culbertson, Executive Producer in the Public Affairs Department, brought intelligence and important persuasiveness to both the critical fund raising and direct management of the project.

Assembling the series actually amounted to a kind of benevolent brokerage by Stanley and Mrs. Culbertson. At his suggestion, she talked to the Fund for the Advancement of Education about using the NBC-TV network for college credit courses. They were "excited." At almost the same time, the American Association of Colleges for Teacher Education (AACTE) approached NBC tentatively. Would it put up $25,000 to study how TV could be used to improve teacher training? "I thought it was a helluva good idea," recalls Stanley. But his vision was broader: Would they be interested in something considerably bigger? Indeed they would, they said. This became vital in the funding arrangements that were to follow.

It seemed wholly apparent that NBC alone could not float the concept. And so, after appeals to the Ford Foundation, it finally agreed to put in $500,000, a major share of the first year's expected cost. Then, following beguiling calls from Mrs. Culbertson, added increments of $100,000 apiece came in from a number of large corporations. As a practical matter, the funds all went to AACTE, which thereupon paid NBC for its facilities, at cost. Stanley didn't let on to his management, but the last of the donations didn't come in until September 4, 1958, just before the broadcasts were to start.

By then, the apt series title had been locked up, as an outgrowth of a conversation between Stanley and noted educator Dr. James Killian, then Science Advisor to President Eisenhower. "What you'd have here," Stanley explained, "would be a continental classroom." Dr. Killian liked the idea, and the coinage stuck.

On October 6, 1958, the daily broadcasts began on the NBC network. That first year, the topic was "Atomic Age Physics," a college-level course 165 lessons long. Says Stanley: "Physics was the subject that was in trouble then. Many people teaching it had received their degrees before atomic energy was invented." And the man to teach these teachers was Dr. Harvey White, Professor of Physics at the University of California at Berkeley. Moving in to the NBC project, he lined up a veritable "Who's Who" of American scientists as guest lecturers, individuals like Dr. Glenn Seaborg, then Chancellor at Berkeley and later head of the Atomic Energy Commission. There's probably never been another national refresher course quite like it.

White and the other "Continental Classroom" teachers who were to follow had to do 130 lectures of their own in a year's time, five a week. They were under fantastic pressure. In spite of the grind, they made out because they were "pros" — fine teachers who displayed little if any temperament. They would work from outlines, rather than from prepared scripts. NBC tried to let their talent go into the studio when they wanted. Largely, this meant afternoon sessions. A four-hour stretch of studio time allowed for camera-blocking, a dress rehearsal, and the tape-recording. Once 6:30 A.M. rolled around, there seemed to be no question that people by the thousands were watching.

NBC's audience-research specialists estimated that 400,000 viewed Physics, while 600,000 tuned in to Chemistry, in the second year. But at no time over the five-year span of "Continental Classroom" did more than 5,000

Flashback: Continental Classroom

sign up for actual credit in a course. Even so, to Lawrence McKune of Michigan State, that first series on Physics was unique:

For the first time in the history of education, 4,905 students...in all parts of the United States, studied precisely the same course with the same teacher at the same hour, using the same outlines and the same texts.

In the second year, NBC repeated Physics at 6 A.M., then ran its new Chemistry course at 6:30 (it had to pay for the full 6-to-7 A.M. hour of network time, anyway). Physicists began watching Chemistry, and the chemists brushed up on their physics, a neat refresher switch.

By 1960, the mathematicians were asking for a course. Ford concurred. So NBC went along. "We had to," says Stanley. "They were the main money people." This time, a new approach was tried. The first half of the year was devoted to Algebra; John Kelley of Berkeley taught three days a week, and Julius Hlavaty took the Tuesday–Thursday pair. Then, in the second "term," Frederick Mosteller, Chairman of Statistics at Harvard, carried the main load on Probability and Statistics, while Paul Clifford of Montclair State College did the "applications" on Tuesday–Thursday. By that particular term, as many as 320 colleges and universities were granting credit for the course. Stanley notes that "few of

them were giving Probability in those days."

At that point, the Ford Foundation decided to cut off its financial support. And even though a number of corporate sponsors stuck with the project, Stanley began to feel a budget squeeze (a cutback to two TV cameras, instead of the normal three). Regardless, Stanley still managed to come up with a star performer for that fourth year, the late Peter Odegard, then Chairman of the Political Science Department at Berkeley and former President of Reed College.

Successful? Stanley says that Odegard's "American Government: Structure and Function" had an audience of 1.5 million. The League of Women Voters, he recalls, "were convinced we did this especially for them!" But then "Continental Classroom" folded. Why? "Money," says Stanley. "The company did lose a little, and wasn't willing to take a chance on raising some money the next year." The series budget—it ran between $1.2 million and $1.5 million annually—was "not a helluva lot for a network, not really." But NBC must have thought so. "American Government" was rebroadcast in the fifth year, and "Continental Classroom" ended officially on May 17, 1963.

*Excerpted from Robert D. B. Carlisle, *College Credit Through TV: Old Idea, New Dimensions*. Lincoln, Nebraska: Great Plains National Instructional Television Library, 1974.

---

entertain and/or inform the general public, but which can be adapted to instructional purposes by classroom teachers. Such programs might include classic and contemporary dramas, dance and musical performances, science programs (such as *The Miracle Months* and *Hidden Universe — the Brain),* dramas based on historical situations (such as *Roots, The Holocaust,* and *Eleanor and Franklin),* documentaries, and in-depth coverage of current news events.

In addition to such programs, commercial television may also provide what might be called incidental instructional opportunities.

Figure 9.4 "Big Bird," a main character on *Sesame Street,* after more than 10 years still the most recognized series from Children's Television Workshop.

Popular programs regularly viewed by students at home may provide experiential background upon which the creative teacher can build learning experiences.

Television, as we know, has considerable potential in the area of attitude formation. Popular dramatic series (even situation comedies) often revolve around moral dilemmas: Should the doctor inform the parents of the unwed

Figure 9.5 *The Electric Company,* designed to improve reading skills for 6- to 9-year-olds, has been the most heavily viewed program in American schools since its inception in the early 1970s.

pregnant teenager about her condition, or should the girl's condition be considered a private and confidential matter between doctor and patient? Should the high school basketball player inform his coach that a teammate is experimenting with drugs, or should he take the attitude that everyone has the right to "do his own thing"? Is the policeman who knows that a brutal murderer will go unpunished justified in taking thes40law into his own hands by, say, planting false evidence against the murderer? More and more teachers are finding popular commercial programs a prime resource for discussion of moral and ethical issues relating to attitude formation.

Programs like these are made more accessible and more adaptable to classroom use through the publication of teacher's guides by organizations such as Prime Time School Television (PTST). These teacher's guides are published as special inserts in periodicals (for example, *Media & Methods)* that reach teachers regularly. In fact, PTST has published a special guide to assist teachers in conducting "values clarification" discussions of the sort described above.*

Broadcasting by Noncommercial Stations

The 270-plus TV stations in the United States that hold noncommercial licenses are referred to collectively as *public television* stations, a term designating their common commitment to operate not for private gain but for the public benefit. Although these sta-

---

*"Televised Values: A PTST Model for Instruction," *Media & Methods.* 13 April 1977, pp. 31–36.

tions have various patterns of ownership, they tend to operate along roughly similar lines. Just as most commercial stations act as outlets for commercial network programming, most public television stations serve as outlets for the network programming of the Public Broadcasting Service (PBS). Their evening schedules feature PBS offerings and other programs aimed at home viewers in general, while during the daytime hours these stations typically carry instructional programs designed for specific school or college audiences.

Home Audience Programming. Public television attempts to offer an alternative type of programming for viewers that are not well served by the mass-audience programs of commercial broadcasting. In reaching out to selected subgroups, public TV programming does not usually attract viewers on a scale comparable to the commercial networks. However, well-produced series such as *Wall Street Week, Alistair Cooke's America, Masterpiece Theatre,* and *Nova* have won critical acclaim and loyal audiences which in recent years have grown to a size comparable to their commercial rivals. On a more general plane, public opinion polls indicate that over 60 percent of American adults can name their local public TV channel and do watch such programs at least occasionally.

As we discussed above in regard to commercial programs, the types of programs carried on public TV—documentaries, dramas, public affairs features, musical performances, science programs, and the like—are often useful as adjuncts to instruction in schools and colleges.

In-School Instructional Programming. Programs for direct classroom use are a mainstay of most public TV stations' daytime schedules. The average station transmits about four-and-a-half hours of such programs every school day. Instructional programs tend to be about 20 to 30 minutes long, and a single program is often repeated at different hours throughout the day to allow for flexibility in classroom scheduling. Public television stations are cited by teachers as by far their primary source of ITV materials for use in their classrooms.

Contrary to the popular image, broadcast ITV programs usually do not present core instruction in basic subject areas, as you can verify by reviewing the statistics in Figure 9.2. A researcher for the Agency for Instructional Television described ITV's emerging role as:

1. *To assist the classroom teachers in those subjects in which they often have the most difficulty (for example, art, music, "new" mathematics, science, and health);*

2. *To supplement the classroom instruction in subject areas in which limited classroom resources may prevent full examination of historical or international events; and*

3. *To bring outside stimulation in subject areas, such as literature, where teachers have difficulty exciting and motivating the students.**

Closed-Circuit Television

The term *closed-circuit television* refers to a TV distribution system in which the sender and receiver are physically linked by wire. At its simplest a connection between a single camera and a receiver within the same room (e.g., for

---

*Saul Rockman, "Instructional Television is Alive and Well," in Cater and Nyhan (eds.), *The Future of Public Broadcasting.* New York: Praeger, 1976, p. 79.

Figure 9.6   Since *Inside/Out* is aimed at helping children cope with personal problems, post-viewing discussions are an important component of the total lesson.

MEDIA FILE: "ThinkAbout" TV Series

Aimed at the fifth-sixth grade level, "ThinkAbout" is directed toward skills essential to learning. The sixty 15-minute programs aim to stimulate reasoning, encourage productive study skills, and to review and extend skills in mathematics and communication. It is considered one of the most ambitious series ever undertaken.
Source: Agency for Instructional Television.

MEDIA FILE: "Anyone for Tennyson?" TV Series

This award-winning series of professional poetry performances is aimed primarily at the college and adult audience and is also used at the secondary school level. It attempts to heighten the appeal of poetry by portraying works in dramatic format. Through 1979 some fifty half-hour programs had been completed.
Source: Great Plains National.

MEDIA FILE: **"Science Demonstrations" TV Series**

Professor Julius Sumner Miller, known as Walt Disney's "Professor Wonderful," conducts interest-grabbing demonstrations which he explains in everyday language. Suitable for all ages, these 45 quarter-hour programs aim to arouse curiosity about the phenomena all around us.
Source: *Western Instructional Television.*

image magnification in a science lab) constitutes closed-circuit TV (CCTV). Or several classrooms could be linked to a studio to form a building-wide CCTV system. Campus-wide and school-district-wide interconnections are also possible. In some areas, South Carolina and Indiana for example, one finds campus and district centers connected by state-wide CCTV linkages forming networks of impressive scope. For special purposes, transcontinental telephone lines can be leased to set up CCTV hookups of national scope. A common example is the showing of championship boxing matches on large-screen TV projection in theaters.

One of the principal advantages of CCTV is that such systems, since they do not operate through the air waves controlled by government agencies, can be set up freely by anyone who has the money to do so. Although the cost tends to increase with the size of the coverage area (unlike through-the-air delivery systems), the freedom, privacy, and multichannel capability of CCTV makes it an attractive option for some educational purposes.

Because cost increases as geographic coverage increases, CCTV is not widely used in large school districts. It has, however, grown to become the leading delivery system for ITV on college and university campuses because of their more compact geography.

Figure 9.7 illustrates three possible configurations of CCTV. Section A shows the most basic

Figure 9.7 *Typical closed-circuit television systems. (a) Basic system: single camera fed to single monitor; (b) intermediate system: camera and microphone mixed and fed to multiple reception points; (c) complex system: multiple program sources mixed, transmitted, and amplified to multiple reception points.*

Camera — Monitor

(a)

Mixer

(b)

Building 1   Building 2

Building 3   Building 4

Transmitter(s)   Amplifier

(c)

configuration: a single camera feeding a single monitor. This setup might be found in a science laboratory, typing classroom, or auto repair shop to provide a group of students with a close-up or even microscopic view of an instructional demonstration. Section B illustrates a more typical pattern: a microphone is added along with the camera mechanism to allow a sight-and-sound presentation to be shown on several monitors located in one large classroom or perhaps in several different rooms in the same building. This configuration is used to present a lecture (or elaborate demonstration) to a larger number of students. It is common in institutions wishing to serve as many students as possible with a limited number of faculty. The configuration can also make an audiovisual presentation clearly visible to larger numbers of viewers. The more complex system shown in Section C illustrates a campus-wide network of closed-circuit studios serving multiple buildings. In this case, film and video tape inputs have been added. Multiple channels may be used simultaneously, thus allowing different subjects or the same subject at different grade levels to be offered at the same time.

Cable Television

The cable concept of television program delivery was first applied commercially in 1950 in Lansford, Pennsylvania, where, due to interference from a mountain overshadowing the town, people were unable to receive a viewable signal from the nearest TV station. A local TV sales and service man came up with the idea of building a master antenna atop the mountain. There the weak signals were amplified and fed into a coaxial cable that ran down the mountain into Lansford. By paying an installation charge and a monthly sub-

scription fee, a customer could have his home connected to the cable. This idea of having a single tall antenna to serve a whole community gave the process its name, *community antenna television,* or CATV as it is commonly abbreviated.

Most CATV systems in operation today still basically resemble the original master-antenna model, in which broadcast television signals are captured by a favorably situated high-mast antenna (see Figure 9.8). The signals are amplified and delivered to the head-end of the system where they are processed, fed into a trunk line, and further amplified. The signals then proceed along feeder lines and

eventually to smaller drop lines that enter individual homes and other buildings. The signal-carrying cables are installed underground in some systems (especially in congested urban areas), but ordinarily they are strung out along telephone poles, with a fee paid to the telephone company for this use of its property.

By 1980, about half the households in the United States could avail themselves of cable television if they wished, and about 20 percent of all homes had opted to do so. The cable subscriber, besides getting an extremely clear video image on his or her screen, has access to several more chan-

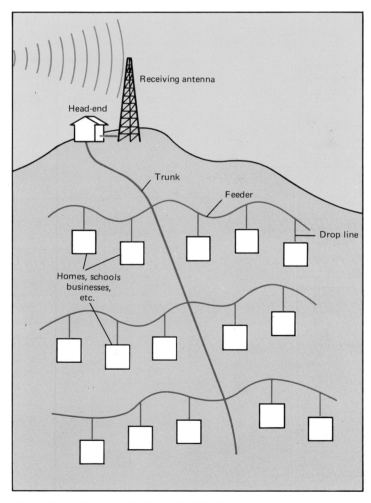

Figure 9.8 Typical cable television distribution system.

nels than are readily available over the air. Some of these channels are "public access" outlets for use by community and special interest groups. Other channels are used for sporting events, special movie showings, programs imported from distant independent stations, etc.

Special Educational Applications of CATV.

Thousands of educational institutions are now plugged into CATV systems, often without charge from the local cable operator. In many cases, schools and colleges are operating public access channels for their own institutional and/or instructional purposes.

The availability of multiple channels facilitates a number of special services: (1) transmission of several programs simultaneously and repetition of programs at different hours for more flexible matching with classroom schedules; (2) aiming specialized programs at small subgroups, for example, those speaking foreign languages or having sight or hearing impairment; (3) retrieval of remotely stored libraries of video materials, allowing teachers—or individual students—access to materials on demand without the logistic struggle often associated with instructional media use.

The Future.

Actually the number of channels available on many cable systems is still small—the average system supplying about seven channels. Developments in the late 1970s, however, such as fiber optics as a replacement for coaxial cable and improvements in the system's other hardware components, foreshadow the development of CATV systems capable of supporting scores, even hundreds, of transmission channels.

But what has caused futurists among educators really to sit up and take notice is the characteristic of CATV which most distinguishes it from other television delivery systems: its ability to transmit signals not only from sender to receiver but also from the receiver back to sender. Although most cable systems today send signals only "downstream" to the home or school, the technology is available to permit return communications "upstream" back to the sender. These return signals can take the form of simple yes–no digital communications, audio signals alone, or full television images with accompanying sound. Each of these feedback possibilities evokes exciting prospects for converting ITV into a two-way, interactive medium of instructional communication. A major on-going demonstration of

cable television's potential for two-way communication, QUBE, was begun in Columbus, Ohio, in 1977. Another promising two-way TV system, this one tied in with telephone facilities, was begun in late 1980 by the Canadian Government and Bell Canada for subscribers in Toronto and Quebec.

Microwave Transmission (ITFS)

The only television delivery system in the United States set up exclusively for educational purposes is also the least well-known.

In 1963, 11 years after the Federal Communications Commission reserved certain VHF (Very High Frequency) and UHF (Ultra High Frequency) channels for noncommercial use, it established the Instructional Television Fixed Service (ITFS), setting aside channels in the microwave band of 2500–2690 MHZ for instructional use by educational institutions. Later rules allowed the ITFS to expand into the areas of audio and hard-copy transmission and into two-way television systems.

The ITFS system has one major technical limitation. Signals broadcast at these high microwave frequencies travel in a line-of-sight pattern. They do not bend with the

CLOSE-UP: Interactive Television Through QUBE.

Since 1977 cable TV subscribers in Columbus, Ohio have been able to talk back to their TV sets—literally. The handheld responder not only allows fingertip channel selection but also has five buttons that can be pressed to respond to specific questions (e.g., game playing, public opinion surveys, and instructional lessons). Responses are tabulated by a central computer and may be displayed on the screen. For instructional lessons, a small light on the responder flashes to indicate "correct" responses.

curvature of the earth, so they cannot travel farther than the horizon. Consequently, coverage of ITFS is limited to areas in direct sightline of the transmission tower.

Nevertheless, this coverage is sufficient for many educational situations. Coverage can generally extend over areas about the size of a large school district, and, unlike closed-circuit television, no wiring is required for connection among classrooms. Like cable, ITFS allows transmission on multiple channels; the average licensee operates about six channels. This greatly expands the broadcasting possibilities in a given locale beyond what would exist merely with VHF and UHF outlets. Because the system operates on frequencies above those that can be received on ordinary sets without a converter, it offers a higher degree of audience selectivity and programming privacy than regular broadcasts. Also, cost of equipment and operation is lower than for regular broadcast television.

At the present time ITFS delivers less of the total ITV used in classrooms than any of the other delivery systems discussed here, but it has been growing slowly over the years. There are now over 100 licensees operating some 600 microwave channels, but geographic distribution is uneven. Twenty-three states and the metropolitan area of Washington, D.C. have no ITFS systems at all. On the other hand, in Milwaukee and Los Angeles, most of the available ITFS channels are already being used by educational institutions. Most of the area channels in the New York and San Francisco area are also in use—not, however, by the city public school districts, but by suburban and parochial schools.

Catholic school systems, having largely missed out on the earlier allocation of VHF and UHF channels for educational purposes, have become prominent users of ITFS. The Catholic schools in New York and Brooklyn operate some 23 channels; the newest system, Chicago, has 10 channels. Other sizable Catholic operations are centered in Milwaukee, San Francisco, Boston, and Miami.

Within higher education, ITFS is used predominantly for graduate and professional school extension purposes. Typical use connects engineering or medical schools (often with two-way links) with professionals out in the field who require continuing education updating. Some of the most sophisticated technical systems in all of ITV are found within this sector.

In short, ITFS is a delivery system with considerable potential. It may well come to play a more prominent role in the future as the available frequencies in the VHF and UHF bands become saturated and educators seek additional channels for distributing video materials.

Portable Video

The final delivery system involves neither wires nor over-the-air broadcasting. We are using the term *portable video* to refer to the several methods of playing back ITV programs right in the classroom by means of video recorders. The distribution system itself—the record/playback machine—is portable and can be set up wherever needed.

Newer recording formats, such as the videocassette and videodisc, now give instructors greater flexibility in choosing what programs they want to use and when and where they want to use them. They even make feasible the use of video materials by students on an individualized basis.

Videocassette. The conventional recording medium for video programs is magnetic tape similar to that used in audio recording. The tape may be used either in an open-reel format or enclosed in a cassette. Currently, the most favored videocassette format is

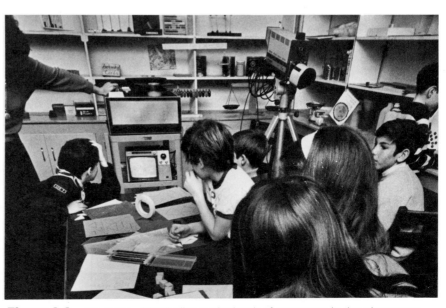

Figure 9.9 "Portable video" allows playback of programs in the classroom without broadcasting or closed-circuit facilities.

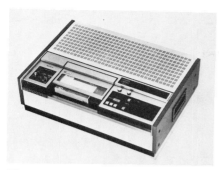

Figure 9.10 The ¾-inch videocassette format.

that using 3/4-in. tape, a format pioneered by Sony's U-Matic system in the early 1970s and now accepted as the standard.

The success of the 3/4-in. videocassette helped stimulate demand for a less expensive home version. The result is the 1/2-in. videocassette which is rapidly gaining in popularity both for home and for institutional use. There are two 1/2-in. videocassette formats on the market, Sony's Betamax and the VHS (Video Home System) offered by a number of competing Japanese manufacturers. Unfortunately, the two systems are incompatible, using different tape speeds and transport mechanisms. So recordings made for one system can not be used with the other.

Figure 9.11 The ½-inch videocassette format.

Videodisc. A more recent addition to video recording and storage systems is the videodisc. As the name implies, audiovisual signals are recorded on plastic discs, rather than on magnetic tape, for playback on television screens. The great promise of videodiscs lies in their ability to store massive amounts of audio-visual information in a compact package. Since videodiscs can have a slow-motion and stop-frame capability, still pictures and even print can be stored as readily as TV presentations. With a storage capacity of some 54,000 frames, one twelve-inch videodisc can hold one hour of color TV programing, about a thousand film-strips, or several thousand pages of print. In addition, some videodisc players contain a microprocessor with memory storage capability, allowing them to be programmed to present branching sequences of programmed instruction. (Programmed instruction is discussed in detail in Chapter 11.)

Given these attributes, plus the very significant fact that discs can be mass produced at low cost, it seems reasonable to suppose that videodiscs are destined to play an increasingly important role in the storage and presentation of instructional materials. However, there are some qualifications you should be aware of. When videodisc players began to be mass marketed in 1980-1981 it became evident that several technically different and *incompatible* systems would compete for consumer acceptance and institutional use. Two different playback systems exist: the optical type, using laser beams either reflected from or passed through the disc, and the capacitive type, using a pickup arm in a way similar to a phonograph. Each has advantages—the optical system having more durable software and the capacitive

system being simpler and less expensive.

Regardless of which technical system is considered, educational users have to decide between interactive and non-interactive (straight playback) systems. The latter offers just straight-ahead playback of conventional video programs without random access or variable speed. This is the system marketed principally to home consumers; it offers educators widespread access to inexpensive off-the-shelf programs for low-cost playback machines. Interactive systems with computer capabilities built in allow rapid access to individual frames, automatic stops in the program for questioning, and branched responses dependent on the learner's answer. The hardware and software costs for interactive systems are considerably higher than for single videodisc players.

Summary. Obviously, accessibility of comparatively inexpensive and highly portable video recording equipment has important logistic implications. Flexibility of scheduling ITV is enhanced even further by ready access to video recorders than it is by access to multichannel delivery systems such as cable television. ITV programs can be taped and put away for use at just the right time to suit

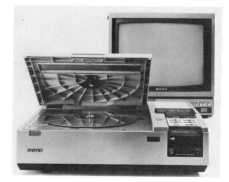

Figure 9.12 The Sony laser-type videodisc player.

specific learning objectives and particular instructional situations. Libraries of recorded material can be built up and stored in centralized banks for retrieval by hand or, if usage justifies, for remote electronic retrieval.

STEPS TO ASSURE EFFECTIVE LEARNING

As with other audiovisual media, the effectiveness of learning from video materials depends heavily on the instructor's planning and utilization practices. The ASSURE model provides a useful outline to carry you through these planning steps. We will assume that you have analyzed your students' characteristics and instructional needs and that your chosen educational goals have been converted into usable performance objective statements. Our discussion here will begin with the third element of the ASSURE model.

Select: Instructional TV Program Selection

In some cases the instructor has no real control over the selection of ITV materials. A program or series may be administratively mandated as an integral part of the curriculum. In most cases, however, instructors do have some discretionary control over selection of ITV materials, either as individual teachers or as members of a selection committee.

The development of sophisticated delivery systems and easy-to-use video tape recorders has stimulated an increase in the number and variety of available televised instructional materials. Program guides and directories can help keep you abreast of available materials in your areas of interest and guide you toward selection of materials best suited to your particular teaching needs. The most comprehensive listing of current educational video recordings is the *Index to Educational Video Tapes* published by the National Information Center for Educational Media (NICEM). *Videolog, Video Source Book*, and

Chicorel Index to Video Tapes and Cassettes are annual directories of programs encompassing both entertainment and educational topics. All are described in greater detail in Appendix A.

As with all other instructional media, however, you should also develop and maintain your own personal ITV program appraisal file. Only you can really know how well the materials work (or don't work) for you and your students. Included here is a suggested ITV program appraisal form. You may wish to use it as is, or to adapt it to your particular needs.

Modify/Design: Local Production of Instructional TV

A feature that separates television from many of the other audiovisual media is that the instructor is not limited to off-the-shelf materials but can with reasonable ease prepare custom materials to fit local needs. "Do-it-yourself" television has become commonplace since the popularization of battery-operated portable video recording systems—the "porta-pak." This technological advance has liberated ITV production from the confines of the engineer-dominated studio. It allows ITV production to be taken "into the field," wherever that might be: the science laboratory, the classroom, the counseling office, the athletic field, the factory assembly line, the hospital, the neighborhood, even the home. Equally important, the simplicity of the system has made it feasible for nonprofessionals, instructors and students alike, to create their own video materials.

APPRAISAL CHECKLIST: TELEVISION

Series title——————————————————————————————

Program title (or number)——————————————————————

Producer/distributo ——————————————————————————

Production date————————————   Program length————min.

Intended audience/grade level————Subject area ——————————————

Objectives (stated or implied):

Brief description:

Entry capabilities required:

—prior knowledge
—reading ability/vocabulary
—math ability

RATING

	High	Medium	Low
Likely to arouse student interest	□ □	□ □	□ □
Technical quality	□ □	□ □	□ □
Provides meaningful viewer participation	□ □	□ □	□ □
Objectives relevant to curricular needs	□ □	□ □	□ □
Focuses clearly on objectives	□ □	□ □	□ □
Evidence of effectiveness (e.g., field-test results)	□ □	□ □	□ □
Teacher's role clearly indicated	□ □	□ □	□ □
Provides guide for discussion/follow up	□ □	□ □	□ □

Strong points:

Weak points:

Reviewer————————————

Position————————————

Recommended action————————————————   Date————————————

Figure 9.13 A porta-pak camera/videocassette recorder system is easily carried and operated by one person.

Applications. Locally produced video could be used for virtually any of the purposes described earlier in relation to still pictures, audio, and film; but its unique capability is to capture sight and sound for immediate playback. So this medium would fit best with activities that are enhanced by immediate feedback: group dynamics sessions, athletic practice, skills training, and interpersonal techniques (e.g. "microcounseling" and "microteaching").

Other applications that emphasize the *local* aspect of local video production are:

- Dramatization of student stories, songs, and poems.
- Student documentaries of school or neighborhood issues.
- Preservation of local folklore.

- Demonstrations, for example, of science experiments, eliminating delays and unanticipated foul-ups.
- Replays of field trips for in-class follow-up.
- Career information on local businesses via field recordings.

Of course, many organizations have more elaborate facilities than the simple single-camera field units that we are describing here. But closed-circuit TV studios and the like are the domain of the media specialist or engineer. Our focus is on the typical sort of system that instructors might expect to be using by themselves.

CLOSE-UP: Applications of Locally Produced Video.

Single-camera field recording video systems open up new possibilities for applications such as: practice with visual feedback for psychomotor skill development, teacher self-improvement through microteaching practice and critique, student documentation of community activities.

Components of the Single-Camera System. A typical single-camera system setup is shown in Figure 9.21. Its basic components are a camera, a microphone, a recorder, and a monitor/receiver.

Camera. The heart of the portable video camera is the vidicon tube, which is basically a vacuum tube that converts light rays into electronic signals that are transmitted through a cable to the video recorder. There is no film or tape inside the camera; all the recording is done in the recorder. The camera may be a viewfinder type. The viewfinder camera is so named because it has built into it a small TV set that allows the operator to monitor the image being picked up by the vidicon tube (See Figure 9.14). Even small hand-held cameras such as that shown in Figure 9.15, typically contain built-in viewfinders with 1-in. screens. The nonviewfinder camera costs several hundred dollars less since it lacks the built-in monitor. It may be used for fixed-camera purposes, however, and it can be used for other local production purposes if it is hooked up to a separate monitor, allowing the operator to aim and focus the camera according to the image shown in the monitor.

Figure 9.14 A compact color television camera complete with viewfinder, zoom lens, and microphone.

Figure 9.15 A typical hand-held color camera; note the pistol grip with on/off trigger, zoom lens, built-in microphone at the front, and eyepiece at the back (used to magnify the built-in viewfinder).

Microphone. Hand-held cameras usually come with a microphone built into the front of the camera. This microphone has "automatic level control," a feature which automatically adjusts the volume to keep the sound at an audible level. The camera, so to speak, "hears" as well as "sees." The problem is that these microphones amplify *all* sounds within their range, including shuffling feet, coughs, street noises, and equipment noise, along with sounds that are wanted. You may, therefore, want to bypass the built-in microphone by plugging in a separate microphone better suited to your particular purpose.

In selecting a microphone remember that television is more than pictures. Indeed, the audio track usually carries more critical information than the visual. (If you doubt this, try watching your favorite TV show with the sound turned off.) So the selection and handling of the microphone is of vital importance. The best advice is to think of your portable video system as an audio recorder plus a video recorder, and to make the same careful preparations as you would for an audio recording session.

Figure 9.16 Two examples of "neck mikes," meant to be clipped to the lapel or necktie.

Figure 9.17 Omnidirectional microphone with windscreen in desk stand.

Figure 9.18 Unidirectional microphone with windscreen, meant to be hand-held.

Figures 9.16, 9.17, and 9.18 illustrate three common microphone options. The lavalier, or "neck mike," is a good choice when a single speaker is being recorded. It can be clipped to a tie or dress, hung around the neck, or even hidden under light clothing. A desk stand may be used to hold a microphone for a speaker or several discussants seated at a table. The microphone might be unidirectional or omnidirectional depending on the number and seating arrangements of the speakers. For situations in which there is unwanted background noise or the speaker is moving, a highly directional microphone should be used, usually held by hand and pointed toward the sound source.

Recorder. You have a wide variety of recorder formats to choose from, including the 3/4-in. and 1/2-in. videocassettes described earlier, but the standard for single-camera local production is the 1/2-in.-*open reel* video tape recorder (VTR). (All current models of the open reel 1/2-in.-VTR are compatible, therefore tapes are interchangeable.) This type of recorder is most commonly encountered either as a table-top deck (as in Figure 9.19) or in the lighter, more compact form of the porta-pak (as in Figure 9.20), intended to be carried over the shoulder or in a backpack position.

Whatever the type of recorder chosen, the recording principle is the same. In fact, it is analogous to audio recording, with both sound and pictures being converted into magnetic impulses that are stored in the metallic oxide molecules in the tape. Although the units pictured here are black-and-white systems, color systems are continually gaining in popularity as their size and price are reduced.

Monitor/receiver. The final major component of the single-camera VTR system is the monitor/receiver, the device on which the recording is played back. The name is derived from the dual capabilities these units usually possess. Television signals may be sent through cables in the form of a "video signal," as in a closed-circuit TV studio. A "monitor" is a TV set built to pick up video signals; a "receiver" is a TV set built

Figure 9.19 A tabletop, open reel ½-inch video tape deck.

Figure 9.20 A porta-pak open reel ½-inch video recording system, including AC power adapter.

Figure 9.21 A generalized, suggested setup for single-camera recording.

to pick up radio frequencies. A "monitor/receiver" is a unit especially adapted to receive both. The flick of a switch allows it to go from off-air pickup to play/back of a VTR connected to it by cable.

Recording Setup for the Single-Camera System. Figure 9.21 shows a typical and effective arrangement for single-camera VTR recording.

1. The monitor/receiver and recorder are set on a sturdy mobile cart. This allows easy movement of the equipment around the room. The cart can be swiveled around so that the monitor/receiver faces the camera operator (to allow monitoring when a nonviewfinder camera is being used). In most cases it is advisable to turn the monitor/receiver away from on-camera subjects to avoid distracting them during recording. It can easily be swiveled back for later "instant replay" viewing.

2. The camera is mounted on a sturdy, wheeled tripod, maximizing mobility and stable support.

3. The camera is outfitted with a zoom lens, an expensive option, but one that adds great flexibility to the single-camera system. The zoom lens, having a variable focal length, can be adjusted to provide a wide-angle view, a medium view, or a close-up view with just a twist of the wrist. You should, however, resist the impulse to zoom in and out during a shot unless there is very good reason for doing so.

4. The camera and mobile cart are placed close to the wall. This kind of arrangement helps reduce the likelihood of passersby tripping over the profusion of cables which necessarily connect all the components to each other and to the power source.

5. The camera is aimed away from the window (or other bright light source). Cameras used in this system usually are equipped with automatic light-level control enabling them to adjust automatically to the brightest light striking the lens. If there is a window in back of your subject, the camera will adjust to that light, thus throwing your subject into shadowy darkness. An important caution when recording outdoors: one of the greatest hazards to the vidicon tube in your camera is exposure to direct sunlight. Aiming at the sun can cause its image to be burned into the vidicon, possibly causing irreparable damage.

6. The subjects are well lighted. If natural light is insufficient, you may supplement it with incandescent or fluorescent lighting in the room. Today's vidicons operate well with a normal level of artificial light.

7. The camera is positioned so that the faces of both subjects can be seen. A common mistake in taping a classroom scene is to place the camera at the back of the room. This provides a nice full-face view of the teacher, but reaction shots of the students are nearly impossible to see. Placement of the camera at the side of the classroom is a reasonable compromise when recording classroom interaction.

8. A desk-stand microphone is being used. This allows pickup of the voices of both subjects, while reducing the pickups of unwanted background noises.

Utilize the Materials

The next step after selecting or producing your video materials is to put them into actual use in the classroom.

Preview. It is not always possible to view a TV program prior to use, but you can usually read about the program in a teacher's guide. In the case of broadcast programs, utilization guides are often published in advance in education journals, as discussed earlier.

Prepare the environment. Before students can learn from any instructional TV presentation they first have to be able to see it and hear it! Provide proper lighting, seating, and volume control.

Television should be viewed in normal or dim light, not darkness. Besides being more comfortable to the eye, normal illumination provides necessary light for student participative activities, for referring to handouts, and for occasional note-taking.

The television receiver should be located so that harsh light from a window or light fixture cannot strike the screen and cause glare. Do not place the receiver in front of an unshaded window that will compete with light from the television screen and make viewing difficult.

An ideal seating arrangement for ITV may sometimes be difficult to achieve. Because of economic constraints, there are often not enough television sets available to give every student an adequate view. Ideally, one 23-in.-screen TV set should serve no more than 30 students seated at desks in an aisled classroom. If conditions are not ideal, the best you can do is do your best. If feasible, seats may be shared or moved closer together so that all may have at least an adequate view of the screen. If possible, stagger seats to help prevent view blockage.

Here are some basic rules of thumb for good seating arrangement (see Figure 9.22):

- Seat no one closer than 7 feet from the receiver.
- Seat no one farther away (in feet) than the size of the TV screen (in inches).
- Seat no one more than 45 degrees from the center axis of the screen.
- Place the TV set no more than 30 degrees above the normal eye level of any seated viewer to avoid having viewers crane their necks uncomfortably.

For proper hearing, the volume of the receiver should be set loud enough to be heard clearly in the rear of the viewing area, but not so loud that it bowls over those in the front. Normally this happy middle ground is not difficult to achieve—if your seating arrangement is within acceptable bounds and your receiver's speaker mechanism is functioning properly.

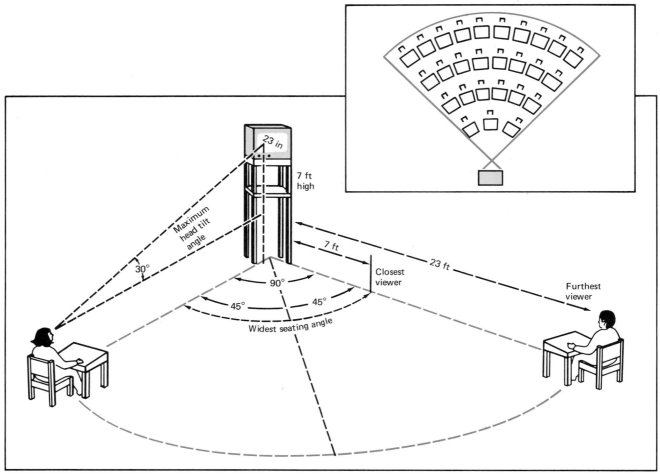

Figure 9.22 Recommended seating arrangements for TV viewing.

Obviously, volume should be kept low enough so as not to disturb neighboring classes. Unfortunately, contemporary "open plan" buildings with only movable room dividers as walls provide a poor environment for TV or other audiovisual presentations. Under such conditions cooperation is critical. Teachers in neighboring areas can mutually agree to lower their decibel level to minimize interference (better than escalating the problem by trying to drown each other out!). Sometimes the only alternative is to seek out an enclosed room that can be reserved for audiovisual use.

Prepare the Audience.
Research in educational psychology as well as the practical experiences of thousands of teachers in all sorts of settings demonstrates that learning is greatly enhanced when learners are *prepared* for the coming activity. No competent instructor would advocate approaching a TV lesson by suddenly stopping the regular lecture, switching on the TV set, and abandoning the classroom for a coffee break. Yet we know that many instructors do just that.

To start the "warmup" before the TV lesson, create a mind-set by reviewing previous related study. Help students see how today's lesson fits into the total picture.

Create a "need to know." Stimulate curiosity by asking questions, and evoke questions the *students would like answered* about this subject.

Clarify the objectives of the lesson. Mention cues—specific things to look for—in the TV presentation. It helps to list such cues on the chalkboard or on a handout so that students can refer to them as the lesson proceeds (and during the follow-up activities). If large amounts of new information are supposed to be retained, give students some "advance organizers"—memory hooks on which they can hang the new ideas. Be sure to preview any new vocabulary needed.

Present the Material. A well-designed ITV presentation will call for frequent student participation. By responding yourself, you provide an example which the students will follow. Learners are quick to detect and act according to your attitude toward the material. Many studies have indicated that the instructor's attitude—often conveyed nonverbally—significantly affects students' learning from TV.

Situate yourself so that you can observe learner reactions. Watch for clues indicating difficulties or boredom. Note individual reactions for possible use in the follow-up discussion. Deal with individual discipline problems as quickly and unobtrusively as possible.

Require Learner Response

If active participation was not explicitly built into the TV lesson it is all the more important to stimulate response after the presentation. The ability to generalize new knowledge and transfer it to real-life applications depends on learner practice under a variety of conditions. The possibilities for follow-up activities are virtually limitless. A few of the common techniques are:

- Discussion—question and answer sessions, buzz groups, panel discussions, debates.
- Dramatization—role-playing, skits, oral presentations.
- Projects—experiments, reports, exhibits, models, demonstrations, drawings, story-writing, bulletin boards, media productions.

Evaluate

Assessment of student learning can be carried out informally by observing performance during the follow-up activities. Individual projects can be good indicators of successful learning. In many cases, though, more formal testing serves a valuable purpose. First, tests that are followed by feedback to answers can provide an efficient review and summary of the main points of the lesson. Second, objective tests can help pinpoint gaps that need to be followed up in the classroom and they can identify individuals who need remedial help. In this way, the instructor can complement the media component by catering to individual differences in ways the media cannot.

AV Showmanship—Television

Let's summarize the key points in using television presentations to the best instructional advantage:

- Check lighting, seating, and volume control to be sure that everyone can see and hear the TV set.
- Get students mentally prepared by briefly reviewing previous related study and evoking questions about today's topic.
- List on chalkboard the main points to be covered in the TV presentation.

- Preview any new vocabulary.
- Most important, get involved in the telelesson yourself. Watch attentively and respond when the presenter asks for a response. Be a good role model. Highlight major points by adding them to the chalkboard during the lesson.
- Support the presentation with meaningful follow-up activities.

REFERENCES

Print References: General

Atienza, Loretta J. *VTR Workshop: Small Format Video* (Paris: UNESCO, 1977).

* Bensinger, Charles. *The Video Guide,* 2d ed. (New York: Esselte Video, Inc., 1979).

Center for Vocational Education. *Present Information with Televised and Videotaped Materials* (Athens, GA: American Assocation for Vocational Instructional Materials, 1977).

Combes, Peter and John Tiffin. *Television Production for Education* (New York: Focal Press, 1978).

Gordon, George N. *Classroom Television* (New York: Hastings House, 1970).

* Hilliard, Robert L., and Hyman H. Field. *Television and the Teacher: A Handbook for Classroom Use* (New York: Hastings House, 1976).

Kuhns, William. *Exploring Television,* rev. ed. (Chicago, IL: Loyola University Press, 1975).

Learning Via Telecommunications, readings from *Audiovisual Instruction-3* (Washington, DC: Association for Educational Communications and Technology, 1978).

Mattingly, Grayson, and Welby Smith. *Introducing the Single-Camera VTR System* (New York: Charles Scribner's Sons, 1973).

Robinson, Richard. *The Video Primer: Equipment, Production and Concepts* (New York: Links Books, 1974).

* Wood, Donald N. and Donald G. Wylie. *Educational Telecommunications* (Belmont, CA: Wadsworth, 1977).

*Key references.

Print References: School Television

Barth, Rodney J., and Thomas Swiss. "ERIC/RCS: The Impact of Television on Reading." *Reading Teacher,* November 1976, pp. 236–239.

Beswick, Chris. "The Video-Cassette Recorder in the Modern Language Classroom." *Visual Education,* October 1977, pp. 25–26.

Charles, Joel. "Interactive Television: Use Your Imagination and Help Students Learn." *Audiovisual Instruction,* May 1976, pp. 23–25.

Dampier, William. "TV Ontario from Dostoyevsky to Donald Duck." *Public Telecommunications Review,* January/February 1978, pp. 20–27.

Dirr, Peter J., and Ronald J. Pedone. *Uses of Television for Instruction 1976-77* (Washington, DC: Corporation for Public Broadcasting, 1979).

Du Bey, Kenneth. "How to Videotape Through a Microscope." *Audiovisual Instruction,* January 1978, p. 33.

Eanet, Alan S., and Sandra M. Toth. "Using TV in a Science Course." *Audiovisual Instruction,* March 1976, pp. 38–40.

Feeley, Joan T. "Television and Reading in the Seventies." *Language Arts,* September 1975, pp. 797, 801, 815.

Fowler, G.C. "Language Arts and Reading Reorientation Via Television." *Educational Broadcasting,* July/August 1976, pp. 8–10, 30.

Genesky, S.M. "A Second-Generation Interactive Classroom Television System for the Partially Sighted." *Journal of Visual Impairment and Blindness,* February 1978, pp. 41–45.

Gibbons, J.F. "Tutored Videotape Instruction: A New Use of Electronics Media in Education." *Science,* March 1977, pp. 1139–1146.

Gould, Edwin, and Vincent Southerland. "TV Typing: Learning the Keyboard Through Instructional Television." *Business Education World,* September/October 1976, pp. 14–15.

Holt, David. "Very Special Students, Very Special Video." *Media & Methods,* January 1978, pp. 46–48.

Kaplan, Don. *Video in the Classroom: A Guide to Creative Television* (White Plains, NY: Knowledge Industry Publications, 1980).

Kundu, Mahima Ranjan. "Visual Literacy: Teaching Non-Verbal Communication Through Television." *Educational Technology,* August 1976, pp. 31–33.

Longworth, Allison. "Cable TV—An Inexpensive Multi-Purpose Communication Vehicle." *Journal of Educational Communication,* September/October 1975, pp. 6–7.

Minow, Newton N., and Lynn M. Mills. "Prime Time School Television: Doing Something About TV." *Phi Delta Kappan,* June 1978, pp. 665–667.

Penman, Brian et al. *Making Television Educational* (Toronto, Canada: Ontario Secondary School Teacher's Federation, 1976).

Shorr, Jon. "Basic Skills of TV Viewing." *Today's Education,* April/May 1978, pp. 72–75.

Smith, Elizabeth Jane, and Karla Hawkins. "Stimulate Reading Through Television." *Instructor,* March 1978.

Stecher, Judith. "TV as a Two Way Street in Learning." *Teacher,* November 1976, pp. 46–52.

Thompson, Margery. "Television May Be Just What's Needed to Teach the 'Basics'." *American School Board Journal,* January 1978, pp. 41–42.

Print References: College and Nonformal Adult Education

Brush, Judith M., and Douglas Brush. *Private Television Communications: 1980 and Beyond* (Berkeley Heights, NJ: International Television Association, 1980).

Dranov, Paula, Louise Moore, and Adrienne Hickey. *Video in the 80s: Emerging Uses for Television in Business, Education, Medicine, and Government* (White Plains, NY: Knowledge Industry Publications, 1980).

Eyster, George W. "ETV Utilization in Adult Education." *Adult Leadership,* December 1976, pp. 109–111.

Field, Hyman F. "Delivery Systems: Meeting the Multiple Needs of Diversified Clientele." *New Directions for Community Colleges,* Spring 1978, pp. 27–33.

Gunter, Jock. "NFE-TV—Television and Nonformal Education." *Educational Broadcasting International,* December 1975, pp. 172–178.

Hatlelid, R.H. "Closed-Circuit TV: Its Potential in Industry (Part 2)." *Canadian Training Methods,* December 1976, pp. 18–19.

Helmantoler, Michael C. "The Non-Traditional College Student and Public TV." *Community and Junior College Journal,* March 1978, pp. 13–15.

McKinney, Fred, and David J. Miller. "Fifteen Years of Teaching General Psychology by Television." *Teaching of Psychology,* October 1977, pp. 120–123.

Print References: Videodiscs

Daynes, Rod et al. "Field Test Evaluation of Teaching with Videodiscs." *Educational & Industrial Television,* March 1981, pp. 54–58.

"Directory of Videodisc Players." *Educational & Industrial Television,* March 1981, pp. 40–53.

Love, John. "The Videodisc—Television's New Horn of Plenty." *Media & Methods,* October 1979, pp. 16–23.

Nugent, Gwen. "Videodiscs and ITV: The Possible Vs. The Practical." *Educational & Industrial Television,* August 1979, pp. 54–56.

Rice, James, Jr. "There's a Videodisc in Your Future." *Library Journal,* January 15, 1978, pp. 143–144.

* Thomas, Willard. "Interactive Video." *Instructional Innovator,* February 1981, pp. 19–20, 44.

Winslow, Ken. "Videodisc Systems—A Retrospective." *Educational & Industrial Television,* March 1981, pp. 38–39.

Winslow, Ken. "Programmable Videodiscs and Videogames—What They Can Mean to Instruction and Training." *Educational & Industrial Television,* April 1977, pp. 23–24.

* Wood, R. Kent, and Kent G. Stephens. "An Educator's Guide to Videodisc Technology." *Phi Delta Kappan,* February 1977, pp. 466–467.

Wooley, Robert D. "A Videodisc/Portable Computer System for Information Storage." *Educational & Industrial Television,* May 1979, pp. 38–40.

Audiovisual References

* "Basic Television Terms: A Video Dictionary," (Santa Monica, CA: Pyramid Films, 1977). (16-mm film or videocassette, 17 minutes, color.)

"Cost Effective Creative Video," (Alexandria, VA: Smith-Mattingly Productions, 1979). (Videocassette, 30 minutes, color.)

"How to Watch TV," (Middleton, CT: Xerox Education Publications, 1977). [Four sound filmstrips (cassette), 12 minutes each, color.]

"Introducing the Single Camera VTR/VCR System," (Alexandria, VA: Smith-Mattingly Productions, 1979). (Videocassette, 30 minutes, color.)

"TV: An Inside View." (Salt Lake City, UT: Media Systems, 1976). [Three sound filmstrips (cassette).]

"Utilizing Instructional Television." (Salt Lake City, UT: Media Systems, 1976). [Two sound filmstrips (cassette).]

Organizations

Agency for Instructional Television (AIT), Box A, Bloomington, Indiana 47401

AIT produces programs as coordinating agency of a consortium that includes most of the United States and the Canadian provinces. It serves as a national distribution center also. It publishes a newsletter and an annual catalog listing dozens of series incorporating several hundred separate programs. Emphasis is on the elementary/secondary levels.

Association for Educational Communications and Technology (AECT), 1126 Sixteenth Street, N.W., Washington, DC 20036

AECT holds conferences, publishes journals and books related to instructional uses of media including TV, and represents the educational communication/technology profession. Its Division of Telecommunications provides a home for members who work in instructional TV and radio.

Corporation for Public Broadcasting (CPB), 1111 Sixteenth Street, N.W., Washington, DC 20036

CPB is a nonprofit, private corporation established and funded in part by the federal government. It performs a broad coordinating function for the nation's public radio and television stations and supports the interests of public broadcasting in general. CPB publishes a biweekly newsletter, *CPB Report.*

Great Plains National Instructional Television Library (GPN), Box 80669, Lincoln, Nebraska 68501

A clearinghouse for ITV recordings since the early 1960's, GPN is now part of the Nebraska Educational Telecommunications complex. GPN's annual catalog describes series for the elementary, secondary, college, and adult levels. Recent emphasis is on college/adult levels.

Regional and Specialized Organizations

Bicultural Children's Television
2150 Valdez Street
Oakland, California 94612

Central Educational Network
5400 N. St. Louis Avenue
Chicago, Illinois 60625

Children's Television Workshop
1 Lincoln Plaza
New York, New York 10023

Division for Film and Broadcasting
U.S. Catholic Conference
1101 First Avenue
New York, New York 10022

Eastern Educational TV Network
1300 Soldiers Field Road
Boston, Massachusetts 02135

International Instructional
Television Co-Op, Inc.
Skyline Center, Suite 1207
5205 Leesburg Pike
Falls Church, Virginia 22021

Midwestern Educational Network
7640 Como Avenue
St. Paul, Minnesota 55108

Ontario Educational Communications
Authority
Canada Square, 2180 Yonge Street
Toronto, Ontario, CANADA M4S 2C1

Prime Time School Television (PTST)
120 South LaSalle St.
Chicago, Illinois 60603

Public Television Library of PBS
475 L'Enfant Plaza North, S.W.
Washington, DC 20024

Southern Educational Network
928 Woodrow Street
Columbia, South Carolina 29250

Western Instructional Television
1549 North Vine Street
Los Angeles, California 90028

Periodicals

Audio-Visual Communications
United Business Publications
475 Park Avenue South
New York, New York 10016

Educational Broadcasting International
IEEE Service Center
445 Hoes Lane
Piscataway, New Jersey 08854

Educational & Industrial Television
C.S. Tepfer Publishing Co.
51 Sugar Hollow Road
Danbury, Connecticut 06810

Instructional Innovator
Association for Educational Communications and Technology
1126 Sixteenth Street, N.W.
Washington, DC 20036

Instructional Broadcasting
Brentwood Publishing
825 South Barrington
Los Angeles, California 90049

Public Telecommunication Review
National Association of Educational Broadcasters
1346 Connecticut Avenue, N.W., Suite 1101
Washington, DC 20036

Teachers Guide to Television
145 East 69th Street
New York, New York 10021

POSSIBLE PROJECTS

9A. Investigate three to five research studies that have been done on the effects of television. Include in your report a description of these studies and the conclusions reached.

9B. Using the *Education Index* read four articles that deal with various ways teachers are utilizing television in the classroom. Report on these readings and give your personal reactions to these attempts.

9C. Interview a teacher who uses television regularly in the classroom and report on this in terms of purposes, advantages, points to adhere to in order to derive the educational benefits, and problems the individual has with the use of the medium.

9D. Select any 3-hour time-block of commercial programs that children and youth are apt to view and report what you observed:

1. Programs seen and your reaction to their potential educational value.

2. Amount and kind of commercial ads during this period.

3. Evidence of sex stereotyping and the number of presentations of a multicultural/multiracial nature.

4. Your overall reaction to what students would have gained from this period of viewing.

9E. Appraise two different television programs for possible use in the classroom. Your critique should include what was the purpose of the program and how you would plan to utilize this program in your classroom.

9F. Examine two of the TV software directories listed in the chapter or in Appendix A and report on areas in which you found materials you might use.

9G. If you are a classroom teacher and have access to a TV recorder, you might plan and produce at least a 10 minute program on a topic of your choice.

9H. Appraise an instructional television program using the "Appraisal Checklist: Television."

CHAPTER 10

MEDIAWARE AND MEDIA FACILITIES

OUTLINE

Projection Setups
Seating Arrangement
Screen Size
Screen Surfaces
Screen Placement
Lenses
Projector Placement
Overhead Projectors
Slide Projectors
Filmstrip Projectors
Audio Setups
Built-in Speaker Systems
Detached Speaker Systems
Feedback
Volume and Tone Setting
Record Players
Tape Recorders (Reel-to-Reel and Cassette)
Motion Picture Projectors
Video Tape Recorders
Recording Problems
Playback Problems

OBJECTIVES

After studying this chapter, you should be able to:

1. Identify and discuss the five variables that affect visual projection and describe how they would be applied in an example situation.
2. State and apply a general rule (the "2-by-6 rule") for matching screen dimensions and audience seating.
3. List the distinguishing characteristics of the four major types of screen surface and apply these variables to specific projection situations.
4. State and apply a general rule for determining the height of screen placement.
5. Relate lens focal length to image size.
6. Relate projector location to image size and shape.
7. Describe the "keystone effect" and state two ways to correct it.
8. Operate each of the following pieces of equipment: tape recorder (reel-to-reel and cassette), overhead projector, slide projector, filmstrip projector, and motion picture projector (16-mm).
9. Indicate the basic care and maintenance procedures which ought to be observed with the pieces of equipment listed in Objective 8.
10. Identify a possible remedy when given a potential problem with any of the pieces of equipment listed in Objective 8.
11. Describe four general factors that should be taken into consideration when using audio equipment for group instruction. Your description should include volume and tone setting, speaker placement, type and size of speaker, and echo/feedback.
12. Relate speaker size to audience size.
13. Describe how to overcome the problem of audio feedback.
14. Discuss the importance of using the proper stylus with a phonograph record. Your discussion should include the way to determine the correct stylus for a record and the consequences of using an improper stylus.

Most media users are not—and do not expect to become—electronic wizards, but they do want to be able to use audiovisual media effectively. The most fundamental element of effective media use is simply keeping the equipment—the mediaware—running and being ready to cope with the snags that always seem to occur at the most inopportune times.

This chapter is intended to give guidelines for the setup of projection equipment, screens, and speakers and then to provide step-by-step operating procedures for the major types of mediaware. Included with each item are hints for the proper care of your mediaware and a troubleshooting checklist to help you cope with the most commonly occurring malfunctions.

Be aware that the equipment operation guides are not intended to be read straight through. They are meant to be *referred to* while you practice with actual AV equipment. Also, the operating instructions in the guides are necessarily somewhat general since they must cover a range of equipment models. If your own mediaware differs markedly from the descriptions given here, refer to the operating instructions provided by the manufacturer.

If you have the responsibility for recommending or actually purchasing mediaware you should become familar with the *Audio-Visual Equipment Directory,* issued annually by the National Audio-Visual Association (NAVA), and with the equipment evaluations published by the EPIE (Educational Products Information Exchange) Institute. These resources are described in the References section at the end of this chapter.

PROJECTION SETUPS

Arranging a proper environment for viewing projected visuals involves several variables, including audience seating pattern, screen size, type of screen surface, screen placement, type of lens, and projector placement.

In most cases, the instructor only has to deal with a couple of these variables, probably seating pattern and projector placement. For everyday teaching situations the classroom often will be equipped with a screen of a certain type attached in a fixed position, and the projector will already have its own lens.

There may be times, however, when you will have to make decisions about any or all of these variables—for instance, setting up an in-service workshop in the school cafeteria or running a film showing at a youth group meeting in a church hall. Let us examine some guidelines for handling each of these variables by looking at a specific hypothetical case.

Seating Arrangement

Let us assume that the room you are to use for projecting visuals is 22 ft. wide and 30 ft. long, a fairly typical room size both for formal and nonformal instructional settings. Let us further assume that you must arrange seating for between 30 and 40 viewers, a fairly typical audience size. Figure 10.1 illustrates a conventional seating pattern for a group of this size (in this case, 36 viewers). Note that the seats are arranged across the narrower room dimension. If the seats were turned to face the left or right side of the room and arranged across its 30-ft. length, viewers along either end of the rows would have a distorted view of the screen. Note too, that the first row of seats is set back somewhat from the desk area, where the screen is to be set up, so that front-row students will not be too close to the screen for comfortable viewing.

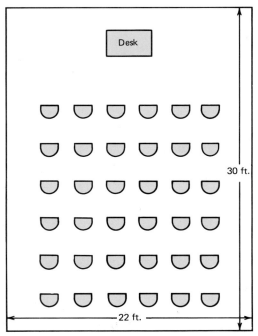

Figure 10.1 Typical size classroom arranged to seat 36.

If the room is closer to a square in shape you might want to consider placing the screen in the corner and seating the audience in diagonal rows. This possibility will be examined later in terms of screen placement.

Screen Size

A general rule of thumb (the "2-by-6" rule) accepted by most audiovisualists dictates that no viewer should be seated closer to the screen than two screen widths or farther away than six screen widths. This means that in our hypothetical case, in which the farthest viewer could be 30 ft. from the front of the room, a screen about 5 ft. wide (60 in.) would be required to ensure that this farthest-away viewer is within six screen widths of the screen (30 ÷ 6 = 5). A square screen is generally preferable, since it can be used to show rectangular images (film, slides, filmstrips, etc.) as well as square images (overhead and opaque projections). Thus, in this case a screen measuring 60-by-60 in. is recommended, as illustrated in Figure 10.2.

Screen Surfaces

Projection screens vary in their surface treatments. Various surfaces have different reflectance qualities and offer different viewing-angle widths.

Matte White Surface. The matte screen has a smooth, nonshiny surface that has the lowest reflectance but provides a constant level of brightness over the widest viewing angle (more than 45 degrees on either side of the center axis). It is durable and inexpensive. Matte white screens can be rolled up for storage or carrying. Because of these qualities the matte white screen is the one most commonly used in instructional settings.

Beaded Surface. The beaded screen is a white surface covered with small glass beads. Approximately two to four times more light is reflected from this surface than from the matte white surface. However, the beads tend to reflect light straight back toward the light source, narrowing the optimal viewing area. In fact, beyond 25 degrees on either side of the center axis the brightness is less than that of a matte white screen. Beaded screens are primarily recommended for long, narrow halls.

Lenticular Surface. The lenticular screen is made from a plastic material that has a pattern molded into the surface, usually a series of very narrow ridges running vertically up the screen. It represents a compromise between the beaded and the matte white surfaces, being nearly as reflective as the former and offering nearly the breadth of viewing angle of the latter. Like the beaded screen, the lenticular screen provides the brightest image within 25 degrees of the center axis and a dimmer image out to about 45 degrees. It must be stretched tight to be effective. It is more expensive than the matte or beaded screen and is seldom used in schools.

Aluminum Foil Surface. Developed by Kodak under the trade name Ektalite, this is the brightest surface available, about 20 times brighter than the matte white surface. However, it has a very narrow viewing angle, with visibility limited to about 20 degrees from the center axis. Screen size is also limited, 40-by-40 in. being the largest standard size. It is rigid and cannot be rolled up. Its greatest advantage is visibility in full room-light. It is particularly recommended for small group use in conditions of high ambient light.

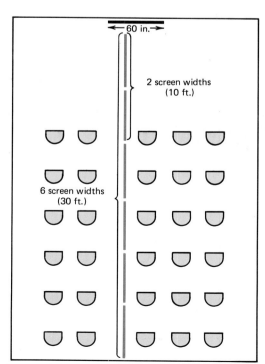

Figure 10.2 Appropriate screen size for typical size classroom, according to the "two-by-six" rule.

The major features of these screen types are shown in comparison in Figure 10.3. Given the room dimensions and audience size in our hypothetical case, a matte white screen would be most suitable.

Screen Placement

In most cases, placement of the screen at the center of the front of the room will be satisfactory. In some cases, however, it may not be. Perhaps light from a window that cannot be fully covered will wash out the projected image (sunlight is much brighter than any artifical light), or you might wish to use the chalkboard during your presentation and a screen so positioned will make it difficult or impossible for you to do so. An alternative position is in a front corner of the room. Indeed, the screen should not be at "center stage" when there is danger that it will attract unwanted attention while nonprojection activities are going on.

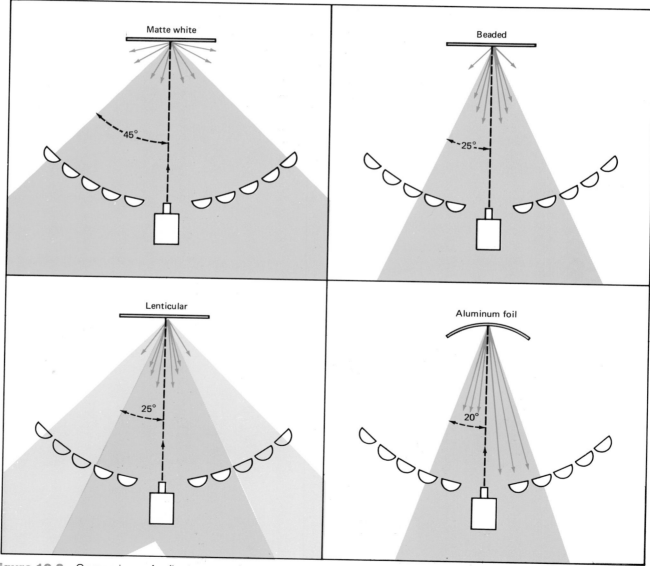

Figure 10.3 Comparison of reflectance and recommended maximum viewing angles for four different screen surfaces.

Corner placement is especially advantageous in a room that is square or nearly so. As illustrated by Figure 10.4, placing the screen in one corner allows more viewers to be seated in the good viewing area.

In any case, nowhere is it written in stone that the screen must be placed front and center. Position your screen wherever it will best suit your purpose.

The height of the screen should generally be adjusted so that the *bottom* of the screen is about level with the heads of the seated viewers. Other inhibiting factors aside, this arrangement will allow reasonably clear sight lines for the most viewers. In general, the higher the screen, the greater the optimal viewing area. Of course, care must be taken that the screen can be seen without viewers uncomfortably craning their necks.

Lenses

For everyday media use you do not have to pay much attention to technicalities about lenses. Whatever lens your projector is equipped with is usually sufficient. Understanding some basic ideas about lenses can help you cope with extraordinary situations.

First, lenses vary in focal length (measured in inches in the United States, in millimeters elsewhere). The *longer the focal length, the smaller the image* at a given distance. Since your objective is to project an image that will fill the screen, this means that the shorter the projection throw, the shorter the lens (in terms of focal length) that will be needed to enlarge the projected image sufficiently. Fortunately, the actual length of most lenses corresponds roughly with their focal length; the longer of two lenses will have the longer focal length. Figure 10.5 illustrates the relationship of lens focal length to the size of its projected image.

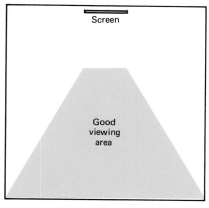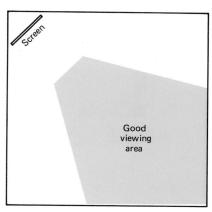

Figure 10.4 In a rather square room, placement of the screen in the corner creates a larger good viewing area.

One type of lens has a variable focal length—the zoom lens. It can, therefore, be adjusted to cast a larger or smaller picture without the necessity of moving the projector or changing its lens. The most commonly encountered zoom lens (found on many slide projectors) has a focal-length range of 4 to 6 in.

When precise specifications are needed in selecting lenses for particular conditions, media specialists use calculation devices prepared by manufacturers, such as the *Da-Lite Lens-Projection*

Screen Calculator or Kodak's *Projection Calculator and Seating Guide.*

Projector Placement

The first requirement in projector placement is to align the projection lens perpendicular to the screen (that is, it must make a 90-degree angle with the screen). Thus, the lens of the projector should be about level with the middle of the screen. If the projector is too high, too low, or off to either side, a distortion of the

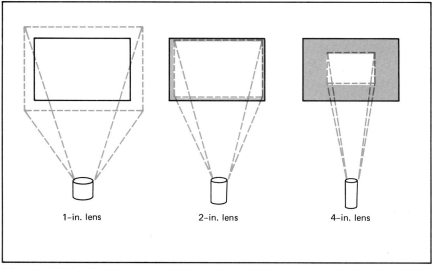

Figure 10.5 The longer the focal length of the lens, the smaller the image.

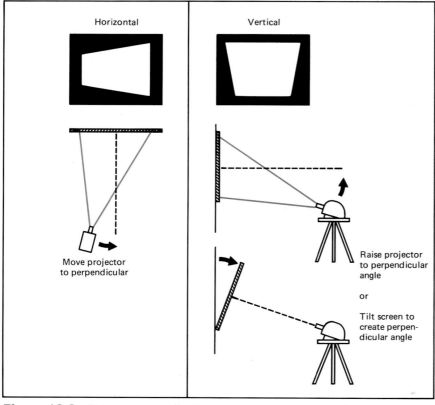

Horizontal	Vertical
Move projector to perpendicular	Raise projector to perpendicular angle or Tilt screen to create perpendicular angle

Figure 10.6   The "keystone effect"—its causes and its remedies.

the image will spill over the edges of the screen. If it is too short, the image will not fill the screen properly. Your goal is to fill the screen as fully as possible with the brightest image possible. The principle to remember here is that the image becomes *larger and less brilliant* with increase in distance between projector and screen. If the projected image is too large for your screen, push the projector closer. If the image is too small, pull the projector back.

Positioning a projector at the proper distance from the screen need not be done solely by trial-and-error. Since classroom-type projectors usually are fitted with certain focal-length lenses, their proper placement can be estimated in advance. Figure 10.8 shows the placement of the overhead, slide, and 16-mm projectors when they are equipped with their most typical lenses.

image will occur, referred to as the "keystone effect." Figure 10.6 illustrates this problem and its remedy: Move either the projector or the screen to bring the two into a perpendicular relationship.

The keystone effect is especially prevalent with use of the overhead projector because it is ordinarily set up very close to the screen and far lower than the screen (to allow the instructor to write on its stage). For this reason, many screens used for overhead projection are equipped with a "keystone eliminator," a notched bar at the top that allows the screen to be tilted forward (see Figure 10.7).

Once you have properly aligned the projector and screen, consider distance between projector and screen. If the distance is too long,

Figure 10.7   Portable tripod screen with "keystone eliminator."

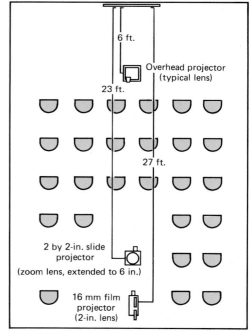

Figure 10.8   Approximate placement of projectors when equipped with typical lenses.

The projection distances described here assume appropriate lighting conditions. Where the room light is so bright that it is washing out the screen image and it cannot be dimmed any further, you must move the projector forward. This will give you a brighter image, but also, unfortunately, a smaller one. In some cases, however, it may be possible to compensate for this reduction in image size by having your audience move closer to the screen.

OVERHEAD PROJECTORS

In terms of its mechanics and electronic components, the overhead projector is a very simple apparatus, with few components requiring special maintenance procedures. Reliable as it is, however, it should not be taken for granted. Take a few basic precautions to ensure that the projector keeps putting on a bright performance.

Keep the overhead projector as clean as possible. The horizontal stage tends to gather dust, fingerprint smudges, and marking-pen traces. It should be cleaned regularly with window spray or a mild solution of soap and water. The lens in the head assembly should also be kept free of dust and smudges. Clean it periodically with lens tissue and a proper lens-cleaning solution. The fresnel lens under the stage may also need cleaning eventually, but this procedure is better left to the specialist. The lens is a precision optical element requiring special care in cleaning. In addition, some disassembly of the unit may be required to get at the lens.

The best way to prolong the life of the expensive lamp in the overhead projector is to *allow it to cool before moving* the projector. Move the projector with care. Keep the projector on a cart that can be rolled from one location to another.

HOW TO... OPERATE AN OVERHEAD PROJECTOR

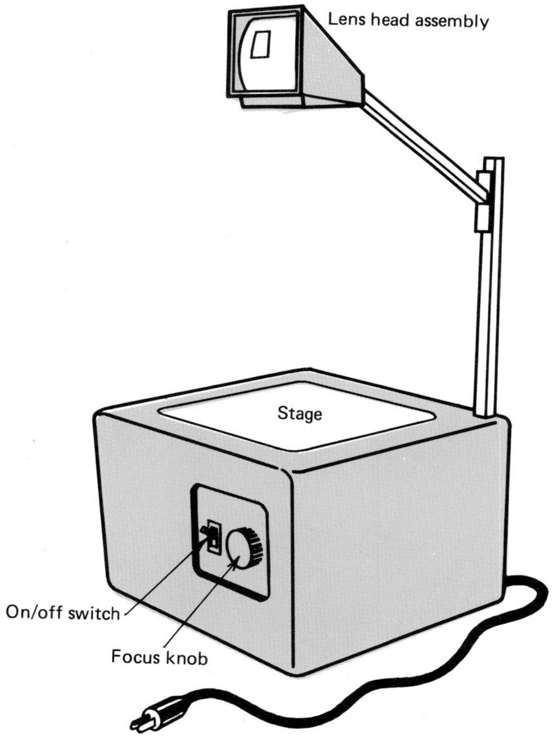

Lens head assembly

Stage

On/off switch

Focus knob

Figure 10.9

Set up
- Connect power cord to AC outlet

Operate
- Turn projector "on." (With some projectors you have to click through two positions to reach the "on" position.)
- Position transparency on stage.
- Adjust lens head to eliminate vertical keystoning:

(Not this

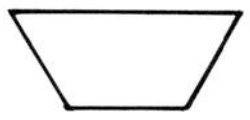

But this)

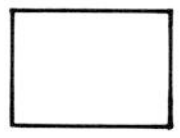

- Adjust the body of the projector to eliminate horizontal keystoning:

(Not this

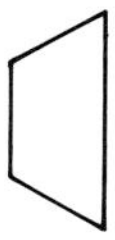

But this)

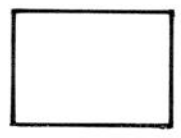

- Focus image.
- Practice writing on the transparency and erasing.

Disassemble
- Restore to storage conformation.

OVERHEAD PROJECTOR TROUBLESHOOTING

PROBLEM	POSSIBLE REMEDY
No light after flipping switch	**1.** Be sure projector is plugged into an electrical outlet. **2.** Turn the switch all the way on. Many overheads have a three-position switch: off, fan, and on. **3.** If lamp is burned out, replace it. Be sure to use a lamp of the same wattage (too high a wattage can cause overheating). Do not handle the lamp while it is hot. Avoid touching the new lamp with bare fingers; this could shorten its life. **4.** Switch may be defective. If so, replace it.
Dark spot on screen or failure of lens to focus despite all adjustment of focus	After determining that it is not simply a matter of dirt on the lens or improper use of the focus control, check for a warped fresnel lens. This lens is plastic and can become warped from excessive heat, usually caused by the fan not running properly. Have a qualified specialist repair the fan or thermostat and replace the fresnel lens.

When hand carrying the apparatus, hold on to the body of the projector, not the thin arm of the head assembly. The head assembly arm is not intended to be a carrying handle. Used as such, it can easily be twisted out of alignment, thus distorting the projector's image.

HOW TO...OPERATE A SLIDE PROJECTOR

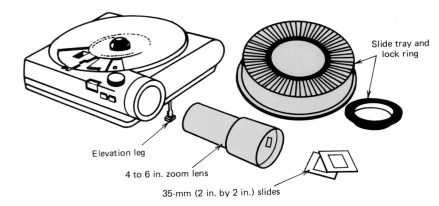

Elevation leg

4 to 6 in. zoom lens

35-mm (2 in. by 2 in.) slides

Slide tray and lock ring

Set up

- Connect power cord to AC outlet (Power cord is stored in a compartment on the bottom of the projector.)
- Plug in remote control cord with white dot on top.
- Insert lens.
- Load slides into tray and tighten the locking ring on the tray.
- Seat slide tray on projector *Note* the notch at "O."

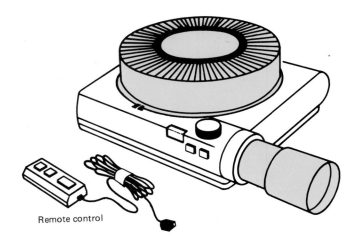

Remote control

Figure 10.10

SLIDE PROJECTORS

In normal use, slide projectors require little special attention to keep working smoothly. The only regular maintenance required of the user is to clean the front element of the projection lens if it

shows finger marks. More likely to cause difficulties are the slides themselves, which should always be stored away from heat and handled only by their mounts. The most frequent cause of foul-ups in slide presentations is a slide which jams because it is warped or frayed ("dog-eared"). Remount slides that could cause jams.

More serious damage can occur if the slide projector falls because it has been propped up precariously on top of a stack of books or on some other unstable base. This happens all too often because the projector's elevation

leg seems never to be quite long enough to raise the image up to the top of the screen. Better solutions are to use a higher projection table or to raise the whole projection table or to raise the whole projector by placing it on a sturdy box or similar platform.

Operate
- Set automatic timer at "m" (manual operation).
- Move on/off switch to "low" or "high" lamp setting.
- Position image on screen, making it smaller or larger by means of the lens barrel.
- Focus image with focus knob.
- Project slides using remote control or buttons on the forward side of the projector.

Disassemble
- Press and hold "select" button while turning the tray to "O."
- Remove slide tray.
- Move on/off switch to "FAN."
- Allow lamp to cool before switching off.
- Remove slides from slide tray.
- Restore to storage conformation.

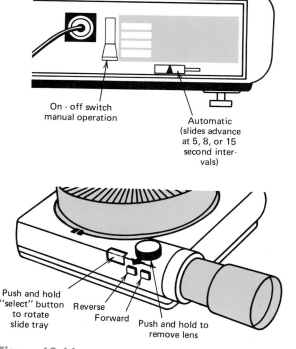

On - off switch manual operation

Automatic (slides advance at 5, 8, or 15 second intervals)

Push and hold "select" button to rotate slide tray

Reverse Forward

Push and hold to remove lens

Figure 10.11

SLIDE PROJECTOR TROUBLESHOOTING

PROBLEM	POSSIBLE REMEDY
Can't find power cord	Look for a built-in storage compartment. On the Kodak Carousel, the power cord is stored in a latched compartment underneath the projector.
No power after plugging in	If you are sure the outlet is "live" (a fuse or circuit breaker may have killed all electrical power in the room), check the circuit breaker on the slide projector. On some models a button on the bottom of the projector must be pressed after changing lamps.
Fan runs but lamp does not light	Some projectors have separate switches for "Lamp" and "Fan" or a two-stage switch for these two functions. Make sure all switches are properly set.
Image not level	Most slide projectors have an adjustment knob on one of the rear feet. Use the knob to raise or lower that side.
Without slides, the blank image is distorted	1. The lenses may be out of alignment or even broken. This is especially likely with the Kodak Carousel, in which several lenses are loosely held in place on the underside of the projector. Often they can be adjusted easily by aligning them correctly in their slots. 2. If an image of the lamp filament is seen on the screen, the lamp has been incorrectly installed and should be seated properly.
Projector gets very hot; slides begin to burn	Stop immediately! The Kodak Carousel has a heat-absorbing glass between the lenses next to the lamp. If this flat glass is broken or missing the heat builds up quickly and can cause damage.
Slide image upside-down or backwards	Remove the slide and reverse it. (Improper loading can be avoided by "thumb-spotting" all slides. See Chapter 5.)
Slide jams in gate	1. Manually remove the slide. On the Kodak Carousel, press the "select" button (power must be on). If the slide does not pop up, the tray will have to be removed. Turn off the power and use a coin to turn the screw in the center of the tray; this unlocks the tray, allowing it to be lifted off and giving access to the gate for manual removal of the slide. 2. Jamming can be avoided by not placing bent slides in the tray. Plastic mounts have a tendency to warp; cardboard mounts fray; glass mounts may be too thick for the slide compartment of the tray. For this reason, jamming is more likely with *narrow* slide compartments, as are found in the 140-slide Carousel trays. Use the 80-slide tray whenever possible.

FILMSTRIP PROJECTORS

A filmstrip projector requires the same sort of care and handling as a slide projector. On the filmstrip projector, however, an additional concern is keeping the film gate clean. Lint and dirt in the gate may be seen around the edges of the projected image and are an annoyance to the viewer. The film gate can be cleaned with a special aperture brush (also used with motion picture projectors) or with some other non-metal, soft-bristle brush.

Filmstrip projectors that come in enclosed cases carry a warning to remove the projector from the case before operating it. This is to ensure that air can circulate freely to the cooling fan located on the underside of the projector. Any interference with the fan, such as a sheet of paper sucked up against the fan grid or an accumulation of dust adhering to the fan grid, can lead to overheating and damage to filmstrips.

HOW TO... OPERATE A FILMSTRIP PROJECTOR

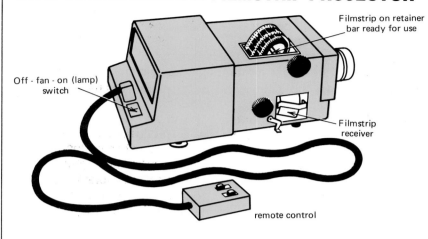

Filmstrip on retainer bar ready for use

Off - fan - on (lamp) switch

Filmstrip receiver

remote control

Framer - advance knob

Film gate

Filmstrip receiver

Figure 10.12

Set up
- Connect power cord to ac outlet.

Operate
- Turn projector "on."
- Place filmstrip on retainer bar.
- Thread filmstrip down into film slot. Be sure that "START" or "FOCUS" appears at head of filmstrip.
- Turn advance knob until "FOCUS" frame appears.
- Adjust framer so the full frame is projected when you click the advance knob.
- Turn projector "off."

Disassemble
- Return filmstrip to container. Do not pull the end of the filmstrip to tighten the roll. Start with a tight roll at the center and continue, holding the film by the edges.
- Restore to storage conformation.

FILMSTRIP PROJECTOR TROUBLESHOOTING

PROBLEM	POSSIBLE REMEDY
Dark areas or smudges projected on the screen	Clean the lens.
Dirt/lint visible at edges of projected image	Foreign matter in the film gate. Clean with an aperture brush or other brush with no metal components.

Filmstrip is not properly framed. Correct with framer knob. **Figure 10.13**

If this is the first frame you see, the filmstrip has been inserted tail-first. Withdraw it and insert the head end. (If the lettering appears backwards, you have threaded it with the wrong side facing the screen; reverse it. The ends of the strip should curl toward the screen.) **Figure 10.14**

AUDIO SETUPS

Built-in Speaker Systems

Most audiovisual equipment intended for use in educational settings comes equipped with a built-in speaker system. The built-in speaker is usually a single-unit "piston" speaker. This kind of unit is suitable for many but not all instructional purposes. Small speakers built into the chassis of table-model recorders, phonographs, filmstrip projectors, and so on, often lack the fidelity necessary for audio clarity throughout the audience area. Because built-in single-speaker units have a limited frequency response, sounds falling outside this range may become distorted—bass sounds, for example, may cause the speaker to vibrate.

Portable cassette recorders are particularly troublesome when used for playback in an average-size classroom. Even under the best conditions, the sound quality of portable cassettes is severely limited by their undersized speakers. If such a unit is used to play back material in which audio fidelity is essential (a musical composition, for example), an auxiliary speaker should be used. A high efficiency speaker, for instance one having a 6- or 8-in. diameter, may be plugged into the earphone or external-speaker jack of the cassette player to provide a suitable listening experience.

Size alone, however, does not guarantee high quality in a speaker. If high fidelity audio is needed, a two-way speaker (bass and treble speaker in one cabinet) or a three-way speaker (bass plus mid-range tweeter plus regular tweeter) is highly desirable. Such speakers may require an auxiliary amplifier when used in conjunction with AV equipment, but they are capable of reproducing the complete frequency range audible to human beings.

Another problem with built-in speakers is that they are often built into the side of the machine containing the controls. This is fine when the operator of the tape recorder or the phonograph is also the listener. But if the apparatus is placed on a table or desk and operated by an instructor for the benefit of an audience, the speaker will be aimed *away from* the audience (see Figures 10.15 and 10.16). A simple way to remedy this situation is to turn the machine around so that the speaker faces the audience and operate the controls from beside rather than in front of the machine.

In the case of film projectors with a built-in speaker facing out of the side, the problem is compounded by the fact that film projectors are usually set up near the back of the room. Thus, the speaker may face away from the majority of the audience. The problem may be even further aggravated by noise from the projector itself. About all you can do

to alleviate such a situation is to move the projector or, if feasible, rearrange your seating pattern so that the built-in speaker will be facing at least the majority of your audience.

If you are operating in a lecture hall or auditorium that has a built-in public address system you will want to plug your projector or player into that system. This might require an adapter to match up the output plug and input jack.

Figure 10.15 A typical tape recorder or record player will often have its speaker facing the operator.

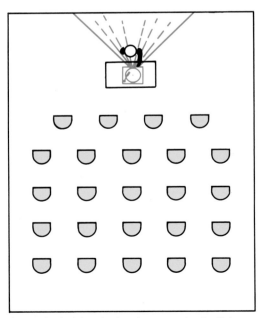

Figure 10.16 An undesirable playback setup: the built-in speaker faces away from the audience.

Detached Speaker Systems

The detachable speakers that accompany some film projectors and stereo tape recorders are generally large and sensitive enough to provide adequate quality sound throughout the instructional area if, as with other separate speaker systems, you give consideration to their individual placement.

Whenever possible, speakers should face toward the center of your audience. If reverberation is a problem, however, especially in long narrow rooms, the speaker may be aimed diagonally across the audience to help alleviate this situation (see Figure 10.17).

In the case of film projection, it is also very important that the speaker be placed as close as possible to the screen. Psychologically, we are conditioned to expect sound to come directly from its source. We are, consequently, most comfortable with film sound when it appears to be coming directly from the screen image that constitutes its source.

Be sure nothing obstructs the sound waves as they travel from the speaker toward your audience. Certainly you would not place the speaker behind an actual sound barrier, but even classroom furniture (desks, chairs) and the audience itself may present physical obstructions to sound. To avoid such interference, place the speaker on a table or some other kind of stand so that it is at or above the head level of your seated audience, as in Figure 10.17.

If you are using a stereophonic system, the speakers should be far enough apart so that the sound is appropriately balanced between the two. As a rule of thumb, the distance between the speakers should equal the distance from the speakers to the middle of the audience. Thus, in the typical 22-by-30 ft. classroom, stereo speakers would be placed 15 to 18 ft. apart—nearly in the corners of the room. (See Figure 10.18.)

Feedback

Feedback is the name given to that annoying squeal that so often intrudes in public address systems or tape recorders being used as voice reinforcers. The usual cause is simple: The signal coming out of the speaker is fed back into the microphone. The most direct remedy is to make sure that the speakers are set up *in front of* the microphone. If the speakers cannot be moved, you may be able to stop the feedback by adjusting the tone and volume controls or even by moving the microphone. (Omnidirectional microphones are more likely to cause feedback problems than unidirectional microphones.)

Figure 10.17 A suggested speaker placement: the detachable speaker is placed near the screen, raised to head level, aimed toward the audience with no obstructions in the way.

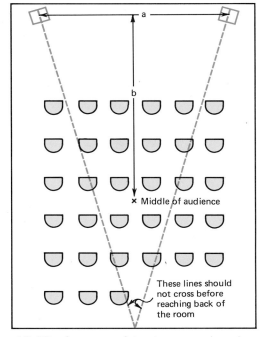

Figure 10.18 An appropriate stereo speaker placement for a typical size classroom: the distance between the speakers equals the distance to the middle of the audience.

Volume and Tone Setting

Because sound wave intensity decreases rapidly over distance, achieving a comfortable sound volume for all listeners can be quite a challenge. This is particularly true in larger rooms, for it is difficult to reach the back of the room without generating a very loud sound at the front. This, of course, can cause considerable discomfort to those seated near the speaker. An ideal solution would be to use several low-power sources rather than a single high-power one. But since this is usually not feasible, you can only strive to achieve a reasonable compromise through proper setting of the volume control. By moving around the room during the presentation (unobtrusively), you can get a feel for the best volume setting to suit your situation. The problem may be further alleviated by not seating students at the extreme front or back.

The tone control can be used to correct certain other acoustical problems. For instance, low frequency (bass) sounds will reverberate annoyingly under certain conditions ("boominess"). This can be compensated for somewhat by turning the tone control of the film projector or tape recorder toward "treble." This also tends to improve the audibility of male speakers' low-pitched voices. Conversely, high pitched sounds can be dampened with the tone control.

RECORD PLAYERS

The component of a record player (phonograh) that is most likely to cause problems for the user is the stylus ("needle") assembly. Fortunately, most of these problems can be recognized and remedied by even the most "nonexpert" of people.

Phonograph records come in three basic types, classified according to the speed at which they revolve on the turntable (RPM = revolutions per minute). Each type has a different groove width:

78 RPM the original standard type, no longer being produced; it has the widest grooves.

45 RPM grooves are about one-half the width of those on 78 RPM records, allowing more recording time per inch.

33⅓ RPM often referred to as "microgroove" because its grooves are narrower than those of 78 and 45 RPM records.

Each of these basic record types requires a stylus whose tip diameter exactly matches the width of the record's grooves. If the tip of the stylus is too narrow for the record, it will ride on the bottom of the groove instead of along its sides (where the signal is encoded) thereby picking up the signal poorly and possibly damaging the groove itself. If the stylus tip is too wide, it will ride too high in the groove, thereby failing to pick up recorded sounds properly, possibly skipping out of the grooves entirely, and causing excessive wear on the grooves. (See Figure 10.19.) It is essential, therefore, that your stylus be one that fits the type of record you wish to play.

Most styli today have tips of diamond or sapphire and are thus extremely durable. They are not, however, damage proof. One frequent cause of damage to the sty-

lus is allowing it to strike down hard upon a record or empty turntable. Do not move or carry the player around without first securely fastening the tone arm (which contains the stylus assembly). Continual playing of cracked or warped records can also damage the needle, as can using it on a wrong RPM recording.

Keep the stylus clean of any dust it may pick up as it glides over records. If your phonograph does not have a cleaning brush that automatically cleans the needle attached to the tone arm, clean your stylus periodically with a quick flick of a soft brush from back to front to avoid dislodging the stylus from its cartridge. Do not use your finger tip for this purpose. You may damage the needle by too heavy a touch. Further, your finger may leave a deposit of oil which will attract additional dust.

Even if your stylus is well cared for, it will gradually wear out and need to be replaced. If you think that a stylus might need changing, inspect it closely with a strong magnifying glass, or a stylus microscope, available at hi-fi shops. A worn stylus will show one

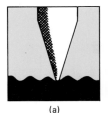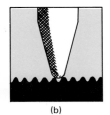

(a)   (b)

Figure 10.19 Mismatches between stylus size and type of record.

HOW TO... OPERATE A RECORD PLAYER

Controls

Tone arm lock

Figure 10.21

Set up
- Open case and connect power cord to ac outlet.

Operate
- Turn amplifier and turntable power "on."
- Set turntable speed control.
- Place record on turntable.
- Release tone arm from the locking screw or locking clip.
- Position tone arm on record.
- Adjust volume control.
- Adjust tone control.
- Turn amplifier and turntable power "off."

Disassemble
- Place turntable speed control in "neutral" (if possible).
- Lock the tone arm into place.
- Return to storage conformation.

or more flattened surfaces instead of a smoothly rounded tip. Removal of the stylus usually involves nothing more complex than unscrewing its mount or unplugging its cartridge from the tone arm. If in doubt, consult an audiovisual or hi-fi specialist about the selection of a proper stylus and its proper installation.

Figure 10.20 Styli and cartridges come in many configurations; this one is a typical plug-in stylus/cartridge combination.

RECORD PLAYER TROUBLESHOOTING

PROBLEM	POSSIBLE REMEDY
Tone arm skates across record	1. Stylus may not be the proper one for the record. If the stylus does match the record speed, the tone arm may not be exerting sufficient pressure; if the machine has an adjustment to correct this, increase the pressure slightly, but only within the limits recommended for your phonograph—usually 2 to 7 g. In many cases the tracking pressure may already be too great, thus guaranteeing even faster wear on records and the stylus. 2. Check the stylus for excessive wear; replace if worn.
Sound is tinny, murky, distorted	1. Replace stylus, if worn. 2. Cartridge may be cracked; if so, replace it.
Turntable revolves jerkily ("wow" sound) or too slowly	The idler wheel may have become flattened on one side or may have oil on it, causing it to make poor contact with the turntable rim. Consult an audiovisual specialist or repairperson to check the idler wheel.

SHURE HI-TRACK

TAPE RECORDERS (REEL-TO-REEL AND CASSETTE)

The part of a tape recorder needing most frequent attention is the record/playback head. To get good quality recording or playback, the tape must make full contact with the record/playback head. Each time the tape passes across the head, small bits of debris are deposited on it. Eventually, this debris will interfere with proper contact between the tape and the head. Therefore, the record/playback head should be cleaned regularly. Most manufacturers recommend cleaning after 5 to 10 hrs. of use. Of course, it should be done more frequently

HOW TO...OPERATE A REEL-TO-REEL TAPE RECORDER

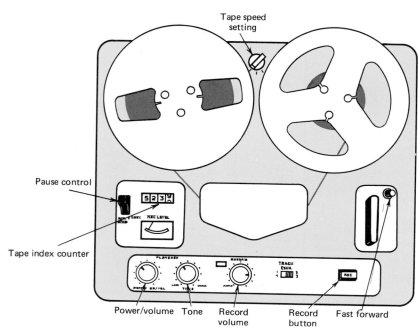

Figure 10.22

Set up
- Open case and connect power cord to ac outlet.
- Position the feed reel (the full one) on the left spindle and the take-up reel on the right one.
- Turn power switch "on."
- Thread tape.
- Press button to set tape index counter at zero.
- Set tape speed.

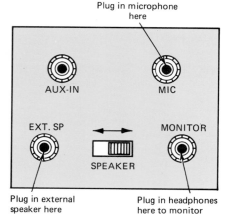

Figure 10.23

Operate
- Plug in microphone.
- Turn record control to "auto" (if your recorder has an automatic record level setting).
- Press "record" button and *hold* while you move lever to "forward" position.
- Record your voice on tape.
- Rewind tape to starting point by moving lever to "rewind."
- Play back your recording.

Disassemble
- Rewind tape.
- Turn power control "off."
- Return to storage conformation.

when the machine is used in dusty areas, such as in a machine shop or woodworking area.

There are two methods for cleaning tape recorder heads. There are specially made head-cleaning tapes available in both open reel and cassette format. If these are not available or not effective for your problem, you can use special head cleaning fluid (available at most stores selling tape recorders or from audiovisual suppliers). Apply with a cotton swab. Do not use carbon tetrachloride, which can damage the heads, or alcohol, which can leave a residue of its own on the head. Alcohol can also damage tapes if they are played immediately after cleaning. In addition, over a period of time, carbon tetrachloride and alcohol can cause rubber parts of the pressure rollers to deteriorate.

The entire tape path should be inspected for dirt or damage which might interfere with proper tape operation. Most importantly, follow the recommended maintenance procedures in the manual that accompanies the recorder. Do not oil any tape recorder unless specifically recommended to do so by the manufacturer. Most tape recorders are designed so that they do not need lubrication.

Audio equipment in general is subject to buildup of carbon or other contaminants on the contacts inside the volume and tone controls. This buildup causes an

TAPE RECORDER TROUBLESHOOTING

PROBLEM	POSSIBLE REMEDY
Recorded voice or music is too low-pitched—sounds like a drawn-out drone	You are playing back at a slower speed than was originally recorded; raise the speed.
Recorded voice or music is too high-pitched—the "chipmunk" effect	You are playing back at a faster speed than was originally recorded; lower the speed.
Sound is faint and indistinct	Record/playback head needs cleaning; use a tape recorder head cleaner.
Hissing in background	Excess noise may be caused by head having become magnetized by long use of recording mode. Have a qualified specialist demagnetize ("degauss") the head(s).
Two different sound sources are heard simultaneously—one normal, the other backwards	Your playback machine has a different head configuration than the original recorder (e.g., yours is single-track, original is dual-track).

HOW TO...OPERATE A CASSETTE RECORDER

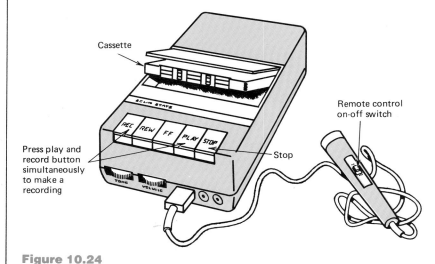

Cassette

Press play and record button simultaneously to make a recording

TONE   VOLUME

REC REW F.F PLAY STOP

Stop

Remote control on-off switch

Figure 10.24

Set up
- Connect power cord to ac outlet.
- Press "stop" key.
- Insert cassette.

Operate
- Press "play" key.
- Press "stop" key.

Record
- Connect microphone to recorder.
- Press "play" and "record" keys simultaneously.
- Record your voice.
- Rewind tape to starting point by pressing "rewind" key.
- Play tape.

Disassemble
- Rewind tape.
- Remove cassette.
- Restore to storage conformation.

CASSETTE RECORDER TROUBLESHOOTING

PROBLEM	POSSIBLE REMEDY
Tape comes out of cassette and snarls around the capstan of recorder	**1.** Very thin tape, as found in longer length cassettes (e.g., C-120) is especially prone to do this. Convert to shorter length (thicker) tapes.
	2. The plastic hub of the take-up reel may be rubbing against the cassette. Try rotating the hub with a pencil to see if you can free it.
	3. Mechanical problem: Take-up spindle is not pulling hard enough because of faulty clutch or belt. Have cassette repaired by qualified specialist.
"Record" button on cassette will not stay down	The "accidental erasure" tab on the back of the cassette has been broken out. Place tape over the gap left by the missing tab if you want to record something new on the cassette.

annoying scratching sound whenever the control knob is turned. Usually the problem can be resolved quickly and easily by spraying "tuner cleaner" (available at hi-fi and electronics supply stores) directly onto the shaft of the control. More stubborn fouling of the contacts might require some disassembly of equipment to get the spray closer to the source of the trouble.

MOTION PICTURE PROJECTORS

Since film projectors and 16-mm films are comparatively expensive instruments of instruction (the typical half-hour educational film costs about $300), it is particularly incumbent upon instructors to prolong the life of these items by taking proper care of them.

The average life of a film is approximately 100 showings. Mishandling, however, can greatly reduce this span of service. On the other hand, careful threading, inspection after each use, periodic lubrication of the film, and proper storage (at room temperature, 40 percent humidity) can lengthen the working life of the film.

Proper care of the projector can also help extend the service span of film. It is important to keep the projector's film path clean to prevent undue wear on the film. An aperture brush or other soft-bristled, nonmetalic brush should be used regularly to clean the film path, the film gate, and around the sound drum.

The lens of the projector should be kept free of dust and smudges by periodic cleaning with lens tissue and cleaner. The projector's volume and tone control mechanisms sometimes develop internal carbon buildup, causing crackling sounds when the knobs are turned to adjust audio. This debris can generally be eliminated simply by spraying around the external extensions of the control knobs with an aerosol tuner cleaner while turning the knobs.

Given the electro-mechanical complexity of the film projector, you should not go much beyond these routine cleaning procedures to help keep your projector in good working order.

HOW TO... OPERATE A 16-MM FILM PROJECTOR

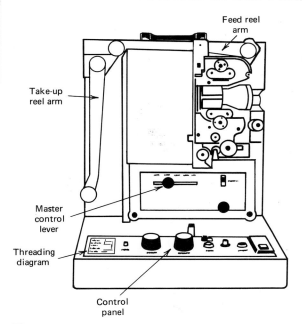

Set up (refer to Figure 10.27)
- Unbuckle and separate speaker from projector.
- Swing *feed reel arm* up and into position.
- Raise *take-up reel arm* into position.
- Attach drivebelt onto pulley on take-up reel arm.
- Place take-up *reel* on spindle and lock spindle.
- Plug power cord into ac outlet.
- Plug *speaker* or headphones into speaker jack.
- Place *film* on feed reel arm spindle and lock spindle.
- Unwind about 5 feet of film.

Threading
- Check to be sure that "rewind" lever is in raised position.
- Follow threading diagram printed on projector. On the Kodak Pageant projector, the steps are as follows:

Figure 10.25

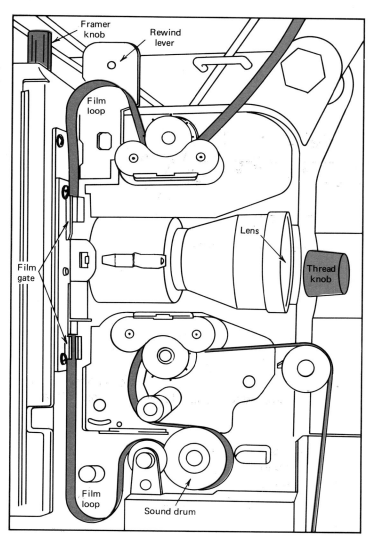

1. Open clamps around upper and lower drive sprockets. See (A) and (B) on picture below.
2. Turn thread knob until white line faces you. See (2) on picture below.
3. Loop film under *upper sprocket* (A) and engage teeth with sprocket holes in film; then close clamp.
4. Open *film gate* and slide film into channel so that it is flat.
5. Close film gate by pressing in on clamp.
6. Form a loop to match red line on rewind lever.
7. Bring film around black *bottom* roller to form loop.
8. Thread film over *pressure roller* and around *sound drum*.
9. Thread film around idler and over lower sprocket (B).
10. Engage sprocket holes with teeth on sprocket (B) and close clamp.
11. Thread film around three remaining *idler rollers*—if more film is needed, turn master control briefly to "motor."
12. Insert end of film leader into slot of empty take-up reel.
13. Double check threading diagram to ensure that film is properly threaded.
14. Rotate threading knob clockwise to check film loops.

Figure 10.26

HOW TO...OPERATE A 16 MM FILM PROJECTOR (continued)

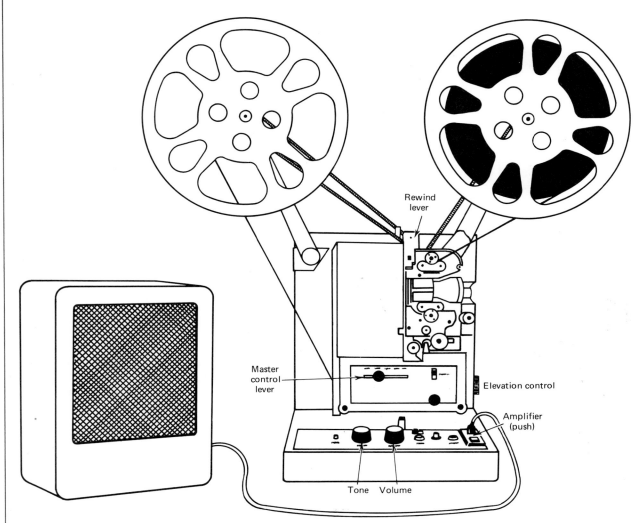

Figure 10.27

Operate

- Turn amplifier "on."
- Move *master control lever* to "motor," then to "lamp."
- Position image on screen by moving projector and adjusting the elevation control.
- *Focus* image by turning lens.
- Adjust volume and tone.
- Rotate *framer knob* if image is not framed properly.
- You may *reverse* film by pulling master control lever to "off," then "reverse."
- Run film *forward* until all film has run through projector.
- Turn master control lever to "off."

Rewind

- Secure end of film in slot of feed reel, and take up slack.
- Pull *rewind lever* down.
- Move master control to "rewind/forward" position, *not* "reverse."
- When film has been rewound onto feed reel, turn master control lever to "off" and lift rewind lever to "up" position.
- Turn amplifier "off."

Dissassemble

- Push rear arm forward to remove belt.
- Lower feed reel arm.
- Press release lever and carefully lower take-up arm.
- Return projector and speaker to storage conformation.

FILM PROJECTOR TROUBLESHOOTING

PROBLEM	POSSIBLE REMEDY
Projector runs but lamp doesn't light	First, be sure that you have turned the operation lever all the way on. It should be in the "Lamp" position. If the lamp doesn't light after being properly switched on, it is possible that it is burnt out and needs to be replaced.
Projector runs but there is no sound	**1.** Be sure that the "Amplifier" switch is turned on. **2.** Be sure that the speaker is plugged in. **3.** Check to see that the film is threaded properly around the sound drum. **4.** Check the other switches, such as "Sound/Silent" and "Micro./Film." If there is still no sound after checking all the above steps, it is likely that the exciter lamp is burnt out and needs to be replaced.
Distorted sound	Make sure that the film is wound tightly around the sound drum.
Flowing blur instead of an image	The film is not properly engaged in the gate. Be sure that the sprockets are meshing with the sprocket holes and that the film gate is closed.
Fuzz around edges of projected image	Dirt and lint collect easily around the aperture (due to the static electricity created by moving film). The film gate should be cleaned with a brush before each showing. If dirt is causing distraction during a showing, it may be cleared away by blowing into the aperture area. This is not recommended as a routine cleaning practice (since the moisture in your breath can harm lenses and delicate metal parts) but only as a "quick fix" in an emergency.
Projector chatters noisily	Lower loop has been lost. Stop the projector and reform the loop, or press down on the loop restorer while the projector continues running.
Film breaks	Stop the projector. If possible, determine and correct the cause of the breaking. Then re-thread the film. The broken end should be overlapped on the take-up reel. Mark the break by inserting a slip of paper into the reel at this point. Do *not* attempt to repair the break with tape, pins, paper clips, etc.
Voice not synchronized with image (lips)	The lower loop is either too tight or too loose, causing the sound track to pass over the sound drum either before or after the image is projected in the aperture. Adjust the lower loop.

VIDEO TAPE RECORDERS

Video record/playback machines are highly sophisticated electronic instruments. Maintenance and repair, consequently, should generally be left to the specialist. In addition, video tape recording systems are far from standardized in their various mechanisms and modes of operation. You should, therefore, refer to the manufacturer's manual for information about the operating principles and procedures of the particular system you happen to be using. The "Troubleshooting" guide included here is limited to general sorts of problems that may occur with virtually any video system and that can be remedied by the nonspecialist.

VIDEO TAPE RECORDER TROUBLESHOOTING

PROBLEM	POSSIBLE REMEDY
Recording. Video tape is running but there is no picture on the monitor	1. Check to see that all components are plugged in and turned on. Make sure the lens cap is off the camera and the lens aperture is open. 2. Check the monitor. Switch it to "TV" and try to tune in a broadcast channel; make sure the brightness and contrast controls are properly set. If you still fail to get a picture, check to see if there is a circuit breaker on the back of the monitor that needs to be reset. If you get a picture while switched to "TV" you should then check the connection between camera and monitor. 3. Check the cable connections from camera to recorder and from recorder to monitor. 4. Check the settings of the switches on the recorder. Is the input selector on "Camera?" Is the "Record" button depressed?
Playback. Video tape is running but there is no picture or sound on monitor	1. Make sure the monitor input selector is set at "VTR" and all units are plugged in. 2. Check connectors between playback unit and monitor (e.g., make sure "Video Out" from playback is connected to "Video In" on monitor). Wiggle the end of the cable to see if there is a loose connection. 3. Check switches on playback unit.
Fuzzy sound and/or snowy picture	1. Video and/or audio heads may be fouled. Clean with approved spray. 2. Brushes under head-drum cover may be fouled or damaged. Have a technician check this possibility.
Picture slants horizontally across screen (the audio may also sound off-speed)	If adjustment of the horizontal hold knob does not clear up the situation, you may have a tape or cassette that is incompatible with your playback unit. The only remedy is to obtain a playback machine that matches the format of the tape or cassette.

REFERENCES

Print References

Aydelotte, Mark. "Lights and Mikes." *Media & Methods,* October 1976, pp. 71–72.

Baker, Dan. "Video Vans." *Educational & Industrial Television,* March 1977, pp. 27–28.

Benson, Laurel D. "Demystifying AV Equipment: A Troubleshooting Workshop." *Audiovisual Instruction,* November 1976, pp. 48–49.

Berliner, Oliver. "Does Your Audio Match Your Video?" *Educational & Industrial Television,* February 1977, pp. 29, 32.

* Bullard, John R., and Calvin E. Mether. *Audiovisual Fundamentals,* 2d ed. (Dubuque, IA: Wm. C. Brown, 1979).

Crocker, A.H. "Equipment for Individual Learning." *Educational Media International,* March 1977, pp. 2–6.

Educational Products Information Exchange. *Videocassette Recorders/Players,* Report No. 89e (Stony Brook, NY: EPIE Institute, 1979).

———. *Audio Cassette Players,* Report No. 91e (Stony Brook, NY: EPIE Institute, 1980).

Gaston, Sarah J. "How to Buy Audiovisual Hardware." *School Shop,* January 1977, pp. 23–26.

Johnson, Warren. "Resources for Hardware Selection." *Audiovisual Instruction,* April 1978, pp. 46–47.

King, Kenneth L. et al. *A Systematic Approach to Instructional Media Competency* (Dubuque, IA: Kendall/Hunt, 1980).

Kodak Projection Calculator and Seating Guide (S-16) (Rochester, NY: Eastman Kodak, 1979).

Lord, Kenniston W., Jr. *The Design of the Industrial Classroom* (Reading MA: Addison-Wesley, 1977).

McVey, Gerald F. "Environments for Effective Media Utilization: Some Design Considerations." *Viewpoints,* September 1975, pp. 59–77.

Mattingly, Grayson, and Welby Smith. *Introducing the Single-Camera VTR System* (New York, NY: Charles Scribner's Sons, 1973).

* Oates, Stanton. *Self-Instruction Manual: Audiovisual Equipment,* 3d ed. (Dubuque, IA: Wm. C. Brown, 1975).

Rosenberg, Kenyon C., and John S. Doskey. *Media Equipment: A Guide and Dictionary* (Littleton, CO: Libraries Unlimited, 1976).

* Schroeder, Don, and Gary Lare. *Audiovisual Equipment and Materials: A Basic Repair and Maintenance Manual* (Metuchen, NJ: The Scarecrow Press, 1979).

Waggener, Joe, and Tim Kraft. "Video Troubleshooting for the Technically Butterfingered." *Audiovisual Instruction,* January 1979, pp. 44–45.

Wilkinson, Gene L. "Projection Variables and Performance." *AV Communication Review,* Winter 1976, 413–436.

* Wyman, Raymond. *Mediaware: Selection, Operation, and Maintenance,* 2d ed. (Dubuque, IA: Wm. C. Brown, 1976).

Yeamans, George T. *Projectionists' Primer* (Pullman, WA: Information Futures, 1979).

Organizations

EPIE (Educational Products Information Exchange) Institute, 475 Riverside Drive, New York, New York 10027

EPIE is a nonprofit, consumer-supported agency functioning like a "consumer's union" and providing analytical information about instructional materials and equipment. EPIE conducts workshops on analyzing instructional materials and publishes *EPIE Reports* bimonthly and a newsletter, *EPIEgram.*

National Audio-Visual Association (NAVA), 3150 Spring Street, Fairfax, Virginia 22030

Trade association for producers and distributors of audiovisual equipment and materials. Publishes annually *The Audio-Visual Equipment Directory.*

POSSIBLE PROJECTS

10-A. Demonstrate the proper setup, operation, and disassembly of the following pieces of equipment: tape recorder (reel-to-reel and cassette), overhead projector, slide projector, filmstrip projector, and motion picture projector (16-mm and film loop).

10-B. Given a piece of equipment from the list in Project 10-A with a "problem," troubleshoot and correct the problem.

10-C. Demonstrate proper care and maintenance for each piece of equipment listed in Project 10-A.

10-D. Set up (or diagram the setup) for a given instructional situation requiring audio and/or projection.

---

*Key references.

CHAPTER 11

TECHNOLOGIES OF INSTRUCTION

OBJECTIVES

After studying this chapter, you should
be able to:
1. Define "technologies of instruction"
and identify five characteristics of such
a "technology."
2. Identify five examples of "technologies of instruction."
3. Discuss the basic application of
reinforcement theory, including a definition of "reinforcer."
4. Describe the relationship between
"teaching machines" and "programmed
instruction."
5. Discuss five characteristics (or elements) of programmed instruction.
Your description should include a discussion of what programmed instruction is and how it differs from other
forms of instruction.
6. Distinguish between "linear" and
"branching" formats of programmed
instruction.
7. Describe an appropriate application
of programmed instruction in an
instructional setting. Include the content field, the audience, and a rationale
for using programmed instruction
rather than some other approach.
8. Discuss five considerations when
using programmed instruction in the
classroom.
9. Describe "programmed tutoring"
indicating what it is, how it is used,
and an instructional situation in which
it could be applied.
10. Discuss why the Personalized
System of Instruction is a technology
for *managing* instruction and compare
and contrast PSI with the other tech-

11. List the three types of sessions
used in the A-T System and briefly
describe the purpose of each.
12. Define "instructional module" and
identify six components of a module.
13. Justify why instructional simulations and games can be considered as
a technology of instruction.
14. Justify why the computer itself is
not a technology of instruction as
defined in this chapter.
15. Synthesize an instructional situation in which *one* of the technologies
of instruction could be used effectively.
Your description should indicate both
how and *when* you would use it.

American economist John Kenneth Galbraith defines *technology* as "the systematic application of scientific or other organized knowledge to practical tasks."* This view of the concept of technology correctly focuses on technology as a *process,* an approach to solving problems, rather than on the *products* of technology—computers, transistors, satellites, bionic devices, and the like. Unfortunately, the debate over the role of technology in education has too often been clouded by a tendency to concentrate on the role of artifacts such as audiovisual hardware, television transmission systems, "teaching machines," and so on. Advocates and critics alike have too often assumed that there is some sort of "magic" inherent in these artifacts. The only question seems to have been whether this "magic" was helpful or harmful to students, teachers, and educational institutions.

This is not to denigrate the educational value of the products of technology. Indeed, much of this book is devoted to helping you choose among and use these products for more effective teaching and learning. But there is nothing magical about the hardware. The magic, if there is to be magic, stems from the selection of materials according to their usefulness in achieving specific learning objectives and their utilization in ways conducive to applying sound learning principles.

This chapter, therefore, highlights *technology as a process.* It will extend Galbraith's definition into the realm of education, showing ways in which materials and activities can be combined to allow a "systematic application of scientific knowledge." These spe-cial arrangements we will refer to as *technologies of instruction.*

A TECHNOLOGY OF INSTRUCTION: a teaching/ learning pattern designed to provide reliable, effective instruction to each learner through application of scientific principles of human learning.

We use this term in the plural because many different arrangements could merit this label, including those which have not yet been invented. The six examples of technologies of instruction explored in this chapter do not by any means comprise a full listing of all technologies of instruction; they are intended merely to be representative of some of the most common formats in widespread use today. Criterion-referenced instruction, competency-based education, and mastery learning are names given to instructional formats that could be classified as technologies of instruction. They share many features in common with each other and in common with the formats elaborated on in this chapter. The four formats discussed in depth in this chapter are programmed instruction, programmed tutoring, the Personalized System of Instruction, and Audio-Tutorial Systems. Two other technologies of instruction will be alluded to only briefly here because they are examined in detail in the two following chapters—simulation and gaming and computer-assisted instruction.

THE ROOTS OF TODAY'S TECHNOLOGIES OF INSTRUCTION

Many of today's methods of instruction have roots in theories that are hundreds or even thousands of years old. Socrates, Comenius, Pestalozzi, and Herbart would find many of their own ideas clearly reflected in contemporary classroom practices. But the body of theory that influenced most strongly the development of today's technologies of instruction is of much more recent origin. In fact, many regard an article published in 1954 in *Harvard Educational Review* as the catalyst that sparked a whole new movement in education. In that article, "The Science of Learning and the Art of Teaching," the author, psychologist B.F. Skinner, challenged educators to modify their traditional practices to put into effect new principles of learning that were emerging from studies in experimental psychology.

Basic Concepts of Reinforcement Theory

Skinner's body of theory, which he referred to as "operant conditioning" but is generally known as reinforcement theory, differs from earlier behaviorist theories in that it applies to voluntary behaviors. He claimed that earlier stimulus-response paradigms were adequate for explaining reflexive responses such as salivation, dilation of the pupil of the eye, the knee-jerk reflex, and the like. However, he was more interested in explaining responses that people emit voluntarily, such as driving a car, writing a letter, and balancing a checkbook.

---

*John Kenneth Galbraith. *The New Industrial State.* Boston: Houghton-Mifflin, 1967. p. 12.

Figure 11.1 Psychologist B. F. Skinner, whose theory of learning gave impetus to the development of programmed instruction.

The backbone of Skinner's theories was the concept of reinforcement. He hypothesized that the *consequences* of a response determine whether or not it will be learned. That is, a behavior that is followed by a satisfying consequence is more likely to recur in the future. Giving such a satisfying consequence is referred to as reinforcement.

A reinforcer is any event or thing that increases the likelihood of a preceding behavior's being repeated: learned. This phrasing is intended to point out that a thing is a reinforcer only if it *works*. An object may be desirable or satisfying to one person at one time but not to another person or at another time. For instance, a chocolate bar might sound quite inviting to you right now, but not if you are a diabetic or are on a diet or have just finished eating a big box of candy.

Also fundamental to reinforcement theory is the notion that complex skills can be broken down into clusters of simpler behaviors.

Each behavior bit can be learned one at a time through skillful arrangement for immediate reinforcement after each correct response. These simple behaviors then become links in a longer, more complex behavior chain. Skinner was able to demonstrate this process dramatically by teaching a pigeon to turn a complete circle clockwise within just a single demonstration session. Closely observing the pigeon's behavior, he rewarded every partial movement of the head or feet toward the clockwise direction with a kernel of corn. Counterclockwise movements went unrewarded. Gradually, the pigeon's clockwise movements became less random, until, by the end of the session, counterclockwise movement ceased and the pigeon moved only in a clockwise direction.

Transferring these basic concepts (overt response, followed by reinforcement) to formal human learning requires adding another element to the formula—a prompt. Rather than waiting around for a desired response to occur spontaneously or randomly, the instruc-

tional material can be structured to hint at or prompt the desired response. The basic formula for applying reinforcement theory to human learning, then, requires a prompt, an overt response, and a reinforcement. For example:

1. PROMPT (e.g., math problem)

2. RESPONSE (e.g., correct answer)

3. REINFORCEMENT (e.g., knowledge of correct response and/or praise)

Emergence of Programmed Instruction

In his 1954 article Skinner pointed out that the elements of his formula were not well represented in traditional classroom instruction. In large-group instruction, students spend much of their time listening, with little opportunity for overt response. Even if an overt response is given, the typical teacher, responsible for large numbers of students at once, has limited opportunity even to observe individual responses, much less to reinforce each one appropriately. How, then, could the principles of response/reinforcement be implemented in the classroom?

Skinner's initial solution to this problem was an innovative method of presenting instructional material printed in small bits or "frames," each of which included an item of information (prompt), an incomplete statement to be completed or question to be answered (response), and provision of the correct answer (reinforcement). A mechanical device—which later came to be referred to as a teaching machine—was used to control the logistics of the process.

This solution—programmed instruction—provided a mechanism for adapting lessons to an individual's pace, thereby circumventing the large-group barrier. Further, it assured that students would be kept actively at work making frequent (and nearly always correct) responses, thus gaining frequent reinforcement. In short, programmed instruction appeared to be a feasible method for putting reinforcement theory into practice in all sorts of real-life classroom situations.

Reinforcement theory has been presented in some detail here not because it is the basis for *all* technologies of instruction but because of its historical primacy in stimulating the concept of a "technology of instruction." And it does lie at the heart of several of the techniques described in the rest of this chapter. The first to be examined in detail is programmed instruction itself.

PROGRAMMED INSTRUCTION

What It Is

Originally, the term *programmed instruction* was used in reference to a particular *format* for presenting printed learning materials to an individual learner. B.F. Skinner's 1954 article, previously mentioned, described a mechanical device consisting of a small box having on its top surface a window through which information printed on a paper roll could be read. The learner responded to a question or blank to be filled by selecting a multiple choice answer. If the right one was chosen, the paper roll would advance to the next question when a knob was turned. Other early devices required written responses. (See Figure 11.2*a, b,* and *c.*)

Since reinforcement theory demanded that reinforcement be given only after a correct response, it was originally considered necessary to use a mechanical monitoring device to enforce this requirement. During the infancy of programmed instruction, much creative energy was invested in developing such "teaching machines" to automate the presentation of frames of information to the learner. Research and practical experience soon indicated, however, that students were quite capable of monitoring their own progress without the help of a cumbersome and expensive page-turning machine. So, in many cases, the "teaching machines" were discarded and their learning contents were put into book formats. The earliest programmed instruction texts arranged the frames across the page in horizontal strips. The correct response for each question could be checked only by turning the page. Later, this method was

Figure 11.2*a*   A teaching machine of the early years of programmed instruction; the paper roll advanced only when the correct multiple-choice response was chosen.

Figure 11.2*b*   Another of the early teaching machines; this type required written ("constructed") responses.

Figure 11.2*c*   In contrast to the original teaching machines, those using the branching format provide remedial pathways for students who give incorrect responses.

relaxed, allowing the frames to be arranged vertically, just as in conventional printed pages. These programmed texts were meant to be read with a piece of paper covering the rest of the page while a frame was being read. After writing in an answer in the blank on the first frame, for example, the cover was moved down to see the confirmation (correct answer) printed in the box to the left of the second frame. You will have a better idea of how programmed instruction works if you go through the following example.

Programmed Instruction as a Technology of Instruction

It is clear that programmed instruction was developed very consciously as a specific pattern of activities designed to put scientific principles of learning into practice. As such, it fits our definition of a "technology of instruction." However, the translation from the laboratory into the classroom was quite direct and unadorned. By the early 1960s an orthodoxy had developed around

the construction of programmed instruction. The elements of this orthodoxy were summarized by Wilbur Schramm (*Programmed Instruction: Today and Tomorrow.* New York: Fund for the Advancement of Education, 1962) as follows:

(a) *an ordered sequence of stimulus items,*
(b) *to each of which a student responds in some specified way,*
(c) *his response being reinforced by immediate knowledge of results,*

	An Example Of Linear Programming
	1. Psychologists differ in their explanations about what learning is and precisely how it occurs. The series of statements or "frames" presented here deal with one particular explanation of the process of _____.
Learning	**2.** We cannot observe learning directly, but we can infer that it has occurred when a person consistently makes a *response* that he or she previously was unable to make. For example, if a student says "nine" when asked "What is three times three?" she is making a _____ that was probably learned through practice in school.
Response	**3.** If you reply "kappa" when asked "What Greek letter is represented by K?" you are making a _____ that you learned through some prior experience.
Response	**4.** The word or picture or other sensory stimulation that causes you to make a response is a *stimulus* (plural: stimuli). Therefore, if "kappa" is your response, "What Greek letter is represented by K?" would be the _____.
Stimulus	**5.** To the stimulus "good," the student of Spanish responds "bueno;" the student of Arabic responds "gayid." To the stimulus "silver," the student of Spanish responds "plata;" the student of Arabic responds "fida." They are responding to English words which are serving as _____.
Stimuli	**6.** In these frames the written statements are the stimuli to which you are writing _____ in the blanks.
Responses	**7.** We learn to connect certain verbal responses to certain stimuli through the process of forming *associations*. We say that the student associates "nine" with "three times three;" he learns to associate "kappa" with "K;" and he _____ "plata" with "silver."
Associates	**8.** Much verbal learning seems to be based on the formation of associations between _____ and responses.
Stimuli	Etc.

(d) *so that he moves by* small steps,

(e) *therefore making* few errors *and practicing mostly correct responses,*

(f) *from what he knows, by a process of* successively closer approximations, *toward what he is supposed to learn from the program.*

Although many of the materials which incorporated these elements were found to be successful with students, in a good number of controlled studies the programmed materials failed to live up to the claims made by their adherents. In some experiments it was found that "large steps" worked better than "small steps." Delayed rather than immediate knowledge of results sometimes yielded just as good results. At times, even scrambling the order of the frames produced better learning than "an ordered sequence." In addition, it was found that some students considered the repetitious pattern of small, easy steps tedious and boring.

Further doubts were raised when Norman Crowder ("On the Differences Between Linear and Intrinsic Programming," *Phi Delta Kappan,* March 1963, pp. 250–254) challenged the programmed instruction orthodoxy with a competing technique of program writing—one which ignored all psychological theory and attempted instead simply to present information to readers in a more efficient, individualized form. He called this technique "intrinsic programming." Its basic method was to present a large block of information followed by multiple choice questions requiring application of the facts or principles presented.

Each choice of answer directed the reader to a different page. If the correct choice was made, the learner skipped ahead to new frames of information. Incorrect choices led to explanations of the correct response and to fresh questions. If the learner had additional difficulty he or she would be routed to sequences of remedial instruction. At each step the learner encountered questions testing mastery of the subject matter and was directed onward to new material only after demonstrating a grasp of the prerequisite skills. Because Crowder's pattern of frames resembled the branches of a tree, this programming technique became known as the branching format. The original Skinnerian format is referred to as linear. The two patterns are compared in Figure 11.3. The major advantage of branching over linear programming is that students who catch on quickly can move through the material much more efficiently, following the "prime path." In the linear format, all learners are expected to go through all the steps.

By the late 1960s it had become clear that programmed instruction was not be confined to the precise formats originally worked out by Skinner. The initial form of programmed instruction was seen to be too literal an application of reinforcement theory to formal learning. For one thing, it was apparent that *knowledge of results* was not consistently reinforcing to all learners all of the time. Its potential for being reinforcing varies with the situation, as is the case with other potential reinforcers such as food, sex, praise, money, and the like. In addition, programmed materials, like any other instructional materials, needed to be made varied and interesting, a need that could not be met by rigid adherence to any single stereotyped "recipe."

In recent years the basic concepts underlying programmed instruction have found expression in a multitude of forms; programmed tutoring, the Personalized System of Instruction, and computer-assisted instruction are

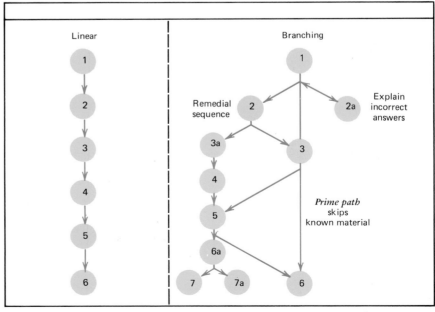

Figure 11.3   Comparison of linear and branching formats of programmed instruction.

63. When you use the binomial probability table, you are making an important assumption that you should be aware of. You are assuming that the observations in your sample are random and independent; that is, you are assuming that every observation in the population has an equal chance of being chosen at any step in the sampling process. Suppose you are going to choose three people out of a population of six that consists of three men and three women. You choose to select them one at a time. On the first draw you choose a man. Does this affect the chances of your choosing a man on the second draw?

Yes, because there are now substantially fewer men in the remaining population. For the first draw $P = \frac{3}{6} = 0.5$; for the second draw $P = \frac{2}{5} = 0.4$.

64. You have a jar containing six marbles, three red and three blue. You draw one marble at random and find that it is blue. You record this observation and replace the marble in the jar. Has your first observation affected the chances of choosing a blue marble on the second draw?

No, because you replaced the blue marble.

65. Can you use the binomial probability table to analyze the marble problem?

Yes. The observations are independent. One observation does not affect the probability of the others.

66. Can you use the binomial probability table to analyze the problem in frame 63?

No. The observations are not independent.

Procedures for dealing with this problem exist, but they are beyond the scope of this book.

Figure 11.4 A contemporary example of linear programmed instruction. Note the use of longer responses—ones that require the learner to think about a problem and apply principles that have been presented earlier.

> Every hue has a tone sequence from its lightest tints to its darkest shades. Through light/dark contrast, color can be controlled to exaggerate form toward three-dimensional effect or to suppress form toward a flattened effect.

Examples

When your hair becomes bleached by summer sun or peroxide, it becomes lighter in value than before. When the bleach grows out, the hair becomes darker in value.

When you roast a marshmallow, it changes in value from white to a very light brown to a darker value of brown. If you are not careful at this point, it will turn black—a still darker value.

Exercise

Indicate the contrasting tones associated with each of the following:

(a) Coffee stain on a white shirt
(b) New blue denim patch on faded denim jeans
(c) Tree shadow on a yellow house
(d) Teeth brushed with "Sparkle-brite" showing through lips with red lipstick

----

(a) Stain is darker in value than white fabric
(b) Patch is darker in value than the jeans
(c) Shadow area is darker in value than the yellow wall
(d) Teeth are lighter in value than lips

You may find it helpful to make a tonal scale of at least one hue. Using blue-colored ink or paint, place the undiluted blue in the center frame. Going to the right of center, add a little water or white paint to dilute the blue for each step of the frame, leaving white in the last frame. Going to the left, add a very little black for each step until you reach black for the last frame. You may even succeed in extending this value scale further than the steps in following the sketch. It is possible to make such a tonal scale for each hue.

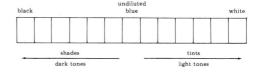

Figure 11.5 Excerpt from a programmed book on art. This program calls for a variety of types of responses, including painting, as seen at the bottom of the page.

SELF-TEST

This self-test is designed to show you whether or not you have mastered the objectives of Chapter 2. Answer each question to the best of your ability, based on what you learned in this chapter. Correct answers are given following the test.

Read the following paragraph. Then answer the following questions that refer to the situation.

Mr. Cee, a sixth grade teacher, is concerned about Bill Boneau, a boy in his class. Bill, a natural leader, can command the respect of his fellow students. However, far too often, he uses this leadership ability to distract students from academics. In addition, he seldom pays attention to the teacher presentations or class discussions, and his homework is seldom done—all of which seem to be affecting his test scores. A notable exception to his lack of interest is science. Bill is interested in scientific projects, and he does well on them. His interest and leadership in this area have carried the entire class to levels of scientific inquiry and understanding far beyond those of any of Mr. Cee's previous classes.

1. List three inappropriate behaviors of Bill's which should be reduced in frequency.
   a. _____
   b. _____
   c. _____

2. List two appropriate behaviors to be encouraged.
   a. _____
   b. _____

3. List the rules for Bill that would be included in a behavioral contract.
   _____
   _____
   _____

Figure 11.6 A review exercise in a programmed book. Previously learned principles are applied to the solving of a hypothetical problem.

---

three concepts that we will be examining more closely. And printed programs are still being produced and used. In fact, today they are more widely used than ever before. But they are not necessarily labeled as "programmed instruction" and they hardly ever follow the rigid formula of earlier linear programming. Note, for example, the variety of programming formats illustrated in Figures 11.4, 11.5, and 11.6.

The most comprehensive listing of commercially available programmed materials is:

Programmed Learning and Individually Paced Instruction—Bibliography. 5th ed. Carl Hendershot, compiler (Bay City, MI: Hendershot Bibliography, 1979).

APPRAISAL CHECKLIST: PROGRAMMED MATERIALS

Series title (if applicable)_____

Individual title_____

Producer/distributor_____   Date_____

Required completion time—range_____ average_____

Intended audience/grade level_____   Subject area_____

Objectives (should be clearly stated in learner performance terms):

Brief description/summary:

Entry capabilities required:

    —prior subject matter knowledge
    —reading ability
    —math ability (or other)

RATING	High		Medium		Low
Likely to arouse student interest (e.g. humor, vivid examples, variety of formats)	☐	☐	☐	☐	☐
Content accurate and timely	☐	☐	☐	☐	☐
Structure is "lean"-sufficient review without unnecessary redundancy	☐	☐	☐	☐	☐
Test (criterion) frames parallel to the stated objectives	☐	☐	☐	☐	☐
Relevant practice is consistently provided	☐	☐	☐	☐	☐
Learner responses require "thought," not just copying given information	☐	☐	☐	☐	☐
Feedback (knowledge of correct response) is well delivered (e.g. consistent, well hidden)	☐	☐	☐	☐	☐
Feedback provides remediation	☐	☐	☐	☐	☐
Validation data are provided (should describe tryout population, time, gains in achievement & attitude)	☐	☐	☐	☐	☐

Strong points:

Weak points: Reviewer_____

                                    Position_____

Recommended action: Date_____

Despite the great diversity of styles and formats evident among programmed materials, there are still a number of features shared in common among them. These include performance objectives stated in advance, clear sequence of activities, frequent response (requiring thinking, not just copying), regular feedback, test items that are parallel to the stated objectives, and validation based on actual learner tryouts. Note that these features are among the criteria included here in the appraisal checklist for programmed materials.

Applications of Programmed Instruction

Programmed materials have been used successfully from the elementary school through the adult education levels and in almost every subject area. By itself or in conjunction with other strategies, a program can be used to teach an entire course or a segment of a course. Many teachers use short programmed units to teach simple principles and terminology. Programmed instruction is particularly useful as an enrichment activity. It can help provide highly motivated students with additional learning experiences that the teacher might ordinarily be unable to provide because of classroom time pressures. Programmed materials have proven to be very effective in remedial instruction. The program can function as a kind of tutor for slow learners in situations where more personalized attention may be virtually impossible (in overcrowded classrooms, for example). Such students may even take this particular tutor with them when they leave the classroom! One of the reasons for the success of programmed materials in remedial instruction is their "failure-proof" design. By being broken into small steps, by allowing the student to take as much time

as needed for each step, and by being evaluated and revised carefully prior to publication, these materials are more likely to provide the slow learner with a successful experience. For some students it may be their first encounter with school work that gives them an immediate and continued feeling of success.

Programmed instruction can be an effective means of providing class-wide competencies in skills prerequisite to successful completion of a unit of study. For example, one high school physics teacher used a small programmed text to allow his students to teach themselves the power-of-ten notation, which is a prerequisite for solving physics problems. At the outset, some of the students were even more proficient with power-of-ten operations than their instructor; others had been introduced to the technique but had lost their competence in it because they had not been required to use the skill; still others had never even been introduced to it. The program on power-of-ten notation eliminated devoting class time to a subject that would have bored some and confused others. Instead, the students were allowed to consider the material on their own. Those who knew the technique could ignore the program; those who had previously learned the skill but were a little rusty could use the program as a review; and those who had never been exposed to power-of-ten notation could master the necessary manipulations on their own and at their own pace. All students were subsequently required to pass a criterion test demonstrating mastery of this skill.

Programmed materials have a wide variety of other more or less specialized uses. They can, for example, be used for make-up

instruction by students who have been absent from school for an extended period of time. They can be used to expand curricular offerings when it might be difficult or impossible otherwise to do so—because of too few interested students, for instance, or no qualified instructor. This could be an important consideration for smaller schools and for training programs in business/industry settings.

It is true that programmed materials are often more expensive than ordinary textbooks, mainly because of the time and effort spent in their careful development and in their validation testing. Their increased efficiency as learning tools, however, may compensate for their higher cost (especially in situations in which the cost of student time and failure is taken into account).

Programmed instruction is by its very nature individualized learning, in which the student advances at his or her own pace. However, as with other techniques for individualized instruction, this does not mean that students are always working alone. Group activities can and should be scheduled to supplement the programmed instruction and to meet other desired educational goals. In addition, and again as with other properly planned individualized activities, programs help release teachers from routine classroom chores in order to interact personally with students and to provide them with human reinforcement.

Utilization of Programmed Instruction

Programmed instruction is basically learner centered. It focuses on the activities of the student rather than the activities of the teacher. The role of the teacher, however, is as important to the success of programmed instruction as it is to any other type of instruction. It is up to the instructor to arrange and maintain conditions conducive to achievement of the program's learning objectives.

Be sure to familiarize yourself with the entire program before implementing it for class use so that you will be in a position to assist students to work through it when and if they need help. Familiarity with the program will also help you coordinate the programmed materials with other instructional activities—lectures, group discussions, etc.

The students' first exposure to programmed materials is particularly important. Be sure to explain the mechanics of using the materials so that the students will not get bogged down with them when they begin to work the program. For example, clarify whether answers are to be recorded directly on the materials or on separate sheets of paper. (Recording answers on separate sheets may allow the materials to be used over and over again.) Once the mechanics of the program are understood, the student is free to concentrate on working the program and to experience the immediate success so important in initial exposure to new learning methods.

Because programmed materials often have the physical appearance of a test, the fact that the program is not a test should be emphasized. Carefully explain that even though the program confronts the student with a series of questions to be answered, users need not be fearful of making errors. If errors are made, the program automatically helps the learner correct them. Explain that students are never evaluated on the basis of their performance in working through the program. Evaluation is based upon student performance on criterion tests administered *after* using the program. Programs are for teaching, not for testing.

It should be established that students will be working at their own pace, neither pushed faster than they can efficiently perform nor held back if they wish to work rapidly. Under no circumstances will a student be assigned a minimum amount of material to be covered in a single class period.

Students should be encouraged to ask questions about the material as they work, especially if they become confused. Confusion may not only indicate misunderstanding on the part of the student. It may also indicate ambiguities and weaknesses in the program itself which you will want to record for future reference.

Stress the importance of being intellectually honest with oneself when working with programmed materials. Inform your students of the futility of just peeking ahead in order to ascertain a correct response rather than thinking it out for themselves. Explain that there is nothing to gain by such actions and much to lose, namely, the opportunity to learn. Human nature being as it is, you will probably find some students unable to resist some initial peeking ahead. But this behavior will likely fade as students discover for themselves that there is no advantage in it and that the program is designed to make certain they can work out the correct responses on their own.

PROGRAMMED TUTORING

What It Is

Programmed tutoring (also referred to as Structured Tutoring) is a one-to-one method of instruction in which the decisions to be made by the tutor are "programmed" in advance by means of carefully structured printed instructions. In a typical program the tutor and student sit down together to go through the lesson material. The "teacher's book" has the answers to the exercises; the "student's book" does not. An excerpt from a typical programmed tutoring teacher's book is shown (opposite). Note how the tutor's role in the program is set forth, step-by-step, to conform with learner response to the materials.

Since the tutor is continually choosing the next step on the basis of the learner's last response, programmed tutoring is a form of branching programming. As such, it shares the basic advantage for which branching was originally developed: the fast learner may skip quickly through the material without tedious, unnecessary repetition.

Programmed tutoring uses what might be called "brightening," as opposed to the "fading" or gradual reduction of prompts used in conventional linear programmed instruction. In "brightening," the item is first presented in a relatively difficult form. If the learner responds correctly he or she is reinforced and goes on to a new item. If not, a series of increasingly clearer prompts or hints are given. For example, in teaching a beginning reader to follow written instructions, the student's book might say, "Point to your teacher."

STEP 1   Tell the student that this exercise will help him learn to sound out new words.
STEP 2   Point to the first word and ask the student to *sound* it out.
    a. If the student reads the word correctly, praise him; then go on to the next word.
    b. If the student is unable to read the word or reads it incorrectly, have him make the individual sounds in the word separately and then assist him in blending the sounds.
    Example:
      Word: "THIN"
    Tutor: Place your finger over the last two letters in the word and ask: "What sound does the *th* make?" If the student answers correctly, praise him and go to the next sound. If he answers incorrectly or fails to answer, tell him the sound and have him repeat it. Follow the same procedure for each sound in the word, and then show him how to blend the separate sounds.
STEP 3   Follow step 2 for each word on the sheet.
STEP 4   At the end of the session, praise the student.
STEP 5   Fill out your tutor log.

Source: Grant Von Harrison, *Beginning Reading 1: A Professional Guide for the Lay Tutor* (Provo, Utah: Brigham Young University Press, 1972), p. 101.

If the learner does not do so when first shown the instructions, the tutor might follow this sequence of "brightening" prompts:

1. "Read it again." (Wait for response.)
2. "What does it say?"
3. "What does it tell you to do?"
4. "Do what it tells you to do."

The sequence of prompts would continue until the learner gives an acceptable response. Then reinforcement would be given. The idea is to lead the student toward the solution with "brightening" hints but to avoid actually giving the correct answer itself.

Programmed Tutoring as a Technology of Instruction

Programmed tutoring shares with programmed instruction the characteristics of individualized pacing, active learner response, and immediate feedback. The use of a live human tutor as a mediator adds immensely to the flexibility of the system, and it adds another major advantage over printed self-instructional material by employ-

Figure 11.7   A typical arrangement for a programmed tutoring session.

ing *social reinforcers* in the form of praise ("That's great." "Oh, what a good answer." "You're really on the ball today.") rather than just simple knowledge of results. Administered flexibly and creatively by a live guide, this technology of instruction can overcome the monotonous pattern sometimes associated with other programmed formats.

Applications and Utilization of Programmed Tutoring

Programmed tutoring combines the qualities of programmed instruction with the warmth and personal attention that only a human tutor can add. The tutor may be a teacher aide, a parent, or another student ("peer tutoring"). Almost anyone can be trained as a tutor since the sequencing of the material and the tutor's responses are carefully programmed into the lesson by the designer. As such, it is particularly attractive for areas in which qualified teachers are lacking. Douglas G. Ellson, a principal developer of programmed tutoring, estimates that over a million young people in less-developed countries have learned to read by this method since its origins in 1960.

Reading and mathematics have been the most popular subject areas for application of tutoring. These subjects lend themselves to this method because of their high degree of structure. Also, being very basic skills, they are frequently the targets of remedial or

Figure 11.8   The directions given in the tutor's guidebook structure the programmed tutoring lesson.

compensatory education programs—the milieu in which volunteer tutoring projects are often mounted. Indeed, Ellson's tutoring program centered at Indiana University has been recognized by American Institutes for Research and the U.S. Office of Education as one of the half dozen most effective compensatory education programs in the United States.

In preparing to utilize programmed tutoring, keep in mind that the research consistently indicates that tutors gain even more than their students. So give everyone a chance to be a tutor, not just the most advanced students. In any case, ensure that the tutors are trained in and do use the correct procedures. The materials are validated for effectiveness only when they are used as directed.

A final utilization hint: Consider using the tutorial method to make productive use of high-absence days. Train those who are present to tutor absentees when they return. Tutors deepen their knowledge; the absentees catch up.

PERSONALIZED SYSTEM OF INSTRUCTION

What It Is

The *Personalized System of Instruction (PSI)* could be described as a technology for *managing* instruction. It puts reinforcement theory into action as the overall framework for a whole course. In the PSI classroom students work individually at their own pace using any of a variety of instructional materials—a chapter in a book, computer-assisted instruction, a loop film, a sound filmstrip, a programmed booklet, etc. The materials are arranged in sequential order and the student must show *mastery* of each unit before being allowed to move on to the next.

Mastery is determined by means of a test taken whenever the student feels ready for it. The content and emphasis of the test should be no surprise because each unit is accompanied by a study guide that spells out the objective and most important points to be learned in that unit.

Study help and testing are handled by *proctors*—usually more advanced students who volunteer to help others. Proctors are a critical component of PSI for it is their one-to-one tutorial assistance that makes the system *personalized*. After scoring each test the proctor reviews it immediately with the student, asking questions to probe weak points and listening to defenses of alternative answers. If performance is below the specified mastery level the student returns at another time to take a second form of the test. Up to four retakes may be allowed.

Group meetings are rare, being used mainly for "inspirational" lectures, film showings, and review sessions. The instructor acts pri-

Figure 11.9 Psychologist Fred S. Keller, originator of the Personalized System of Instruction.

marily as a planner, designer, manager, and guide to students and proctors.

PSI as a Technology of Instruction

Like programmed tutoring, PSI strives to implement the learning principles that programmed instruction originally envisioned: (a) the presentation of information appropriate to the student's current ability, (b) frequent opportunities to respond to the material, and (c) immediate feedback/correction. To these principles PSI adds the philosophy of mastery—the student may not tackle new material until the prior skills have been mastered—and the person-to-person contact with a proctor and instructor.

Unlike programmed tutoring and programmed instruction, PSI does not revolve around the design of specially structured materials; it manipulates the *framework* in which instruction occurs. It consciously puts into play a number of "generalized reinforcers," rewards that tend to work well with humans despite differences in preference or current need. These include grades, diplomas, and other similar tokens of achievement, personal attention, social approval, affection, and deferent behavior of others. The designers of PSI aimed to maximize rewards for conscientious study, minimize frustration, and eliminate the fear connected with not knowing where you are going, how well you are doing, and what surprise the instructor is going to pull on the final exam.

Applications and Utilization of PSI

Since its origins in Fred S. Keller's psychology course at the University of Brasilia in the mid-1960s, PSI has been successfully used at all grade levels and in virtually every subject area. It is also widely known in military training and in business/industry education. The validity of the PSI approach has been attested to by extensive research. Kulik, Kulik, and Smith ("Research on the Per-

Figure 11.10 Interaction with the proctor "personalizes" the Personalized System of Instruction.

sonalized System of Instruction," *Programmed Learning and Educational Technology,* Spring 1976, pp. 13, 23– 30) prepared a review of studies in which PSI had been compared with conventional

instruction. Their conclusion was as follows:

In a typical published comparison, PSI and lecture means are separated by about two-thirds of a standard deviation. How large a difference is this? Let us take an average student, Mary Smith, who may take her introductory physics course, for example, by either a conventional method or by PSI. If she takes a typical lecture course, her achievement in physics will put her at the 50th percentile on a standardized test. She is an average student in an average course. If she takes the same course in a PSI format, she will achieve at the 75th percentile on the standardized test. This increment is what PSI has to offer the individual student...In our judgment, this is the most impressive record achieved by a teaching method in higher education. It stands in stark contrast to the inconclusive results of earlier comparisons of college teaching methods.

Flashback: Serendipity and Botany 108

In the fall of 1961, S.N. Postlethwait, a professor of botany at Purdue University, began preparing supplementary lectures on audio tape to provide an opportunity for students with inadequate academic backgrounds to keep up with his introductory botany class. Any student could listen to these recordings at the university audiovisual center. Soon Dr. Postlethwait decided that he could improve the effectiveness of these tapes by having the students bring their botany textbooks to the audiovisual center when they came to listen to the tapes. On the tapes he could refer them to the photographs, diagrams, and drawings in the text as he discussed the concepts and principles under study.

Later, the tapes included instructions that the students check views contained in the recorded

lectures against views expressed in the text. Thus the author's point of view could be considered along with the lecturer's. Then Dr. Postlethwait decided to add a new dimension to his instructional approach. He placed plants in the audiovisual center so that students could observe and handle the plants when they were being discussed on the tapes. Ultimately, the students were instructed to bring their laboratory manuals to the center and conduct experiments in conjunction with study of their texts and listening to the tapes. Consciously or unconsciously, Dr. Postlethwait had moved his instructional technique from one focusing on abstract learning experiences (lectures) toward a multimedia system emphasizing concrete experiences—an integrated lecture-laboratory approach.

Flashback: Serendipity and Botany 108

Biologist Sam Postlethwait, originator of the Audio-Tutorial System of Independent Study.

During the spring of 1962 an experimental group of 36 students was chosen to receive all of the instruction via the integrated lecture-laboratory approach. The experimental class met with Dr. Postlethwait only once each week, to take quizzes and for a general discussion of the week's subject matter. They were required to take the same examinations given the conventionally taught group. At the end of the semester the experimental group scored just as well on the exam as the group that had received traditional instruction.

The students' reactions to the "supplementary" material were so positive that in the fall of 1962 Postlethwait decided that rather than carrying plants and other materials from the biology greenhouse to the audiovisual center each week, he would set up a botany learning center in the biology building. A conventional science laboratory was converted to a learning center with the addition of 22 learning carrels equipped with tape recorders. At this time, Postlethwait was covering the same content in his classroom lectures that was being presented on the tapes in the learning center. By the end

of the semester most of the students were going to the learning center instead of coming to the lectures! In spite of the fact that Postlethwait missed their "sitting at his feet" to learn about botany, he candidly admitted that all the students missed by not coming to the lectures were his smiling face and West Virginia jokes.

Eventually, Postlethwait did away with his traditional lectures and restructured his Biology 108 course to give the students maximum freedom for independent study and to pace themselves according to their individual interests and capabilities. Students could come in at their convenience and spend as much time as necessary for them to master the material under study.

A significant aspect of Postlethwait's audio recordings was the conversational tone and relaxed atmosphere he deliberately cultivated. He would sit among the materials gathered for the particular lesson and speak into the recorder as if he were having a conversation with a friend whom he wished to tutor through a sequence of pleasant inquiries. Later, in their carrels, students would examine duplicates of the same materials while they listened to Postlethwait's chat.

Group meetings were later added to the program to supplement the independent study sessions. Students were brought together periodically in small groups (the "small assembly session") to discuss what they had learned in independent study and to present their own "lectures" on the current subject matter. Larger meetings (the "general assembly sessions") were scheduled for guest lectures, films, review sessions, and the like.

Serendipity is the faculty of making fortunate and unexpected discoveries by accident. Dr. Postlethwait turned out to be embarking on a seredipitous journey when he set out to tinker with the traditional format of his botany course. What began simply as audio tapes to supplement his classroom lectures eventually evolved into a full-scale technology of instruction—the Audio-Tutorial System.

AUDIO-TUTORIAL SYSTEMS

What They Are

The term *Audio-Tutorial Systems* is used in the plural here to acknowledge that many variations have evolved from the original tape-controlled independent study method developed by S.N. Postlethwait at Purdue University in the early 1960s. Like PSI, this is a technology for *managing* instruction. But it springs from different roots and has different emphasis than the preceding methods, which derive from programmed instruction.

As described in the accompanying "Flashback," the Audio-Tutorial System had its birth in expediency. It was an intuitive response to a felt problem. It evolved into an identifiable, systematic method of instruction through years of experimentation and refinement by instructional developers.

Specific guidelines for setting up and running courses according to the PSI system can be found in the books and articles listed in the References section at the end of this chapter. A few cautions about implementing a PSI approach are in order. First, PSI involves a great deal of time in planning and developing supplementary materials. Even though less lecture time is involved, instructors should be prepared to spend about half again as many hours conducting a PSI course as conducting a conventional course. Second, a willingness and ability to state objectives specifically is a prerequisite. Third, the "mastery" point-of-view built into PSI rejects norm-referenced grading (the "normal curve") and insists on complete mastery as the criterion of success. It aims to elevate all students to the "A" level.

The most visible aspect of most Audio-Tutorial (A–T) courses is the study carrel equipped with specially designed audio tapes that direct students to various learning activities. This component is known as the Independent Study Session. The taped presentation is *not* a lecture but a tutorial conversation by the instructor, designed to facilitate effective communication. A live instructor is nearby to assist students when needed. Learners proceed at their own pace, sessions beginning and ending to suit their own schedules.

Since the students are proceeding individually, there seldom is more than one student at any given point in the study program. So, often only one or two pieces of equipment are necessary to accommodate many students in a laboratory situation. Demonstration materials are set out at a central location; again, one set may be

Figure 11.11 The independent study carrel is the most visibly distinctive feature of the Audio-Tutorial approach.

sufficient to serve a large class. Motion and color are provided when necessary by means of 8-mm film and/or videocassette. Instructions on how to perform a laboratory procedure, for instance, can be viewed coincident with handling the apparatus itself. The student can view the first step in a procedure, do that step, view the second step, turn the projector to "hold" while carrying out that step, and so on.

In addition to the Independent Study Session, there are two other basic components in most A–T systems: a General Assembly Session and a Small Assembly Session.

The General Assembly Session is a large-group meeting with no fixed format. It may include a presentation by a guest lecturer, a long film showing, an orientation to subject matter, an opportunity for review or emphasis of critical materials, help sessions, a major exam, or any other activity appropriate to a large-group setting.

During the Small Assembly Session, six to ten students and an instructor meet for a modified seminar. Students are seated informally around a table with the instructor. The primary purpose of the session is to exploit the principle that one really learns a subject when one is required to teach it. For this session each student is expected to prepare a little lecture about each of the objectives being covered that session. Each student is asked to discuss at least one of the objectives in turn. The other students then have an opportunity to correct or add comments concerning any item. This session has proven to be an effective feedback mechanism for both the students and the instructor. It lets the students know how they did and often provides clues to the instructor for improving the

study program. The miniature seminar enables many students to see relationships and concepts which may not have been evident from the Independent Study Session.

Audio-Tutorial Systems as a Technology of Instruction

Unlike programmed instruction, programmed tutoring, and PSI, A–T did not originate from a particular theory of learning. Its development was pragmatic. What worked was kept; what didn't work was pruned away. The resultant system, though, does fit our definition of a technology of instruction. It takes the form of an identifiable, unique pattern of teaching/learning. Its procedures provide consistent (replicable), effective instruction on an individualized basis. And, most importantly, A–T puts into action a number of scientifically based principles of human learning:

1. The conversational audio tapes embody principles of communication theory (source credibility, personalization in the form of address, etc.).
2. The special emphasis on concrete media, such as slides, films, and realia applies what cognitive psychology advocates regarding realistic, meaningful messages.
3. Self-pacing and varied media alternatives cater to individual differences in learning style and rate.
4. The pervasive concern for individual success embodies the "whole person" emphasis of humanistic psychology.

These attributes differentiate A–T from the other systems discussed in this chapter. What unifies all of these systems is their common technological approach, characterized by such qualities as modular units, requirement of active

student participation, and provision of rapid feedback and correction.

Applications and Utilization of Audio-Tutorial Systems

The A–T approach is still most prevalent in science education, where it began. But during the two decades since its inception, it has also been successfully applied in many other areas, at many levels, and in both formal and nonformal educational settings. One indication of its widespread diffusion is the existence of a professional association, the International Congress for Individualized Instruction, devoted to sharing ideas and research on audio-tutorial and related systems of instruction.

As a result of these many and varied experiences with A–T, a number of generalizations can be recommended to anyone considering implementing such a system. First, as is true of PSI, setting

Figure 11.12 Multisensory materials and varied activities help maintain student interest in the Audio-Tutorial approach.

up an audio-tutorial system requires a great deal of preparation. However, A–T materials need not always be invented locally. Commercial publishers now offer sizable collections of packaged A–T materials.

Individualization and personalization are critical elements of this sort of system. Self-pacing and frequent corrective feedback must be designed into the system and vigilantly maintained. One aspect of personalization is the conversational tone of the audio materials; "lecture" style is not very appealing on a one-to-one basis.

Active participation by the learner is essential. A varied menu of activities—viewing films, manipulating real objects, field trips,—helps keep interest high.

A NOTE ON MODULES

For generations teachers have spoken in terms of "lessons" and "units" when talking about the parts of a course of instruction, but the age of space travel and computer technology has given us a new way of looking at the basic building blocks of instruction: the concept of the module.

In order to create complex electronic systems, engineers had to think in terms of small interchangeable units that could be easily plugged into and detached from the total system. Thus the concept of modules (as in "lunar module" and "modular designed TV") was born and popularized. Carried over into education, *instructional module* has become the generic name for free-standing instructional units dealing with a single concept of a larger subject. Modules carry a wide variety of labels, including unipack, individualized learning package, and learning activity package.

Modules are usually designed as self-instructional units for independent study. However, group-based modules (for example, built around a simulation, a game, or a field experience) are also found. The Personalized System of Instruction and Audio-Tutorial Systems, discussed in this chapter, are two types of course management systems that are designed around the concept of modules. However, it must be pointed out that the module itself is not a technology of instruction. It is a building block, more or less neutral, which can become *part of* a technology of instruction.

The reading materials used in a PSI course, for example, may be designed in the module format. If so, those modules become part of the PSI technology of instruction. If a module embodies the prompt/response/reinforcement pattern characteristic of programmed instruction, it becomes part of that technology of instruction. How-

Figure 11.13 More and more modular materials are being offered by commercial publishers.

ever, it is also possible for modules to be designed in a conventional prose style and to be used in a conventional teaching method. Then they are merely small bits of conventional instruction, not elements of a technology of instruction.

Characteristics of Modules

There are many different formulas for designing instructional modules, but certain components are virtually universally agreed upon:

1. *Rationale.* An overview of the content of the module and explanation of why the learner should study it.
2. *Objective.* What the learner is expected to gain from studying the module, stated in performance terms.
3. *Pre-Test.* To determine if the learner has the prerequisite skills needed to enter the module, and to check whether the learner already has mastered the skills to be taught.
4. *Learning Activities.* Resources to be used in attaining the objectives; materials not contained in the module per se, such as textbooks, audio tapes, filmstrips, and laboratory materials.
5. *Self-Test.* A chance to review and check one's own progress.
6. *Post-Test.* An examination to test whether the objectives of the module have been mastered.

Specific guidelines on selection criteria, design steps, and utilization principles for instructional modules can be found in the References listed at the end of this chapter.

SIMULATION AND GAMES

What They Are

We will not dwell long on defining simulation and games at this point. These concepts are described in detail in Chapter 12. It will suffice to define *simulation* as any scaled-down representation of some real-life happening. A *game* is an activity entailing competition within clearly defined rules toward a specified goal. As used in instruction, these two concepts can be applied separately, or together in the form of a *simulation game.* For present purposes the two will be grouped together to allow us to consider simulation/gaming (S/G) in general.

Simulation/Gaming as a Technology of Instruction

Recalling our basic definition of technology of instruction as a teaching/learning pattern that puts into effect scientific understandings about human learning, we find that S/G can embody a number of principles that are fundamental in the psychology of learning.

Meaningful Organization of Subject Matter. By placing the learner in a more or less realistic setting, simulation presents the subject matter in context. Facts, principles, and problems are viewed in their interaction rather than being presented singly as separate unrelated items.

Repetition. Repetition has always played a major role in school learning. The problem has been to maintain student interest in drill exercises. The game format, with its repetitive cycles of play (e.g. dealing out new hands in a card game), can direct learn-

ers through extensive drill-and-practice exercises while keeping interest high by means of variation in the pattern and the excitement of chance.

Reinforcement. S/G can be employed as a framework for reinforcement just as well as printed programmed materials. In a well-designed game the participants are required to make frequent responses related to the instructional objectives, for example, classifying items, making value judgments, making decisions. Each of these responses can be connected with certain preordained consequences—favorable consequences for correct responses and unfavorable consequences for less correct actions. Through such trial-and-error patterns the participant's behavior can be "shaped" toward the desired learning goals. In addition, like programmed tutoring, S/G goes beyond just "knowledge of results" in its array of possible reinforcers. It capitalizes on the social context of game play to incorporate such generalized reinforcers as achievement, dominance, and social approval.

COMPUTER-ASSISTED INSTRUCTION

Any discussion of technologies of instruction would be incomplete and woefully out-of-date if the revolution in computer applications were omitted. Because of its importance, Chapter 13 will be devoted to this topic. Our purpose at this point is to call attention to the computer's unmatched ability to *manage information* with such speed and accuracy that teaching/learning interactions can now be handled with much greater efficiency and effectiveness.

The computer, like the modular concept, *is not in itself a technology of instruction.* It is a physical tool that can be used to present programmed instruction, programmed tutoring, simulation/gaming, and other instructional formats on demand to individual learners without the necessity of a human helper being immediately present. Further, it can take such technologies of *managing* instruction as PSI and A–T and carry out their management functions far more efficiently than human paper shufflers and materials dispensers.

These functions, usually referred to as computer-assisted instruction and computer-managed instruction respectively, will be examined in detail in Chapter 13.

Figure 11.14 The Kee keyboard trainer combines simulation of a typewriter keyboard with a computer-controlled instructional program.

SUMMARY

In this chapter we have examined six teaching/learning formats, analyzing their differences in emphasis and their similarities as examples of technologies of instruction. These characteristics are summarized in the table below. You can see how each of these formats fulfills the requirements of the definition given at the beginning of the chapter. In addition, it should now be clearer why other teaching/learning formats do not meet these requirements. A conventional lecture, for example, lacks reliability (it is not repeatable unless recorded), ordinarily lacks prior testing, does not accommodate individual differences, and allows little practice/feedback or other instructionally desirable traits. Much the same could be said of a sound-slide presentation or other multi-media show.

A computer or other machine in itself is not a technology of instruction although it can be a contributing element when coupled with a program with certain special qualities.

CHARACTERISTICS OF TECHNOLOGIES OF INSTRUCTION

	Programmed Instruction	Programmed Tutoring	Personalized System of Instruction	Audio-Tutorial Systems	Simulation and Gaming	Computer-Assisted Instruction
A teaching/ learning *pattern*	Small units of information requiring practice, followed by feedback	Small units of information requiring practice, followed by feedback	Large units of information in sequential order; passing a test is required before proceeding (mastery)	Core of instruction is on audio tape, used in lab setting independently; small group and large group sessions are added	Small group activity, may entail representation of reality and/or competition	Small units of information presented on display screen, frequent practice required, followed by immediate feedback
Designed to provide *reliable,*	Program recorded in printed form	Tutor follows directions; learner uses structured workbook	Course organization is clearly spelled out; based on print materials and standardized tests	Core material recorded on audio tape and other audiovisual materials	Procedures are enforced by means of game directions and play materials	Instructions are coded into a computer program and displayed on a screen
Effective instruction	Programs must be learner tested and revised during development process	Programs are learner tested and revised during development process	Materials themselves are not validated, but mastery is assured by testing/correction cycle	Materials themselves are not validated, but mastery is encouraged by small group test/review sessions	May be learner tested for effectiveness	Programs must be learner tested and revised during development process; computer capability facilitates data gathering
To *each* learner	Allows individual pacing	Allows individual pacing plus highly flexible, responsive branching via human tutor	Allows individual pacing plus one-to-one discussion of test errors and questions	Allows individual pacing in independent study portion of course	Usually group paced, with individuals assigned to compatible groups	Allows individual pacing and some branching
Through application of *scientific* principles of human learning	Reinforcement theory: verbal response followed by knowledge of results	Reinforcement theory: verbal or other overt response followed by knowledge of results plus social reinforcers Constant personalized human contact Variety	Rather frequent response to tests over content followed by immediate correction Occasional personalized human contact Mastery requirement ensures that learner is working at his level of comprehension	Conversational relationship with instructor via tape High use of audiovisual and other concrete media Occasional personalized human contact Active involvement in challenging tasks	Meaningful organization of content (in simulation) Frequent practice with immediate feedback Social interaction with small group Emotional involvement Repetition of drill-and-practice without tedium High motivation	Reinforcement theory: verbal response followed by knowledge of results plus branching May involve audiovisual display Appearance of personalized human contact May apply mastery concept Highly motivational for at least some learners

REFERENCES

Print References: Programmed Instruction

The Center for Vocational Education. *Employ Programmed Instruction* (Athens, GA: American Association for Vocational Instructional Materials, 1977).

The Center for Vocational Education. *Employ Reinforcement Techniques* (Athens, GA: American Association for Vocational Instructional Materials, 1977).

Cram, David. *Explaining "Teaching Machines" and Programmed Instruction* (Belmont, CA: Fearon, 1961).

* Crowder, Norman A. "On the Differences Between Linear and Intrinsic Programming." *Phi Delta Kappan,* March 1963.

Deterline, W.A. *An Introduction to Programmed Instruction* (Englewood Cliffs, NJ: Prentice-Hall, 1962).

* Hartley, James. "Programmed Instruction 1954-1974: A Review." *Programmed Learning and Educational Technology,* November 1974, pp. 278–291.

"Instructor Workshop in Print 5: How to Design Programmed Learning Sequences." *Instructor,* February 1978, pp. 124–128.

Pereira, P.D. *Introduction to Programmed Learning* (Geneva, Switzerland: International Labor Organization, 1967).

* Skinner, B.F. "The Science of Learning and the Art of Teaching." *Harvard Educational Review,* Spring 1954, pp. 86–97.

Williams, Robert E. "Programmed Instruction for Creativity." *Programmed Learning and Educational Technology,* February 1977, pp. 50–64.

―――――――
*Key references.

Print References: Programmed Tutoring

* Ellson, Douglas G. "Tutoring." In *The Psychology of Teaching Methods,* 75th yearbook of the National Society for the Study of Education (NSSE) (Chicago, IL: NSSE, 1976).

Harrison, Grant, and Ronald Guymon. *Structured Tutoring,* Volume 34, Instructional Design Library (Englewood Cliffs, NJ: Educational Technology Publications, 1980).

Thiagarajan, Sivasailam. "Programming Tutorial Behavior: Another Application of the Programming Process." *Improving Human Performance Quarterly,* June 1972.

Print References: Personalized System of Instruction

Freemantle, M.H. "Keller Plans in Chemistry Teaching." *Education in Chemistry,* March 1976, pp. 50–51.

Johnson, Kent R., and Robert S. Ruskin. *Behavioral Instruction: An Evaluative Review* (Washington, DC: American Psychological Association, 1977).

Keller, Fred S. "Good-Bye, Teacher..." *Journal of Applied Behavior Analysis,* Spring 1968, pp. 79–88.

* Keller Fred S., and J. Gilmour Sherman. *The Keller Plan Handbook* (Menlo Park, CA: W.A. Benjamin, 1974).

"The Personalized System of Instruction (PSI)—Special Issue." *Educational Technology,* September 1977, pp. 5–60.

Sherman, J. Gilmour, and Robert S. Ruskin. *The Personalized System of Instruction,* Volume 13, Instructional Design Library (Englewood Cliffs, NJ: Educational Technology Pubs., 1978).

Terman, Michael. "Personalizing the Large Enrollment Course." *Teaching of Psychology,* April 1978, pp. 72–75.

Print References: Audio-Tutorial Systems

Postlethwait, S.N. "Principles Behind the Audio-Tutorial System." *NSPI Journal,* May 1978, pp. 3, 4, 18.

Postlethwait, S.N., J. Novak, and H. Murray. *The Audio-Tutorial Approach to Learning* (Minneapolis, MN: Burgess Publishing Company, 1972).

* Russell, James D. *The Audio-Tutorial System,* Volume 3, Instructional Design Library (Englewood Cliffs, NJ: Educational Technology Pubs., 1978).

Sturgis, A.V., and Cary H. Grobe. "Audio-Tutorial Instruction: An Evaluation." *Improving College and University Teaching,* Spring 1976, p. 81.

Print References: Instructional Modules

Fisher, Kathleen M., and Brian Mac-Whinney. "AV Autotutorial Instruction: A Review of Evaluative Research." *AV Communication Review,* February 1976, pp. 229–261.

* Johnson, Rita B., and Stuart R. Johnson. *Toward Individualized Learning: A Developer's Guide to Self-Instruction* (Reading, MA: Addison-Wesley, 1975).

Moore, David M. "Self-Instruction and Technology: A Review." *Journal of Educational Technology Systems,* No. 1, 1976-1977, pp. 51–56.

Radway, Bonnie, and Betty Schroeder. "Modular Instruction is the Way of the Future!" *Journal of Business Education,* March 1978, pp. 247, 249–50.

Russell, James D. *Modular Instruction* (Minneapolis, MN: Burgess Publishing Company, 1974).

* Russell, James D., and Kathleen A. Johanningsmeier. *Increasing Competence Through Modular Instruction* (Dubuque, IA: Kendall/Hunt, 1981).

Sussman, Miriam L. "Making Tracks with LAP's." *Florida Vocational Journal,* April 1978, pp. 17–19.

Audiovisual References

* "The Audio-Tutorial System—An Independent Study Approach," (West Lafayette, IN: Purdue University, 1968). (16-mm film, 25 minutes, color.)

"Individualized Learning Using Instructional Modules," (Englewood Cliffs, NJ: Educational Technology Publications, undated). (Set of six audio cassettes, 20 minutes each.)

"The Personalized System of Instruction," (Washington, DC: Center for Personalized Instruction, 1974). (16-mm film, 20 minutes, color.)

"Programmed Instruction: The Development Process," (Austin, TX: University of Texas, 1969). (16-mm film, 19 minutes, color.)

"Programmed Tutoring," (Austin, TX: University of Texas, 1969). (16-mm film, 19 minutes, color.)

"PSI" (Washington, DC, Center for Personalized Instruction, 1976). [Sound slide set (cassette), 80 slides, 20 minutes.]

Organizations

Center for Personalized Instruction
Loyola Hall, Room 29
Georgetown University
Washington, DC 20057

International Congress for
    Individualized
    Instruction (ICII)
c/o Physics Department
East Stroudsburg State College
East Stroudsburg, Pennsylvania 18301

National Society for Performance and
    Instruction (NSPI)
1126 Sixteenth Street, N.W.
Washington, DC 20036

Programmed Tutoring Center
2805 East Tenth Street
Indiana University
Bloomington, Indiana 47401

Periodicals

British Journal of Educational Technology (quarterly)
Council for Educational Technology
10 Queen Anne Street
London W1, England

Educational Technology (monthly)
Educational Technology Publications
140 Sylvan Avenue
Englewood Cliffs, New Jersey 07632

Journal of Educational Techology Systems (quarterly)
Baywood Publishing Company
43 Central Drive
Farmingdale, New York 11735

Performance and Instruction (monthly)
National Society for Performance
    and Instruction (NSPI)
1126 Sixteenth Street, N.W.
Washington, DC 20036

POSSIBLE PROJECTS

11-A. Appraise a commercially available program using the "Appraisal Checklist" in the chapter, or one from another source or of your own design.

11-B. Construct a short (10 to 15 frame) program on a subject of your choice. Use either the linear or branching style of programming. Describe exactly how you would use your program and under what conditions.

11-C. Submit a bibliography of at least 10 titles of commercially available programs which could be used in your subject field.

11-D. Observe a programmed tutoring session and write up your analysis of the session including strengths and weaknesses of the approach as you observed it being used.

11-E. Interview an instructor or students who have used the Personalized System of Instruction. Determine their reaction to using the system and ascertain what they perceive as the advantages and disadvantages of the approach.

11-F. Visit an Audio-Tutorial learning center. Interview students using A–T materials as well as the instructors. Prepare a report describing the center and the reactions of the students and the instructor(s).

11-G. Utilize an instructional module as though you were a student. Be sure to do all the activities and complete the exercises. Prepare an appraisal of the module from your point of view. Submit the module with your appraisal, if possible.

11-H. Take some teaching/learning format not discussed in the chapter and analyze it according to the criteria shown in the summary table at the end of the chapter.

CHAPTER 12

SIMULATION AND GAMES

OUTLINE

OBJECTIVES

After studying this chapter, you should be able to:

1. Define *game, simulation, simulation game,* and *instruction.*

2. Diagram the relationship between game, simulation, and instruction.

3. Discuss briefly how games can provide a framework for learning.

4. Describe an instructional situation in which you could use a game. Your description should include the objectives, the audience, the nature of the game, and anticipated outcomes.

5. Explain why and how simulations can be used in the areas of (a) cognitive, (b) affective, (c) psychomotor, and (d) discovery learning.

6. Describe an instructional situation in which you could use a simulation. Your description should include the objectives, the audience, the nature of the simulation, and anticipated outcomes.

7. Discuss the relationship between simulation games and holistic learning.

8. Identify five limitations of instructional games and simulations.

9. Relate the process of (a) selecting and/or (b) modifying instructional simulation/games to the ASSURE model. Include specific examples to the procedures described.

10. Describe the process of using simulation/gaming for instruction with specific references to those procedures which apply specifically to simulation/gaming.

11. Discuss techniques for requiring learner response during and after using a simulation/game.

12. Outline the four steps of the debriefing process with a short description of each step.

13. Appraise an example of a simulation/game using the "Appraisal Checklist" provided in the chapter.

14. State three appraisal criteria that apply specifically to simulations and games.

15. Identify two general references for locating simulation and game materials.

Instructional simulation and games are currently enjoying perhaps the fastest rate of growth in popularity among instructors of all media and technologies of instruction discussed to this point. There is, indeed, some danger of their taking on the qualities of a fad, uncritically accepted as a panacea for all educational problems. They are no such thing, of course. They can make a powerful contribution to learning—if they are properly understood and properly used.

The reasons that simulation and game enthusiasts give to explain their interest in these techniques are as varied as the kinds of simulation and game materials. Some express their concern that learning should avoid the drudgery too often associated with the classroom. Others emphasize the sociological point that play is a natural and necessary component of young children's learning; play should be encouraged and melded with academic objectives. Adult educators and trainers are interested in simulation as a cost-effective method of practicing complex skills. Futurists, along with educational psychologists, cite the importance of learning to view problems as a whole. These and other claims need to be appraised critically before deciding whether to use simulation and game materials. We will begin by examining some basic concepts in this area.

BASIC CONCEPTS: GAME, SIMULATION, AND INSTRUCTION

Game

A game is an activity in which players strive toward the attainment of a goal within prescribed rules. Usually implied in the notion of a game is that it is entertaining. What makes games "fun" is difficult to define objectively. People's tastes differ. A hypothesis is that it is diverting to be removed from the logic of everyday reality. Games create an artificial environment with a different set of operating principles. Most centrally, games prescribe *inefficient* procedures for attaining goals. This can be seen clearly in athletic games. The most efficient way of propelling a golf ball into a hole might be to pick it up and drop it in by hand. Forcing the player to strike it with a stick having an enlarged end prescribes an inefficient (and entertaining) procedure.

Attaining the goal may or may not involve competition. Communication games and "encounter" games exemplify a whole array of activities in which players agree to alter the normal pattern of interpersonal communications in order to pursue such goals as self-awareness, empathy, and leadership development. No competition is involved in these games. In games that do involve competition, the competition may be individual against individual, group against group, or individual against a standard. Each type entails different dynamics and different possibilities for conflict or cooperation among players.

Simulation

A simulation is an abstraction or simplification of some real-life situation or process. In simulations, participants usually play a role that involves them in interactions with other people and/or with elements of the simulated environment. A business management simulation, for example, might put the participant into the role of production manager of a mythical corporation, provide him or her with statistics about business conditions, and direct him or her to negotiate a new labor contract with the union bargaining team.

Simulations can vary greatly in the extent to which they fully reflect the realities of the situation they are intended to model. A simulation that incorporates too many details of a complex situation might be too complicated and time-consuming for the intended audience. On the other hand, if the model is oversimplified it may fail completely to communicate its intended point. A well-designed simulation provides a faithful model of those elements that are most salient to the immediate objective and it informs the instructor and participants about elements that have been simplified or eliminated completely.

Simulation Game

A simulation game combines the attributes of a simulation (role-playing, a model of reality) with the attributes of a game (striving toward a goal, specific rules). Like a simulation, it may be relatively high or low in its modeling of reality. Like a game, it may or may not entail competition.

Instruction

Any of the types of activities described so far may be designed to *help someone learn new skills or values applicable beyond the game itself.* Most commercially developed games intend to provide diversion, not instruction. A person who plays *Clue* or *Thinking Man's Golf* enough times probably learns more and more about the game itself but little in the way of usable skills.

Admittedly, the attribute of being "instructional" is often a matter of degree. The stated intentions of the designer would have to be examined closely.

Many game activities contain some modeling of reality and the distinction between simulations and games is not always clear. Many role-playing exercises take on game-like qualities as participants maneuver toward a good outcome for themselves. Yet the distinctions are worth making because they have significant implications for when and how these different types of materials are used. Figure 12.1 illustrates how the basic concepts of game, simulation, and instruction may overlap and interact; it shows that seven different classifications can be given. The following sections of the chapter will deal with the three classifications of most direct relevance to our interests: instructional games, instructional simulations, and instructional simulation games.

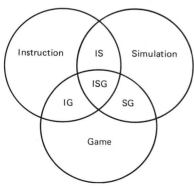

Figure 12.1 "Instruction," "Simulation," and "Game" are three separate concepts; certain activities may overlap two or more of these concepts.

INSTRUCTIONAL GAMES

Play in Human Development

Games are, above all, a form of play. As such, they may be looked upon with suspicion by those who think learning and playing are incompatible. But as viewed by developmental psychologists, play can be a useful mechanism indeed, the deprivation of which can impede cognitive and creative growth.

In fact, playing appears to be correlated with phylogenetic development—that is, the incidence of playing increases as one goes up the scale of animal development, with humans being the most playful.

Anthropologists note that primitive societies often use the playing of games to acculturate their members and to teach survival skills. It is certainly reasonable to assume that play in more advanced societies serves similar functions. Freudian interpretations of play see it as a symbolic reenactment of a threatening event, a safety valve for relieving pressures placed on children by the child-rearing practices of a culture. Child psychologist Jean Piaget views play as being a manifestation of "assimilation," one of the mental processes fundamental to intellectual growth. All observers agree that play is an adaptive mechanism important for human development.

Games as Learning Frameworks

Games can provide attractive and instructionally effective frameworks for learning activities. They are attractive because they are fun! Children (even most grown-up ones) have an immediate, positive response to an invitation to play. Games are a welcome break

in the day-to-day classroom routine. Indeed, positive response to instructional games is probably directly proportional to student boredom with the regular classroom routine. In short, games can help produce a happy, relaxed environment and thus an environment highly conducive to learning.

Many sorts of skills require repetitive practice in order to be mastered. Drills and practice exercises can become tedious, possibly turning off the student to the whole subject. Putting the skill practice into a game format makes the drill palatable, allowing the student to remain "on task" longer.

Figure 12.2a A bingo-type game using letters of the alphabet can get everyone in the class actively involved in a spelling drill.

Figure 12.2b Board games have to be examined critically to determine if player time is spent actively practicing relevant skills.

Of course, to be instructionally meaningful the game activity must provide actual practice of the intended academic skill. An instructionally fatal shortcoming of poorly designed games is that players spend a large proportion of their time exercising the "skill" of waiting for their turn, throwing dice, moving markers around a board, and similar trivial actions.

The element of competition must be handled very thoughtfully in choosing and using instructional games. Individual-versus-individual competition can be a highly motivating device as long as the contenders are fairly matched and the conflict does not overshadow the educational goal. Group-versus-group competition entails the same cautions, but it has the added attraction of providing practice in cooperation and teamwork. For instructional purposes, competition versus a standard may be the best option. It allows individualization, setting different standards for different players. In fact, one of the most effective standards can be the student's own past performance, the goal being to continually raise the level of aspirations.

In any event, in cases in which competition is an element, the scoring system provides a clue as to what type of competition is being fostered. Is one individual or group declared the "winner?" Or is it possible for all players to attain equally high scores? For educational purposes, the latter certainly is preferable. An example is the *Planet Management Game* (described in detail later), in which it is possible for all play groups to achieve a similar level of prosperity for the inhabitants of their planet.

Applications of Instructional Games

Instructional games are particularly well suited to:

MEDIA FILE: "Tuf" Instructional Game

Content area: Mathematics
Age Level: Grade 3 through college

Players roll cubes containing numbers and mathematical symbols, and attempt to form these into equations. "Tuf" might be used throughout a whole course in algebra; it can be played at increasing levels of sophistication. *Source: Avalon Hill.*

MEDIA FILE: "On-Words" Instructional Game

Content area: Language arts, spelling
Age level: Grade 4 through adult

In "On-Words" players roll letter and number cubes, then attempt to form words of a specified length. Intersecting words are formed, as in a crossword puzzle. Can be played at Basic, Advanced, or Adventurous levels, progressing from simple spelling and counting through word analysis. *Source: Wff 'N Proof.*

- Attainment of cognitive objectives in general, particularly those involving recognition, discrimination, or repetitive drill, such as grammar, phonics, spelling, arithmetic skills, formulas (chemistry, physics, logic), basic science concepts, place names, terminology, etc.
- Adding motivation to topics which ordinarily attract low student interest, for example, grammar rules, spelling, math drills.
- Small-group individualized instruction; instructional games allow students to work in a structured activity with a minimum of teacher direction.

In the book *Deal Me In!** Margie Golick, a psychologist specializing

in learning disabilities, argues persuasively for the use of card games to promote a wide variety of useful skills. She points out how various games played with ordinary playing cards can contribute to learning motor skills, rhythm, sequence, sense of direction, visual perception, number concepts, verbal skills, problem-solving, and social skills. Most of these skills are ordinarily taught at the elementary school age level, although some are also taught on a "remedial" basis to older learners.

In a similar vein, there are a number of commercial games, such as *Boggle, Fluster, Scrabble,* and *Probe,* that have been used successfully by teachers for vocabulary building although they were designed merely for fun.

---

*New York: Jeffrey Norton Publisher, 1973.

INSTRUCTIONAL SIMULATIONS

Simulation and Discovery Learning

A particular value of simulation is that it provides a specific framework for implementing what has become known as *discovery learning, the inquiry approach, experiential learning,* and other such terms denoting *inductive* teaching/learning strategies.

The typical conventional classroom teaching/learning approach (we could call it a *deductive* strategy) proceeds something like this:

Presentation of information
(The Point)
↓
Reference to particular examples
↓
Application of the knowledge to the student's experiences

This is an efficient and economical way to learn. One of its weaknesses, though, is its heavy dependence on language for transmission of information, which can be a real handicap for students with limited verbal skills. Another drawback to the deductive method is the difficulty many students have in applying the symbolically coded concept ("The Point") to everyday experience. They may be able to pass a written test (knowledge on a verbal–symbolic level) but they cannot solve real-life problems.

In contrast, the discovery or inductive strategy proceeds more like this:

Immersion in a real or contrived problematic situation
↓
Development of hypotheses
↓
Testing of hypotheses
↓
Arriving at conclusion (The Point)

In the inductive approach the learner is led toward "The Point" through trial-and-error grappling with a problem. Cause-and-effect relationships are discovered by observing the actual consequences of actions. This sort of immersion in a problem is the core of most simulations. Through simulations we can offer students a laboratory in areas such as social sciences and human relations as well as in areas related to the physical sciences, where laboratories have long been taken for granted. True, it tends to be more time consuming than the straightforward lecture approach but the payoff is a higher level of comprehension that is likely to be retained longer.

Simulation and Physical Skills

Skills in the psychomotor domain require practice under conditions of high feedback–giving the learner the feel of the action. Although it might be ideal to practice such skills under real-life conditions, some skills (for example, piloting an airplane or driving a car) can be practiced much more safely and conveniently by means of simulated conditions.

One familiar example of a *simulator* is the flight trainer, a mock-up of the interior of the cockpit, complete with controls and gauges. Today the flight crews of most major airlines receive a large proportion of their training in flight simulators, which are often controlled by computers and offer highly realistic audiovisual effects. Besides eliminating the possibility of loss of life and aircraft, these simulators allow significant savings of energy—millions of gallons of fuel annually—and other costs. One recent study estimated that in-air training costs about $4000 per hour compared to only $400 per hour on the flight simulator, with no loss in effectiveness.

Another example, which more people have experienced personally, is the automobile driver-training simulator. One of the best known of such systems is the AEtna Drivotrainer, shown in Figure 12.3. This system typically consists of a number of simulated car-driving units complete with all the controls of a real automobile.

Figure 12.3 Students training on driver education simulators learn to deal with potentially hazardous conditions in the safety of the classroom.

At the front of the room is a screen. At the rear are a film projector and audio console used to simulate the sights and sounds of actual driving conditions. Students "drive" on filmed streets and highways and their individual responses to filmed driving conditions are recorded and scored. From its inception in 1953 through the end of the 1970s, over 10 million students had sharpened their driving skills by means of this particular system.

Simpler simulators are in widespread use in areas such as training workers in a broad range of manual skills. A full discussion of such devices, including a number of examples, can be found in A. J. Romiszowski's *The Selection and Use of Instructional Media**

Simulation for Cognitive and Affective Learning

Probably the most prevalent use of instructional simulations is in the broad area of interaction with other people and with the environment in general. Role-playing is usually a major element of these activities. The role descriptions may be very general, leaving great latitude for the participant; for example, in *Actionalysis* (see "Media File") the person playing the role of "teacher" is given only a one-word description of the attitude he or she is supposed to be reflecting. The purpose here is to allow the person's own traits to emerge so that they may be discussed and possibly modified. In other simulations, such as historical recreations, highly detailed roles are described in order to project the realities of life in that period.

The great advantage of this sort of first-hand immersion in a topic is that students are more likely to be able to apply to real life what

they have practiced applying in simulated circumstances. This raises the issue of the degree of realism captured by a simulation. A common defect in poorly designed simulations is an overemphasis on *chance* factors in determining outcomes. Much of the reality is spoiled if "Chance Element" cards cause players to gain or lose great quantities of points or other resources regardless of their strategic decisions. An overemphasis on chance or an overly simplified representation of real relationships might end up teaching lessons quite contrary to what was intended.

Figure 12.4 A simulator used for railroad engineer training—a psychomotor skills application.

MEDIA FILE: "Actionalysis" Instructional Simulation

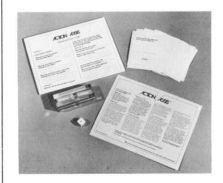

Content area: Education (adaptable to others)
Age level: College and other adult

"Actionalysis" provides two rather simple and flexible structures for role-playing related to teaching or supervision. Participants break into triads for each round: a "teacher," a "student," and an observer; each follows role instructions on a card. Roles and situations change each round.
Source: Randa, Inc.

MEDIA FILE: "Starpower" Instructional Simulation

Content area: Social studies, government
Age level: High school and above

"Starpower" revolves around the trading of tokens which have been distributed "randomly" at the start. During each round participants try to increase their wealth and move upward in the three-tiered class structure which evolves. Later in play, the "rich" make the rules.
Source: Simile II.

---

*London: Kogan Page, 1974, p. 305–329.

Applications of Instructional Simulations

Instructional simulations are particularly well suited for:

- Training in psychomotor skills, including athletic and work skills, and complex skills which might otherwise be too hazardous or expensive to practice in real-life settings.
- Instruction in social studies and human relations, where empathy and coping with the motivations of other people are major goals.
- Development of decision-making and personal interaction skills (e.g. microteaching in teacher education, mock court in law school, management simulations in business administration).

Figure 12.5 Professional decision-making skills are tested in simulations such as this mock court conducted at Suffolk Law School, Boston.

INSTRUCTIONAL SIMULATION GAMES

Simulation Games and Holistic Learning

Since they combine the characteristics of both simulations and games, instructional simulation games have advantages and applications in common with both formats. As such, they exemplify one of the major rationales for the use of simulation and gaming: the provision of holistic learning. That is, through the modeling of reality and through the players' interactions as they strive to succeed, learners encounter a whole and dynamic view of the process being studied. Conventional instruction tends to segment reality into separate packages (biology, mathematics, psychology, etc.), but that is not how the real world is organized. Through participation in simulation games we can see the whole process and its dynamic interrelationships in action. In addition, our emotions are allowed to get involved along with the thinking process. Participants commonly experience excitement, elation, disappointment, even anger, as they struggle to succeed. This, of course, is how learning takes place in the world outside the classroom.

Applications of Instructional Simulation Games

As indicated earlier, instructional simulation games are found in curricular applications that require both the repetitive skill practice associated with games and the reality context associated with simulations. Societal processes

---

MEDIA FILE: "Planet Management" Instructional Simulation Game

Content area: Ecology, social planning
Age level: Junior high school through adult

Participants play in teams, each representing the governing body of a mythical planet. They must decide the annual budget allocations for agriculture, manufacturing, social welfare, etc. An elaborate feedback system shows the effects of their decisions on food, income, population, and environment.
Source: Houghton Mifflin.

MEDIA FILE: "Empire" Instructional Simulation Game

Content area: History
Age level: Junior high through college

"Empire" demonstrates the operation of the eighteenth century British mercantile system as it affected colonial farmers, merchants, planters, and others. Teams compete to trade their products under rules representing the realities of 1745.
Source: Denoyer-Geppert.

(e.g., *Ghetto, Democracy*), cultural conflicts (e.g., *Bafa Bafa*), historical eras (e.g., *Empire, Manchester*), and ecological systems (e.g., *Extinction, Planet Management Game*) are popular topics.

In general, instructional simulation games are frequently used to provide an overview of a large, dynamic process. The excitement of play stimulates interest in the subject matter, and the holistic treatment of the game gives students a feel for the total process before approaching parts of it in a more linear form.

LIMITATIONS OF INSTRUCTIONAL GAMES AND SIMULATIONS

As with all of the other instructional media and formats discussed earlier, simulations and games have their limitations as well as potential strengths. Any materials-based instruction is only as good as the materials themselves. The simulation/game format is not magical. The effectiveness of the learning depends on the quality of the particular material and its utilization.

The use of simulation/game materials usually demands special grouping arrangements—pairing, for instance, or small groups. Some learners might not be able to exercise the responsibility and self-discipline necessary to the success of self-directed instruction.

Obtaining all the needed materials can be expensive and time-consuming. Sometimes costs can be kept down by making local modifications (e.g., altering the procedures so that consumable materials are not consumed). But effort will still be needed to get all the materials together and keep them together before, during, and after play.

Some simulation/game activities depend heavily on post-game discussion ("debriefing") for their full instructional effect. This debriefing must be skillfully planned and conducted. If the instructor lacks discussion-leading skills the whole learning experience is diminished.

Time can be a significant obstacle. Inductive learning is more time-consuming than straightforward lectures or reading assignments. A principle that can be stated in a single sentence might require an hour of play plus discussion to be conveyed experientially. You have to decide whether the added richness of the learning experience is worth the time.

As discussed earlier, some games entail competition in some form. A cultural setting which discourages competitiveness would not be a very compatible place for using competitive games. Likewise, a culture in which achievement is not valued might not provide the motivation required for students to get "into the spirit" of the game. On an individual level, there will be students for whom competition would be uncomfortable, unfair, or instructionally ineffective. This is true, of course, of every type of instructional treatment. It emphasizes the need to always be prepared to deal with individual differences.

FLASHBACK: Gaming—From Ancient Battlefields to Modern Classrooms

It is ironic that educational simulation/gaming, which is now prominently associated with the promotion of mutual understanding and cooperation, traces its ancestry to games designed to teach military tactics and strategies.

One of the earliest known examples of war gaming is *wei-chi* (meaning "encirclement") the existence of which can be traced back to at least 2000 B.C. The game was introduced into Japan around the eighth century A.D. and survives throughout the world today in the popular game, *go*. A variation of the encirclement game evolved in India as *chaturanga*. In this game, representations of foot soldiers, horsemen, chariots, and elephants faced each other on a board representing a battlefield. The Western version of *chaturanga*, chess, evolved into its current form during the Middle Ages. Although chess has long since lost its specific functions as a military training tool, tactics and strategic moves are still at its core, and the object of the game remains a "military" one: to capture (or checkmate) the opponent's king.

Following military defeats in the Napoleonic wars, the Prussians throughout the nineteenth century invested great ingenuity in the refinement of war games that would allow greater latitude for experimentation at lower cost than actual military exercises. Terrain models of battlefields replaced checkered boards; rules for the value of movement of pieces were more realistically prescribed; teams of opposing forces replaced individual players; judges monitored the observance of rules. The resounding Prussian victory in the Franco–Prussian War of 1870 to 1871 and the subsequent Prussian reputation for military genius may be attributable in part to their preparedness born out of years of practice in *Kriegspiel*.

In the years immediately following the Franco–Prussian War, the competition began to catch up. War gaming took root in England and was introduced soon afterward at the United States Military Academy, where the data from the American Civil War added further precision to the components of war games.

By the early twentieth century, war gaming had spread to all the technologically advanced nations of the world. Germany and Japan raised war-gaming techniques to a high art as part of their preparations for World War II. At Japan's Total War Research Institute, for example, highly elaborate simulation games were used to plot both military and civilian strategies to be employed in the conflict which lay immediately ahead.

A breakthrough in war-gaming technique came toward the end of World War II with the advent of the electronic computer. The high speed calculating power of the computer vastly increased designers' ability to deal with complexity. It became possible to include in the games, with a good deal of precision, social and political variables as well as military data.

Crisis Games

An important step in the evolution of war games toward educational games came with the development in the mid-1950s of so-called "crisis games." Growing largely out of experimentation at the RAND Corporation to deal with potential Cold War problems, crisis games are simulations of hypothetical crisis situations, with participants trying to solve or alleviate the crises within a framework of rules structured to reflect the conditions of the simulated crisis situation.

Not long after the original RAND experiments, crisis games were in use at several universities. Gaming became a popular instructional technique in which students of international relations could adopt the roles of government decision makers and play out hypothetical crises.

Business Games

Since economists and business management theorists already possessed well-defined, quantitative models upon which simulation/gaming could be based, it is not surprising that business games were among the first academic games to be developed. The linkage of business games with military games is quite clear. In 1956 the American Management Association (AMA) launched a research project to consider the possibility of developing a simulation that would allow management trainees to experience the same kind of strategic decision-making practice as military officers were then experiencing. Following a visit to the Naval War College, the research group set to work on its project. Its efforts culminated in the creation of the AMA Top Management Decision Simulation,

FLASHBACK: Gaming (continued)

a computer-assisted simulation game in which teams of players representing officers of companies make business decisions and receive "quarterly reports" on the outcomes of their decisions. Business executives and business educators reacted to the game with great enthusiasm.

By the end of 1959 variations of the AMA game had been developed at IBM and the University of California at Los Angeles, and within three years the development of over 85 such games had been noted in professional journals.

To a great extent, business games and crisis games were an extension of war games into new "battlefronts"—the marketplace and the diplomatic arena. Further development was needed to encourage the use of simulation/gaming for more "peaceful" academic purposes, that is, for the understanding and minimization of conflict rather than simply the achievement of supremacy within the conflict situation. This transition can perhaps best be illustrated by considering the career odyssey of one of the major figures in contemporary simulation gaming.

Clark C. Abt, a systems engineer, became involved in the 1950s with the design of computer simulations of air battles, space missions, disarmament inspection systems, and other military problems. He and his colleagues at the Missile Systems Division of the Raytheon Company began to apply war-gaming techniques to increasingly complex problem—problems which became more and more involved with human factors—the social, economic, and political causes and consequences of military actions.

Seeking to better understand these human factors, Abt returned to M.I.T. to earn a Ph.D. in the social sciences. Restrictions on the pursuit of such humanistic concerns within the military-industrial setting led him in 1965 to found his own company, Abt Associates.

Classroom Simulation Games

Within the next few years Abt Associates became a major fountainhead of classroom simulation games, some of the better-known examples being *Pollution, Neighborhood, Empire, Manchester, Colony,* and *Caribou Hunting Game.*

As Abt Associates was developing the techniques for classroom simulation/gaming, many educators, especially in the social studies, were becoming interested in inquiry-oriented approaches to teaching. Jerome Bruner and other instructional theorists, working in the same vein as John Dewey had a generation earlier, were advocating the importance of active student involvement in learning. Immersion in a problem, informed guessing, and hypothesis testing were the methods best calculated to promote "discovery" learning.

This theoretical viewpoint activated a number of reform-minded curriculum development projects. Bruner's own contribution was *Man: A Course of Study*, a total curriculum package developed from the Social Studies Curriculum Program, and incorporating the Abt Associates' *Caribou Hunting*, and *Seal Hunting*. Other such projects including the High School Geography Project and the Holt Social Studies Program yielded several simulation games.

Another historical influence critical to the establishment of the academic respectability of simulation/gaming in the classroom was the Academic Games Program at Johns Hopkins University. Headed by eminent educational sociologist James S. Coleman from 1966 to 1973, the Johns Hopkins group developed a number of ground-breaking games (including *Life Career, Democracy, Generation Gap,* and *Ghetto*) and conducted many studies of game-playing and the learning associated with it. Their general conclusions confirmed the advantages of simulation/gaming and also helped identify some of the problem areas in simulation/game utilization.

SIMULATION/ GAMING AND THE ASSURE MODEL

Putting simulations and games into use can be organized by turning again to the ASSURE model. Again, it is assumed that you have analyzed the needs, interests, and learning characteristics of your audience and clearly specified your objectives. So we will begin here with the third element of the model: select, modify, or design the materials.

Selection of Materials

Selection of any particular simulation or game involves the same considerations as selection of media materials in general. How does the material fit your curricular objectives? Does it address those objectives in a way no other media format can? Is the cost in money and time worth the benefit?

Other considerations that apply particularly to simulation and gaming are noted in the "Appraisal Checklist" included here. You will note that emphasis is placed on identifying whether the item really does provide *relevant practice* of *meaningful skills* within a *valid representation of reality*. These are aspects of simulation/game materials most likely to prove faulty.

Even more than with most other instructional materials, you will not be able to judge the appropriateness and effectiveness of simulation/gaming materials on the basis of superficial examination. You really can't judge a simulation/ game by its "cover." A trial runthrough by yourself or with friends is the only relatively sure way of determining how the game flows and what it teaches.

One discouraging aspect of simulation/gaming instruction is the difficulty of locating and acquiring simulation/gaming materials. Many such materials are marketed by their individual developers, so they do not get into regular trade distribution channels and are likely to be publicized only by word-of-mouth. Others are distributed by small commercial houses which have an annoying tendency to move and/or go out of business very rapidly. Only a minority are sold through regular publishing outlets. So the prospective simulation/game user may need good detective skills and perseverance to obtain exactly the sort of material discussed. Fortunately, there are two reference aids that can help you in this task and which are updated regularly: *The Guide to Simulations/Games for Education and Training*, edited by Robert E. Horn and Ann Cleaves and *Handbook of Simulation Gaming in Social Education*, edited by Ron Stadsklev. Both books are described in detail in Appendix A.

Modification of materials

Although the supply of commercially developed simulation and game materials is growing, you might find it necessary or desirable to *modify* some existing materials to fit your instructional objectives more closely.

Role-play and other less structured activities (e.g., communication games) can be modified easily by changing role descriptions, changing the setting of the activity, or simplifying the interaction pattern in the original activity.

Some games are designed for adaptation to varying age or grade levels. Several of the games in the *Wff 'N Proof* series, such as *On-Words* and *Equations*, begin as simple spelling or arithmetic drills. The instruction manual contains directions for progressively

raising the objectives and rules to higher cognitive levels, ending with games of transformational grammar and symbolic logic.

Familiar parlor games (e.g., bingo, concentration, tic-tac-toe, and rummy) which were never intended for instructional purposes can be viewed as potential frameworks for carrying your own instructional content. Television game shows often have been modeled after such parlor games; they in turn suggest additional frameworks. Game formats that lend themselves to multipurpose modification have been referred to as "frame games." Here are some sample adaptations:

Safety tic-tac-toe—A three-by-three grid is used; each row represents a place where safety rules pertain—home, school, street; each column represents the level of question difficulty. Teams take turns selecting and trying to answer safety related questions, attempting to fill in three squares in a row.

Spelling rummy—Using alphabet cards instead of regular playing cards, players attempt to spell short words following the general rules of rummy.

Reading concentration—This game uses about a dozen matched picture-word pairs of flash cards. Cards are placed face down. On each turn the player turns over two cards, seeking to match a pair. Both reading ability and memorization ability are exercised.

Word bingo—Each player's card has a five-by-five grid with a vocabulary word in each square. The leader randomly selects words, then players seek the words on their boards and if found, the square is marked. Winner is first player with five correctly marked squares in a row.

APPRAISAL CHECKLIST: SIMULATION/GAME

Title_____

Publisher/distributor_____

Publication date_____

Number of players_____

Special equipment or facilities needed:

Intended audience/grade level_____

☐ Has gaming features
(competition, scoring)

☐ Has simulation features
(role playing)

Playing time_____

Subject area_____

Objectives (stated or implied):

Brief description:

Entry capabilities required
—prior knowledge:
—reading ability:
—math ability:

RATING	High	Medium		Low	
Likely to arouse student interest?	☐	☐	☐	☐	☐
Players practice meaningful skills	☐	☐	☐	☐	☐
(Game) Winning dependent on player actions (vs. chance)	☐	☐	☐	☐	☐
(Simulation)Validity of game model (realistic, accurate)	☐	☐	☐	☐	☐
Technical quality (durability, attractiveness, etc.)	☐	☐	☐	☐	☐
Evidence of effectiveness (e.g. field-test results)	☐	☐	☐	☐	☐
Clear directions for conducting game?	☐	☐	☐	☐	☐
Players' instructions clear and concise?	☐	☐	☐	☐	☐
Debriefing guide included?	☐	☐	☐	☐	☐

Strong points:

Weak points:

Recommended action_____

Reviewer_____

Position_____

Date_____

Design of Materials

As indicated above, simple simulation/gaming materials may be adapted by an imaginative teacher with little more than pencil and paper. This does not mean, however, that designing simulation/gaming materials is a simple process. A great deal of careful thought is required for the planning and development of *effective* materials. Good simulation/gaming materials do not just happen.

Figure 12.6 presents a model for the design of simulation and game materials. As you can see, many individual steps are involved in the process and the relationships between and among these steps can be quite complex.

The outline of a simulation/game design that puts this model into practice follows. It is intended to give you some idea of the controlled complexity of effective simulation/gaming materials and to acquaint you with some of the factors you must be prepared to deal with in designing your own materials. (The simulation game described here is intended for adults and was developed by the participants in a workshop at the International Congress of Ecology in 1978.)

SIMULATION/GAME DESIGN: Putting the Model into Practice

I. Select content and delimit scope of S/G activity.
EXAMPLE: The subject will be the sociopolitical conflicts involved in establishing a nature reserve, the "Mountain Park Nature Reserve;" focus will be on developing some interpersonal skills to deal with such conflict situations. This activity will have both simulation *and* game characteristics. It should be playable within one session (e.g., 2 to 3 hours). It will not deal with the scientific aspects of nature reserves themselves.

II. Specify target audience.
EXAMPLE: This game is intended to be played by environmental educators; that is, adults probably possessing formal training in some aspect of ecology.

III. Specify objectives.
EXAMPLE: The general objectives (not yet refined into behavioral outcomes) are that participants will (1) "understand" the sociopolitical complications involved in establishing a nature reserve, and (2) "appreciate" the legitimate contrary points of view likely to be raised by critics and supporters of the planned nature reserve.

IV. Develop simulation/game model.

A. Create a scenario (for a simulation).
EXAMPLE: A public hearing will be simulated. This hearing has been set up to discuss the pros and cons of proceeding with the establishment of the "Mountain Park Nature Reserve." The setting is a

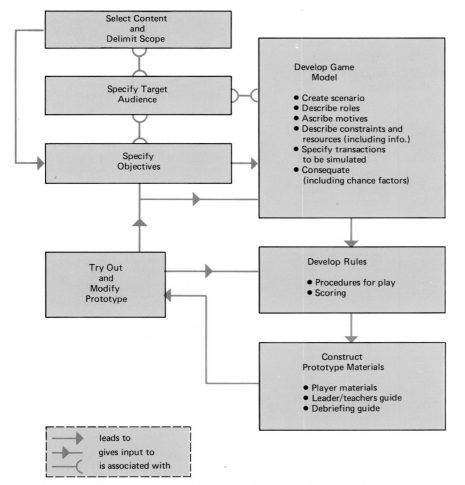

Figure 12.6 Instructional Simulation/Game Design Model.

small country with limited resources but a rather high degree of technological development. The time is now.

B. Describe roles (for a simulation).

EXAMPLE: The number of roles represented in the "Mountain Park Nature Reserve Game" can vary with the size of the playing group. Some of the possible roles are: representatives for concerned government agencies— Agriculture, Tourism, Industry, Conservation, etc.; residents of the impacted area; scientific experts; potential users; environmental activists; and others.

C. Ascribe motivations (for a simulation).

For each of the roles selected for representation, a role description will be developed to inform the player what his motives are as an aid to realistic role-playing.

D. Specify *transactions* to be carried out.

In order to achieve productive learning, players must be engaged in behaviors directly associated with the game's instructional objectives. This means activities such as data-gathering, classifying, choosing, discussing, testing, thinking, etc. Players should *not* be spending most of their time waiting for turns, throwing dice, spinning spinners, or moving markers around a playing board.

EXAMPLE: Since the objectives specified in Step III. call for developing skills in the analysis and "appreciation" of conflicting viewpoints, the main transactions will be *presenting* and critically *listening to* arguments for and against the "Mountain Park Nature Reserve."

E. Arrange appropriate *consequences* for player actions.

Participants should experience consequences for their moves. The point is to reward actions which are consonant with the game's aims.

EXAMPLE: Players will receive points depending on their ability to (1) present a logical argument consistent with their role, (2) use data to support their arguments, (3) paraphrase the contrary arguments of others, and (4) gain supporters to their viewpoint.

V. Develop rules.

A. Procedures for play.

EXAMPLE: This game will be played in two major phases— a series of small-group mini-debates and a public hearing which will conclude with a vote being taken. The debates will be carried out in triads consisting of two different roles plus an observer. The observer will award points to each role based on the criteria stated in Step IV.E. above. Each round of mini-debates will last five minutes, after which everyone rotates into a new triad. About six rounds might be used. The public hearing will allow the various roles to present testimony and be questioned by the other participants. The aim here will be to consolidate support for one's position.

B. Procedures for scoring.

EXAMPLE: As outlined in Steps IV.E. and V.A. above, points will be distributed by the triad "observers" according to the given criteria; another, perhaps separate, scoring system could rate success in the public hearing (e.g., do the proponents or opponents win the final vote?) Ideally, a system will be worked out in which points gained in the "debate" phase can be translated into political strength in the "hearing" phase.

VI. Construct prototype materials.

The developers will create the needed player materials, teacher's guide, and debriefing outline.

VII. Tryout and modify prototype.

The developers will try out the prototype to test for errors or rough edges. Perhaps running time will be longer than expected. Perhaps the original objectives will be reexamined and restated. Players' reactions to the prototype will be observed and recorded as clues to needed modifications.

Utilization of Materials

For simulation/gaming, the Utilization step of the ASSURE model entails procedures that are quite different at some points from those suggested earlier for other media.

Preview. Familiarize yourself with the materials, preferably going through a "dry run" with some friends or a few selected students. Acquaint yourself with the rules. Note individual phases of the simulation/game. Be sure you are aware of exactly when and where important instructional points are made. Practice any activities that the game director is responsible for (e.g., providing tokens, computing scores for each round).

Set a time schedule for use of the materials. Your first concern is to have enough time for a successful session. A "good" game squeezed into too short a time can become a "bad" game. Some games, *Starpower* for example, cannot be broken down to fit into separate class periods; they must be played through continuously. If you have to divide play into separate periods, try to have the breaks come at natural stopping points.

Figure 12.8 Avoid stifling student eagerness by dwelling overlong on rules and strategies; five minutes is a reasonable rule of thumb for rule explanations.

Figure 12.7 Successful learning from simulation/game activities is heavily dependent on the instructor's utilization procedures, especially being well prepared.

Prepare the Environment. Check over all the materials to be certain that everything is ready in sufficient quantities. Before the participants arrive count everything again! If any audiovisual equipment is involved give it a last minute checkout, too. As with any other kind of teaching, students will judge you harshly if they sense that *you* haven't done your homework.

Prepare the Audience. Inform your audience of the learning objectives of the simulation/game activities. Relate the simulation/game to previous studies. Announce the time schedule for completion of the activities. Run through the rules concisely and clearly. If the procedures are somewhat complex, walk the students through one initial round of activities. Resist the urge to lecture about content or to give hints about strategies. Get into the game as quickly as possible.

Present the Simulation/Game. Once the simulation/game is rolling, your job is to keep the mood and the tempo upbeat. Stay in close touch with the action. Be ready to intervene, but only when intervention is clearly called for.

Some participants in simulation/game activities may feel a bit confused in the initial stages and be hesitant to get into the swing of things. Reassure such students that initial confusion is not uncommon and that they will soon pick up on rules and procedures.

Watch for individuals or teams who have fallen behind in the activities or even dropped out of them. They may need additional help in mastering the game mechanics. Withdrawal often signals some basic disagreement with the game's approach to the subject matter. Rather than stifling or suppressing the dissent, discuss the disagreement on a one-to-one basis. Ask the dropout to suspend criticism until the end of the activities.

Watch out for personality clashes; they may require switching of partners or teammates for successful completion of the activities.

Keep track of elapsed time. The excitement and fascination of simulation and game activities make it easy to forget that time is passing. If necessary, remind participants of time limitations. Resist the temptation to extend simulation/game play at the expense of debriefing time.

If announcements must be made during utilization, try not to bluntly interrupt the activities by shouting above the hubub. Dimming room lights or flashing your message on the overhead projector can attract the attention you need.

Record significant participant reactions and comments for discussion during the debriefing period.

Require Learner Response

A unique attribute of simulations and games is that participants are continuously responding *throughout* the activity. Indeed, without response there can *be* no activity. Why, then, should we be concerned with the response element of our ASSURE model when dealing with simulations and games?

The truth is that attention to learner response is perhaps more important in simulations and games than in any other instructional medium we have discussed in this book. The reason? Learner response in simulation/gaming is of a different order than is response in most other media. During the hurly-burly or determined concentration of intense involvement in simulations and games, there is little opportunity to intellectualize or verbalize what one is learning or failing to learn from the activity. The overlay of emotion inherent in simulation/gaming militates against cognitive awareness.

Consequently, it is imperative that learner response during utilization of simulation/gaming materials be raised to conscious level. This is usually done in post-utilization debriefing. Post-activity debriefing may be conducted on either an individual or group basis, or a combination of both may be employed.

Individual Debriefing. In situations in which participants finish simulation/gaming activities at different times or in which the classroom schedule prevents immediate group discussion, some form of individual debriefing may be used.

Theodore Smith, developer of *Consumerism*, has worked out a simple sentence completion activity intended to be completed by each player individually on paper immediately at the conclusion of role-playing.* It is designed to help participants "get in touch with their feelings prior to group debriefing discussions." Learners simply write completions to each of the following sentences:

(a) I was_____. (the role the participant played in the game)
(b) I did_____. (major activities performed)
(c) I felt_____. (emotions felt during play)
(d) I wish_____. (open response)

Given the reality of fifty-minute class periods faced by most teachers, some such individualized response sheet at least allows some of the participant's immediate reactions to be intellectualized and verbalized while they are still fresh in the memory. If group debriefing is postponed until another day, the response sheet can help the participant recapture impressions felt at the time of the activity. Smith reports that comparison of response sheets with the course of group discussion shows that most of the points recorded on the sheets are brought up in later group debriefing.

Group Debriefing. As noted earlier in this chapter, some instructors may have difficulty in guiding group discussions, especially discussions designed to encourage verbalization of concepts not yet fully intellectualized, perhaps because of emotional overlay. Careful planning, beginning with the moment of selection of materials, is necessary for successful debriefing after simulation/gaming activities. Key questions and leading statements must be formulated in advance.

Ron Stadsklev, an experienced simulation/game director (see his *Handbook of Simulation Gaming in Social Education*) has developed a step-by-step debriefing format upon which the following similar format has been modeled.

Figure 12.9 For social simulations and similar activities, the group debriefing is crucial for bringing out the main points of the experience.

---

*Theodore F. Smith "'Was/Did/Felt/Wish' Bridges Gap When Debriefing Has to Be Delayed," *Simulation/Gaming*, January/February 1978, pp. 5–6.

Step 1. Releasing Emotions

Your first step in the group debriefing session should be to relieve any tensions that may have been built up during the simulation/gaming activity. Some roles played by participants may engender conflict and anger. Some games such as *Starpower* and *Ghetto* pit the player against "the system," arousing frustration. Players who feel they did not succeed very well in the game may be experiencing anxiety and feelings of inadequacy. In any event, learners are not likely to be able to think about your questions and concerns until these built-up feelings simmer down to a manageable level.

In order to release some of these pent-up feelings, start with some "safety valve" questions. In many cases the players will have attained some sort of score, so you can start simply by asking for and recording the scores. (You will find it useful to have a chalkboard handy so that you can write down the scores and other comments that participants make. The information on the chalkboard will help build up a "data base" you can refer to in subsequent portions of the debriefing.)

From tabulations of the scores you will be able to declare the winner of the game, if the game calls for winners and losers. Let the winner(s) show off a little bit by asking them how they managed to score so highly. Then the lowest scorers should have a chance to explain their tale of woe—what went wrong for them?

At this point be sure to explain any "dirty tricks" the designer may have built into the game to unfairly influence certain scores. In many simulations modeled on the social class structure, for instance, certain players start out as "disadvantaged" and are consistently impeded from advancing. The scoring system intentionally dooms them from the beginning. Obviously, in simulations such as these the final scores are not meant to reflect player skills. Also, you may want to point out that chance plays some part in the scoring—as it does in real life—so that two players might have followed the same strategy and have come out with different scores. In many cases, a score just a small margin ahead of another does not necessarily represent higher achievement.

To deal further with the emotional residue, ask one or two players how they felt while playing the game. Did anyone else feel that way too? Let all those chime in freely who want to.

Step 2. Description

Review and elaborate on the symbolic intent of the simulation or game. The nature and purpose of the activity will, of course, have been explained before the beginning of play. But some students may not have fully appreciated or fully understood the symbolic intent of the activity at this initial stage. Others may have lost track of it in the heat of participation. For example, children who have played *Pink Pebbles* may have to be reminded that they have been through a simulation of the development of a money economy; players of *Triangle Trade* might need to be reminded that they have simulated the experiences of British colonists of the seventeenth century. Make certain that all participants are fully conscious of the real-world situation or experience that the activity was intended to represent or simulate. Ask basic questions such as, "What real-life situation was represented in this activity? What real-life experiences? What was so-and-so or such and such intended to symbolize?"

Step 3. Transfer

Help the participants transfer the lessons learned in the game to reality. Encourage them to compare and contrast the activities of the simulation or game with the actual dynamics of the real-life situation or experience symbolized by the simulation game. Ask questions such as "How does the scoring system compare with real-world rewards? What elements of reality were missing from or muted in the simulation or game? Were some elements of reality given more weight than they would have in real life? Were some given less weight?"

Step 4. Drawing Generalizations

You are now ready to hit paydirt in your post-activity debriefing session. Get the participants to intellectualize and verbalize exactly what they have learned from the activity. Verbalization will reinforce what has been learned in the activity and strengthen insights that have been gained. Sample questions: "What conclusions can you draw from the simulation/game experience? What did you learn about what specific real-life problems? Did the simulation/game change any of your previous attitudes or opinions?"

Evaluate

The final element of the ASSURE model for teaching/learning is, of course, evaluation. As we have pointed out throughout this text in connection with other instructional media, although full evaluation must await completion of a learning activity, the process begins much earlier.

The notes made during utilization and the records kept of student response to the simulation/gaming materials used will contribute to your final evaluation. The debriefing session, however, will probably provide the most precise and useful data upon which your final evaluation will be based. When all is said and done, the acid test of the propriety and effectiveness of any instructional medium, including simulation/gaming is: Did my students achieve the learning objectives of the activity, or did they not?

REFERENCES

Print References: General

Abt, Clark C. *Serious Games* (New York: The Viking Press, 1970).

The Center for Vocational Educaton. *Employ Simulation Techniques* (Athens, GA: American Association for Vocational Instructional Materials, 1977).

Coleman, James et al. "The Hopkins Games Program: Conclusions From Seven Years of Research." *Educational Researcher,* August 1973, pp. 3–7.

Cruickshank, Donald R., and Ross A. Telfer (eds.). *Simulations and Games: An ERIC Bibliography* (Washington, DC: ERIC Clearinghouse on Teacher Education).

Dukes, Richard L., and Constance J. Seidner (eds.). *Learning with Simulations and Games* (Beverly Hills, CA: Sage Publications, 1978).

Gagne, Robert M. "Simulators." In Robert Glaser (ed.), *Training Research and Education* (New York: John Wiley & Sons, 1962).

Gibbs, G.I. (ed.). *Handbook of Games and Simulation Exercises* (Beverly Hills, CA: Sage Publications, Inc., 1974).

Glickman, Carl D. "Problem: Declining Achievement Scores, Solution: Let Them Play!" *Phi Delta Kappan,* February 1979, pp. 454–455.

* Greenblat, Cathy S., and Richard D. Duke. *Gaming-Simulation: Rationale, Design, and Applications* (New York: Halsted Press Division, John Wiley & Sons, 1975).

* Heyman, Mark. *Simulation Games for the Classroom* (Bloomington, IN: Phi Delta Kappa, 1975).

Hoper, Claus et al. *Awareness Games* (New York: St. Martins Press, 1975).

Krupar, Karen R. *Communication Games* (New York: The Free Press, 1973).

Metzner, Seymour. *One-Minute Game Guide* (Belmont, CA: Pitman Learning, 1968).

_____

*Key references.

Michaelis, Bill, and Dolores Michaelis. *Learning Through Noncompetitive Activities and Play* (Belmont, CA: Pitman Learning, 1977).

* Stadsklev, Ron. *Handbook of Simulation Gaming in Social Education,* Part One, textbook (University, AL: Institute of Higher Education Research and Services, The University of Alabama, 1974).

Sullivan, Dorothy. *Games as Learning Tools: A Guide for Effective Use* (New York: McGraw-Hill, 1978).

* Taylor, John, and Rex Walford. *Learning and the Simulation Game* (Beverly Hills, CA: Sage Publications, Inc., 1978).

Thiagarajan, Sivasailam. "Keep That Delicate Balance." *Simulation/Gaming,* September-October 1977, pp. 4–8.

Thiagarajan, Sivasailam, and Harold D. Stolovitch. *Instructional Simulation Games,* Volume 12, Instructional Design Library (Englewood Cliffs, NJ: Educational Technology Publications, 1978).

Print References: Curricular Applications

Clark, Todd. "Reality in the Classroom." *Social Education,* April 1977, pp. 353–368.

Creamer, Robert C., Richard B. Cohen, and Manuel Escamilla. "Simulation: An Alternative Method for Bilingual-Bicultural Education." *Contemporary Education,* Winter 1977, pp. 90–91.

Ellington, H.I., and F. Percival. "The Place of Multidisciplinary Games in School Science." *Science Review,* September 1977, pp. 29–35.

Ellington, H.I., and E. Addinall, and F. Percival. *Games and Simulations in Science Education* (New York: Nichols, 1980).

Hoffman, Thomas R. "Training: Games Corporations Play." *Audio-Visual Communications,* January 1977, pp. 32, 34.

Hotchkiss, Gwen, and Margaret Athey. "Music Learning Grows with Games." *Music Educators Journal,* April 1978, pp. 48–51.

Hulsey, John Adler, Jr. "New Insights into Simulation as an Effective Method of Teaching Social Studies." *High School Journal,* March 1977, pp. 243–246.

Keller, Clair W. "Role Playing and Simulation in History Classes." *History Teacher,* August 1974, pp. 573–581.

Kiser, Michael, and Larry Stuart. "Putting Games into English and English into Games." *Media & Methods,* April 1974, pp. 26–29.

Spencer, Jan. "Games and Simulations for Science Teaching." *School Science Review,* March 1977, pp. 397–413.

Steiner, Karen. "Child's Play: Games to Teach Reading." *Reading Teacher,* January 1978, pp. 474–477.

Wertlieb, Ellen. "Games Little People Play." *Teaching Exceptional Children,* Fall 1976, pp. 24–25.

Print References: Design

Gillespie, Perry. "A Model for the Design of Academic Games." In Loyda M. Shears and Eli M. Bower (eds.), *Games in Education and Development* (Springfield, IL: Charles C. Thomas).

Greenblat, Cathy S. "The Design of Gaming-Simulations." *Improving Human Performance Quarterly,* Fall 1975, pp. 115–121.

McLean, Harvard W., and Michael J. Raymond. *Design Your Own Game,* 2d ed. (Lebanon, OH: Simulation and Gaming Association, 1976).

* Maidment, Robert, and Russell H. Bronstein. *Simulation Games: Design and Implementation* (Columbus, OH: Charles E. Merrill, 1973).

Olmo, Barbara G. "Simulations—Do It Yourself." *Social Studies,* January/February 1976, pp. 10,14.

Rausch, Erwin. "30,000 Ways to Invent Your Own Group Games." *Successful Meetings,* March 1976, pp. 533–536.

Audiovisual References

"Finding Values Through Simulation Games," (Hollywood, CA: Media Five, 1977). (16-mm film, 20 minutes, color.)

"How to Design Educational Games," (San Jose, CA: Lansford Publishing, 1972). (10 transparencies.)

Periodicals

Journal of Experiential Learning and Simulation (quarterly)
Elsevier North-Holland, Inc.
52 Vanderbilt Avenue
New York, New York 10017

Simages (quarterly)
North American Simulation and Gaming Association (NASAGA)
Box 100
Westminster College
New Wilmington, Pennsylvania 16142

Simgames: The Canadian Journal of Simulation and Gaming (quarterly)
Champlain Regional College
Lennoxville, Quebec
Canada

Simulations and Games: an International Journal of Theory, Design, and Research (quarterly)
Sage Publications, Inc.
275 S. Beverly Drive
Beverly Hills, California 90912

Organizations

COMEX (Center for Multi-Disciplinary Education Exercises)
University of Southern California
Davidson Conference Center
Los Angeles, California 90007

International Simulation and Gaming Association (ISAGA)
U.S. representative: Richard Duke
321 Parklake
Ann Arbor, Michigan 48103

National Gaming Council
c/o Clark Rogers
3R24 Forbes Quad
Graduate School of Public & International Affairs
University of Pittsburgh
Pittsburgh, Pennsylvania 15260

North American Simulation and Gaming Association (NASAGA)
Box 100, Westminister College
New Wilmington, Pennsylvania 16142

POSSIBLE PROJECTS

12-A. Design a simulation/game. Submit the game components along with a description of the intended audience and objectives.

12-B. Play an instructional simulation/game and describe the objectives, results, and your reaction (evaluation) to the game.

12-C. Use an instructional simulation/game in your teaching. Describe the game, its objectives, results, and the reaction (both yours and your students') to the game.

12-D. Appraise an instructional simulation/game using the "Appraisal Checklist" given in the chapter.

12-E. Using the sources and references provided in the chapter, identify games and simulations that you could use in your instructional situation.

CHAPTER 13

COMPUTERS

OBJECTIVES

After studying this chapter, you should be able to:

1. Distinguish between "computer-assisted instruction" (CAI) and "computer-managed instruction" (CMI).

2. Relate the invention of the microprocessor to the lowering of two of the major barriers to adoption of computer-based learning.

3. Graph a comparison of changes in cost for computer hardware to changes in cost for human services over the past three decades.

4. Explain how the modern computer can assist in the individualization of instruction.

5. Describe a concomitant learning (unintended side effect) that may be developed through interaction with computer programs.

6. Defend the position that achieving computer literacy is an immediate priority for teachers.

7. Identify and briefly describe the eight common components of a computer system, given a generalized schematic diagram.

8. Distinguish between "ROM" and "RAM."

9. Discuss two common mass storage media formats used with microcomputers.

10. Compare microcomputers, minicomputers, and mainframes with regard to cost and capability.

11. Suggest five criteria besides cost that might be important considerations in purchasing a computer for instructional purposes.

12. Discuss five advantages and five limitations of computers.

13. Describe how you might use the computer in (a) the computer-managed instruction mode, and (b) the computer-assisted instruction mode.

14. Apply the "Appraisal Checklist" to a sample CAI program.

15. Name a major directory of computer-based learning materials.

The computer with its virtually instantaneous response to student input, its extensive capacity to store and manipulate information, and its unmatched ability to serve many individual students simultaneously is becoming more and more widely used as an aid to instruction. The computer has the ability to control and manage a wide variety of learning material—films, filmstrips, random access slides, audio tapes, and printed information. The computer can also record, analyze, and react to student responses that are typed on a special typewriter keyboard or indicated with a "light pen" on a cathode ray tube (television display screen). Some display screens will even react to the touch of a student's finger.

There are two types of computer-based instruction: computer-assisted instruction (CAI) and computer-managed instruction (CMI). In CAI the student interacts directly with the computer which stores the instructional material and controls its sequence. In CMI the computer helps teachers administer and guide the instructional process. The student is *not* "on line" (directly connected) with the computer system, and the instructional material is *not* stored in the computer. The computer does, however, store information about students and about relevant instructional materials that can be retrieved rapidly. In addition, the computer can diagnose the learning needs of students and prescribe optimal sequences of instruction for them. We will take a closer look at each of these forms of computer-based instruction later in this chapter.

THE EMERGING ROLE OF COMPUTERS IN EDUCATION

Development of the Technology

The computers developed in the 1950s were awesome creations. Their vacuum tubes and miles of wiring filled several large rooms, dwarfing the sizable crew of attendants needed to keep them working. Not highly reliable but fabulously expensive, they were designed for carrying out complicated mathematical manipulations and did this very efficiently for those who were able to speak their highly specialized mathematical language.

The possibility of educational applications was mainly conjectural at that time, although important instructional experiments were conducted throughout the 1950s and 1960s. These experiments were spurred by the development of FORTRAN, a more easily learned computer language, and B.F. Skinner's research in programmed instruction. It was seen that the step-by-step format of linear programmed instruction lent itself well to the logical "mentality" of the computer. The factors of cost, hardware reliability, and the availability of adequate materials remained major barriers to the widespread adoption of computers for instruction.

The advent of the *microcomputer* in 1975 altered this picture dramatically. The microcomputer was made possible by the invention of the microprocessor, a tiny chip of silicon that contains within itself all the information processing ability of those roomfuls of original computer circuitry. The microcomputer was an immediate success in the marketplace, especially for use in small businesses and in the home. By 1980 the number of units in use was approaching one million.

Figure 13.1 The tiny microprocessor fostered the microcomputer revolution. Chips like this one are being built into home appliances, automobile components, and dozens of other machines in addition to computing machines, giving each a "brain" of its own.

The development of the silicon chip reduced the cost of computers to a truly remarkable degree. As illustrated in Figure 13.4 the cost of "people services" has crept constantly upward while computer expenses have been plunging. For certain kinds of tasks, computers are clearly less expensive than people.

The acceptance of microcomputers by the schools has been unusually rapid compared with other educational innovations. By 1981, figures compiled by the National Center for Education Statistics indicated that fully half of the secondary schools in the United States and about one out of seven elementary schools had one or more microcomputers.

The Computer and Individualization

The recent emergence of computer technology coincides with a heightened awareness among educators of the importance of individualization. Research into new instructional methods consistently indicates that certain treatments work for certain people under certain conditions. There are no panaceas. The great quest

Figures 13.2 and 13.3 The old and the new in computer technology: the huge "mainframe" system with its large, separate components versus the self-contained microcomputer.

in the field of media and technologies of instruction is to find ways of matching individual learners with the appropriate subject matter, pitched at the right level, and presented in a compatible medium at the optimal pace in the most meaningful sequence.

True individualization, therefore, imposes a tremendous burden of decision-making and resource management. One instructor might approach an ideal level of individualization with a handful of students. But when dealing with 20, 30, 40, or more students the logistics of individualization overwhelm any single teacher's capacity.

The computer gives promise of overcoming these and other logistic barriers to individualization of instruction. Its electronic circuitry can accurately make the myriad of decisions necessary to the planning and implementation of an individualized program of instruction on a mass basis and in a fraction of the time required by the human mind.

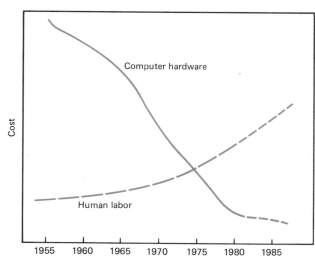

Figure 13.4 Comparison of trends in the cost of human labor versus the cost of computer hardware.

Concomitant Skills Springing from Computer Programming

"Reading," said seventeenth-century philosopher Francis Bacon, "maketh a full man, conference a ready man, and writing an exact man." If Bacon were alive today he might well add that "writing a computer program maketh an even more exact man." One serendipitous effect of working with computers is that they literally force us to communicate with them in an orderly and logical way. Any departure from precision is rejected by the computer.

Observers who have watched the development of young people as they work with computers, particularly in computer programming, note a tendency for orderly, logical thinking to be carried over into other areas of the students' work. Deductive reasoning thus becomes the "hidden curriculum" or concomitant learning—an unintended but welcome side-effect of contact with computers.

Computer Literacy

With microcomputers demonstrating their mass appeal it is certainly within the realm of possibility that computers will become as much a household fixture as the stereo set or the telephone. Lacking some of the inhibitions of their elders, young people are adapting rapidly to the new possibilities of computers. Many young people, particularly those from more privileged homes, are coming to the schools and colleges and world of work more "computer literate" than their adult mentors.

An interesting bit of evidence for a computer literacy gap among teachers comes by way of a recent study conducted by Michael R. Cohen with a group of elementary school teachers.* The

Figure 13.5 Young people who work with computers, particularly with programming, are practicing skills of logic, organization, and systematic thinking.

teachers were asked to draw a picture of an instructional computer, including themselves in the picture, and to list educational objectives that an instructional computer might achieve. Analyzing the drawings, Cohen concluded that many teachers hold an image of the computer that is at least ten years out of date in terms of size and configuration. Further, they tend to equate computer instruction with rote learning and similar low level objectives.

For years, authoritative groups connected with math and science curricula have been advocating that the high school curriculum include computer literacy skills. This advice is beginning to be heeded not only at the high school level, but increasingly even at the elementary school level. The remaining challenge is to attain computer literacy among the *teachers*.

This chapter is intended to offer first steps toward basic computer literacy. It describes the components that make up a computer, compares the various available hardware systems, suggests possible applications of computers in instruction, and recommends some criteria for selecting both hardware and software.

---

*"Improving Teachers' Conceptions of Computer-Assisted Instruction," *Educational Technology*, July 1979, p. 32.

COMPUTER HARDWARE

Basic Computer Components

(Note: There is a brief glossary of computer terminology at the end of this chapter. You may wish to consult it in conjunction with this overview of technical components.)

Regardless of the size of the computer or the number and complexity of peripheral (add-on) devices, computers have a number of standard components. These are diagrammed in Figure 13.6.

CPU (Central Processing Unit).

This is the "brain" that carries out all the calculations and controls the total system. In a microcomputer the CPU is just one of the tiny chips inside the machine.

Memory. This stores information for manipulation by the CPU. The memory contains the *control* function, that is, the programs (detailed sequential instructions) that are written to tell the CPU what to do in what order.

In microcomputers, control instructions are stored in two types of memory:

ROM (Read-Only Memory)—

control instructions which have been "wired" *permanently* into the memory. Usually stores instructions that the computer will need constantly, such as the programming language(s) and internal monitoring functions.

RAM (Random Access Memory)—the flexible part of the memory. The particular program or set of data being manipulated by the user are *temporarily* stored in RAM, then erased to make way for the next program.

Mass Storage. This is a way of storing all the programs that you are not immediately using. In microcomputers, the computer can process only one program at a time, so you need some place to store the other programs and sets of data for future use. There are two common mass storage media:

Cassette tape—an adaptation of the audio cassette recorder/playback. The information is stored magnetically, just as on an audio recording. Also as on an audio tape, you have to play through the whole tape to get to any single portion of it.

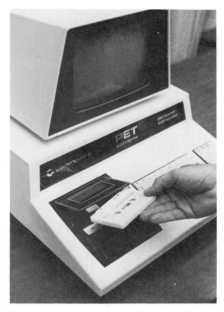

Figure 13.7 An adaptation of the audiocassette tape is a common form of mass storage for the microcomputer.

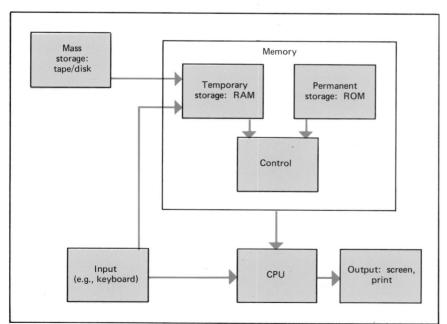

Figure 13.6 Basic elements of a microcomputer system.

Figure 13.8 The "floppy disk" method of microcomputer mass storage.

Disk—resembles a phonograph record except that computer disk information is stored magnetically, not mechanically. The disk gives the advantage of fast access to programs stored on different bands of the disk without playing all the way through the other bands. Early disks were referred to as "floppy disks" because of their nonrigid construction. More recently, "hard disks" have been developed that contain vastly more information and retrieve it faster than the older "floppies."

Input. This is a means of "talking to" the computer. The most common means of inputting new information is through a keyboard. Through the keyboard you can write or modify a cassette or disk program. After that, the cassette or disk can serve as the input.

Output. This is a means of displaying the results of your calculations. A television set, referred to as a CRT (Cathode Ray Tube), is the usual output device for a microcomputer. It may be built into the total package, as the Commodore PET, or be a separate component, as the TRS-80. Microcomputers designed primarily for home use plug into TV sets. Large computers and minicomputers commonly provide output by means of data printed on paper sheets ("hard-copy"). This option is also available on many microcomputer systems, but is quite expensive.

As mentioned before briefly, instructions are relayed to and throughout the computer via programs. Originally, since computers were used basically as high-powered calculators, the programs were written strictly in mathematical terms. But over the years, as a broader variety of business and educational applications have sprung up, new computer languages have been developed. Certain of these languages have incorporated terminology more and more resembling the English language. The language used by most microcomputers is BASIC. A newer language, Pascal, permits more sophisticated programming using less memory. It has been adopted by U.S. government agencies and is the primary language used in computer science instruction in universities. Pascal is likely to have a major impact on microcomputers as well.

Types of Computers

Although there are no hard and fast boundaries to classify the different types of computer systems, most users base the classification on the *size* of the machine's computing ability. To understand the comparisons, a little technical jargon is necessary: the term *bit* refers to the smallest unit of information; the term *byte* technically means eight bits, but in practice usually refers to the information in one character (number or letter). A computer's memory size is usually described in terms of how many bytes it can store at one time. A thousand bytes is a "kilobyte," usually abbreviated "K." Thus, if a computer can store 16,000 bytes it is said to have a 16K memory. Texas Instruments, for example, describes its microcomputer as having "16K RAM and 26K ROM."

In 1970 the 1000-byte (1K) RAM silicon chip was introduced. In 1980 a 64,000-byte (64K) chip was available, with a 256,000-byte (256K) chip not far behind!

Selecting Hardware

It is becoming increasingly common for instructors to be involved in the selection of an instructionally related computer for their institution. This section is meant to give you at least some general guidelines for participating intelligently in such a selection process.

To begin with, computers can be classified into three main groups according to their general capabilities: mainframe computers, mini-computers, and microcomputers.

COMPARATIVE ATTRIBUTES OF THREE MAIN COMPUTER TYPES

	GENERAL DESCRIPTION	CAPABILITIES	HARDWARE COSTS (per learner hour)	LIMITATIONS
MICROCOMPUTERS (e.g., Apple II, Commodore PET, Radio Shack TRS-80)	Microprocessor as CPU;8-bit per byte memory. TV set for display output. Cassette or disk for add-on memory. Portable. May be self-contained or have separate components.	Handles drill and practice and simple branching programs well. Game playing is a major strength. Music and motion graphics (usually in color). Designed to use simple languages such as BASIC.	$1,000 can buy basic package. (Per learner hour cost under $1, assuming five year life of machine and heavy schedule of usage.)	Relatively slow speed makes them unsuitable for "number-crunching" or even handling the voluminous records needed for CMI.
MINI-COMPUTERS (e.g. Digital Equipment, Data General)	Between micro and mainframe in size; 16-bit per byte memory.	Can support up to several dozen terminals. Larger memory means higher speed and accommodation of higher power CAI author languages like Pascal.	Costs more than $4,000 depending on number of terminals and peripherals. (Per learner hour cost, $1.50 to $2.50 depending on single or multiple users.)	Situated between micros and mainframes in terms of capacity. Smaller systems suffer same limitations as micros.
MAINFRAMES (e.g., IBM, Control Data, Sperry Univac)	High speed, flexible machines for business and scientific computing; 32 to 60 bit per word memory. Usually multiple users share time. Designed for "number-crunching"—processing huge amounts of numerical data.	Great computing capability. High speed permits many simultaneous users. Large memory allows extensive data bases and complex programs to be stored.	Cost usually in multi-million dollar range. (Per learner hour cost varies widely but $4 per hour is not unusual.)	Sharing time with multiple users can mean inconvenience. Machine failure wipes out *all* users. Communications costs continue to escalate.

Based on Richard W. Davis, "Computer Instruction: Basic Hardware Alternatives," *NSPI Journal*, November 1977, pp. 7–10.

Note that the more powerful machines are capable of using a larger word size (more bits per byte), thus increasing their processing capacity. Most mini-computers have 16-bit RAM memory, double the 8-bit RAM memory of the microcomputer.

The general rule of computer selection is to begin by specifying your objectives in advance—just how much is your computer system expected to do? The comparison chart allows you to compare capabilities with costs and arrive at a rough estimate, at least, of the type of system you ought to be considering. Once that is established you can begin to look at specific models of equipment. In comparing models, many different

criteria may be considered. Which criteria will be most salient to you depends on the specifics of your situation. The criteria that have been found meaningful by experienced users are:

- Cost.
- Reliability.
- Expansion potential. Can additional output and input mechanisms be added? Can internal

memory be expanded? Can peripherals (add-on devices) such as a hard-copy printout device or a modulator/demodulator device (MODEM) that allows computer signals to be transmitted via telephones be added to the basic system?

- Software (program) availability.
- Ease of operation.
- Physical features, such as portability, tamper-proof design, etc.
- Support system availability. Does the supplier have a local representative to answer user's questions and to take care of maintenance problems?

MEDIA FILE: Plato computer system

Control Data's Plato

Plato represents the special breed of computer system especially designed for and dedicated to educational applications. Not a microcomputer, Plato falls into the category of the large mainframe system. Individual terminals are connected to a powerful main CPU by means of telephone lines (note the MODEM in the photo).

Plato is the most widely disseminated CAI system, with over 1300 terminals in North America, Europe, Africa, and Australia. It also offers the most comprehensive range of instructional software. Plato programs cover the span from kindergarden through graduate school levels in every conceivable subject area, including business/industry training. Begun in 1960 at the University of Illinois, Plato (originally known as PLATO—Programmed Logic for Automatic Teaching Operation) pioneered in CAI research and development.

With the advent of microprocessors, the Plato hardware has been changing, moving away from its original plasma display screen toward high resolution CRT display screens. Terminal hardware may be purchased or leased; users pay monthly charges for continued service.

Control Data Corporation now also offers Micro PLATO, a microcomputer version of Plato that can stand alone without connection to the Plato communications network. A limitation is that the library of Plato instructional software is not directly transferable to Micro PLATO.

MEDIA FILE: Commodore PET microcomputer

Commodore PET

The PET is representative of the self-contained home or school microcomputer. It has a 16K memory (expandable to 32K). The black/white TV set, keyboard, and cassette memory unit are all combined together with the CPU.

Because of its reliability and portability the PET has become popular for school use. Although direct instruction lessons are not nearly as abundant as they are with more established systems such as Plato and TICCIT, this software gap is made up by teachers' authoring their own programs and sharing them through "user groups."

MEDIA FILE: Apple II microcomputer

Apple II Microcomputer

Introduced in 1977 as the first programmable personal computer that could be bought fully assembled, the Apple II is one of several microcomputers considered an industry "standard."

Like other competing microcomputers, the Apple II is built around a low-cost basic system that can be expanded by adding memory capacity (up to 48K bytes) and other peripherals, such as disk drive and hard-copy printer.

Its major special features include built-in capability for color graphics and audio—from computer music to synthesized human speech.

The manufacturer, Apple Computer Inc., has shown a commitment to educational applications by funding an Apple Education Foundation and by publishing a good deal of supporting literature, including a newsletter, *Apple Education News*. Several different clearinghouses have arisen to facilitate interchange of locally produced Apple programs.

MEDIA FILE: Radio Shack microcomputer

Radio Shack TRS-80

Like stereo systems, microcomputers can be found in single-unit, highly portable packages, such as the PET, or in components, such as the TRS-80 shown here. The advantage of the latter is the ability to customize an arrangement to fit your special needs.

The TRS-80, can be hooked up with a number of different peripherals including disk memory, hard-copy (paper) printer, voice synthesizer, and multiplexer (to feed several terminals from the same CPU). Within the lowest price range, Radio Shack is a leader in software development and in hardware accessibility through its thousands of local electronics supply dealers.

ADVANTAGES OF COMPUTERS

The computer can be viewed generally as a tool for enhancing the various technologies of instruction (through CAI) and of instructional management (through CMI). Specific advantages are:

The novelty of working with a computer raises student motivation.

Color, music, and animated graphics can add realism and appeal to drill exercises, laboratory activities, simulations, etc.

High speed personalized responses to learner actions yield a high rate of reinforcement.

Memory capacity allows students' past performance to be recorded and used in planning next steps.

The patient, personal manner that can be programmed provides a more positive affective climate, especially for slower learners.

The record-keeping ability of the computer makes individualized instruction feasible; individual prescriptions can be prepared for all students (particularly mainstreamed special students) and their progress can be monitored.

The teacher's "span of control" is enlarged as more information is put easily at the teacher's disposal, helping to keep control close to the point of direct contact with the learner.

Figure 13.9 Students are intensely, actively absorbed as they participate in an interactive computer-assisted lesson.

LIMITATIONS OF COMPUTERS

As we have seen with all the other media and technological innovations, there are always trade-offs to be made and limitations to consider. Some of the major limitations of computers in instruction are:

- Despite the dramatic reduction in cost of computers and computer use, computerized instruction is still relatively expensive. Careful consideration must be given to the costs and benefits of computers in education. Maintenance can also be a problem, especially if equipment is subjected to heavy use.
- Design and production of computers specifically for instructional purposes has lagged behind design and production for other purposes.
- There is a lack of high-quality direct-instruction materials for use with computers, especially for use with microcomputers. There is also a compatability problem. Often, software developed for one computer system cannot be used with another. (The ease with which software—especially on cassette—can be duplicated without permission has inhibited commercial publishers and private entrepreneurs from producing and marketing instructional software.)

- Teacher design of instructional materials for use with computers can be a laborious task, even for teachers with computer literacy.
- Creativity may be stifled in computerized instruction. The computer is slavish in its obedience to its program. Creative or original learner responses will be ignored or even rebuked if the program's designer has not anticipated such possibilities.
- Some learners, especially adult learners, may resist the linear, lock-step control of the learning process typical of run-of-the-mill computer instruction materials.

APPLICATIONS OF COMPUTERS

The potential uses of computers in educational settings go far beyond just the provision of direct instruction. There is the obvious administrative role of keeping school records, scheduling classes, making out paychecks, and the like. A computer facility often serves as a vocational training tool—giving students the opportunity to develop computer science skills or at least computer literacy. Guidance programs use computers to deliver career planning assistance. Science instructors and students make use of the computational ability of computers to help work out mathematical problems. But all these applications are ancillary to our main interest.

In the domain of instruction we can set forth two broad classes of applications: *computer-managed instruction* (CMI), in which the

Figure 13.10 The most obvious application of computers is as a calculating aid.

computer gathers, stores, and manages information to guide students through individualized learning experiences and *computer-assisted instruction (CAI)*, in which the computer interacts directly with learners in presenting lessons. Both applications will be explored at greater length.

Computer-Managed Instruction

There is considerable impetus for CMI these days because of the increasing emphasis being placed on individualized instruction. Both in formal education and in nonformal settings such as the military, business/industry, and government, there is recognition that greater efficiency, effectiveness, and equal opportunity can be reached in instruction only to the extent that teachers can accommodate the individual differences that cause each student to have different learning patterns.

Individualized instruction means that students will be moving through the checkpoints in the educational process at different times via different paths. You can imagine the management problem this entails if you think of one teacher responsible for teaching five subjects or major topics, with 20 objectives in each subject, to 30 students. This adds up to a minimum of 3000 checkpoints.

The computer can help solve this management problem by administering diagnostic tests, scoring them, prescribing appropriate next steps, and monitoring the progress of the student all the way along the route. This is essentially what CMI attempts.

There are some difficulties with CMI, though. Over the years a number of different CMI systems have been developed and tried out, among them PLAN developed by Westinghouse (in Iowa City schools), TIPS (at the University of

Figure 13.11　In computer-managed instruction a major function of the computer is automated test scoring.

Wisconsin), CISS (at New York Institute of Technology), Advanced Instructional System (for the U.S. Air Force), Plato Learning Management (Control Data Corp.), and TICCIT (developed by Mitre Corp. and Brigham Young University). Each of these systems is designed for a different environment, makes different assumptions about the instructional setting, and emphasizes different strengths. Finding the right match with your own institutional needs surely would demand a careful

Figure 13.12　A well-designed CMI program keeps track of individual student progress, prescribing remedial activities as needed.

analysis of the available products on a number of dimensions, including computer system compatibility. The available packages cannot really be regarded as fully standardized.

Whatever the merits of the various CMI systems, they generally suffer from a lack of adequate instructional materials (referred to as "courseware"). Two exceptions are Plato Learning Management and TICCIT. Since both of these systems began as CAI packages, they are strong in instructional software. Time-sharing mainframe systems like Plato tend to offer more courseware because the expense of developing such materials can be spread out over a larger number of users. The key, though, is that you can't have computer-managed instruction without *instruction* to manage.

Hardware cost is another factor to bear in mind. Up to now the microcomputer breakthrough has not benefitted CMI in a major way. Because microcomputers trade off speed for smaller size, current models are not capable of processing efficiently all the data needed to serve large numbers of students. Access to a mainframe computer or a mini-computer is still desirable for efficient CMI. This picture will change, though, as mass storage techniques improve (see the previous discussion of "hard disks") and more efficient programming languages are developed for the microcomputer.

Computer-Assisted Instruction

Computer systems can deliver instruction directly to students by allowing them to interact with lessons programmed into the system; this is referred to as computer-assisted instruction (CAI). The various utilization possibilities can best be discussed in terms of the various instructional modes that the computer can facilitate most effectively: tutorial, drill and practice, discovery, simulation, and gaming. According to a recent index of computer-based instruction,* these categories account for some 90 percent of the instructional programs available from various agencies. The distribution in each category is shown in the following table.

PERCENTAGE DISTRIBUTION OF COMPUTER-BASED LEARN-ING PROGRAMS

Tutorial[a]	32%
Drill and practice	22
Discovery	20
Simulation	13
Gaming	3
Other	10
Total	100%[b]

[a]Some categories represent combinations of Wang's original categories.

[b]Wang's 4287 entries represent multiple listings of some programs in more than one category.

Source: Anastasia C. Wang (ed.). *Index to Computer Based Learning, 1978 Edition.* (Microfiche.) (Milwaukee, WI: University of Wisconsin, 1978).

Tutorial Mode. In this mode the pattern followed is basically that of branching programmed instruction (see Chapter 11); that is, information is presented in small units followed by a question. The student's response is analyzed by the computer (compared with responses plugged in by the author) and an appropriate feedback is given. A complicated network of pathways or "branches" can be programmed. The more alternatives available to the com-

*Anastasia C. Wang (ed.), *Index to Computer Based Learning, 1978 Edition.* Microfiche. Milwaukee, WI: University of Wisconsin, 1978.

puter, the more adaptive the tutorial can be to individual differences. The extent to which a skilled live tutor can be approximated depends on the creativity of the author.

Drill and Practice Mode. Use of this mode assumes that a concept, rule, or procedure has already been taught to the student. The program leads the learner through a series of examples to increase dexterity and fluency in using the skill. The key is to reinforce constantly all correct responses. The computer can display infinite patience, going ahead only when mastery is shown. Drill and practice is prominently used for math drills, foreign language translating practice, vocabulary building exercises, and the like.

Discovery Mode. Discovery is a general term to describe activities using an inductive approach to learning; that is, presenting *problems* which the student solves through trial and error. It approximates laboratory learning and much real-life learning outside the classroom.

The opposite of rote or drill learning, the aim of the discovery approach is the deeper understanding that results from grappling with a puzzling problem. Through the complex branching and data storage capabilities of the computer, more students will be exposed to "laboratory" learning in such areas as math, social sciences, and other science areas.

Simulation Mode. The simulation mode of instruction is described in detail in Chapter 12. In this mode, the learner confronts a scaled-down approximation of a real-life situation. It allows realistic practice without the expense or risks otherwise involved. A well-known computer simulation, *Ham-*

Figure 13.13 Drill and practice exercises can be made more motivating on the computer.

murabi, puts the player in charge of economic decisions for a small agrarian country in pre-Biblical times.

In the modern realm of aeronautics, we find airline companies using sophisticated computerized simulations of airplane performance as an integral part of flight crew training. Business management problems and laboratory experiments in the physical sciences are other popular subjects for computer simulations.

Figure 13.14 Highly realistic, challenging simulations are possible when the microcomputer is connected with a video player such as a videodisc, as shown here.

Gaming Mode. In Chapter 12 we discussed the distinction between gaming and simulation. A game activity may or may not entail simulation elements. Likewise, a game may or may not be instructional. It depends on whether or not the skill practiced in the game is an academic one, that is, related to a specified instructional objective.

At the moment, recreational games of the *Star Wars, Battleship,* and *Blackjack* variety are major attractions to home computer buyers and young school users. They can serve a useful purpose in building up computer literacy in an enjoyable, nonthreatening manner. But the ultimate goal of useful learning must be kept in mind. Teachers experienced in computer utilization recommend rationing purely recreational game use, using it as a reward for completing other school work.

Still, when applied to *instructional* tasks, gaming can be a highly motivating framework, especially for repetitious drills. Another common instructional game application is in management training. Participants form management teams making decisions regarding a mythical corporation. The winning team is the one reaping the highest corporate profits.

SELECTION OF CAI PROGRAMS

As has happened before in the field of instructional media, the development of the hardware for CAI has outstripped the pace of software development. It is clear that the ability to compose computer programs is not synonymous with the ability to design effective instruction. Reviewers who have had the opportunity to appraise critically a portion of the flood of CAI programs being offered in the marketplace dismiss 80 percent of them as "junk."

Several agencies are attempting to help teachers cope with the CAI software selection task by conducting independent reviews and evaluations of materials, including CONDUIT at the University of Iowa and MicroSIFT at the Northwest Regional Education Lab. (Further information on these organizations is given in the References at the end of this chapter.) The most comprehensive directory of CAI programs is *Index to Computer Based Learning* edited by Anastasia C. Wang. This nonevaluative index is published annually on microfiche at the University of Wisconsin—Milwaukee. (See Appendix A for further details.)

As we have pointed out in reference to the other media and technologies of instruction, each format of media/technology has particular attributes that contribute to a unique set of criteria by which to judge the associated materials. In the case of CAI materials, we find many of the same concerns that affect programmed instruction materials—active participation, consistent reinforcement, and field test data. To these we add criteria based on the special capabilities of computers—branching, use of graphics, and random variations to allow repeated use. Finally,

there are descriptive data related to the different physical variations among computer systems. What type of CPU is the program designed for? What language is it coded in? What size memory is required? Is the software on cassette, disk, or some other storage device?

These criteria are summarized on the "Appraisal Checklist" included here.

APPRAISAL CHECKLIST: COMPUTER-ASSISTED INSTRUCTION

Series title (if applicable)_____

Individual title_____

Distributor_____

Format: ☐ cassette ☐ disk ☐ other _____

Designed for what system?_____

Language?_____

Memory size?_____

Length of lesson_____

Intended audience/grade level_____Subject area_____

Objectives (stated or implied)

Brief description:

Entry capabilities required

- —prior subject matter knowledge
- —reading ability
- —math/computer skill

RATING

	High		Medium		Low
Focuses clearly on its objectives	☐	☐	☐	☐	☐
Relevance to curricular needs	☐	☐	☐	☐	☐
Continuously *interactive*	☐	☐	☐	☐	☐
Branches to adapt to varying aptitude levels	☐	☐	☐	☐	☐
Motivating presentation format	☐	☐	☐	☐	☐
Appropriate graphics	☐	☐	☐	☐	☐
Directions simple and complete	☐	☐	☐	☐	☐
Reinforces positive responses	☐	☐	☐	☐	☐
Reusable (involves random elements to provide varied replays)	☐	☐	☐	☐	☐
Evidence of effectiveness (e.g. field tests)	☐	☐	☐	☐	☐

Strong points:

Weak points:

Reviewer_____

Position_____

Recommended Action:

Date_____

A BRIEF GLOSSARY OF COMPUTER TERMINOLOGY

BASIC (Beginner's All-purpose Symbolic Instruction Code) a simple programming language based on the English language.

bit smallest unit of information (from BInary digiT).

byte generally, a single, alphanumeric character (e.g., one letter of the alphabet).

CRT (Cathode Ray Tube) a computer display screen, same as television set.

hardware physical components of computer system.

mainframe a large, high speed business/scientific computer; often entails time sharing.

microprocessor a tiny chip incorporating an integrated circuit that is able to execute complex instructions electronically.

MODEM (MOdulator/DEModulator) device that translates computer signals for transmission over telephone lines.

peripherals auxiliary devices that can be attached to a basic computer (e.g., a voice synthesizer, hard-copy printer, MODEM).

PLAN (Program for Learning in Accordance with Needs) a computer-based instructional management system for diagnosis and record-keeping developed in 1967 by Westinghouse with American Institutes for Research and 13 school districts.

Plato a powerful computer system designed especially for instructional use; begun in 1960 at University of Illinois, now marketed by Control Data Corp.

RAM (Random Access Memory) the major memory mechanism of a computer; a "blank slate" to hold the program currently being used and then to be erased.

ROM (Read Only Memory) contains program(s) permanently wired into the circuitry of the computer (e.g., the BASIC language).

software the programs that control the computer operation.

TICCIT (Time-shared Interactive Computer-Controlled Information Television) like Plato, a computer system custom designed for instructional purposes; it was developed by Mitre Corp. and Victor Bunderson of Brigham Young University, and is now marketed by Hazeltine Corp.

REFERENCES

Print References

Blaisdell, F.J. "Historical Development of Computer Assisted Instruction." *Journal of Educational Technology Systems*, No. 2, 1976-1977, pp. 155–170.

Davis, Richard W. "Computer Instruction: Basic Hardware Alternatives." *NSPI Journal*, November 1977, pp. 7–10.

* Doerr, Christine. *Microcomputers and the 3 R's: A Guide for Teachers* (Rochelle Park, NJ: Hayden, 1979).

* Frederick, Franz J. *Guide to Microcomputers* (Washington, DC: Association for Educational Communications and Technology, 1980).

Gawronski, Jane Donnelly et al. "Computer Assisted Instruction in the Elementary School." *School Science and Math*, February 1976, pp. 107–109.

* Gleason, Gerald T. "Microcomputers in Education: The State of the Art." *Educational Technology*, March 1981, pp. 7–18.

A Guide to the Selection of Microcomputers (London, England: Council for Educational Technology for the United Kingdom, 1980).

Hall, Keith A. "Computer-Based Education: Research, Theory, and Development." *Educational Communications and Technology*, Spring 1978, pp. 79–93.

Handler, Kenneth. "The Computer Comes to the English Classroom: Computerized Monitoring of Pupil Progress in Reading." *Educational Technology*, November 1975, pp. 34–35.

* "The Illinois Series on Educational Application of Computers." Sample titles: *A Teacher's Introduction to Educational Computing, Computer Applications in Science Education*, and *Computer Applications in the Teaching of English* (Urbana, IL: Department of Secondary Education, University of Illinois, 1979).

*Key references.

Kearsley, Greg P. "Some 'Facts' About CAI: Trends 1970-1976." *Journal of Educational Data Processing*, No. 3, 1976, pp. 1–12.

McLagan, Patricia, and Raymond Sandborgh. "Computer-Aided Instruction." Special Report, *Training*, September 1977, pp. 48–57.

Magidson, Errol M. "Student Assessment of PLATO: What Students Like and Dislike about CAI." *Educational Technology*, August 1978, pp. 15–18.

Magidson, Errol M. "One More Time: CAI is Not Dehumanizing." *Audiovisual Instruction*, October 1977, pp. 20–21.

"Microcomputers in Education." Special theme issue, *Educational Technology*, October 1979.

"Microcomputers." Special theme issue, *Instructional Innovator*, September 1980.

"Microcomputers—The Future is Now." Special theme issue, *The Practitioner* (National Association of Secondary School Principals), October 1979.

Miller, Inabeth. "The Micros are Coming." *Media & Methods*, April 1980, pp. 32–43, 72–73.

Milner, Stuart D. "Teaching Teachers About Computers: A Necessity for Education." *Phi Delta Kappan*, April 1980, pp. 544–546.

Milner, Stuart D. "How to Make the Right Decisions About Microcomputers." *Instructional Innovator*, September 1980, pp. 12–19.

Molnar, Andrew. "The Next Crisis in American Education: Computer Literacy." *Journal of Educational Technology Systems*, No. 1, 1979.

Moody, Robert. *First Book of Microcomputers* (Rochelle Park, NJ: Hayden, 1978).

Rice, Jean. *My Friend the Computer* (Minneapolis, MN: T.S. Dennison Company, 1976).

Spencer, Donald D. *Fun with Computers and BASIC* (Ormond Beach, FL: Camelot Publishing, 1976).

Spivak, Howard, and Stuart Varden. "Classrooms Make Friends with Computers." *Instructor*, March 1980, pp. 84–90.

Waite, Mitchell, and Michael Pardee. *Microcomputer Primer* (Indianapolis, IN: Howard W. Sams, 1976).

Audiovisual References

* Adventures of the Mind," (Bloomington, IN: Indiana University Audio-Visual Center, 1980. [A series of 16-mm films (or videocassettes) about microcomputers, 20 minutes each. Individual titles are: "Data Processing Control Design" "Extending Your Reach" "For Better or For Worse" "Hardware and Software" "Speaking the Language".]

"Computer-Rage," (Morristown, NJ: Creative Computing). (Game.)

"Computers for Kids," (Ormond Beach, FL: Camelot Publishing, 1979). (Kit including slides, cassette, and teacher's manual.)

"Visual Masters for Teaching About Computers," (Ormond Beach, FL: Camelot Publishing, 1978). (Overhead transparency master set.)

"Visual Masters for Teaching BASIC Programming," (Ormond Beach, FL: Camelot Publishing, 1978). (Overhead transparency master set.)

Organizations

Association for Educational Data Systems (AEDS) 1201 Sixteenth Street, N.W., Washington, DC 20036

The largest of the organizations dedicated to the use of computers in education. Its emphasis is on the secondary-school level and its interests include both administrative and instructional uses of computers.

Association for the Development of Computer-Based Instructional Systems (ADCIS), Computer Center, Western Washington University, Bellingham, Washington 98225.

CONDUIT P.O. Box 388, Iowa City, Iowa 52244

Evaluates and distributes computer-based instructional materials and publishes a periodical, *Pipeline*.

Human Resources Research Organization (HumRRO) 300 N. Washington Street, Alexandria, Virginia 22314

Ongoing research on computer-based education; publishes a directory of CBE projects it considers to be successful.

Periodicals

AEDS Journal
Educational Data Systems
1201 Sixteenth St., N.W.
Washington, DC 20036

Creative Computing
Box 789-M
Morristown, New Jersey 07960

Computer Cassette Review
c/o Robert Elliott Purser
P.O. Box 466
El Dorado, California 95623

Computers and Education (quarterly,
   international journal edited in
   England)
Pergamon Press Inc.
Maxwell House, Fairview Park
Elmsford, New York 10523

Cursor—Programs for PET Computers
c/o The Code Works
Box 550
Goleta, California 93017

Journal of Computer-Based Instruction
   (quarterly)
Association for the Development of
   Computer-Based Instructional
   Systems
Western Washington University
Bellingham, Washington 98225

*Microcomputing (Kilobaud
   Microcomputing)*
P.O. Box 997
Farmingdale, New York 11737

Microsift
Northwest Regional Education Lab
710 S.W. Second Street
Portland, Oregon 97204

Suppliers of Equipment and Materials

Apple Computer, Inc.
10260 Bandley Drive
Cupertino, California 95051

Atari, Inc.
1265 Borregas
Sunnyvale, California 94086

Bell & Howell Co.
7100 McCormick Road
Chicago, Illinois 60645

Commodore Business Machines
901 California Avenue
Palo Alto, California 93404

Compucolor Corp.
P.O. Box 569
Norcross, Georgia 30071

Control Data Corp.
P.O. Box 0
Minneapolis, Minnesota 55440

Data General Corp.
Route 9
Westboro, Massachusetts 01772

Digital Equipment Corp.
146 Main Street
Maynard, Massachusetts 01754

Mattel Toys
5150 Rosecrans Avenue
Hawthorne, California 90250

Radio Shack
Division, Tandy Corp.
700 One Tandy Center
Fort Worth, Texas 76102

Texas Instruments, Inc.
8600 Commerce Park Drive
Houston, Texas 77036

POSSIBLE PROJECTS

13-A. Read and summarize an article on the use of computers in education or training.

13-B. Interview a student and/or teacher who has used computers for instruction. Report on how the computer was used including user's perceptions as to strengths and limitations.

13-C. Locate computer programs suitable for your subject area using the information sources available to you.

13-D. Appraise an instructional computer program using the Appraisal Checklist provided in the chapter.

13-E. Synthesize a situation in which you could use computer-based materials. Include a description of the audience, the objectives, the role of the computer, and the expected outcomes (or advantages) of using the computer.

CHAPTER 14

LOOKING AHEAD

OBJECTIVES

After studying this chapter, you should be able to:

1. Describe how the miniaturization of media forms and equipment has increased their use for educational purposes. Cite specific examples.

2. Discuss three technological techniques for reaching students wherever they might be.

3. Describe two recently developed special technological adaptations of television that help the handicapped learn.

4. Justify the need for life-long learning in our society.

5. Cite three recent responses to the need for life-long learning using television.

6. Describe four professional specialities in educational technology.

7. Compare the relationship of four professional organizations to educational technology.

8. Identify five professional journals which deal with educational technology.

9. Discuss three "pros" and three "cons" in reference to accountability in education and instruction.

Having studied the preceding chapters of this book, you are certainly now aware that instructional technology is a rapidly developing and rapidly changing area, if for no other reason than that it has developed and changed apace with technology in our broader society. It would be pointless here to reiterate the many individual trends in education—the trend toward individualization of instruction, toward innovations in traditional teaching methods, toward the teacher as manager rather than purveyor of instruction, etc.—which have already been detailed throughout this book and which will undoubtedly continue on into the future.

Instead, we will concentrate our attention in this our final chapter on two technological trends of general and major importance and on two major educational trends certain to be profoundly affected by developments in educational technology. The technological trends we will discuss are miniaturization of mediaware and electronic systems for the delivery of instruction. The educational trends we will consider are the development of life-long learning systems, and increasing insistence on accountability in education.

The chapter continues with a discussion of future technologies of instruction, the growing role of instructional technology in the education of the handicapped, a discussion of professional careers in the field of instructional technology, and concludes with a consideration of professional organizations and journals dedicated to the advancement of educational technology.

MINIATURIZATION: MAKING INSTRUCTION PORTABLE

Perhaps the most important single technological trend affecting the use of instructional media has been the movement toward miniaturization of mediaware formats and equipment. This trend has led to lower cost, increased ease of operation and portability of equipment, and hence to increased access to and use of instructional media in the formal and nonformal learning situation.

Even 16-mm film equipment has become more portable and easier to operate. For example, many such projectors now on the market feature automatic threading, whereas two decades ago all machines had to be manually threaded. The machines have become smaller because mechanical parts have become more reliable and smaller. Reduction in amplifier size has been made possible by the introduction of, first, transistors and printed circuits, and, more recently, integrated circuits. Standard reel-to-reel tape recorders have gotten progressively smaller also. To take but one further example, many schools and colleges now use small-screen television viewers in individualized and small-group instructional situations, an impossibility two decades ago because television monitors for classroom use were not available in small-screen size.

Figure 14.1 Shown (from left) are: an early silent 16-mm film projector manufactured by Victor, a 1950s model sound 16-mm projector by the same company, and a contemporary self-threading sound film projector.

Figure 14.2 Classroom television sets were originally considered large-group presentation devices. Miniaturization made personal portable sets available; individualization of the curriculum made them necessary.

Another example of miniaturization opening up new opportunities for the educational use of electronic technology was the development of the 8-mm cartridged silent film, to which sound was later added. Originally developed for home use, the system offered the advantage of having one's film returned from the processor in a handy cartridge that could be inserted in a special projector and displayed on a home screen with a minimum of fuss. Educators soon found an educational use for this new format. The three minutes of film that could be contained in the cartridge was sufficient to present basic instructional concepts, and the ease of operation of the equipment made it highly suitable for presenting motion picture instruction to individual students and small groups. Although the 8-mm cartridged film was not widely adopted in the schools (mainly because it was not particularly less expensive than 16-mm film and equipment, which schools already had), it did help to further sensitize educators to the instructional potential of miniaturization and to increase their demands for more such handy media formats.

Technology met these demands to a hitherto undreamed of extent with the development of the cassette tape recorder. Very few technological innovations have been more quickly or universally adapted to instructional purposes than the cassette tape recorder. The advantages of the cassette were immediately obvious. First, the whole cassette is considerably smaller than a comparable reel-to-reel tape and its box. The principal reason for this reduction in size is that the tape itself is half the width of the standard ¼-in. recording tape. The next obvious difference between the cassette and reel-to-reel format is convenience of operation. No longer does the user have to thread the tape into the machine. The car-

Figure 14.3 Repeated viewings of short segments of filmed action have long been considered instructionally useful. Prior to the 1960s the showing of film loops required a cumbersome attachment to a standard 16-mm projector. The development of the 8-mm cartridged film loop greatly simplified this process, speeding its adoption into the schools.

tridge is simply placed in the machine and the "play" or the "play-record" buttons pushed and the tape is in operation. Finally, the machine is considerably smaller than reel-to-reel tape recorders. The most widely sold form of cassette tape recorder today can be carried in one hand. This is a vast change from the 15-to 30-lb. reel-to-reel tape recorders that had to be carried around before.

In the early days of cassette development, recording quality left a good deal to be desired. Even so, teachers were quite willing to trade quality for miniaturization. But, as the cassette format became widely adopted, making further technological improvements economically feasible for producers of cassettes, the quality of the recording improved. With today's hi-fidelity systems, it is difficult to tell the difference between

Figure 14.4 Shown (from left) are: an early classroom type reel-to-reel tape recorder, a cassette recorder, and a microcassette recorder, held by Calvin E. Mether, archivist for the Association for Educational Communications and Technology.

the audio quality of a well-recorded cassette tape and a well-recorded reel-to-reel tape with similar quality speakers.

Miniaturization of electronic components has today resulted in video tape recorders portable enough to be carried on a shoulder strap, a development that has contributed immensely to the use of videotaped materials for instructional purposes. Video tape, itself, has also been improved remarkably in recent years. When it was first introduced, the tape had to travel at a very high speed in order to record with any degree of fidelity. However, today's video tape recorders record at a relatively slow speed, allowing much more recording time per standard reel. Today, videocassette machines for school and home can record up to six hours per reel. When video tape was originally introduced the tape was 2 in. wide; today ½-in. tape is very common for school and home, with little difference in *discernible* quality. The ½-in. videocassette system is rapidly becoming the standard format in both education and training. Recording in this format is simple and of acceptable quality.

It is very likely that the video format of the future for commercially produced and marketed programs will be the videodisc. As discussed in Chapter 9, there are several technically different videodisc systems currently contending for acceptance in the marketplace. It may well develop that different systems become adopted as standards for home and institutional use. In any case, videodiscs lend themselves to mass production more simply and inexpensively than do film or video tape and hence can be expected to spur the wider use of video materials at home and in school.

Miniaturization has also had its effect on the print medium, making the printed word more easily and widely available for instructional and other purposes than the developers of movable type could have imagined. Perhaps the most universally used micro-form for reducing the size of the printed word so that it can be more widely disseminated is microfiche. In dif-

Figure 14.5 Videocassette systems make it easy and economical for educational users to record and play back programs as needed.

Figure 14.6 The videodisc, coupled with microcomputer capabilities (now built into some videodisc players), makes *interactive video* feasible for widespread, economical application. Learner responses may be given by means of a keyboard, voice-response unit, or light pen; the system reacts by branching to the appropriate information stored on the videodisc. Pictured here is the American Heart Association's videodisc system for CPR (cardio-pulmonary resuscitation) training. The mechanisms inside the mannequin are connected with the videodisc player to provide feedback on the correctness of the learner's performance.

ferent microfiche formats, dozens, even hundreds, of pages of print can be recorded on a single piece of film. The contents of the entire *Encyclopaedia Britannica*, for example, can be reduced to a stack of microfiches small enough to be thrust into one's pocket.

Recent advances in the photographic quality of microfiches have raised the possibility of using microfiches as still projection media. Microfiches containing color transparent images and the projectors to show them are now available, suggesting a new format for future packaging of filmstrips and slide sets. Up to 98 images fit on one 4 by 6 in. fiche, making production, mailing, storing, and handling easier and less expensive than ever before for visuals of this type.

Another striking manifestation of miniaturization is to be seen in the area of computer technology. Mainly because of advances in micro-chip technology, computers, which used to be obtainable only in extremely cumbersome form and at extremely high cost, are now available in formats taking up no more space than a television set and costing about the same amount of money. The educational

Figure 14.7 One volume of a typical encyclopedia can be reduced to a small handful of microfiches, as shown here.

importance of this development is discussed in Chapter 13. Schools and small organizations that not many years ago could not have dreamed of using computer technology for administrative and instructional purposes, are now finding this tool logistically and economically feasible. We can certainly expect that computer-based instruction will continue to grow rapidly in the years to come.

Miniaturization has, of course, also meant that the products of electronic technology have moved into the home. Most of your students will be familiar with devices such as pocket calculators, cassette recorders, electronic games, and possibly microcomputers from being exposed to them in their homes or in other nonschool settings long before they may be required to use similar devices for instructional purposes. This should make your teaching task somewhat easier, but it also means that you will have to keep abreast of mediaware developments—if only to avoid the embarrassment of having your students know more about such matters than you do. (A recent newspaper story told about a 10-year-old who magnanimously offered to instruct his teacher in how to handicap horse races via computer, a skill he claimed to have learned from a pocket calculator designed for this purpose which his father had purchased.)

ELECTRONIC DELIVERY SYSTEMS: REACHING ALL LEARNERS

Another technological innovation that has already had tremendous impact on education and that undoubtedly will have even greater impact in the future is that of electronic systems for the delivery of instruction. Just a few years ago, the individual classroom teacher was practically the sole "distributor of instruction" on the educational scene. Today we have instruction via open broadcast by radio and television stations, microwave systems, satellite, and closed-circuit systems such as cable television and the telephone.

Figure 14.8 Satellite distribution systems make television available even in remote Eskimo village schools in Alaska.

Although instruction via open broadcast by radio and television, especially television, has been and will continue to be a significant force in education, there is presently a trend toward wider applications of closed distribution systems to the instructional situation. Closed distribution systems—microwave, closed-circuit, satellite—unlike open systems, have the advantage of being able to transmit a number of instructional programs simultaneously. In addition, they have the significant advantage of being able to overcome broadcast television's inherent limitation in coverage area. For example, satellite signals can be sent to virtually any spot on the face of the earth and once received can be carried by cable and/or microwave systems to any instructional setting, including the home. Direct reception of satellite transmissions by schools, business and industrial facilities, hospitals or any other likely instructional setting is now a reality with the proper receiving equipment, eliminating the need for redistribution by cable. Satellite signals can now also be received and transmitted via telephones equipped with optical fibers capable of transmitting hundreds of messages simultaneously. Appropriate equipment attached to such telephones permits local display of the signals. A recent survey disclosed that telecommunications networks of the type described here are already in widespred use throughout all parts of the United States.*Looking only at educational networks within individual states, researchers found 98 organizations operating networks in 44 of the 50 states.

The successful operation of the Space Shuttle in 1981 signals another breakthrough in the cost of providing the satellites that are the backbone of these electronic delivery systems covering broad geographic areas. With the lowered costs of the recyclable Shuttle and its ability to carry multiple satellites into orbit on a single trip, the cost of placing and maintaining satellites will be cut many-fold.

Computer technology is adding yet another dimension to electronic distribution of instruction. Along with the instructional capabilities of localized computers, we can expect the growing use of large centralized computer facilities offering instructional programming to be used in "real time" or stored in microcomputer systems for delayed use.

Electronic distribution systems have also given rise to the technique of *teleconferencing* for instructional purposes. Pioneered in the Scandinavian countries, teleconferencing can provide an interactive learning experience between instructor and students without the instructor (or other resource person) having to leave his or her home base. For example, an instructor may video tape a lesson for transmission via a closed-circuit distribution system and after it is shown, or even while it is being shown, engage in a dialogue with the audience through a telephonic communication system specially designed for this purpose.

Interest in this technique has grown with the high cost and growing inconvenience of travel due to energy shortages in many parts of the world. The Center for Interactive Programs and Instructional Communications at the University of Wisconsin, for example, has been offering seminars in teleconferencing since 1975. Even without assuming that energy resources will remain in short supply in much of the world, teleconferencing and similar telecommunication instructional techniques are likely to grow in use in the coming years.

In the long run the development of electronic systems for the distribution of instruction will have a profound effect on the organization and administration of our educational facilities. For the last half-century educators and the public have been assuming that in order to increase access of each child to a full range of instruction and in order to make better use of personnel and to increase cost efficiency (economy of scale), smaller schools had to be replaced by larger ones. However,

Figure 14.9 Although larger schools provide "economies of scale," they also bring a threat of depersonalization. Technology-based delivery systems help make smaller units economically feasible.

*Jerold Gruebel, W. Neal Robison, and Susan Rutledge, "Intrastate Educational Telecommunication Systems: A National Survey," *Educational Technology*, April 1981, pp. 33–36.

advances in technology have now made it administratively and economically feasible to educate smaller groups of students in a large number of small instructional settings. Proponents of "decentralization" as a step toward greater public participation in the control of public education may well have found an unexpected and powerful ally in technological advances such as the development of electronic systems for the distribution of instruction.

Figure 14.10 This Tennessee one-room schoolhouse of 1936 was designed primarily for lecture instruction but had to accommodate individual and small-group study for children at different grade levels.

Figure 14.11 This modern Toronto classroom contains only one grade level but is easily adaptable to a variety of learning modes. In comparison to Figure 14.10, what differences has technology made in terms of, for instance, the role of instructional materials, the physical environment, study facilities, and other visible factors?

FUTURE TECHNOLOGIES OF INSTRUCTION

Shifting our attention from "technology as product" to "technology as process" we can recognize that new scientific understanding of human learning will also be contributing to changes in how instruction is carried out in the future. Conventional educational research and development has already yielded the sorts of technologies of instruction described in Chapter 11: programmed instruction, programmed tutoring, audio-tutorial methods, and the like. Looking into the future, though, breakthroughs in improved learning may well be coming from less conventional sources.

Meditation has long been associated with religious practices and religious training in India and the Orient. In the 1960s these religious influences began to attract popular attention in North America. Experimentation since that time has built up a sizable body of evidence that meditative techniques can have physiological and psychological effects on humans, and that these effects can have instructional consequences. For example, some studies have shown that meditation reduces anxiety, thereby facilitating complex problem-solving by groups under stress. Individuals often report that the relaxation and fresh perspective lent by meditation heightens their study abilities.

The meditative state and other "altered states of consciousness" are already being integrated into new teaching/learning approaches being developed in North America and elsewhere. One of the most advanced—known as "suggestive-accelerative learning and teaching"—has recently been described in detail in Volume 36 of the Instructional Design Library.* This approach grows out of earlier research done by Georgi Lozanov in Bulgaria. Lozanov found that by inducing a state of conscious relaxation prior to a lesson, and by using special techniques involving music and drama during a lesson, adults could learn foreign languages with unusual ease and high rates of retention. Similarly impressive results have been reported by experimenters in Eastern and Western Europe, Canada, and the United States. In the References at the end of the chapter there are further readings that provide additional information on what may become new technologies of instruction of the future.

---

*Owen L. Caskey, *Suggestive-Accelerative Learning and Teaching*, Englewood Cliffs, NJ: Educational Technology Publications, 1980.

NEW DEVICES, NEW TECHNIQUES FOR TEACHING THE HANDICAPPED

Under the auspices of the Office of Special Education of the U.S. Department of Education, a great deal of research has gone into the development of special devices to help the handicapped overcome physical and sensory limitations; for example, a carpenter's level constructed to give audible signals so that a blind or partially sighted individual can level a surface without help. The Office of Special Education has also developed a number of devices and materials that help the handicapped acquire new information and skills. It is these developments with which we are primarily concerned.

In order to make television more useful to the hearing impaired, for example, a technique has been developed called closed captioning that adds titles or captions to television programs. The captions are recorded on a magnetic disc by an agency called the National Captioning Institute. The disc is mailed to any television station requesting the service. The station inserts the caption into line 21 of the TV picture area, a line which does not carry picture information. The caption data are transmitted along with the regular picture and sound, but become visible only if a decoder unit is attached between the antenna (or cable) and the antenna terminals on the set or if the television set has a built-in decoder. The Public Broadcasting System, which helped develop the technique, currently includes several hours of closed-captioned programs in its schedule. The networks—ABC, CBS, and NBC—also broadcast a considerable number of closed-captioned programs.

Also in the area of TV, use of a subchannel for audio signals has been approved by the Federal Communications Commission so that descriptive audio material can be received to substitute, at least partially, for the picture. As with closed captions, the audio signal cannot be heard without the use of a special decoding device. Programming the subchannel requires considerably more production work than simply translating dialogue and narration into captions. What is appearing on the screen must be described without interfering with the normal audio part of the program. Therefore the subchannel audio has to be inserted into those parts of the program that have no narration or dialogue. Although still in its developmental stage, this technique shows great promise and undoubtedly presages further advances in efforts to help the handicapped take advantage of the instructional potential of television.

Another promising development in efforts to bring the benefits of instructional technology to the handicapped is the Kurzweil Reading Machine. This electronically complex device scans a printed page, analyzes letter components via a computer, and reads back the printed page via a voice synthesizer. (If the user of the machine has trouble understanding a spoken word, the machine can be switched to "spell" and the word will be spelled out.) The Kurzweil Reading Machine represents an important advancement in the development of recording and playback devices to bring the instructional potential of *all* print media to the visually handicapped.

Figure 14.12 A Kurzweil Reading Machine in use at the New York Public Library.

The devices and techniques noted above are, of course, but a scant sampling of the products currently in use or being developed, both by government and private industry, to make it possible for the handicapped to benefit from instructional technology. Public Law 94-142 not only mandates education in the "least restrictive environment," but also has provided schools with funds to purchase equipment and materials to make such education possible. Instructional media will make a positive and growing contribution to the education of the handicapped in the years to come.

ACCOUNTABILITY IN EDUCATION AND INSTRUCTION

For almost two decades there has been a trend in education toward what has come to be referred to as *accountability*. Basically, accountability is a demand for some form of public demonstration that schools do what they are supposed to do and do it effectively. But beyond that, each teacher is accountable for the progress or lack of progress in his or her class.

Much of the impetus toward accountability has come from increasing competition for the tax dollar of the American public—a general social and political phenomenon which is certain to continue in the foreseeable future. Taxpayers hard pressed for money to support schools want to be assured that their taxes are being well spent. They are concerned both with the cost–benefit of instruction (whether or not we are getting the right kinds of benefit from instruction for the money that is being spent on it) and with the cost–effectiveness of instruction (whether or not these benefits are being achieved as effectively as possible at the lowest possible cost).

Not only a large segment of the public but also many educators support the idea that the schools should be held accountable for the learning progress of students. These educators claim that some teachers are too easily diverted from concentration on the learning tasks at hand to unnecessary and unrelated class activities. Some educators further claim that society has asked the schools to do so many jobs that the main purpose, instruction, is lost, or at least lessened, in the process.

This demand by the public and by concerned educators for some sort of accountability seems reasonable. Accountability has, however, met with considerable resistance from many members of the education profession. They argue that the really vital outcomes of the educational process cannot be quantified or measured, that the only learning outcomes which can be measured are trivial ones—dates, names of historical personages, rules of grammar, multiplication tables, etc. They further argue that accountability requires rigid determination of goals in advance of instruction, thus ruling out serendipitous opportunities that arise during instruction to teach material not specifically covered by predetermined goals. Opponents also claim that accountability will lead to public onus being put upon dedicated teachers working with low-ability students who will naturally have far greater difficulty achieving specific predetermined objectives than will high-ability students.

These and other objections to accountability have a certain validity and we hope the concept will develop in such a manner that legitimate qualms will be allayed. In any case, it seems reasonable to assume that the educational establishment, and individual teachers within the establishment will become more and more publicly accountable for the outcome of the educational enterprise.

Perhaps the most widely known and highly publicized manifestation of the trend toward accountability has been the National Assessment of Educational Progress (NAEP) program. Under this program, general achievement tests are given periodically at various grade levels throughout the country. The tests are intended for long-range comparisons between groups of students at various periods of time. They compare how well students do on standard measures of learning in different parts of the country and in various kinds of schools. So far the results have been used simply to determine whether the schools in general are achieving what they are supposed to achieve. No attempt has yet been made to use NAEP to compare specific schools for instructional effectiveness, but many educators are naturally apprehensive that the program may in the future come to be used for this purpose. Despite opposition from the organized teaching profession, some form of national assessment is likely to continue on the educational scene.

A number of states have developed similar assessment mechanisms. In 1977, for example, the state of California inaugurated its own educational assessment program. In March of 1977, all students at designated grade levels in the state of California took the same achievement tests in reading, arithmetic, social science, and science. The reports were processed and distributed in April, 1977, not only to the schools and school districts but also to the parents of each child taking the test. Parents received a computer printout that indicated where their children stood in relation to other members of their grade levels throughout the state of California. While, again, this assessment movement was resisted by professional educators in California, parents of California school children responded favorably to the program. A number of other states that do not yet have assessment programs are currently considering establishing them.

Other states have developed minimum competency tests to determine promotion from one cluster of grades to another and/or graduation from high school. Although some of these efforts have been challenged in the courts (most notably in Florida), the assessment and minimum competency movements will probably continue to gain strength.

The trend toward accountability and public disclosure of educational achievement will result in closer ties between the general public and the educational enterprise. Educators will be called upon to explain their selection of instructional methods and materials in terms of attainment of instructional objectives. They will

also be called upon to defend their selections in terms of cost–benefit and cost–effectiveness. Education and evaluation of education will become public processes rather than purely private ones between teachers and stu-

Figure 14.13 Technology tends to make instruction visible. As parents and other community members get involved in the schools as reading tutors, volunteer aides, and the like, structured materials make their help more effective. By the same token, teachers' use of well-designed materials heightens their credibility in the eyes of the general public.

dents. It behooves all instructors, then, to be prepared to defend their choices of materials and methods. If they are not prepared to do so, they run the increasing risk that those materials and methods will be publically judged as dispensable frills.

Fortunately for those particularly concerned with the use of media in the schools, instructional technology allows instructors to construct flexible yet structured designs for achievement of specific educational objectives that can be laid out for public inspection. As pointed out throughout this text, such designs, when properly planned and adhered to, can be demonstrated to result in consistent and readily apparent learning experiences—readily apparent to the teacher, the student, and the public. Accountability need not necessarily make us apprehensive. We can, rather, look upon it as an opportunity to further the trend toward partnership between home and school in the educational enterprise, a trend which innovative technology itself has done so much to foster.

LIFE-LONG LEARNING SYSTEMS

Life-long learning has long been an ideal of professional educators. Advances in the products and processes of instructional technology have brought us to the verge of making that ideal attainable for millions of our citizens. Indeed, we might say that in this respect, at least, our society has "lucked out." Never before in our development as a people have we had a greater need for life-long learning.

Fifty years ago, it was possible for a doctor, a teacher, a scientist, or for that matter, an electrician or a typewriter-repair person to be trained in a field and remain reasonably competent in it with little or no updating for the rest of his or her life. However, scientific and technological knowledge is increasing at such a rapid pace that this is no longer possible.

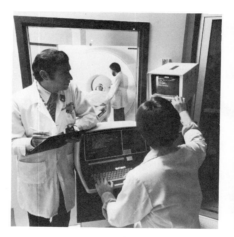

Figure 14.14   Jobs at all societal levels, from neurosurgery to police work to auto mechanics, are being affected by technological advances. People will have to change as jobs change; life-long learning becomes a practical necessity, not just a utopian ideal.

Indeed, for millions of us, life-long education is something more than an ideal—it has become a necessity.

In our mobile society today, many people switch from the field in which they were trained to another, or to several others, during their working lives. Early retirement systems in some professions and businesses have contributed to this trend, and many people in our present-day economic system become what economists call "structurally unemployed" and must seek new jobs and careers outside the fields of their expertise and/or training. For all these people, access to an educational system geared to life-long education is virtually a necessity.

Then there are the rest of our people—millions of ordinary members of our society who wish to keep up with a rapidly changing world, many of whom are beyond the age of formal schooling. These people, too, will more and more be demanding access to life-long learning; and, indeed, there will be more and more such people as the average age of the population continues to climb.

Obviously, the products and processes of instructional technology are destined to play a major role in the development of life-long learning systems. Audio and video cassettes and discs, electronic learning devices, electronic systems for delivery of instruction to wherever the life-long learner may be (the formal learning institution, the factory, the business office, the community center, the home), and numerous other kinds of instructional technology will necessarily be in the forefront in society's efforts to establish such systems.

Without the products and processes of instructional technology, life-long learning would likely be destined to remain an ideal. With them, we at least have reason to hope that it will soon become a reality for the millions of our people who need and desire it.

Television in Life-Long Learning

Television is particularly useful in reaching people who are not engaged in formal educational programs but who want and need information, new techniques, and new methods. Many of these people find it impossible to fit into the scheduling patterns of colleges and universities. Others do not live close enough to the institutions best equipped to serve them. As a society becomes more dependent on information, the demands for continuing education of people engaged in professional and white-collar occupations increase tremendously. Teachers, doctors, engineers, nurses, accountants, and executives are examples of the kinds of people who need continual updating to keep up with their fields, but who may also find regular contact with a college or university difficult. In recognition of this situation, a number of agencies have been set up and are being set up to serve the life-long learning needs of the population through television.

Among the recent developments in this area are:

- The National University Consortium for Telecommunications in Education, headquartered at the University of Maryland, has underway a pilot project to offer courses for undergraduate degrees via television and other nontraditional delivery systems.
- The University of Mid-America, a consortium of 11 state universities with headquarters in Lincoln, Nebraska, has begun planning for the establishment of a nationwide "open university" that would offer both undergraduate and graduate programs on television.
- The Appalachian Community Service Network, a project originally started as an experiment by the Appalachian Regional Commission, has become an independent nonprofit corporation that will distribute 64 hours of programming each week by way of satellite to cable television systems across the country. About half that total will be undergraduate and graduate courses for credit. Fifteen hours will be devoted to continuing education for professionals.
- The Central Education Network, which comprises public television stations in 10 Midwestern states, has formed a "post-secondary council" that includes higher education and public broadcasting representatives from each state. The council will attempt to determine the needs for telecommunications at the 821 colleges and universities in the 10-state area, and to realize savings by group purchasing of "telecourses" and equipment.
- The American Educational Television Network, a profit-making corporation with offices in Irvine, California, and McLean, Virginia, began broadcasting continuing-education courses for professionals during the fall of 1981.
- With the assistance of the American Association of Community and Junior Colleges, the two-year colleges that have produced many of the television courses, or "telecourses," used in higher education have begun to work together on both course development and marketing.

In 1981 publisher Walter Annenberg granted $150 million to the Corporation for Public Broadcasting to create a "national university of the air." The intention is to use the full capabilities of television— including broadcasting, cable, videocassettes, and videodiscs—to make higher education accessible to people for whom traditional college studies are economically or geographically inaccessible.

When these programs are all in full operation, virtually everyone in the United States will be in reach of a distance education program.

PROFESSIONAL CAREERS IN EDUCATIONAL TECHNOLOGY

This book has been dedicated to helping you become a more effective instructor (manager of instruction, if you will) through application of instructional media and technology to your teaching tasks. You may, however, wish to specialize in this fascinating and fast-growing field. (A directory of graduate programs in instructional technology is available from the Association for Educational Communications and Technology). If so, what opportunities for professional employment are likely to be open to you? Unlike the situation in some education areas, instructional technology is becoming more and more pervasive in formal and nonformal education with each passing year, and, correspondingly, an ever larger number of people are being employed in this specialty.

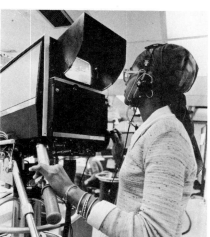

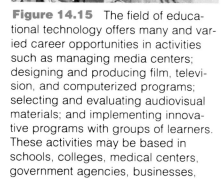

Figure 14.15 The field of educational technology offers many and varied career opportunities in activities such as managing media centers; designing and producing film, television, and computerized programs; selecting and evaluating audiovisual materials; and implementing innovative programs with groups of learners. These activities may be based in schools, colleges, medical centers, government agencies, businesses, industries, or wherever there are people who need to learn.

Traditionally, the areas in which the growth of instructional technology has created career opportunities are the various media programs at school, district, regional, and state levels. At all of those levels, media professionals are employed to run programs and, depending on the size of the organization, produce materials for use in schools. As school districts and regional media centers have built up their collections of audiovisual materials for distribution, they employed instructional media professionals as selectors of these materials. In formal education, media selection specialists not only determine what materials will be added to collections but also how well collections of materials are serving the curricular and instructional needs of the institution. In training programs, media specialists frequently evaluate the effectiveness of the programs as well as determine the materials to be used in them. Another major career area at all education levels is the professional management—classification, storage, distribution—of media collections.

Instructional product design—the development of validated and reliable instructional materials—has been an important specialty in the field of instructional technology for some time. Publishers and producers of instructional materials, along with school districts, community colleges, and colleges and universities, are constantly on the alert for specialists trained in the skills of product design. Computer-assisted instruction, interactive video, and other emerging forms of individualized instruction comprise an important growth area within the instructional product design field.

And we must not overlook fields other than education that require specialists in educational technology. The health sciences, for example, are heavily involved with instructional technology and have been employing an increasing number of professionals to help develop the instruction used in those programs. Industrial training also prevents a growing area of employment. In this area, skills in developing instructional materials are very advantageous. As service industries have increased in importance in our economy, training programs for service personnel have correspondingly increased. Aside from employment opportunities within such industries, organizations that design programs for training service personnel employ, both on a permanent and a free-lance basis, people skilled in designing instructional media.

Training programs in fields other than formal education require teachers. Most teacher trainees in schools of education tend to focus on formal educational institutions, public, private, or parochial, as their locus of future employment. However, training programs in business and industry and in government and private institutions have been employing an ever-growing number of professionally trained teachers in recent years. Many if not most of these programs rely heavily on instructional technology and instructional media. Consequently, specialists in instructional technology are in considerable demand as teachers in these programs, as are nonspecialists who nevertheless have secured for themselves some academic background in the basic principles and techniques of instructional technology.

PROFESSIONAL ORGANIZATIONS IN EDUCATIONAL TECHNOLOGY

Whether your interest in instructional technology is general or whether you intend to specialize in this area of education, you should be familiar with some of the major organizations dedicated to its advancement.

The Association for Educational Communications and Technology (AECT). AECT is an umbrella organization intended to encompass all of the substantive areas of instructional technology. These various areas are expressed as divisions within the organizational structure of the Association. For example, the Division of Educational Media Management is concerned with the administration of media programs and media collections. The Industrial Training and Education Division is concerned with the application of instructional technology to training programs. The Division of Instructional Development is concerned with analysis of instructional problems, and the design of effective solutions. The Division of Telecommunications is concerned with instruction delivered via radio, television, and other telecommunications media. Oher divisions of AECT reflect other professional concerns within instructional technology.

AECT publishes a monthly journal, *Instructional Innovator,* and a research quarterly, *Educational Communication and Technology Journal.* Its annual convention features a major exhibition of audiovisual hardware and software in addition to a broad-ranging program of educational seminars and workshops.

American Library Association (ALA).

The ALA is an organization of professionals concerned with the organization, classification, storage and retrieval, and distribution of print and non-print materials, including instructional materials. The ALA has divisions for particular interests. The American Association of School Librarians, for example, is concerned with management of materials collections at the school level.

American Society for Training and Development (ASTD).

ASTD is an association composed primarily of professionals engaged in training programs in business and industry.

ASTD is by far the predominant association for people working in training and management development programs in business, industry, government, and similar institutions. Between 1970 and 1980 its membership grew fourfold to more than 20,000 individuals. During this period the original name, American Society of Training Directors, was changed to reflect the broadened base of interests of its members. The society publishes a monthly journal, *Training and Development,* sponsors studies of problems in the training field, and conducts an annual convention that includes a varied and significant educational program. ASTD is organized into divisions; the Media Division is of primary interest to professionals working in instructional media production.

National Society for Performance and Instruction (NSPI).

This organization originally was called the National Society for Programmed Instruction, but its name was changed to reflect broadened interests. NSPI members are interested in the study and application of performance and instructional technologies. NSPI membership includes a mixture of people in business, industry, the military, allied health professions, government, and formal education. The Society publishes a monthly journal, *Performance and Instruction.*

The International Visual Literacy Association (IVLA).

The IVLA is an organization dedicated to exploring the concept of visual literacy—how we use visuals for communication and how we interpret these visuals. As such, it is particularly concerned with the development of instructional materials designed to foster skills in interpreting visuals.

The National Association of Educational Broadcasters (NAEB).

Instruction via telecommunication systems is the primary concern of the NAEB. Although the organization in the past tended to be dominated by the public television stations, it now primarily represents individuals who work in some area of educational telecommunications, including public radio, school television, university closed-circuit systems, and the like.

State Organizations.

Several of the national organizations cited above have state affiliates (e.g., AECT, ALA), or local chapters (e.g., NSPI). By joining one or more of these, you will be brought quickly and personally into contact with nearby professionals who share your particular concerns.

PROFESSIONAL JOURNALS IN EDUCATIONAL TECHNOLOGY

All of the above organizations publish journals of interest to their members. There are a number of other periodicals of special interest to teachers interested in using instructional media. *Media & Methods,* for example, is a journal of particular interest to teachers of social studies and English. *Booklist* will keep you current on the availability of new instructional materials. *Learning* magazine gives practical ideas for improving instruction. *Educational Technology* addresses both teachers and media specialists with articles on a broad range of topics from the theoretical to the practical. For the business/industry setting, *Training* covers new developments in training techniques in a lively, popular style.

By this time we hope that you have made the acquaintance of all these journals—and many more. But if you haven't, take the opportunity to browse through them in the periodical room of your university or public library. It will be time well spent.

Figure 14.16 A sampling of journals in educational technology.

As you work with instructional media and technology and as you gain experience in whatever instructional position you find yourself, you may want to explore the possibility of deepening your professional interest in one of the specialties in instructional technology. Through regular reading of one or more of the journals in the field, you will be kept informed about developments in instructional technology. You will find it a fascinating area within education and one with exciting career possibilities.

REFERENCES

Print References

Ashby, Eric. *Adapting Universities to a Technological Society* (New York: Jossey-Bass, 1974).

Boraiko, Allen A. "Fiber Optics: Harnessing Light by a Thread." *National Geographic,* October 1979, pp. 516–535.

Brooks, Jean S., and David L. Reich. *The Public Library and Non-Traditional Education* (Homewood, IL: ETC Publications, 1974).

* Carnegie Commission on Higher Education. *The Fourth Revolution: Instructional Technology in Higher Education* (New York: McGraw-Hill, 1972).

* Caskey, Owen L. *Suggestive-Accelerative Learning and Teaching,* Volume 36, The Instructional Design Library (Englewood Cliffs, NJ: Educational Technology Publications, 1980).

Dede, Christopher J. "Educational Technology: The Next Ten Years." *Instructional Innovator,* March 1980, pp. 17–23.

Harrison, Shelley A., and Lawrence M. Stolurow (eds.). *Improving Instructional Productivity in Higher Education* (Englewood Cliffs, NJ: Educational Technology Publications, 1975).

Heyman, Mark. *Places and Spaces: Environmental Psychology in Education* (Bloomington, IN: Phi Delta Kappa, 1978).

* Holmberg, Borje. *Distance Education* (New York: Nichols, 1977).

Holmberg, Borje. *Status and Trends of Distance Education* (London: Kogan Page, 1981).

Lozanov, Georgi. *Suggestology and the Outlines of Suggestopedy* (New York: Gordon and Breach Science Publishers, 1978).

Lucas, Jerry. *Ready, Set, Remember* (White's Creek, TN: Memory Press, 1978).

Macken, E. et al. *Home-Based Education: Needs and Technological Opportunities* (Washington, DC: U.S. Government Printing Office, 1976).

"Microelectronics: Their Implications for Education and Training." *Audiovisual Instruction,* September 1979, pp. 13–17.

Monson, Mavis, Lorne Parker, and Betsy Riccomini (eds.). *A Design for Interactive Audio* (Madison, WI: University of Wisconsin—Extension, 1977).

Oettinger, Anthony G., and Nikki Zapol. "Will Information Technologies Help Learning?" *Teachers College Record,* September 1972, pp. 116–126.

* Polcyn, Kenneth A. *An Educator's Guide to Communication Satellite Technology* (Washington, DC: Academy for Educational Development, 1973).

Racle, Gabriel L. "Can Suggestopaedia Revolutionize Language Teaching?" *Foreign Language Annals,* February 1979.

"Satellites Will Be Flying High in the 1980s." *Educational & Industrial Television,* January 1980, pp. 31–33.

* Scanlon, R., and JoAnn Weinberger. *Symposium on Improving Productivity of School Systems Through Educational Technology* (Philadelphia: Research for Better Schools, 1974).

* Shane, Harold G. "Future-Planning as a Means of Shaping Educational Change." In Robert M. McClure (ed.), *The Curriculum: Retrospect and Prospect, The Seventieth Yearbook of the Society for the Study of Education, Part I* (Chicago, IL: University of Chicago Press, 1971), pp. 185–218.

Toffler, Alvin. *The Third Wave* (New York: Morrow, 1979).

Tunstall, Jeremy (ed.). *The Open University Opens* (Amherst: University of Massachusetts Press, 1974).

Van Horn, Royal W. "Environmental Psychology: Hints of a New Technology?" *Phi Delta Kappan,* June 1980, pp. 696–697.

* Key references.

POSSIBLE PROJECTS

14-A. Read an article on trends in media formats and equipment, then write or record a review/summary of the article. The report should be approximately 2 1/2 double-spaced pages or 5 minutes in length. Possible journals include: *Instructional Innovator* (formerly *Audiovisual Instruction)* and *Media & Methods.*

14-B. Survey three professional media specialists and assess their role in the total functioning of the school. Include the results and your questionnaire, along with a brief summary of the implications that can be drawn from your results.

14-C. Discuss five important trends in media from your point of view. Include in your dicussion both hardware (equipment) and software (materials) advances and indicate how they relate to the trends you have indentified.

14-D. Review several professional journals that deal with educational technology. Write a brief (one page) description of the types of articles and information contained in each journal.

14-E. Predict five ways in which your role as a teacher/trainer might change in the next five years. Look into your "crystal ball" and let your imagination take over based upon the information presented in this chapter.

APPENDIX A

INFORMATION SOURCES

Instructors ordinarily begin their search for needed audiovisual materials in the media collection at their own location. School people would turn next to the catalogs of media collections housed at the school district or regional educational service center. But where can you turn to beyond your own organization? This appendix will help you gain access to the wealth of audiovisual resources available for rental or purchase from commercial and noncommercial sources. (Appendix B focuses on sources that give away or loan materials for free or for a nominal cost.)

COMPREHENSIVE INFORMATION SOURCES

Assuming that you had identified an instructional need for which audiovisual materials were not available within your organization or from a free loan source, where might you begin searching for another supplier? The most comprehensive information source is the set of indexes published by the National Information Center for Educational Media (NICEM), University of Southern California, University Park, Los Angeles, California 90007. NICEM provides indexes for each media format and for several popular subject areas plus a producer/distributor index. All are revised periodically and are updated by a supplement service. Arranged by subject as well as by title, these annotated indexes give a comprehensive view of what is available in the marketplace.

NICEM indexes covering still picture formats are:

Index to Educational Overhead Transparencies
Index to Educational Slides
Index to 35mm Filmstrips

Audio materials are indexed in:

Index to Educational Audio Tapes
Index to Educational Records

Films are covered by two indexes:

Index to 16mm Educational Film
Index to 8mm Motion Cartridges

Video tapes appear in:

Index to Educational Video Tapes

NICEM indexes covering multiple types of media on a given topic are:

Index to Environmental Studies
Index to Health and Safety Education
Index to Psychology
Index to Vocational and Technical Education

The University of Southern California also maintains the nation's largest and most comprehensive bibliographic information retrieval system for special education, the National Information Center for Special Education Materials (NICSEM). NICSEM provides information on the content of materials and their applicability to specific handicaps. The NICSEM material is helpful in the construction of individualized programs for handicapped children. To provide better access to the information stored in their data bank, NICSEM now publishes four indexes plus a thesaurus:

Special Education Index to Learner Materials
Special Education Index to Parent Materials
Special Education Index to In-Service Training Materials
Special Education Index to Assessment Devices
NICSEM Special Education Thesaurus

The NICSEM data base can also be accessed through several computerized search services, for example, Lockheed Dialog. Any library subscribing to such a search service would have a terminal through which you could sift the NICSEM references on-line.

Other reference works covering a broad range of media and content areas are:

Brown, Lucy Gregor. *Core Media Collection for Elementary Schools*. 2nd edition (New York: R. R. Bowker, 1978).

Brown, Lucy Gregor. *Core Media Collection for Secondary Schools.* 2nd edition (New York: R. R. Bowker, 1979).

Elementary School Library Collection: A Guide to Books and Other Media. Annual. Lois Winkel, ed. (Greensboro, NC: Bro-Dart Foundation).

Multimedia Approach to Children's Literature: A Selective List of Films, Filmstrips and Recordings Based on Children's Books. 2nd edition. Ellin Greene and Madalynne Schoenfeld, eds. (Chicago: American Library Association, 1977).

A Reference List of Audiovisual Materials Produced by the United States Government. (Washington, DC: National Audio Visual Center, 1982).

The Seed Catalog: A Guide to Teaching/Learning Materials. Jeffrey Schrank, ed. (Boston: Beacon Press, 1974).

SPECIALIZED INFORMATION SOURCES

Many information sources are restricted to a particular media format, content area, or audience:

AAAS Science Film Catalog (Washington, DC: American Association for the Advancement of Science, 1975).

American Folklore Films and Videotapes: An Index. Bill Ferris and Judy Peiser, eds. (Memphis, TN: Center for Southern Folklore, 1976).

Bibliography of Nonprint Instructional Materials on the American Indian. (Provo, UT: Brigham Young University Press, 1972).

Chicorel Index to Video Tapes and Cassettes. Annual. Marietta Chicorel, ed. (New York: Chicorel Library). An annotated index of more than 4000 commercially available video recordings. Emphasis is on entertainment rather than educational items.

Collier Marilyn. *Films for 3 to 5's.* (Berkeley, CA: California University Department of Education, Instructional Laboratories, 1975). Cover title: *Films for Children Ages 3 to 5.*

Educational Sound Filmstrip Directory. Annual (St. Charles, IL: Dukane Corp., Audiovisual Division).

Feature Films on 8mm and 16mm and Videotape. 6th edition. James Limbacher, ed. (New York: R. R. Bowker, 1979).

Film Resources for Sex Education. (New York: Sex Information and Education Council of the United States, distributed by Human Sciences Press, 1976).

Films for Children: A Selected List. 4th edition (New York: Children's and Young Adult Section of the New York Library Association, 1977).

Films Kids Like: A Catalog of Short Films for Children. Susan E. Rice, ed. Published for the Center for Understanding Media by the American Library Association (Chicago: American Library Association, 1973).

The Guide to Simulations/Games for Education and Training. 4th edition. Robert E. Horn and Anne Cleaves, eds. (Beverly Hills, CA: Sage, 1980). Aims for comprehensive coverage of formal education and the business/industry training sector. All listings carry full descriptions including, in some instances, evaluations and/or testimonials of users.

Handbook of Simulation Gaming in Social Education. 2nd edition. Ron Stadsklev, ed. (s.l. : Institute of Higher Education Research and Service, University of Alabama, 1979). Published in two volumes—the first being an introductory textbook on simulation/gaming, particularly as it relates to objectives in the social sciences arena, and the second being a directory of individual materials with extensive descriptive annotations. Coverage is limited to "social education," interpreted quite broadly.

Index to Computer Based Learning. 1981 edition. Anastasia C. Wang, ed. (Microfiche) (Milwaukee, WI: Educational Communication Division, University of Wisconsin, 1981). Contains on microfiche approximately 3000 entries arranged by subject, including, for example, accounting, botany, Chinese, driver education, graphic arts, journalism, logic, music, social studies, welding, and zoology. All of the entries are cross-indexed according to program language, type of central processing unit required, instructional strategy, source, and program category.

More Films Kids Like. Maureen Gaffney, ed. (Chicago: American Library Association, 1977). A sequel to Susan Rice's *Films Kids Like.*

Movies for Kids: A Guide for Parents and Teachers on the Entertainment Film for Children. Edith Zornow and Ruth M. Goldstein, eds. (New York: Frederick Ungar, 1980).

National Center for Audio Tapes Catalog, 1974–76. (Boulder, CO: National Center for Audio Tapes, 1974).

Parlato, Salvatore J., Jr. *Films—Too Good for Words: A Directory of Non-Narrated 16mm Films.* (New York: R. R. Bowker, 1973).

Positive Images: A Guide to Non-Sexist Films for Young People. (San Francisco: Booklegger Press, 1976).

Programmed Learning and Individually Paced Instruction—Bibliography, 5th edition. Carl H. Hendershot, compiler (Bay City, MI: Hendershot Bibliography, 1979). Supplements are issued periodically.

Schwann Record and Tape Guide (137 Newberry Street, Boston MA 02116). Also available from many record stores.

Selected Films for Young Adults, 1979. Media Selection and Usage Committee, Young Adults Services Division, American Library Association (Chicago: American Library Association, 1979).

Videolog. Three volumes: "Programs for Business and Industry," "Programs for General Interest and Entertainment," "Programs for the Health Sciences" (Edison, NJ: Esselte

Video, Inc.). Program information on over 15,000 videotapes and videocassettes in a broad range of categories.

Video Source Book. Annual (Syosset, NY: National Video Clearinghouse). Computer-generated catalog of 18,000 video programs, encompassing entertainment, sports, fine arts, business/industry, and education.

RENTAL SOURCES

The media formats that are generally available for rental for a fee are 16-mm films and videotapes. Several universities maintain large libraries of educational films (some of them are also available as videotapes). Indiana University, the University of Illinois, Syracuse University, and University of Southern California are among these libraries. Each publishes a catalog of titles available and their rental prices. But there is one "umbrella" publication that pulls together rental information as well as purchase information on each of 40,000 current films. It is:

The Educational Film Locator of the Consortium of University Film Centers and R. R. Bowker Co. 2nd edition (New York: R. R. Bowker, 1980).

COMMERCIAL INFORMATION SOURCES

Commercial producers and distributors of audiovisual materials publish promotional catalogs of their wares. Companies often assemble a special "school and library" catalog, arranged by subject or medium, to display their offerings more effectively. When you use these catalogs keep in mind the bias of the seller. The descriptions given and the claims made do not pretend to be objective. Any purchases should be guided by objective evidence such as field test results, published reviews, and local appraisals based on previews.

A sampling of major audiovisual producers and distributors is given below. The alphabetical lists of companies are grouped roughly according to the media format(s) with which they are identified.

Study Prints
David C. Cook, School Products Division, 850 North Grove Avenue, Elgin, IL 60120.

Encyclopaedia Britannica Educational Corporation, 425 North Michigan Avenue, Chicago, IL 60611.

Silver Burdett Company, 250 James Street, Morristown, NJ 07690.

Society for Visual Education (SVE), Inc., 1345 Diversey Parkway, Chicago, IL 60614.

Overhead Transparencies
Allyn & Bacon, Inc., AV Dept., 470 Atlantic Avenue, Boston, MA 02110.

Creative Visuals Division, Games Industries, P.O. Box 1911, Big Spring, TX 79720.

Denoyer-Geppert Audiovisuals, 5235 Ravenswood Avenue, Chicago, IL 60640.

Encyclopaedia Britannica Educational Corporation, 425 North Michigan Avenue, Chicago, IL 60611.

Hammond, Inc., 515 Valley Street, Maplewood, NJ 07040.

Instructo Products Company, 1635 North 55th Street, Paoli, PA 19130.

Lansford Publishing Company, P.O. Box 8711, San Jose, CA 95155.

McGraw-Hill Film Division, 1221 Avenue of the Americas, New York, NY 10020.

Milliken Publishing, 1100 Research Boulevard, St. Louis, MO 63132.

Rand McNally & Co., P.O. Box 7600, Chicago, IL 60680.

3M Company, Visual Products, 3M Center, St. Paul, MN 55119.

Tweedy Transparencies, 208 Hollywood Boulevard, East Orange, NJ 07018.

United Transparencies, P.O. Box 688, Binghamton, NY 13902.

Filmstrips
Argus Communications, 7440 Natchez Avenue, Niles, IL 60648.

Audio Visual Narrative Arts, Inc., Box 9, Pleasantville, NY 10570

BFA Educational Media, 2211 Michigan Avenue, Santa Monica, CA 90404.

Communacad, The Communications Academy, Box 541, Wilton, CT 06897.

Coronet Instructional Media, 65 East South Water Street, Chicago, IL 60601.

Denoyer-Geppert Audiovisuals, 5235 Ravenswood Avenue, Chicago, IL 60640.

EMC Corporation, 180 East Sixth Street, St. Paul, MN 55101.

Educational Images, P.O. Box 367, Lyons Falls, NY 13368.

Encyclopaedia Britannica Educational Corporation, 425 North Michigan Avenue, Chicago, IL 60611.

Eye Gate Media, Inc., 14601 Archer Avenue, Jamaica, NY 11435.

International Film Bureau, 332 South Michigan Avenue, Chicago, IL 60604.

January Productions, 124 Rea Avenue, Hawthorne, NJ 07506.

McGraw-Hill Film Division, 1221 Avenue of the Americas, New York, NY 10020.

National Film Board of Canada, 1251 Avenue of the Americas, New York, NY 10020.

Paramount Communications, 5451 Marathon Street, Hollywood, CA 90038.

The Reading Laboratory, Inc., Content Materials Division, P.O. Box 681, South Norwalk, CT 06584.

Society for Visual Education (SVE), Inc., 1345 Diversey Parkway, Chicago, IL 60614.

Sunburst Communications, Suite 81, 41 Washington Avenue, Pleasantville, NY 10570.

Time-Life Multimedia, 100 Eisenhower Drive, Paramus, NJ 07652.

Weston Woods Studio, Weston, CT 06883.

Slides
American Museum of Natural History, Central Park West at 79th Street, New York, NY 10024.

Art Now, Inc., 144 North 14th Street, Kenilworth, NJ 07033.

The Center for Humanities, Inc., Communications Park, Box 100, White Plains, NY 10602.

Clay-Adams, 229 Webro Road, Parsippany, NJ 07054.

Harcourt Brace Jovanovich, 757 Third Avenue, New York, NY 10017.

Harper & Row Media, 2350 Virginia Avenue, Hagerstown, MD 21740.

Hester and Associates, 11422 Harry Hines Boulevard, Suite 212, Dallas, TX 75229.

Instructional Resources Corp., 12121 Dove Circle, Laurel, MD 20811.

Metropolitan Museum of Art, Fifth Avenue at 82nd Street, New York, NY 10028.

Museum of Modern Art, 11 West 53rd Street, New York, NY 10019.

National Audubon Society, 950 Third Avenue, New York, NY 10022.

National Geographic Educational Services, 17th and M Street, N.W., Washington, DC 20036.

Sandak, Inc., 18 Harvard Avenue, Stamford, CT 06902.

Society for Visual Education (SVE), Inc., 1345 Diversey Parkway, Chicago, IL 60614.

United Scientific Co., 216 South Jefferson Street, Chicago, IL 60606.

Ward's Natural Science Establishment, Inc., 3000 Ridge Road East, Rochester, NY 14603.

Wilson/Lund, Inc., 1830 Sixth Avenue, Moline, IL 61265.

Audio Materials

Audio Book Co., Box 9100, Van Nuys, CA 91409.

Bilingual Educational Services, Inc., P.O. Box 669, 1603 Hope Street, South Pasadena, CA 91030.

Books on Tape, P.O. Box 71405, Los Angeles, CA 90071.

Bowmar Records, 622 Rodier Drive, Glendale, CA 91201.

Broadcasting Foundation of America, 52 Vanderbilt Avenue, New York, NY 10017.

Caedmon, 1995 Broadway, New York, NY 10023.

Capitol Records, 1750 North Vine, Hollywood, CA 90028.

Columbia Records, 51 West 52nd Street, New York, NY 10019.

Coronet Instructional Media, 65 East South Water Street, Chicago, IL 60601.

Decca Records, 445 Park Avenue, New York, NY 10022.

Walt Disney Educational Media Company, 500 South Buena Vista Street, Burbank, CA 91521.

Educational Corp. of America (now Rand McNally), P.O. Box 7600, Chicago, IL 60680.

Grolier Educational Corp., Sherman Turnpike, Danbury, CT 06816.

Imperial Educational Resources, Inc., 19 Marble Avenue, Pleasantville, NY 10570.

Imperial International Learning, Box 548, Kankakee, IL 60901.

Language Master Systems, Bell & Howell, 7100 North McCormick Road, Chicago, IL 60645.

Learning Systems Corporation, 60 Connolly Parkway, Hamden, CT 06514.

Listening Library, Inc., 1 Park Avenue, Old Greenwich, CT 06870.

Miller-Brody Productions, 342 Madison Avenue, New York, NY 10017.

RCA Educational Division, Front and Cooper Streets, Camden, NJ 08102.

Science Research Associates (SRA), 155 North Wacker Drive, Chicago, IL 60606.

Society for Visual Education (SVE), Inc., 1345 Diversey Parkway, Chicago, IL 60614.

3M Company, 3M Center, St. Paul, MN 55144.

Variable Speech Control (VSC) Corporation, 185 Berry Street, San Francisco, CA 94107.

Films (Distributors)

BFA Educational Media, 2211 Michigan Avenue, Santa Monica, CA 90404.

CRM/McGraw-Hill Films, 110 15th Street, Del Mar, CA 92014.

Churchill Films, 662 North Robertson Boulevard, Los Angeles, CA 90069.

Coronet Instructional Media, 65 East South Water Street, Chicago, IL 60601.

Walt Disney Educational Media, 500 South Buena Vista Street, Burbank, CA 91521.

Encyclopaedia Britannica Educational Corporation, 425 North Michigan Avenue, Chicago, IL 60611.

Films, Inc., 1144 Wilmette Avenue, Wilmette, IL 60091.

Indiana University, Audio-Visual Center, Bloomington, IN 47405.

International Film Bureau, 332 South Michigan Avenue, Chicago, IL 60604.

Learning Corporation of America, 1350 Avenue of the Americas, New York, NY 10019.

Modern Learning Aids, P.O. Box 1712, Rochester, NY 14603.

National Audiovisual Center, General Services Administration, Washington, DC 20409.

National Film Board of Canada, 1251 Avenue of the Americas, New York, NY 10020.

Perspective Films, 369 West Erie Street, Chicago, IL 60610.

Phoenix Films, 470 Park Avenue South, New York, NY 10016.

Pyramid Films, Box 1048, Santa Monica, CA 90406.

Time-Life Multimedia, 1271 Avenue of the Americas, New York, NY 10020.

Simulations and Games

Avalon Hill Co., 4517 Harford Road, Baltimore, MD 21214.

CONDUIT/Central, Box 388, Iowa City, IA 52240.

Denoyer-Geppert, Inc., 5235 Ravenswood Avenue, Chicago, IL 60640.

Didactic Systems, Inc., Box 457, Cranford, NJ 07016.

Edu-Game, P.O. Box 1144, Sun Valley, CA 91352.

Houghton-Mifflin Co., One Beacon Street, Boston, MA 02107.

Interact Co., P.O. Box 262, Lakeside, CA 92040.

Simile II, P.O. Box 910, Del Mar, CA 92014.

Simulations Publications Inc., 44 East 23rd Street, New York, NY 10010.

Teaching Aids Co., 925 South 300 West, Salt Lake City, UT 84101.

Wff 'N Proof, 1490-TZ South Boulevard, Ann Arbor, MI 48104.

John Wiley & Sons, Inc., 605 Third Avenue, New York, NY 10158.

REVIEW SOURCES

Your search-and-sift process can be aided greatly by drawing on the evaluative judgments made by other professionals. A number of periodicals are devoted to reviewing audiovisual materials; others publish reviews in addition to their other editorial content. These periodicals are listed below.

Booklist. American Library Association, 50 East Huron Street, Chicago, IL 60611.

EFLA Evaluations. Educational Film Library Association, Inc., 43 West 61st Street, New York, NY 10023.

EPIE Report. EPIE (Educational Products Information Exchange) Institute, Box 620, Stony Brook, NY 11790. Includes *EPIE Gram: Materials* and *EPIE Gram: Equipment,* which may also be received separately.

Film Library Quarterly. Film Library Information Council, Box 348, Radio City Station, New York, NY 10019.

Film News. Suite 2202, 250 West 57th Street, New York, NY 10019.

Landers Film Reviews. Landers Associates, Box 69760, Los Angeles, CA 90069.

Library Journal. R.R. Bowker, 1180 Avenue of the Americas, New York, NY 10036.

Media & Methods. American Society of Educators, 1511 Walnut Street, Philadelphia, PA 19102.

Media Review. Professional Evaluations of Instructional Materials, 343 Manville Road, Pleasantville, NY 10570. Available for grades K-8 and 9-college.

Rockingchair. The review newsletter for librarians and popular music fans who buy records. Cupola Productions, Box 27, Philadelphia, PA 19105.

School Media Quarterly. American Association of School Librarians, American Library Association, 50 East Huron Street, Chicago, IL 60611.

Science Books and Films. Variant title: *AAAS Science Books and Films.* American Association for the Advancement of Science, 1515 Massachusetts Avenue, N.W., Washington, DC 20005.

Sightlines. Educational Film Library Association, 43 West 61st Street, New York, NY 10023.

For more extensive, annotated guides to media reviews or descriptions of other audiovisual information sources, consult:

Chisholm, Margaret E. *Media Indexes and Review Sources* (College Park, MD: School of Library and Information Services, University of Maryland, 1972).

Multi-Media Indexes, Lists and Review Sources. A Bibliographic Guide. Thomas L. Hart, Mary A. Hunt, and Blanche Woolls, eds. (New York: Marcel Dekker, 1975).

Media Review Digest (Ann Arbor, MI: The Pierian Press).

Rufsvold, Margaret I. *Guides to Educational Media* 4th edition (Chicago: American Library Association, 1977).

Sive, Mary Robinson. *Selecting Instructional Media* (Littleton, CO: Libraries Unlimited, 1978).

APPENDIX B

FREE AND INEXPENSIVE MATERIALS

With the ever increasing costs of instructional materials, teachers should be aware of the wide variety that can be obtained for classroom use at little or no cost. These free and inexpensive materials can supplement instruction in many subjects, or they can even be the main source of instruction on certain topics. For example, many films are available for loan without a rental fee; the only expense is the return postage. By definition, any material that you can borrow or purchase for instructional purposes without a significant cost (usually less than a couple of dollars) can be referred to as "free and inexpensive."

The types of free and inexpensive materials are almost endless. The more commonly available items include posters, games, pamphlets, brochures, reports, charts, maps, books, filmstrips, audiotapes, films, videotapes, multimedia kits, and realia. The more costly items, such as films and videotapes, are usually sent only on a free-loan basis and must be returned to the supplier after use. In some instances, single copies of audio cassettes and filmstrips will be donated to your school to be shared among all the teachers.

ADVANTAGES

Free and inexpensive materials can provide up-to-date information that is not contained in textbooks or other commercially available media. In addition, they often provide more in-depth treatment of a topic. If classroom quantities are available, printed materials can be read and discussed by students as textbook material would be. If quantities are limited, they can be placed in a learning center for independent study. Audiovisual materials lend themselves to classroom presentation by the teacher. Individual students who want to explore a subject of interest can use the audiovisual materials for self-study or for presentation to the class. Posters, charts, and maps can be combined to create topical displays. These can be motivational or can be used for direct instruction. Materials that are given and do not have to be returned can be modified and adapted for varied instructional or display purposes.

Materials that are expendable have the extra advantage of allowing learners to get actively involved with them. Students can cut out pictures for notebooks and displays. They can assemble printed information and visuals in scrapbooks as reports of group projects. Of course, when treating free materials as raw materials for student projects, you will have to develop your own objectives and plan appropriate learning activities to go along with the materials.

LIMITATIONS

Several potential limitations of free and inexpensive materials must be taken into consideration. First, many free and inexpensive materials can be described as sponsored materials because their production and distribution are sponsored by particular organizations. These organizations—whether private companies, non-profit associations, or government agencies—often have a message to convey. That message might be in the form of outright advertising. If so, you will have to be aware of your own school's policies on the use of advertising matter in class. You may consider covering or removing the advertisement, but that, too, raises ethical questions in view of the effort and expense that the sponsor has incurred in providing the materials to you.

What may be even more troublesome to deal with is sponsored material that does not contain outright advertising but does promote some special interest in a less obvious way. As discussed in Chapter 8 in regard to sponsored films, a recent study by the Center for the Study of Responsive Law* disclosed a persistent tendency for privately sponsored materials to convey self-serving messages. Propagandistic or more subtly biased materials can thus enter the curriculum through the "back door." Careful previewing and caution are advisable when considering sponsored materials.

---

*Sheila Harty. *Hucksters in the Classroom: A Review of Industry Propaganda in the Schools*. Washington, DC: Center for Study of Responsive Law, 1980.

APPRAISAL CHECKLIST: FREE AND INEXPENSIVE MATERIALS

Topic_____   Type of Material_____

Source_____   (booklet, filmstrip, tape, film, etc.)

Cost_____ Date_____

Objectives (stated or implied)

Brief Description:

RATING

	High		Medium		Low
Free from undesirable advertising and/or bias	☐	☐	☐	☐	☐
Accurate, honest and up-to-date	☐	☐	☐	☐	☐
Useful in meeting objectives	☐	☐	☐	☐	☐
Appropriate level for the audience	☐	☐	☐	☐	☐
Potential uses (alone or with other media)	☐	☐	☐	☐	☐
Readability	☐	☐	☐	☐	☐
Illustration quality (well done and eye-catching)	☐	☐	☐	☐	☐
Durability (if to be re-used)	☐	☐	☐	☐	☐

Strong Points

Weak Points   Reviewer_____

                                                         Position_____

Recommended Action_____   Date_____

As with any other type of material, appraise the educational value of these materials critically. Some are very "slick" (technically well presented) but are not educationally sound. The Appraisal Checklist above is intended to help you make these judgments.

The final potential limitation is a logistical one. With the increasing expense of producing both printed and audiovisual materials, your supplier may have to impose limits on the quantities of items available at one time. You may not be able to obtain a copy of the material for every student in the class.

LOCAL SOURCES

Many local government agencies, community groups, and private businesses provide informational materials on free loan. Public libraries often make films, prints, and filmstrips available. Even libraries in small communities may have access to films through a statewide network. These materials usually can be loaned to local schools. However, public library collections are often entertainment-oriented, as should be expected in a service designed for the general public, so you will probably not find in them a great many strictly instructional materials. Other government agencies, such as county agricultural agents, public health departments, and parks departments, make materials available for use in schools.

Community organizations, such as the Red Cross, League of Women Voters, medical societies, and the like, welcome opportunities to spread information about their special interests. Films, slide-tapes, printed material, and guest speakers are frequently offered.

Among business organizations, utilities—telephone, electric, gas, and water companies—are most likely to employ education specialists who can inform you about what instructional services they offer. Chambers of commerce often can suggest private corporations that might supply materials of interest to you.

NATIONAL AND INTERNATIONAL SOURCES

Nationally, one of the most prolific sources of free and inexpensive materials is the federal government. In the United States, two federal agencies offer special access to materials, the U. S. Government Printing Office and the National Audiovisual Center. Your key to the tremendous wealth of posters, charts, brochures, books, and other printed government documents that are available to the general public is "Selected US Government Publications," a monthly catalog of all new listings. You can have your name added to the free mailing list by sending a request to: Superintendent of Documents, U. S. Government Printing Office, Washington DC 20402.

The National Audiovisual Center is the central clearinghouse for all federal government-produced audiovisual materials. Its catalog, *A Reference List of Audiovisual Materials Produced by the United States Government* is issued every four years (most recently, 1982) with a supplement every two years. It lists more than 12,000 titles of films, videotapes, slide sets, audiotapes, and multimedia kits that have been produced by or for government agencies. All are available for purchase; the 16 mm films (constituting 80% of the collection) can be rented; some of the materials are made available for *free loan* from regional sources. For further information, write to: National Audiovisual Center, Reference Section RL, General Services Administration, Washington DC 20409.

Trade associations and professional associations also aim to acquaint the general public with their own fields of interest and the causes they promote. Some

examples are the National Dairy Council, the American Petroleum Institute, National Wildlife Federation, American Heart Association, and National Association for the Advancement of Colored People.

Private corporations that operate on the national or even international basis offer sponsored materials, as discussed earlier in this appendix. Examples of these businesses include: American Telephone and Telegraph, Goodyear Tire and Rubber Company, Exxon, and US Steel.

Most foreign governments disseminate information about their country to promote trade, tourism, and international understanding. They typically offer free posters, maps, and informational booklets plus films on a free-loan basis. To find out what is available for any particular country, write to the embassy of that country in Washington, DC. International organizations such as the Organization of American States (OAS), United Nations, and the North Atlantic Treaty Organization (NATO) also operate information offices. Popular sources of posters of foreign countries are the airline and cruise ship companies.

COMPREHENSIVE INFORMATION SOURCES

It would be impractical to list here all of the thousands of suppliers of free and inexpensive materials, much less to offer up-to-date addresses. Instead, we recommend that you consult one of the many books and catalogs devoted specifically to free and inexpensive materials. They are updated regularly and contain full name, address, and cost information.

The most comprehensive information source on free and inexpensive materials is the series of catalogs published by Educators Progress Service, Box 497, Randolph, Wisconsin 53956. Revised annually, the titles in this series include:

Educators Index of Free Materials
Educators Guide to Free Films
Educators Guide to Free Filmstrips
Educators Guide to Free Teaching Aids
Educators Guide to Free Audio and Video Materials
Educators Guide to Free Social Studies Materials
Educators Guide to Free Science Materials
Educators Guide to Free Guidance Materials
Educators Guide to Free Health, Physical Education and Recreation Materials
Elementary Teachers Guide to Free Curriculum Materials

Books that list sources of free and inexpensive materials are:

Aubrey, Ruth H. *Selected Free Materials for Classroom Teachers* (Belmont, CA: Fearon Publishers). *Updated periodically.*

Blakely, Pat, Barbara Haislet, and Judith Hentges. *Free Stuff for Kids* (Wayzata, MN: Meadowbrook Press, 1979).

Feinman, Jeffrey. *Freebies for Kids* (New York: Wanderer Books, 1979).

Jackson, Joe L., ed. *Free and Inexpensive Learning Materials* (Nashville: George Peabody College). Updated periodically.

Monahan, Robert. *Free and Inexpensive Materials for Preschool and Early Childhood* (Belmont, CA: Fearon Publishers, 1977).

Weisinger, Mort. *1001 Valuable Things You Can Get Free* (New York: Bantam Books). Updated periodically.

Where to Get Hundreds of Educational Materials—Free! (Greenwich, CT: Frances Press, 1975).

National level services for free-loan films are:

Association-Sterling Films, which provides free-loan films from its 12 offices in the United States and Canada.

Modern Talking Picture Service, which provides sponsored films for free loan from its 25 offices in major cities throughout the United States.

HOW TO OBTAIN FREE AND INEXPENSIVE MATERIALS

When you have determined what you can use and where you can obtain it, correspond on official school stationery. Some agencies will not supply free and inexpensive materials unless you do. For classroom quantities (when they are available), send just one letter. Do not have each student write individually. If a single student is requesting one copy of something for a class project, the student can write the letter, but you should also sign it. We recommend that you request a preview copy of the material before requesting multiple copies. Don't send a request for "anything you have!" Be specific and at least specify the subject area and the grade level. Only ask for what you need. Don't stockpile materials or take advantage of a "free" offer. Somebody is paying for those materials, so don't waste them. Follow up with a "thank you" note to the supplier and let them know how you used the materials and what the students' reaction was to them. Be courteous, but be honest. Many suppliers attempt to improve free and inexpensive materials on the basis of user comments.

APPENDIX C

COPYRIGHT GUIDELINES

To protect the financial interests of the creators, producers, and distributors of original works of information and/or art, nations adopt what are referred to as copyright laws. These laws set the conditions under which anyone can copy, in whole or in part, original works transmittable in any medium. Without copyright laws, writers, artists, film makers, and the like, would not "...receive the encouragement they need to create and the remuneration they fairly deserve for their creations" (from the legislative 1976 Omnibus Copyright Revision Act). The flow of creative work would be reduced to a trickle, and we would all be the losers.

The first copyright law in the United States was passed by Congress in 1790. In 1976, Congress enacted the latest copyright law, taking into consideration technological developments that have occurred since the passage of the previous Copyright Act of 1909. For example, in 1909, anyone who wanted to make a single copy of a literary work for personal use had to do so by hand. The very process imposed a limitation on the quantity copied. Today, a photocopier can do the work in seconds; the limitation has disappeared. Nor did the 1909 copyright law provide full protection for films and sound recordings, nor anticipate the need to protect radio and television. As a result, violations of the law, and abuses of the intent of the law, have made serious inroads on the financial rewards of authors and artists. We are all aware (and probably guilty) of photocopy abuse, but did you know that more than one out of three 8-track cartridges of pop music sold in the open market are pirated copies of the original production? Or that under-the-counter video tapes of new feature films are available *before* general distribution of the films to theaters takes place? Clearly, corrections in the 1909 law were in order.

If you have been reading about the new copyright law in the professional literature, you are aware of the confusion about interpretation of the act caused by claims, counterclaims and, frankly,righteous breast-beating by both copyright holders and consumers. We must remember that the fine points of the law will have to be decided by the courts and by acceptable common practice over an extended period of time. As these decisions and agreements are made, we can modify our behavior accordingly. As of now, then, we need to interpret the law and its guidelines as accurately as we can, and to act in a fair, judicious manner.

Although detailed examination of the law is beyond the scope of this text, here we describe the basic framework of the law and present examples of violations and examples of reasonable interpretation of "fair use" to help guide you in the decisions you need to make about copying protected works for class use. The law sets forth in section 107 four basic criteria for determining the principle of fair use:

1. The purpose and character of the use, including whether such use is of a commercial nature or is for nonprofit educational purposes.
2. The nature of the copyrighted work.
3. The amount and substantiality of the portion used in relation to the copyrighted work as a whole.
4. The effect of the use on the potential market for or value of the copyrighted work.

The following are based on several sets of guidelines issued to spell out the criteria in section 107.

For educational use, an instructor may make a single copy of a chapter from a book; an article from a periodical or newspaper; a short story, short essay, or short poem whether or not from a collective work; an illustration from a book, periodical, or newspaper. The context in which the term "teacher" is used seems to be broad enough to include support personnel working with teachers.

The guidelines further stipulate the amount of material that may be copied and the special circumstances that permit multiple copies. Fair use is defined as one illustration per book or periodical, 250 words from a poem, and 10 percent of a prose work up to 1000 words. Multiple copies cannot exceed the number of students in a class, nor can there be more than nine instances of multiple copying for one course during one class term. No more than one short poem, article, story, essay, or two excerpts may be copied from the same author. The limitations of nine instances and one item or two excerpts do not apply to current news periodicals, newspapers, and current news sections of other periodicals.

However, multiple copies must meet a "spontaneity" test. The copying must be initiated by the individual teacher, not directed or suggested by any other authority. The decision to use the work, *and* the "inspiration" for its use, must be close enough to the moment of use to preclude waiting for permission from the copyright holder. This means, of course, that the same "inspiration" cannot occur the same time next term.

The last guideline, market value, means that copying must not substitute for purchase of the original, or create or replace an anthology or a compilation of works protected by copyright. It also prohibits copying works intended to be consumable, for example, workbooks or standardized tests.

If a work is "out of print," that is no longer available from the copyright holder, then you are not affecting the market value of the work by copying it. The market value guideline can act in favor of the user as we will see from the examples given below.

Unfortunately, neither the law nor the guidelines spell out fair use of media other than print. Eventual fair use criteria, therefore, may evolve more out of acceptable common practice than out of the law and guidelines.

As for music, the new copyright law protects the performance of the work as well as the work itself. For example, Beethoven's Fifth Symphony may be in the public domain but the recorded performance by the Chicago Symphony Orchestra is protected.

The term, or period of time, of the copyright has been changed by the new act. For an individual author, the copyright term will continue for his or her life and for 50 years after death. If a work is made for hire, that is, by an employee or by someone comissioned to do so, the term is 100 years from the year of creation or 75 years from the year of first publication or distribution, whichever comes first. Works copyrighted prior to January 1, 1978 are protected for 28 years and then may have their copyrights renewed. The renewal will protect them for a term of 75 years after their original copyright date.

As we stated before, final interpretation of the provisions of the 1976 Copyright Act will have to wait for future court decisions to define the language and to resolve internal contradictions or conflicts in the law. For example, under the 1976 law, a suit was brought against Sony to prohibit the company from stating in its ads that videotape recorders may be used to record television programs for future viewing. The court ruled that the copyright law does not prevent a private party from videotaping a television program for later personal use.*

Until the courts decide otherwise, it would seem reasonable that teachers (and media professionals) can use the fair use criteria to copy materials that would seem otherwise to be protected. Some examples follow:

1. If the school media center subscribes to a journal or magazine to which you refer students and you want to make slides of several graphics or photos to help students understand an article, it would seem that this is fair use based on the following:
   a. The nature of the work is general, its audience (and market) is not predominantly the educational community,
   b. The character of use is nonprofit,
   c. The amount copied is small,
   d. There is no intent to replace the original, only to make it more useful in a class in conjunction with the copyrighted words.
2. If *you* subscribe to a journal and want to include several pictures from it in a presentation in class, it would seem reasonable to do so for the same reasons.
3. Suppose a film you frequently use drops out of the distributor's catalog; it is "out of print." To protect the print you have, it would seem reasonable, after unsuccessful attempts to reach the copyright owner to get permission, to videotape the film and use the video tape in class. If, at a later date, the film is put back on the market by the same or another distributor, you must go back to using the film. This is not uncommon. For example, *Pacific 231*, an effective film to demonstrate editing, was originally distributed by Young America Films. After Young America Films was purchased by another company, *Pacific 231* was dropped from the catalog. It was not available for almost 20 years. Then Pyramid Films secured the distribution rights and it is now available for purchase. During the long period of unavailability, it would have been reasonable to use a videotape copy.
4. From experience you know that recordings of literary works put out by major record labels may disappear from their catalogs in a few years. For example, RCA Victor once made available a recording of Shakespeare's *Midsummer Night's Dream* with Mendelssohn's incidental music inserted at the appropriate places. It is no longer available. If you had taped the records, put the tapes on the shelf as a contingency, and used the records in class, you would at least now have the tape available if your records were damaged. You have not intended to deprive anyone of income; you simply have used the technology to guarantee availability to yourself.
5. You have rented a film for a specific date but circumstances beyond your control prevent your using it before it is due back. It would seem reasonable, after requesting permission (a telephone call could clear it), to videotape the film, use the videotape, and then erase the tape after

---

Universal City Studios v. *Sony Corporation of America*

use. Again, you have not deprived anyone of income. (This should **never** be done if the film is in on a preview basis!)

6. You are a Consumer Education teacher and you have advance notice that a documentary series on TV is going to deal with a young married couple in financial trouble due to excessive use of credit cards. The "spontaneity" section of the guidelines would seem to cover videotaping the program for use in class within the next few days after the broadcast. Much of the "common law" of fair use comes about by general agreement among affected parties. The general agreement among broadcasters and representatives of users is that a videotaped TV program may be used for 45 days, then erased*.

There are not any guidelines in regard to nonprint materials in contrast to printed matter. Until the courts decide otherwise, it would seem reasonable to extend the print guidelines to nonprint material in judicious fashion.

We are not advocating deliberate violation of the law. On the contrary, we support the intent of the copyright law to protect the financial interests of copyright holders. What we are saying is that the proper balance in the application of the guidelines eventually has to be decided by the courts and by accepted common practice. In the meantime, reasonable interpretations of fair use may permit you to do copying that might seem on the face of it to be prohibited.

SEEKING PERMISSION FOR USE OF COPYRIGHTED MATERIALS

Aside from staying within the guidelines that limit but recognize our legal right to free use of copyrighted materials, what else can we do to assure our students access to these materials. We can, obviously, seek permission from the copyright owners and, if required, pay a fee for their use. Certain requests will ordinarily be granted without payment of fee—transcripts for the blind, for example, or material to be tried out once in an experimental program. (Use of materials in the public domain—materials on which copyright protection has run out, for instance, or materials produced by federal government employees in the course of their regular work—needs no permission.)

In seeking permission to use copyrighted materials, it is generally best to contact the producer or publisher of the material rather than its creator. Whether or not the creator is the holder of the copyright, the producer or publisher generally handles permission requests and sets fees. The address of the producer (if not given on the material) can be obtained from various reference sources, including the *Literary Market Place*, the *Audio-Visual Market Place*, and *Ulrich's International Periodicals Directory*.

Be as specific as possible in your request for permission. Give the page numbers and exact amount of print material you wish to copy. (If possible, send along a photocopy of the material.)

Describe nonprint material fully. State how you intend to use the material, where you intend to use it, how you intend to reproduce it, your purpose in using it, and the number of copies you wish to make.

Remember that fees for reproduction of copyrighted materials are sometimes negotiable. If the fee seems to you to be too high or otherwise beyond your budget, do not be hesitant about asking that it be lowered.

If for *any* reason you decide not to use the requested material, make this fact known to the publisher or producer. Without this formal notice it is likely to be assumed that you have in fact used it as requested, and you may be dunned for a fee you do not in fact owe.

Keep copies of all your correspondence and records of all other contacts that you made relevant to seeking permission for use of copyrighted instructional materials.

*See pages 36–37 of the September, 1981 *Instructional Innovator* for the off-air copying guidelines that have been agreed upon.

THE TEACHER AND VIOLATION OF THE COPYRIGHT LAW

What happens if an educator knowingly and deliberately violates the copyright law? The 1976 Act contains both criminal and civil sanctions. The criminal penalty can be a fine up to $1000 and a year in jail. Copyright owners may recover up to $50,000 in civil court for loss of royalties due to infringement. Furthermore, in any infringement lawsuit, the employing institution can be held liable along with the instructor.

Although individual teachers are not likely to be brought into court on charges of copyright infringement, flagrant violation *can* get the teacher's employer in difficulty. A Board of Cooperative Educational Services was taken to court and found guilty of distributing videotapes of copyrighted material. The media personnel in this case flagrantly violated the law.* Punitive damages aside, in a profession devoted to promoting ethical behavior, deliberate violation of the copyright law is unacceptable.

Encyclopaedia Britannica Education Corporation v. The Board of Cooperative Educational Services (BOCES)

REFERENCES

We have concentrated here on the problem of copying copyrighted materials for educational purposes and on the guidelines set up under the 1976 Act to help assure that such duplication does not violate the law or otherwise infringe on copyright ownership. The Act itself contains hundreds of these provisions covering all aspects of copyright law and ownership. Some of these other provisions are of particular interest to educators—provisions covering copying by libraries, for example, or use of copyrighted materials for instruction of the visually handicapped and the hearing impaired. Other provisions may be of interest to those who have authored or plan someday to author or produce instructional materials. In any case, it behooves each of us to be familiar at least with those aspects of the law likely to affect our own special activities and interests.

Copyright and Educational Media: A Guide to Fair Use and Permission Procedure (Washington, DC: Association for Educational Communications and Technology, 1977).

Explaining the New Copyright Law (Washington, DC: Association of American Publishers, 1977).

Gary, Charles L. *The New Copyright Law and Education* (Arlington, VA: Educational Research Services, 1977).

General Guide to the Copyright Act of 1976, L. C.-3.7/2:C79, available from the Copyright Office Library of Congress, Washington, DC 20559. The following pamphlet materials are also available from the Copyright Office: *Copyright and the Librarian, Reproduction of Copyrighted Works for the Blind and Physically Handicapped, Highlights of the New Copyright Law.*

Johnston, Donald. *Copyright Handbook* (New York: R.R. Bowker, 1981).

Librarian's Copyright Kit: What You Must Know Now (Chicago: American Library Association, 1978).

Lieb, Charles H. *New Copyright Law: Overview* (Washington, DC: Association of American Publishers, 1976).

The Visual Artist's Guide to the New Copyright Law (New York: Graphic Artists Guild, 1978).

PHOTO CREDITS

Chapter 1

Figure 1.1: (a) NASA (b) Children's Television Workshop (c) Courtesy Atari Inc. (d) © Ira Berger 1981/Woodfin Camp (e) © Donald Dietz 1980/Stock, Boston (f) Jack Prelutsky/Stock, Boston. Figure1.2: Susan Szasz. Figure 1.3: © Paramount Pictures Corporation. All Rights Reserved. ABC Television Network. Figure 1.4: © Michal Heron 1981. Figure 1.5: © Peter Menzel/Stock, Boston. Figure 1.6: © Michal Heron 1981. Figure 1.9: Michael Neff. Figure 1.10: George Bellerose/Stock, Boston. Figure 1.11: William Vandivert. Figure 1.13: Shirley Zeiberg/Taurus Photos. Figure 1.14: Michael Neff. Figure 1.15: Deane Dayton. Figure 1.16: New York University Education Quarterly. Figure 1.17: Deane Dayton. Figure 1.18: Sybil Shackman/Monkmeyer. Figure 1.19: Bell and Howell Company. Figure 1.20: Research for Better Schools, Inc. Figure 1.21: Response Systems Corporation. Figure 1.22: Courtesy PBS. Page 26: Jim Owens. Figure 1.23: © Peter Menzel/Stock, Boston. Figure 1.24: Rhoda Sidney/Monkmeyer. Figure 1.25: (a) Strickler/Monkmeyer (b) Paul S. Conklin/Monkmeyer.

Chapter 2

Page 34: (left) Terry McKoy/Taurus Photos (center) Kenneth Karp (right) © Jim Anderson 1978/Woodfin Camp. Page 35: (left) Courtesy of Eastman Kodak Company (center) Laimute E. Druskis/Taurus Photos (right) Hugh Rogers/Monkmeyer. Page 43: Pitman Learning, Inc. Figure 2.2: Jim Owens. Figures 2.13 and 2.14: © Michal Heron 1981.

Chapter 3

Figure 3.1: © Michal Heron 1981. Page 54: © Karsh, Ottawa/Woodfin Camp. Figure 3.5: © Richard Kalvar/Magnum. Figure 3.7: The Bettmann Archive. Figure 3.9: Minox U.S.A. Figure 3.10: Konica Corporation. Figure 3.11: Pentax Corporation. Page 69: William Orisich. Figure 3.12: © 1967 Eastman Kodak Company. Figure 3.13: © Michal Heron 1981. Figure 3.16: Michael Neff. Pages 73, 74 and 75: Thomas Cecere.

Chapter 4

Figures 4.1 and 4.2: Jim Owens. Figure 4.3: Michael Neff. Page 87: Jim Owens. Figure 4.4: Department of Psychology, Duke University. Figure 4.5: Courtesy of Lesney/AMT Corp., Baltimore. Figure 4.6: Denoyer-Geppert Audio-Visuals. Figure 4.8: Mike Mazzaschi/Stock, Boston. Page 94: Jim Owens. Figure 4.9: Patricia Hollander Gross/Stock, Boston. Figure 4:10: Jim Owens. Figure 4.11: © Michal Heron 1981. Page 100: Michael Neff. Figures 4.12 and 4.13: © Michal Heron 1981. Figure 4.14: Oravisual, Inc. Figure 4.15: Jerome Oehler. Figure 4.16: Strickler/Monkmeyer. Figures 4.17, 4.18 and 4.19: Jim Owens.

Chapter 5

Figures 5.2 and 5.3: Michael Neff. Figure 5.6: (a) Swan Pencil Company (b) 3M Company. Page 118: Milliken Publishing Company. Page 119: Denoyer-Geppert Audio-Visuals. Figures 5.9 and 5.10: Michael Neff. Figures 5.11, 5.12 and 5.13: Courtesy of Eastman Kodak Company. Page 127: (top) Adapted and reproduced by permission of the publisher from *Concepts in Science 5: Experiences, A Workbook* by Paul F. Brandwein, et al. © 1966 by Harcourt Brace Jovanovich, Inc. (bottom) © 1979 Art Now, Inc. Figure 5.14: Michael Neff. Figures 5.15, 5.16 and 5.17: Dennis Short. Figure 5.20: Jim Owens. Figure 5.21: (a) Michael Neff (b) Bell and Howell Company. Figure 5.22: Jim Owens. Figure 5.23: (top) Viewlex Audio-Visual International (bottom) Singer Educational Division. Figure 5.24: Dukane Corporation. Page 134: (top) Aims Media Inc. (center) Society for Visual Education, Inc. (bottom) Denoyer-Geppert Audio-Visuals.

Chapter 6

Figure 6.1: (left) Ken Heyman (right) © Martha Stewart. Figure 6.4: Courtesy Folkways, Photo by Lorinda Morris. Figure 6.6: G.T.E. Sylvania. Figure 6.7: Michael Neff. Figure 6.8: Bell and Howell Company. Figure 6.9: Audiotronics. Figure 6.10: VOXCOM. Figure 6.11: American Printing House for the Blind, Inc. Page 148: (top, center) UPI. (bottom) Courtesy Random House, Inc. Page 149: (top) Audiotronics (bottom) Courtesy of Eastman Kodak Company.

Page 150: (top) P and H Electronics, Inc. (center) Michael Neff (bottom) © Michal Heron 1981. Page 151: © Michal Heron 1981. Figure 6.12: Wollensak 3M. Figure 6.13: Michael Neff. Figure 6.14: © Bruce Roberts/Photo Researchers. Figure 6.20: Recordex Corporation. Figure 6.21: VSC Corporation. Figure 6.22: Michael Neff.

Chapter 7

Figure 7.1: Singer Educational Division, Society for Visual Education. Figure 7.3: Visual Horizons. Figure 7.5: Hugh Rogers/Monkmeyer. Figures 7.6 and 7.8: Michael Neff. Figure 7.10: Courtesy of Eastman Kodak Company. Figure 7.12: Indiana University, Audio-Visual Center. Figures 7.14 and 7.15: Courtesy of Eastman Kodak Company. Figure 7.16: Charles Beseler Company. Figure 7.17: Retention Communications Systems. Figure 7.18: Encyclopedia Britannica Educational Corporation Sales Promotion. Page 175: Interpretive Education Inc. Figure 7.19: Dennis Short. Page 177: Michael Neff. Page 178: Kit developed at the Boston Children's Museum. Figure 7.20: Hugh Rogers/ Monkmeyer. Figure 7.21: F. Bernstein/Leo deWys. Page 179: Dennis Short. Figure 7.22: Peter Vandermark/Stock, Boston.

Chapter 8

Page 189: (left) The Bettmann Archive (right) From *Teaching With Films* by George H. Ferns and Eldon Robbins. The Bruce Publishing Company © 1946. Page 190: From *Teaching With Films* by George H. Ferns and Eldon Robbins. The Bruce Publishing Company © 1946. Figure 8.5: National Film Board of Canada. Figure 8.6: From the Encyclopedia Britannica Educational Corporation. Figure 8.7: Courtesy of Eastman Kodak Company. Figure 8.8: Indiana University, Audio-Visual Center. Figure 8.9: Pyramid Film and Video. Figure 8.10: National Film Board of Canada. Figure 8.11: International Film Bureau, Inc. Figure 8.12: Counselor Films, Inc. Figure 8.13: Roger Werth/Woodfin Camp. Figure 8.14: Kalmia Company. Figure 8.15: Produced by CRM Productions. Distributed by CRM/McGraw Hill Films. Figure 8.16: Wide World Photos. Figure 8.17: Agency for Instructional Television. Figure 8.18: Museum of Modern Art-Film Stills Archives. Figure 8.19: Produced by CRM Productions. Distributed by CRM/McGraw Hill Films. Figure 8.20: *U.S. Congress.* From the Encyclopedia Britannica Educational Corporation. Figures 8.21 and 8.22: National Film Board of Canada. Figures 8.23 through 8.32: Museum of Modern Art—Film Stills Archives. Figure 8.33: Copyright, Des Moines Register and Tribune Company. Figure 8.34: *Death of a Princess,* WGBH Educational Foundation. Figures 8.35 through 8.38: © Michal Heron 1981. Figure 8.39: Michael Neff. Figure 8.40: William Orisich. Figure 8.41: Frank Siteman/Stock, Boston. Page 207: (top) Encyclopedia Britannica Educational Corporation (center) Aims Media, Inc. (bottom) Churchill Films. Page 208: (top) Pyramid Film and Video (center) Janis Films (bottom) Films Inc. Ballet dancer photo sequence (pages 187 through 211): From the film *Movement in Classical Dance,* Indiana University, Audio-Visual Center. Basketball photo sequence (pages 186 through 210): From an Indiana University television series, animation sequence by Bill Orisich, Indiana University, Audio-Visual Center.

Chapter 9

Figure 9.1: © Teri Leigh Stratford/Photo Researchers. Page 216: The School Board of Broward County, Florida. Instructional Television Center. Page 217: University of Mid-America. Figures 9.4 and 9.5: Children's Television Workshop. Figure 9.6: Agency for Instructional Television. Page 222: (center) Agency for Instructional Television (bottom) Great Plains National Instructional Television Library. Page 223: Western Instructional Television. Page 225: Photo courtesy Warner Amex Qube. Photography by Larry Phillips. Figure 9.10: Sony Video Products Company. Figure 9.11: Panasonic Company. Figures 9.12 and 9.13: Sony Video Products Company. Page 230: © Michal Heron 1981. Figures 9.14 and 9.15: Sony Video Products Company. Figures 9.16, 9.17 and 9.18: Audiotronics. Figures 9.19 and 9.20: Michael Neff.

Chapter 10

Figure 10.7: Michael Neff. Figure 10.15: Wollensak 3M. Figure 10.20: Courtesy Shure.

Chapter 11

Figure 11.1: Kathy Bendo. Figure 11.2: (a and b) Photo from *Teaching Machines and Programmed Learning,* published by Association for Educational Communications and Technology (c) Hugh Rogers/Monkmeyer. Figure 11.4: From *Statistics,* second edition, by Donald J. Koosis, © 1977 John Wiley & Sons, Inc., page 60. Figure 11.5: From *Art As You See It,* by Ione Bell, Karen M. Hess, and Jim R. Matison, © 1979 by John Wiley & Sons, Inc., page 77. Figure 11.6: From *Psychology of Learning,* by James M. Royer and Richard G. Allan, © 1978 John Wiley & Sons, Inc., page 64. Figures 11.7 and 11.8: Michael Neff. Figure 11.9: J.S. Keller, Kalamazoo 1968. Figure 11.10: © Donald Dietz 1980/ Stock, Boston. Page 278 and Figure 11.11: Dennis Short. Figure 11.12: Hugh Rogers/Monkmeyer. Figure 11.13: © Jean-Claude Lejune/Stock, Boston. Figure 11.14: Kee Incorporated.

Chapter 12

Figure 12.2: (a) © Bohdan Hrynewych/Stock, Boston (b) Ed Malitsky/The Picture Cube. Page 292: Deane Dayton. Figure 12.3: Doron Precisions System, Inc. Drivotrainer System. Figure 12.4: © Al Stephenson 1980/Woodfin Camp. Figure 12.5: Frank Siteman/The Picture Cube. Page 294: Thomas Cecere. Page 295: (center) Thomas Cecere (bottom) Denoyer-Geppert Audio-Visuals. Figure 12.7: Thomas Cecere. Figure 12.8: Rick Friedman/The Picture Cube. Figure 12.9: Jean-Claude Lejune/Stock, Boston.

Chapter 13

Figure 13.1: Michael Neff, Figures 13.2, 13.3, 13.5, 13.7, 13.8 and page 316: Deane Dayton. Page 317: (top) Apple Computer, Inc. (bottom) Deane Dayton. Figure 13.9: Deane Dayton. Figure 13.10: George Bellerose/Stock, Boston. Figures 13.11 and 13.12: Michael Neff. Figure 13.13: Deane Dayton. Figure 13.14: MCA Disco Vision, Inc.

Chapter 14

Figures 14.1 through 14.4: AECT Archives, The University of Iowa. Figure 14.5: Michael Neff. Figure 14.6: Jim Sheldon ©. Figure 14.7: Michael Neff. Figure 14.8: Pro Pix/Monk-meyer. Figure 14.9: Jay Hoops/Leo deWys. Figure 14.10: The Bettmann Archive. Figure 14.11: George S. Zimbel/Photo Researchers. Figure 14.12: Kurzweil Computer Products. Figure 14.13: (top) © Michal Heron 1980/Woodfin Camp (center) Agency for Instructional Television (bottom) Bell and Howell Company. Figure 14.14: (top left) © John Blaustein 1980/Woodfin Camp (top right) Harvey Barad/Monkmeyer (bottom) Nancy J. Pierce/Photo Researchers. Figure 14.15: (top left) Perry Ruben/Monkmeyer (top right) © Ellis Herwig/Stock, Boston (center left) J. Berndt/Stock, Boston (center right) Bill Grimes/Leo deWys (bottom) Mimi Forsyth/Monkmeyer. Figure 14.16: Michael Neff.

INDEX